Pluralism at Yale

PLURALISM AT YALE

The Culture of Political Science in America

RICHARD M. MERELMAN

The University of Wisconsin Press

The University of Wisconsin Press
1930 Monroe Street
Madison, Wisconsin 53711

www.wisc.edu/wisconsinpress/

3 Henrietta Street
London WC2E 8LU, England

Library of Congress Cataloging-in-Publication Data
Merelman, Richard M., 1938–
Pluralism at Yale : the culture of political science in America / Richard M.
Merelman.
pp. cm.
Includes bibliographical references and index.
ISBN 0-299-18410-2 (cloth : alk. paper)
ISBN 0-299-18414-5 (pbk. : alk. paper)
1. Yale University. Dept. of Political Science—History. 2. Political science—
Study and teaching (Higher)—United States—Case studies. 3. Pluralism (Social
sciences)—United States—History. I. Title.
JA88.U6 M38   2003
320′.071′17467—dc21   2002010197

A dog starv'd at his Masters Gate
Predicts the Ruin of the State
—William Blake, *Auguries of Innocence*

Contents

Preface

This book offers a novel theoretical approach to the role of political scientists in the American political regime. By extension, it treats the perennially interesting question of the relationship between intellectuals and politics. It does so through a case study of one set of political scientists at one university during one time period. After tracing many connections between these political scientists and American political culture, I conclude that pluralism at Yale provided useful legitimation for the American political regime.

Skeptics may reasonably wonder how so delimited a study can illuminate larger questions about intellectuals and politics. Ultimately, the answer depends on each reader's evaluation of this work. Nevertheless, there is among many, I am sure, a more serious prior reservation: namely, the suspicion that academics are virtually invisible in the daily push and pull of politics in the United States.

Reaction to the horrific events of September 11, 2001, should dispel this reservation. Academics of all kinds—legal scholars, historians, sociologists, literary critics, anthropologists, students of religion, of the Middle East and Asia, and, yes, political scientists—have taken a conspicuous public role in discussing these events. My reading of their journalistic ruminations on the subject is that legitimation—especially the protection and vindication of the American regime—is uppermost in the academic mind. Also, their responses incorporate the theories of liberal democracy that abound in the academy, including pluralism.

I have accumulated many debts in this project. First and foremost, of course, I am grateful to the 129 Yale political scientists and former graduate students whom I interviewed. I appreciate their willingness to talk with me for longer or shorter periods and to allow their comments and—in most cases (105, out of 111 quoted)—names to be utilized. I also want to thank David Cameron, former chair of the Yale Department of Political Science, for allowing me access to useful departmental records from the 1955–70 period.

I also wish to thank Dan Lipson, Spencer Jones, and T. J. Mertz, graduate students at the University of Wisconsin, who assisted me in compiling the material for chapter 8. As usual, Diane Morauske and Dawn Duren did yeoman work in translating my dog-eared drafts into impeccably word-processed text. Finally, grants from the Spencer Foundation and the American Philosophical Society and a semester's sabbatical from the University of Wisconsin provided monetary and temporal resources necessary to conduct this work.

David Canon, Leon Epstein, Michael Schatzberg, and Crawford Young, longtime friends and valued colleagues at the University of Wisconsin, provided indispensable feedback to an earlier draft of this book. The finished product is much the better for their contributions.

For the sake of truth in advertising, I confess that, in terms of the categories I introduce in chapter 5, I fit most easily into the Rejecter category. I was persuaded by pluralism while I was a graduate student at Yale, but I have become unpersuaded over the years. I retain great admiration for most of the people whom I knew at Yale and am grateful for the excellent education I received there. I have no particular axes to grind or scores to settle, other than those that any academic in his sixties acquires in his dealings with himself. It would be foolish for me to defend here my "objectivity," for I claim no such thing in the first place. I do, however, assert my utmost commitment to as balanced, nuanced, and thoughtful an argument as I can muster.

All research undertakings encounter barriers and impediments. This project is no exception. Indeed, at a number of points I intended to abandon the enterprise. I would have done so had it not been for the intercession of my wife, Sally Hutchison, who insisted I continue. Every scholar should have a muse of such charm and sternness.

Pluralism at Yale

1

Yale Pluralism and the American Political Regime

INTRODUCING THE PROBLEM

In the mid-1950s, often characterized as bland and harmonious, the following tumultuous political events occurred: Citing a dangerous Communist presence within American government, Senator Joseph McCarthy initiated an attack upon leading members of the Democratic Party, officials in the State Department, and high-ranking military officers. McCarthy claimed that the Communists had deceived many influential Americans, who had fallen victim to a powerful, insidious conspiracy (Rovere, 1959). Robert Taft, the respected and influential Republican senator from Ohio, and Dean Acheson, the former American secretary of state, opposed each other on McCarthy's charges. Acheson, an indirect target of McCarthy, "later liked to joke about the awkward ballet that Taft would go through in order not to have his photograph taken next to him at Yale [University] Corporation meetings" (Halberstam, 1993: 58).

In the resulting turmoil, suspected Communists in Hollywood, Washington, and New York were "blacklisted," that is, denied jobs on political grounds. To secure academic positions, many scholars were required to sign loyalty oaths, stating their allegiance to the United States. Congressional hearings subjected numerous celebrities to inquiries about their friends and associates and their loyalty to the United States. Most who were targets of these practices claimed they were victims of witch-hunts conducted by powerful but unscrupulous politicians. Finally, a series of dramatic spy trials culminated in the electrocution of Julius and Ethel Rosenberg, who had been convicted of conveying military secrets about the atomic bomb to the Soviets (Radosh and Milton, 1983).

Elsewhere, in a very different political arena, white southerners, enraged by recent Supreme Court rulings, organized so-called Citizens Councils to protect themselves from the federal government. Washington, they claimed, was creating by force a racially integrated society against the legitimate desires of a majority of ordinary white southern citizens. Symbols of southern defiance against federal power came out of mothballs; moreover, southern governors and legislators enacted legislation meant to protect the South in its struggle against the administration in Washington (James, 1981).

Meanwhile, black southerners—largely disenfranchised, poor, and uneducated—resisted these same white southerners. Blacks organized boycotts, filed lawsuits, and undertook demonstrations, protest marches, and acts of civil disobedience. In return, blacks suffered arrest, intimidation, injury, and even death (Branch, 1988). Like whites, blacks believed themselves to be victims of oppressive and unjust power, but they blamed the very white southerners who believed *they* were oppressed by the federal government.

These events demonstrate that even in supposedly peaceful times there exists a struggle between those with more power and those with less. McCarthy could exert power over suspected Communists. White southerners could exert power over black southerners. And the federal government could exert power over white southerners.

More generally, these events of the 1950s indicate two things: that in all political systems power is distributed unequally, and that political inequality is often unstable because, as Dennis Wrong puts it, "Any exercise of power by one group over another may be experienced as oppressive and lead to open or latent resistance by the subordinate group" (1994: 205–6). Given these facts, how then do political systems manage to persist over time? The obvious answer to this question is the exercise of power through force. Another, quite opposed, possibility, however, is the idea of a *legitimating discourse.*

In this book I examine one legitimating discourse: the pluralist theory of American politics that flourished at Yale University between 1955 and 1970, when many of the events just described occurred. What generated this discourse? How did it diffuse? How did it actually function? Does it survive? What are its implications for contemporary politics? This case study of Yale has ramifications for the role

4

of intellectuals in politics; for the relationships between political ideas and personal experiences; for the study of legitimacy; for the analysis of culture and politics; and for the condition of American politics in the new millennium. I address all of these subjects in the present work.

As Wrong's remark illustrates, most writers concerned with the place of ideas in the persistence of political systems concentrate on the beliefs of the weak (e.g., Gramsci, 1971). By contrast, I direct attention to the beliefs of those who rule. Accounting for the beliefs of power holders is important, understudied, and misunderstood. Moreover, our primary existing approach to this subject—that of a "dominant ideology"—is inadequate. Therefore, I introduce the concept of a legitimating discourse. Let me briefly justify the need for this concept, describe it, and then apply it to pluralism at Yale.

PROBLEMATIZING THE BELIEFS OF DOMINANTS

By concentrating on the weak, writers on ideas and power have overlooked the question of how the strong gain and retain the self-confidence to rule. What, for example, persuaded the federal government, white southerners, and McCarthy that they could rightly exert power over their opponents? The question is important; unless the powerful rule with conviction, the weak are unlikely to submit peaceably to their subordination. Indeed, the weak may resist even the most determined of power holders (e.g., Scott, 1998). Why then would the weak defer to an *un*confident set of rulers? In short, we must inquire into the beliefs of dominants as part of any inquiry into ideas and politics.

Of course, some may argue that I have identified a nonproblem. Isn't it obvious that the mere exercise of power can provide its own justification for the right to rule? Certainly there are autocracies where the dramatic display of awesome power is part of the legitimation process. Yet in democracies few power holders are content with such a legitimation strategy. Thus, neither McCarthy nor white southerners nor the federal government claimed power simply on the grounds that they could exert it. Indeed, in democracies authorities seldom advance such claims as, in effect, "Might makes right" or "Someone has to make this decision, and it might as well be me" (but see C. Young, 1994: 284). The reason is obvious: such arguments concede the possibility that power is exploitative and thus could possibly disturb "the composure [power holders] need to rule confidently" (Cohen, quoted in Torrance, 1995: 69). Moreover, this claim would create resentment among the ruled. As a result, at least in democracies, justifications for the wielding of power commonly reach beyond the simple holding of power itself.

But understanding the generation of legitimating justifications is surprisingly problematic. For one thing, power holders do not assert legitimating justifications monolithically. According to Boudon, even Marx believed that the ruling class was *conscious* of the distinction between the truth and the usefulness of the *theories* to which it subscribes" (1989: 40; emphasis in the original). In some cases this distinction between truth and utility has troubled power holders enough to alienate them from the system of power upon which they have depended. Some even become propagandists for and leaders of insurgencies (Abercrombie, Hill, and Turner, 1980: 157). In short, the strong vary both in the intensity and the unanimity with which they hold beliefs favorable to their own power. Ultimately, even white southerners debated each other about their right to dominate blacks (e.g., Pride, 1995). Thus, holders of power must continually construct self-justifications.

We know surprisingly little about how this process of self-justification—what Bennett Berger (1995: 49) calls "ideological work"— proceeds. There are several potential stimulants to the process: group interest, group competition, personal need, and a desire for group cooperation. Yet none assures the ultimate result: power holders who are fully convinced of their right to rule.

The most commonly cited stimulant for legitimation among dominants is group interest. Theories of group interest assert that power holders share economic interests, political interests, or both. In the 1950s, the federal government, for example, possessed a political interest in enforcing Supreme Court decisions against white southerners. These shared interests motivate power holders to form groups and cooperate with each other. In pursuit of these interests, power holders develop justifications for their rule (Torrance, 1995: 154; Dant, 1991: 10; Abercrombie, Hill, and Turner, 1980: 22; Boudon, 1989: 133).

But shared interests do not assure that power holders actually produce legitimating justifications. For one thing, inferring shared group interests is no simple matter. As Marx pointed out in reference to the proletariat, there is a fundamental distinction between a class *in* itself and a class *for* itself. Similarly, occupants of power positions must first develop a consciousness of their shared interests if they are to produce justifications for their rule. By itself, the concept of group interest cannot account for or produce such a consciousness; therefore shared group interests cannot assure the appearance of legitimacy justifications (Dant, 1991: 39; Archer, 1996).

In addition, attempts by the strong to develop justifications for their power may not always succeed. McCarthy, for example, developed only a rudimentary set of legitimating ideas. After all, the strong are primarily engaged in *exerting* power, not thinking about it. Even Marx and Engels recognized this problem; however, they argued that the division of labor created a specialized group—intellectuals—who concentrate on producing legitimating justifications for the powerful (1970: 65). Yet how intellectuals are connected to power holders is itself an object of debate (H. Williams, 1988: 104; Aronowitz, 1988: 326; Eyerman, 1994). There is no convincing reason to believe that intellectuals always aid those with power.

Another oft-cited stimulant of legitimating justifications is group competition. According to Mannheim, a group in competition with others will "draw upon particular conceptual resources," which include "styles of thought" (Longhurst, 1988: 95; Mannheim, 1936: 269). Styles of thought are, in Mannheim's phrase, "total ideologies" (59), which include "not just the content of belief but also the conceptual apparatus of an individual or group" (Morrice, 1996: 64). Interestingly, one such conceptual apparatus, in Mannheim's view, was social science.

Yet group competition cannot explain the production of legitimating justifications. Competition between *groups* does not ensure that *individual* members of any single group of power holders will agree on legitimating justifications. In addition, by definition, group competition ensures that at any moment a *multiplicity* of ideas circulates about how society is and should be organized. Given this fact, members of every group will likely be exposed to many different perspectives, promoting disagreement within any particular group. Indeed, at the extreme, a group may never adopt any common point of view at all.

A further potential explanation of legitimating justifications is personal need or motivation. All people are motivated to understand the world around them and to explain to themselves why they either have power or lack power. Arguably, this disposition is particularly strong among power holders; if those in power cannot justify their power to themselves, their exercise of power over others may become tenuous (Merelman, 1986). Indeed, theories of cognitive dissonance and of social dominance (Sidanius and Pratto, 1993) provide evidence to support this view (see also Cohen, 1998: 186–87).

Yet the motivational theory of legitimating justifications will not do the job either. Motivation is essentially an emotional condition; by contrast, legitimating justifications are articulate beliefs, ideas, and theories. The motivation to create and embrace legitimating justifications does not ensure that such justifications will emerge. After all, not everyone is able to construct legitimating justifications. Furthermore, power holders may not settle on any single justification. According to Boudon (1989), not motivation, but contemplation, socialization, and education account for shared legitimating justifications.

A final candidate for the explanation of the development of legitimating justifications is the need for power holders to cooperate. In any political system the holders of power depend on each other. For example, bureaucrats rely on legislators for money to conduct agency business, and legislators expect bureaucrats to implement laws efficiently. McCarthy depended heavily on the Republican Party in Congress, and the GOP hoped to benefit from McCarthy's attacks on Democrats. Obviously, legitimating justifications can facilitate cooperation among holders of power (Cormack, 1992: 16).

However, like its predecessors, this explanation for legitimating justifications is insufficient. It assumes unwarrantedly that power holders work together on entire sets of issues. But different power holders make decisions on different issues sequentially (Lindblom, 1965). Furthermore, rules meant to regulate the actions of power holders rarely cover all situations (Boden, 1994). Most often, ad hoc language strategies accomplish the task of coordination. Hence, coordinated actions do not depend entirely upon legitimating justifications; nor do legitimating justifications necessarily coordinate all action. Thus, legitimating justifications may exist, but not necessarily because of the need for coordination (see also Olson, 1965).

To summarize briefly, it is mistaken to believe that holders of power automatically produce legitimating justifications. Theories of group interest, group competition, individual motivation, and coordination cannot explain the appearance of legitimating justifications. In short, as Gramsci (1971) pointed out, power holders can achieve hegemony only through a continuous process of intellectual invention. We need innovative conceptualizations and novel empirical studies to understand this process. For this purpose I propose the idea of a "legitimating discourse."

CONCEPTUALIZING A LEGITIMATING DISCOURSE

A legitimating discourse is *any body of ideas, images, or practices that portrays a political regime to be functioning as its power holders claim it to be functioning, and, in so doing, provides support to those who exert power in the regime.* On seven counts the concept of a legitimating discourse differs from the idea of a "dominant ideology" (Marx and Engels, 1970: 64; Althusser, 1969: 235; Mannheim, 1936), its chief competitor. It is especially helpful in examining Yale pluralism between 1955 and 1970.

First, unlike dominant ideology theories (Abercrombie, Hill, and Turner, 1980: 29; Longhurst, 1988: 14), a legitimating discourse does not require that the weak adopt the ideas of the powerful, nor even that the powerful agree on basic legitimating justifications. The definition above says nothing about whether power holders actually adopt legitimating discourses. Obviously, people with power normally gravitate toward beliefs that portray themselves favorably. Whether they in fact do so, however, is a matter of empirical investigation.

Second, unlike most dominant ideology theories (Barrett, 1991: 4–6; Torrance, 1995: 191), a legitimating discourse assumes no determinate relationships between social position and beliefs. For example, despite its power, the federal government did not assert full civil rights authority over the South until the 1960s. Because power holders desire to be seen as legitimate, they will normally try to generate and support legitimating discourses. However, this is a problematic process with no guarantee of success.

Third, unlike dominant ideologies, which are usually thought to distort reality (Boudon, 1989: 36, Longhurst, 1988: 14; Cormack, 1992: 10; H. Williams, 1988: 4), a legitimating discourse may be entirely false, entirely true, or, to varying degrees, both false and true. Perhaps power holders *are* living up to their stated aspirations, however self-interested such aspirations may be. For example, perhaps, as white southerners argued, the federal government *was* bent upon racial integration at any cost. The point is that regardless of its actual truth value, a legitimating discourse simply provides ammunition for dominants to support their claims of truthfulness and effectiveness.

Fourth, unlike dominant ideology theories (Oliga, 1996: 93–94; H. Williams, 1998: 48; Morrice, 1996: 48–119; Boudon, 1989: 52), the idea of a legitimating discourse does not presume power holders are irrational. The strong *may* be irrationally disposed to embrace comforting ideas, but they may also abandon these ideas in the face of convincing counterarguments. Indeed, faced with evidence that blacks were not intellectually inferior, some white southerners altered their perspectives.

Fifth, in contrast to a dominant ideology, a legitimating discourse does not necessarily mystify reality (Barrett, 1991: 167; Cormack, 1992: 26–27; Agger, 1992: 274; Torrance, 1995: 201). For example, instead of falsely portraying coercion as inevitable, a legitimating discourse may admit that coercion is a fallible human decision. Nor does a legitimating discourse necessarily reify or rigidify ideas; instead, it may highlight the evolving quality of such concepts as liberty and equality. The question is whether these concessions to reality deprive a legitimating discourse of its capacity to justify domination. The answer is no. A legitimating discourse asserts that power holders are doing the best that can realistically be expected (but see Connolly, 1984). Thus, where a dominant ideology professes falsely to the public that "everything is fine," a legitimating discourse announces with apparent sincerity that "this is as good as you can get."

Sixth, unlike dominant ideology theories (H. Williams, 1988: 5; Swartz, 1997; Gramsci, 1971; Aronowitz, 1988: 297), the concept of a legitimating discourse does not maintain that intellectuals are necessarily part of or controlled by the holders of power. It proposes, instead, that intellectuals are a "status group" (Weber, 1978: 306), often allied with, but sometimes arrayed against, political power holders. True, power holders influence intellectuals. Moreover, intellectuals often "select themselves" into the orbits of dominant groups. Many intellectuals are, indeed, predisposed to produce legitimating discourses. But some are not. For example, not all law professors supported the federal government's exertion of power over the South.

Why are intellectuals partially autonomous politically? Partly because many belong to professional associations (Brint, 1994) that shield them from the direct control of outside political forces. In addition, "Intellectuals seem no less prone to ideological effects in their thought than other groups" (Balkin, 1998: 133). Intellectuals are mainly interested in justifying their *own* positions, not in justifying the power of others. Finally, power holders actually depend upon the freedom of intellectuals. In liberal democracies typified by norms of intellectual exchange and public debate, any ideas that are too obviously sponsored, censored, or controlled offer comparatively little benefit to their patrons. Only when legitimating discourses have emerged *independently* can dominants employ them effectively (Brym, 1980: 56).

Seventh and finally, where dominant ideologies evaluate power holders favorably (Abercrombie, Hill, and Turner, 1980: 18; Boudon, 1989: 119; Swartz, 1997: 39), a legitimating discourse may not contain any explicit value statements. Yet this absence does not detract from the power of legitimating discourses. In fact, the opposite is true; the avoidance of explicit evaluations actually *increases* the power of legitimating discourses.

Ludwig Fleck first conceptualized this phenomenon. Based on his study of how the Wasserman reaction to syphilis was presented to the public, Fleck concluded that "scientific rationality is embedded within the broader cultural world view" (O'Rand, 1989: 105). O'Rand applies Fleck's precept by demonstrating that, in the analysis of gender, preconceptions about giftedness, norms, and underlying causes "undergird *both* the scientific investigation and the social acceptance of gender-related capacities" (107; emphasis added). Her analysis shows that "the esoteric circle of the scientist and the broader cultural context interpenetrate" (118).

So far as academic legitimating discourses are concerned, this interpenetration takes several forms. For one, legitimating discourses reassure power holders that their policies are feasible, thus indirectly commending such policies. In addition, legitimating discourses imply that power holders are neither liars nor conspirators. Lastly, legitimating discourses usually accept for research purposes the operational definitions preferred by power holders (but see Peterson and Hassel, 1998). In so doing, legitimating discourses indirectly incorporate the values that generate these operational definitions. Because practices that conform to these operational definitions allegedly "work," legitimating discourses indirectly promote the values of power holders.

In summary, legitimating discourses provide cultural ammunition for holders of political power. While some legitimating discourses are indistinguishable from dominant ideologies, others are quite different. Academic intellectuals—including political scientists—sometimes produce the latter type of legitimating discourses, one of which, Yale pluralism, is the topic of this study. Other legitimating discourses that academics have produced include Keynesian economics (with its commendation of New Deal fiscal policies), traditional public administration theory (with its commendation of Progressive civil service reforms, but see McSwite, 1997: 13), functionalist sociology and systems theory (with their theorization of an allegiant public), Whig history (with its progressive view of social change), liberal constitutionalism (with its commendation of the American state), and, more recently, supply-side economics (with its endorsement of Republican tax policies in the 1980s). Although many social scientists, policymakers, and journalists have argued that economic theories like Keynesianism, monetarism, and supply-side theory have influenced policymakers and political elites, little attention has been paid to such political science discourses as pluralism. My study corrects this omission.

AMERICAN POLITICS AT YALE, 1955–1970: A RESEARCH PERSPECTIVE

Between 1955 and 1970 the Yale University Department of Political Science was a national leader in the study of American politics. Indeed, the American Council on Education rated the Yale graduate faculty in American politics first among all American universities in both 1964 and 1969. In those years such Yale thinkers as Robert Dahl, Charles Lindblom, Robert E. Lane, Herbert Kaufman, Harold Lasswell, David Barber, Karl Deutsch, and Gabriel Almond spearheaded the insurgent and ultimately powerful "behavioral approach" to the study of politics. Also, many Yale thinkers developed a pluralist account of the American political system (Purcell, 1973: chapter 13). All but Deutsch and Almond remained at Yale throughout the period. Dahl, Lindblom, Lane, Lasswell, Deutsch, and Almond served as presidents of the American Political Science Association, solidifying Yale's eminence.

While these Yale faculty produced the foundational works associated with the Yale department, graduate students who were at Yale during this period, such as David Barber, William Muir, Fred Greenstein, Nelson Polsby, Aaron Wildavsky, Raymond Wolfinger, and Russell Murphy also made major contributions to behavioralism and pluralism. Indeed, these younger writers became important disseminators of the ideas developed at Yale. (For a list of the major works in Yale pluralism, see the appendix).

The significance of Yale political science can also be seen in a recent study of scholarly reputation in American political science (Miller, Tien, and Peebler, 1996). Based on a *Professional Visibility Index* composed of scholarly citations, the study reports that approximately 10 percent of the top seventy scholars between 1954 and 1994 were Yale political scientists. This figure undoubtedly understates the prominence of Yale between 1954 and 1970, a conclusion supported by the fact that three of the top fifteen article contributors to the *American Political Science Review* between 1954 and 1973 were members of the Yale department. Only Michigan equaled Yale in *APSR* publication during the 1955–70 period. Finally, the *Social Science Citation Index* contains more references to Robert Dahl in the 1956–65 period than to his principal scholarly antagonist, C. Wright Mills. The disparity between the two grew from 1960 to 1970, no doubt in part because of Mills's death during the period. Nevertheless, citations of Dahl's principal pluralist writings equaled 518 between 1960 and 1970, as compared to but 132 references to Mills's *The Power Elite*. Nor was Yale's stature confined to American politics. To the contrary, Karl Deutsch was the most widely cited scholar in the study of international politics between 1960 and 1970, far outdistancing his competitors (Coser, 1984: 208). Indeed, his 437 citations come close to Dahl's, a feat that Coser calls "amazing".

Also, through teaching, Yale behavioralism and pluralism directly reached many Yale students who today are major actors in American politics. For example, at a gathering of state governors in 1998,

Robert Dahl was surprised to encounter six former students, including George Pataki of New York and Pete Wilson of California. George W. Bush, a Yale undergraduate in the late 1960s, took political science courses. Both Joseph Lieberman and Richard Cheney attended Yale, as did Hillary Rodham Clinton and Lani Guinier. And Bill Clinton graduated from Yale Law School, some of whose faculty and students played active roles in the political science department. Yale has always emphasized careers in public service for its students. A steady stream of Yale graduates regularly flows to positions of political power in Washington and state capitals.

Of course, Yale political science during this time was part of a *national* movement toward behavioralism and pluralism. Seminal participants in this movement—such as Seymour Lipset, Louis Hartz, Heinz Eulau, David Truman, David Easton, Angus Campbell, and Philip Converse—had no continuing connection to Yale, although Lipset and Truman taught as visitors to the department. But Yale produced a larger core group of behavioral, pluralist scholars than did other political science departments, whose "new" political scientists often found themselves a beleaguered minority. Moreover, the Yale department conceptualized behavioralism and pluralism more broadly than did political scientists elsewhere (see, for example, Ware, 1998: 14–16). As a result, pluralist work in the department encompassed many aspects of American politics—from the Supreme Court (Muir) to working-class men (Lane) and young children (Greenstein); from political culture (Almond) to local politics (Dahl, Kaufman); from the policymaking process (Lindblom) to legislatures (Polsby, Barber), political parties (Greenstein), school boards (Muir), and government bureaucracies (Kaufman, Wolfinger, Murphy).

Certainly, Yale pluralist scholarship was by no means as popular nationally as the writings of, for example, John Kenneth Galbraith (1958) and Arthur Schlesinger (1949), who also expounded versions of pluralism. However, research by Yale political scientists contributed necessary scholarly foundations for the arguments advanced by these two writers. Indeed, as Norman Cantor (1991: 18) points out about scholars of medieval history, they "provide the base upon which highly readable accounts of the medieval world are constructed" for a general audience. The same thing was true for Yale pluralism and popular accounts of American politics.

In an ideal world, my study of pluralism would investigate all the academic sites where pluralism developed, not just Yale. However, for both practical and analytical reasons, I chose to concentrate on Yale. Practically, I could not examine every promising site. Also, Yale was sufficiently prominent to justify a single-case examination. Finally, because I received my doctorate in political science from Yale in 1965, I expected good access to the department. Analytically, my concept of a legitimating discourse necessitates detailed, micro-analytic investigation. A single academic department—in this case, the Yale political science department—was an ideal setting for the empirical application of my concept.

From a research standpoint, my task is to understand how Yale political scientist faculty and graduate students produced and employed pluralism as a legitimating discourse. To accomplish this task, I rely on several sources of information: writings by and about the Yale scholars, including published and unpublished recollections of the period; secondary literature, such as studies of pluralism and behavioralism; analyses of American politics and society between 1955 and 1970; representations of pluralism in American political culture; and archival materials in departmental records.

Most important, I rely heavily upon interviews with faculty members and graduate students of the Yale political science department in the 1955–70 period. I conducted interviews with 27 faculty from July 1997 to October 1999. I also conducted 102 interviews with former graduate students from the 1955–70 period. These represent about half of all those students in the graduate program. The interviews probed reflections upon, memories of, and feelings about the department in the 1955–70 period. These open-ended interviews lasted from 45 minutes to two hours. I conducted most by telephone and tape-recorded all. Each was "on the record" except for small portions some interviewees asked to keep off-the-record. The interviews probed such subjects as the internal operations of the department, the generation of specific pieces of research, the effects of personal, professional, and political events on scholarship, the intellectual and emotional climate of the department, and the impact of salient events within the department. I did not limit these interviews to Americanists. I wished to capture, insofar as possible, the full creative milieu of the department. Interviewing peripheral as well as core scholars and students not only reveals this milieu but also provides novel, unexpected insights into pluralism as a legitimating discourse.

I realize these interviews are not objective, factual representations of the department between 1955 and 1970 but are retrospective, subjective interpretations. Does this subjective, retrospective quality weaken my analysis? No. For one thing, my checking of interviewee recollections against archival materials reveals few factual discrepancies of consequence. More important, I regard the subjective reality of my interviewees as an important aspect of the department. Not only do people act on their perceptions, but their perceptions also form part of the department's collective memory (on collective memory, see Schwartz, 1996; Schudson, 1992; Cruz, 2000). Put differently, I do not assume there is a common, uniform, stable "Yale political science department." Instead, my interviews bring the department to life as the constructed, diverse, lived experience of its members.

My reliance on interviews does not slight published accounts of pluralism, of Yale, of behavioralism, or of political science, including those produced by Yale scholars themselves. However, I add an important dimension to these accounts. For example, consider Dahl's well-known 1961 discussion of behavioralism's ascent (1961a). In this article, Dahl not only highlights several factors that appear in my account but also describes the contributory impact of the Second World War, when a "great many American political scientists temporarily vacated their ivory towers and came to grips with day-to-day political and administrative realities in Washington" (764). In this piece Dahl does not mention his own Washington experience; by contrast, this experience, which emerges in my interview with him, constitutes an example of what the next chapter calls the "performance" of pluralism. These performances or "improvisations," *along* with written texts, are in fact the heart of pluralism as a legitimating discourse.

Why do I concentrate on the 1955–70 period in the life of the Yale department? As the appendix shows, the 1955–70 period incorporates much of the work the Yale department created within the pluralist paradigm. In addition, this period saw important changes in the relationship between social scientists and American politics (Ball, 1993; Wood, 1993; Aaron, 1978; Eyerman, 1994: 167–68). The period begins at the tail end of the McCarthyite crusade against domestic Communism, a movement that placed considerable pressure on universities and scholars. Yale itself felt these pressures (Kalman, 1986: 125–29). Soon, however, John Kennedy ascended to the presidency, bringing with him many Ivy League academics, some of whom had already played roles in programs such as urban renewal, for which Yale's hometown of New Haven, Connecticut, was a national leader. Following Kennedy's assassination, social scientists contributed to Lyndon Johnson's War on Poverty and Great Society programs. Of this period Robert Wood writes, "At least for most of one decade, the politics of innovation stood alongside the politics of distribution and redistribution" (1993: 177). Wood demonstrates that academic intellectuals played key roles in the politics of innovation.

The period ends with the eruption of domestic civil rights protests, bursts of civil disobedience, urban riots, and anti–Vietnam War demonstrations. As is well known, many academics and their students took part in these events (on Yale at the time, see Hersey, 1970; Taft, 1976; Kernan, 1999). The 1968 presidential election of Richard Nixon initiated a conservative reaction against the policies most academic social scientists supported; meanwhile, domestic turmoil spurred many social scientists to reconsider the American political system. Given this history, it is easy to understand why the 1955–70 period is fertile ground for examining the legitimating discourse of Yale pluralism.

The scholarship of Robert Dahl is a microcosm of the era. In fact, two of Dahl's works provide "bookends" for the period I analyze. In 1956 Dahl published *A Preface to Democratic Theory;* in 1970, his *After the Revolution?* appeared. The latter book begins by stating that a political era has ended. "Old patterns of authority are losing out, and . . . if I may use a bold new revolutionary expression, 'things will never be the same again'" (4). Ironically, the "old patterns" to which Dahl referred in 1970 included many features of the American political system his 1956 *Preface* had praised. In fact, *Preface* was itself part of the earlier system's political culture.

The concluding sentences of the two books reveal clearly the rationale for my 1955–70 periodization. On the penultimate page of *Preface* Dahl praises the American political system: "With all its defects, it does nonetheless provide a high probability that any active and legitimate group will make itself heard effectively at some stage in the process of decision. This is no mean thing in a political system" (150). And the concluding paragraph of the book reads, "This is no negligible contribution, then, that Americans have made to the arts of government—and to that branch which of all the arts is the most difficult, the art of democratic government" (151).

By contrast, *After the Revolution?* ends on a more ambivalent note. The final chapter, entitled "From Principles to Problems," details needed reforms in the American political system. In the last two sentences Dahl comments:

> In thought and rational discussion, we must move back and forth along this path, which is not straight but triangular, with sides marked Principles, Problems, Solutions, except that at any point you may and almost certainly will generate a new triangle.
> Well, we really are at the end or the beginning. (166)

Ironically, *After the Revolution?* is itself a preface to renewed debate and innovation; by contrast, *Preface* ends in a celebratory afterword on an *earlier* revolution, that of 1776. What *Preface* considers settled in 1956 *After the Revolution?* considers up for grabs by 1970. Thus, the 1955–70 period encompasses a crucial intellectual era in Yale political science—and in the United States.

YALE PLURALISM AS A LEGITIMATING DISCOURSE

The pluralist approach to American politics is multifaceted and nuanced (see, for example, Purcell, 1973; Shapiro and Reeher, 1988; Katznelson, 1997: 311–33; McLennan, 1995; A. Eisenberg, 1995; McFarland, 2001). At root, however, pluralism consists of four basic premises. These four propositions describe an American polity consisting of multiple centers of power. Competing policymakers, who are mutually tolerant, forge political coalitions that respond to public demands and social problems by producing moderate, reformist policies. The result of this process is gradual, piecemeal, but undeniable political progress. The four key assertions in this formulation are that political power is distributed in multiple, competing centers of power; that policymaking is reactive rather than proactive; that political leaders are tolerant coalition builders; and that the outcome of this process is gradual, moderate, political reform, not deadlock or radical change. Of these four premises the first two predate the 1950s (see Schlossberg, 1998); the second two are largely products of the 1950s and the Yale influence. I call these four assertions the pluralist premise, the reactive premise, the elite tolerance premise, and the reformist premise.

Together, these four premises fit the definition of a legitimating discourse offered earlier. That is, they support the claims American political leaders typically make to justify their power. American politicians regularly proclaim their responsiveness to citizens, their alertness to public needs, their openness to reasonable compromise and coalition building, their respect for limited, shared power, and their ability to create progressive change and political reform. Thus, the four pluralist premises generally support the American political regime.

Let us examine these premises one by one. The most important contention of the pluralist approach, of course, is the pluralist premise, which claims that political power is dispersed among competing groups, rather than concentrated in the hands of a single dominant oligarchy. Here are several versions of this thesis from Yale political scientists. In his *Community Power and Political Theory* (1963) Nelson Polsby writes: "Pluralists see American society as fractured into a congeries of hundreds of small special interest groups, with incompletely overlapping memberships, widely differing power bases, and a multitude of techniques for exercising influence on decisions salient to them" (118). In this passage Polsby does not use the term *pluralism;* six pages later, though, he does. In fact, he cites three other Yale political scientists—Robert Dahl, Raymond Wolfinger, and Herbert Kaufman—to support his claim that, at least in local communities, pluralism is the rule rather than the exception (124, 128–29).

Among Yale political scientists, Robert Dahl offers the seminal statement of the pluralist premise. Dahl characterizes New Haven as a "pluralist democracy" (1961c: 305) in *Who Governs?* However, he cautions that pluralism does not create political equality among New Haven citizens. Still, pluralism provides limited, but crucial, power to citizens. In an essay published the same year as *Who Governs?* Dahl expands this argument to the entire United States: "To the extent that inequalities are dispersed rather than cumulative—as I am suggesting they are in the United States—the growth of a unified oligarchy is inhibited. For the pattern of dispersed inequalities means that an individual or a group at a disadvantage with respect to one resource may compensate for his handicap by exploiting his superior access to a different resource. . . . I believe this to be true in the United States" (1961b: 83).

Other Yale political scientists extend the pluralist assertion to specialized governmental institutions. Readers interested in the law, bureaucracies, and urban policy encounter pluralist assertions in the following formulations by three Yale political scientists:

> The organization of the legal profession, the written judicial opinion, and the tradition of the civic remedy—these three distinctively legal factors, coupled with the social factors of pluralism, voluntarism, and literacy, account in large part for the potential power of law in the United States. (Muir, 1967: 137–38)

> Although pluralist views of public administration are common, improved mutual adjustment is hardly recognized as a systematic alternative to improved central coordination in public administration. (Lindblom, 1965: 303)

> [Community Progress Incorporated (a poverty agency)] was a world in which power and influence were extraordinarily fragmented. . . . The decentralization of power was a positive advantage, particularly in the agency's efforts to weld a bureaucratic coalition. (Murphy, 1971: 139)

These three passages also associate pluralism with positive values. Muir connects pluralism to the "rule of law," a central value of the American legal tradition. Lindblom argues that improved mutual adjustment is a valuable alternative to central coordination in public administration. Murphy states that, through pluralism, Community Progress Incorporated advanced programs to attack urban poverty. Thus, pluralism helps achieve worthwhile goals.

A second group of Yale political scientists concentrated on the reactive premise. Within the Yale political science department—and, perhaps, political science as a whole—Charles Lindblom's statement is the strongest version of the reactive argument. In 1963, with David Braybrooke, Lindblom propounded an influential theory of "incremental politics" to depict "the decisions typical of ordinary political life" (71). As the authors explained, incremental decision making is "better described as moving *away* from known social ills rather than as moving *toward* a known and relatively stable goal" (71). In other words, policymakers normally react to immediate, tangible social problems; they do not implement elaborate programs to achieve future goals. This statement captures the essence of the reactive premise.

Other members of the Yale department put forth similar arguments. Consider, for example, Fred Greenstein's seemingly critical formulation of the reactive premise regarding political parties: "One *shortcoming* of American party politicians, with their keen sensitivities to group pressures, is their tendency to neglect making policies if group pressures are not forthcoming" (1970: 117; emphasis added). To Greenstein, party leaders are not visionaries; instead, they respond only if pressures are placed upon them. Greenstein laments the consequences of this reactive pattern for unorganized citizens, whom the system poorly represents. However, in his concluding statement, Greenstein actually praises reactivity among parties: "At a minimum, it is unlikely that effectiveness of policy-making, stability, and democracy would be better advanced if there were *no* American party system. Furthermore the *presently constituted* American party system makes contributions that do not readily meet the eye" (119–20; emphasis in original).

A third statement of the reactive premise is Robert E. Lane's description of political thinking in "Eastport" (New Haven). Lane writes, "In two senses we must say that Eastport tends not to ideologize: first, the use of forensic ideologies, of theoretical constructs with well-defined referents, is minimal; second, the smaller and vaguer theories, the segments of ideologies employed, are used more as guides to interpretation than as defenses against the real world" (1962: 355–56). Thus, Lane's working-class subjects are in touch with the world; they do not use ideologies to escape reality. Nor do they lose themselves in abstractions. In sum, they react flexibly and realistically to immediately felt problems.

The third premise of Yale pluralism is that political leaders are mutually tolerant and able to cooperate with each other. There is general agreement among political leaders on "the rules of the game," namely the values and constitutionally defined institutions and procedures of the American political regime.

The elite tolerance premise appears prominently in the writings of Robert Dahl. Consider these two statements, the first from *A Preface to Democratic Theory* and the next from *Who Governs?*:

> In a sense, what we ordinarily describe as democratic "politics" is merely the chaff. It is the surface manifestation, representing superficial conflicts. Prior to politics, beneath it, enveloping it, restricting it, conditioning it, is the underlying consensus on policy that usually exists

21

in the society among a predominant portion of the politically active members. (1956: 132)

> Democratic beliefs, like other political beliefs, are influenced by a recurring *process* of interchange among political professionals, the political stratum, and the great bulk of the population. The process generates enough agreement on rules and norms so as to permit the system to operate, but agreement tends to be incomplete, and typically it decays. So the process is frequently repeated. (1961c: 316; emphasis in original)

Another version of the elite tolerance premise emerges in James David Barber's study of the Connecticut state legislature. Barber identifies four types of legislators, of which the lawmaker type contributes most to the legislature's performance. According to Barber, "The Lawmaker's ways of relating to others reflect a fundamental respect for and empathy with persons unlike him, an expectation that others will return these feelings, a conviction that reasoning is effective in cooperative work, and an ability to work out personal guidelines for conducting such relations. . . . Lawmakers can listen to others without surrendering to them, hold back something in social intercourse without withdrawing to a quiet corner, and challenge an adversary without making him an enemy" (1965: 254). Barber's description singles out tolerance ("fundamental respect," "empathy") as a necessary personal quality that enables policymaking to proceed effectively in the Connecticut state legislature.

In his seminal cross-cultural study of democratic political culture, written at Yale, Gabriel Almond (with Sidney Verba) asserts the elite tolerance premise indirectly: "In the United States and Britain, where a large proportion of the respondents express pride in the political characteristics of their nation, this proportion was higher among the better-educated respondents. In the United States 92 percent of those with some university education responded with political objects of pride" (1965: 67). This prideful consensus among the highly educated assures that substantive policy differences will not subvert the American political process.

Fourth, and finally, many Yale political scientists assert the reformist premise. Contrary to Olivier Zunz, who argues that Dahl's *Who Governs?* presents pluralism as "maintaining the status quo" (1987–88: 214), Dahl actually enunciates the reformist premise in

New Haven: "When [Mayor] Lee took office in January 1954, there was evidently latent agreement within the political stratum of New Haven on the need for redevelopment. . . . Lee converted this latent agreement into active support for a huge program . . . but the program that the political stratum almost unanimously supported could not be executed under the old highly decentralized pattern of petty sovereignties. In effect, then, Lee converted support for redevelopment into acquiescence in a new pattern of influence, the executive-centered order" (1961c: 202).

Of course, Dahl asserted the reformist premise for only a single city. However, other Yale political scientists extended the premise. For example, Herbert Kaufman found that the U.S. Forest Service carried out successful reform programs in land conservation. Kaufman summarized the reform achievements of the service: "Overall performance comes remarkably close to the goals set by the leadership. There are timber sales targets and timber cut targets; maximum acceptable burn targets for controlling fires; grazing targets; wildlife targets; revenue targets; targets for the number of visitors to be accommodated; and many others. Over the years, the averages of actual performance figures fall within a few percentage points of the objectives" (1960: 203). Importantly, unlike Dahl, Kaufman attributed successful reform not to fortuitous intervention by gifted leaders but to embedded organizational practices. Thus, Kaufman inserts a pattern of *institutionalized* reform within pluralism.

Charles Lindblom also advanced the reformist premise. In his short volume titled *The Policy-Making Process* (1968), Lindblom described "reconstructive leadership," which he contrasted favorably with "the simple compromise of unreconstructed preferences" (106). Lindblom praised reconstructive leadership because it undertakes necessary reforms. Though by no means common in the United States, reconstructive leadership nevertheless does occur with some frequency. Lindblom cites Lyndon Johnson's presidency as an example; however, his chief illustration is Franklin Roosevelt and the New Deal. In describing reconstructive leadership and reform during the New Deal, Lindblom observes: "What every modern political system requires is *moving* compromise—specifically, a never-ending sequence of compromises, each successive one responding to a new alignment of preferences or interests. Leadership that understands this fact, and that molds the moving structure of preferences, opens up significant new departures in policy, as Franklin Roosevelt did" (106).

Perhaps the most confident assertion of the reformist premise at Yale occurs in William Muir's study of how New Haven public schools complied with the Supreme Court's 1963 decision outlawing school prayer: "Can law change deep-rooted attitudes? Of course it can. It has done so—in reshaping in less than a generation this nation's views about racism; in altering in even a shorter time police attitudes toward criminal behavior; in ennobling the city dweller as the backbone of American democracy; in imparting an understanding of poverty . . . in stemming religious prejudice; in establishing heightened standards of honesty and public service" (1967: 138). The rhetorical tone of Muir's statement is extravagantly positive. The attitudinal changes he attributes to law are obviously progressive and promote political reform. As we can see, the reformist premise played a significant role in the pluralist writings of Yale political scientists.

CONCLUSION

This chapter shows that groups exerting power stand to benefit from legitimating discourses. Yale pluralism was just such an academic legitimating discourse between 1955 and 1970. How did this discourse emerge, and how did it operate among Yale political scientists? What helped Yale political science generate pluralism? These are the questions I investigate in chapter 2.

2

Performing Pluralism

ANALYZING YALE PLURALISM AS A
LEGITIMATING DISCOURSE

In this chapter I argue that for most of the 1955–70 period the practices of the Yale political science department faculty stimulated and
reenacted major assertions in the department's writing about the
American political system. Pluralist scholarship embodied the department's internal dynamics, and the department's dynamics embedded
pluralist theory in action. In their collegial roles members of the department "performed" the American political system their texts described. In this way, Yale political scientists became legitimators of
the regime their works portrayed. As a single ensemble, scholarly
texts and department practices became a legitimating discourse for
the American political regime (Bauman, 1987; Beetham, 1991). The
integration of theory and practice comprises the heart of my interpretation of pluralism at Yale. This interpretation, I suggest, sheds light
not only on Yale pluralism but perhaps also on American political
science as a whole. There is truth in Rogers Smith's description of
American political science's "long-standing but perennially unfulfilled
longings to found a grand new science of politics that will also make
American democracy flourish." I agree with Smith that most political
scientists, not just Yale pluralists, "have . . . genuinely wished to aid
American democracy, however deep their reservations might run
about its current form" (1997: 273). The "elective affinity" (Weber,
1958: 284–85) between American liberal democracy and American
political science is by now almost axiomatic. I join the many writers
who assert this affinity, including Lowi (1992: 1–7), Ricci (1984), Farr
(1995), Gunnell (1993), Easton (Easton, Gunnell, and Stein, 1995),

25

Seidelman with Harpham (1985), Lacey and Furner (1993: 3–63), Ross (1991), and Parenti (1996: 221–35).

Yet these broad characterizations about American political science and liberal democracy are unsatisfying for three reasons: they do not recognize _variations_ in this supportive relationship over time; they do not capture the _process_ through which supportive ideas emerge; and, finally, they do not illuminate the complex, double-sided role of political science within American political culture. My interpretation of Yale pluralism is meant to remedy these deficiencies. Let me explain.

As to _variation_, American political science has often wavered on major features of the American political regime. Take, for example, the question of the democratic public. As Terence Ball points out, "There has been something of a seesawing back and forth between a hopeful and a despairing view of the rationality and educability of the citizenry" (1995: 41). Political science has vacillated between _denouncing_ qualities of the public and _dismissing_ these same qualities (e.g., Brooks and Cheng, 2001), a process stimulated by behavior-alism's attack on the rational citizen myth in the 1950s and 1960s. This debate continues today. For example, theorists of "social capi-tal," such as Robert Putnam (1996: 34–46), view with alarm the pub-lic's disengagement from politics. By contrast, theorists of rational choice, following Anthony Downs (1957), treat nonparticipation as an entirely acceptable feature of a liberal democratic regime.

This oscillation even extends to democratic institutions. Some writers, such as Theda Skocpol (Finegold and Skocpol, 1995), see governmental institutions as engines of progressive reform in Ameri-can society. By contrast, others, such as John Chubb and Terry Moe (1990), turn away from institutions and rely upon the market to effect needed reforms in the United States.

Both sides of these two arguments can justly be characterized as friendly to liberal democratic politics. Yet certainly the social capital theorists and Chubb and Moe are more critical of the democratic polity than are—in their quite different ways—Downs or Skocpol. Thus, particular perspectives determine how much support American political science provides to the liberal democratic regime. My ana-lytic framework recognizes this fact. Yale political science in the 1955–70 period provided an unusually strong defense of American liberal democracy. By investigating why this was so, I hope to illuminate American political science more generally.

As to *process,* most studies of scholars do not inquire into their everyday experiences (but see Hollinger, 1996; Verdery, 1991). Even the few studies that consider mundane experience do not investigate the actor's point of view (e.g., Collins, 1998). Instead, writers fall back on two deficient strategies. Some assert that social contexts or political conditions "determine," "shape," "condition," "select," or "account for" the production of ideas. Others treat ideas solely as singular mental constructs, picturing the work of one writer as an unmediated, direct response to that of another. The former "contextualist" approach is characteristic of the sociology of knowledge (McCarthy, 1996); the latter "idealist" approach is characteristic of traditional intellectual history.

I agree with John Gunnell (1995), who implicitly criticizes contextualism for underestimating the freedom social conditions afford actors. Although contexts exert influence, they do so only through personal experiences. Thus, all scholars bring their own distinctive experience of "capitalism" or "the state" or "liberal democracy" to their scholarship on those issues. Hence, Yale pluralism cannot be understood entirely as a response to such general conditions as, say, McCarthyism, the Cold War, or post–World War II prosperity. The point is that personal experiences inevitably differ; therefore, there is no uniform or monolithic "response" of scholars to large social or political events.

Scholars differ from one another in their local circumstances, their professional disciplines, their universities, their departmental colleagues, and their friends and family (Brint, 1994). Also, as Burton Bledstein puts it, "The American university has served as a primary service organization, a professional service institution which has made possible the functions of many derivative institutions serving the middle class" (1976: 289). Therefore university life filters and cushions larger social and political events. In addition, colleagues, friends, and families all refract the effects of capitalism, the state, liberal democracy, McCarthyism, the Cold War, and so on. These filters create distinctive "takes" within seemingly identical contexts. For example, David Calleo—a Yale political scientist from 1960 to 1967—had been a Yale undergraduate honors student. By contrast, Robert Dahl had not attended Yale as an undergraduate. Therefore, the meaning of Yale for Calleo inevitably differed from that of Dahl. Partly for this reason, the two developed different perspectives on Yale pluralism.

If contextualism is an incomplete account of scholarship, so also is idealism. Rarely do intellectual historians incorporate personal experiences within their accounts of ideas. Gunnell himself falls victim to this tendency. For example, he observes that among Austrian émigré social scientists, "a general intellectual orientation . . . facilitated integration" into the United States in the 1930s (1993: 183). But his inferences do not rest on a detailed examination of particular individuals, nor on personal accounts by the actors. Therefore, how are we to know if his assertion is correct?

By contrast, I explore the situationally specific production of a legitimating discourse in a narrow but deep case study. I examine a single political science department in a delimited, but especially fertile, period of its history. One innovation of this framework is that it focuses attention not only on the best-known scholars but also on quite "ordinary" scholars. Why? Because both groups form the context that generates scholarship. True, the Yale political science department between 1955 and 1970 contained such influential scholars as Robert Dahl, Robert Lane, Harold Lasswell, Karl Deutsch, Gabriel Almond, and Charles Lindblom. But it was also home to lesser-known scholars, such as Peter Lupsha, Robert Dix, Willis Hawley, John May, Hayward Alker, Richard Merritt, Irwin Gertzog, and James Fesler. All constituted the "community of experience" that fostered Yale pluralism. Each therefore contributed to Yale scholarship. Exploring this community of experience (see also Wuthnow, 1987) sheds new light on the production and dissemination of scholarly ideas. Indeed, now the ideas appear to be less the products of a few "great minds" than the fruits of a larger collective endeavor.

Applying my analytic framework to Yale political science generates a distinctive description of the way scholars produce and disseminate ideas. Just as supporting characters such as Rosencrantz and Guildenstern see *Hamlet* quite differently from Hamlet himself (in Tom Stoppard's *Rosencrantz and Guildenstern Are Dead*), so also do William Muir or Jonathan Casper see Yale pluralism quite differently from Robert Lane or Charles Lindblom. Academic knowledge is an iceberg, most of whose mass lies submerged beneath the sea. I wish to reveal what lies under the iceberg's tip. Bennett Berger sums up my argument:

> A case study, like a handful of interviews, does not conclusively "prove" anything general. But by focusing on how macro-regularities are experienced by living persons and on how macro-cultural constraints are interpreted . . . in specific situations, micro sociologies give us the rare . . . opportunity to know something about how socially located persons struggle with "conditions" that, in Marxist terms, they did not entirely choose. (1995: 89)

But the micro-analytic focus of a case study does not exhaust its advantages. Instead, as John Walton argues, "Generalizations in social science are developed from case study methods" (1992: 126). I propose some tentative generalizations throughout this study. In particular, I relate political science to *American political culture*. I view this relationship as double-sided. That is, like other academic disciplines, political science "is *in* the same world that it is *about*" (Fuller, 1993: 125); in short, it is embedded in the political culture it analyzes.

What does this double-sidedness, or reflexivity, imply for American political science and American liberal democracy? In one of its two guises, American political science is about American liberal democracy. This is the only aspect most historians of American political science consider (e.g., Fowler, 1999). These writers focus primarily on what political science—as a collection of literary texts—has to say about American liberal democracy. Texts, then, constitute the sole cultural "supports" political science provides for the American political regime.

But, as Fuller's comment implies, political science also participates within the American political regime. Through professional activities and policy advice, political scientists constantly encounter political institutions. Moreover, as teachers, political scientists influence millions of students. In addition, as researchers and writers, political scientists influence both each other and their readers. Indeed, because scientific, rather than religious, legitimation is a principal feature of liberal democracies (Robbins, 1993), the university has taken on a singularly important legitimating role. Finally, as intellectuals, political scientists help to "provide democracies with their political vocabularies" (Goldfarb, 1998: 81). Political science is therefore not only a collection of texts or ideas about American liberal democracy but also a set of practices that helps constitute American liberal democracy. As a single ensemble, text and practice express the full contribution of American political science to American political culture. Therefore, to "do" political science is simultaneously to write a theme for, and to improvise a variation on, American politics.

Many readers will recognize how this theoretical formulation resembles Anthony Giddens's discussion of "structuration" (for an overview, see Layder 1994: chapter 8). According to Giddens, "The concept of structuration involves that of the *duality of structure,* which relates to the *fundamentally recursive character of social life, and expresses the mutual dependence of structure and agency.* By the duality of structure, I mean that the structural properties of social systems are both the medium and the outcome of the practices that constitute those systems" (Giddens, 1979: 69; emphasis in original). "Structuration" is Giddens's attempt to overcome the structure-agency dichotomy that has long plagued the social sciences.

For our purposes, the concept of structuration addresses how political science "agents" (or actors) help to produce the "structures" of American liberal democracy. I argue that Yale political scientists helped to generate—as scholars—and to play out—as colleagues and citizens—the features of American liberal democracy their texts described. Structure and action—literary theme and experiential improvisation—crucially supported each other, producing a legitimating discourse for the American political regime (Boudon, 1989: 123).

However, mine is not a determinist position. Actors do not always conform to structures. Nor do favorable academic environments inevitably produce legitimating discourses. The political scientists who created their version of liberal democratic political culture at Yale in the late 1950s no longer did so by 1970. Instead, Yale political science increasingly departed from its earlier pluralist themes. Thus, the relationship between structure and action—literary theme and experiential improvisation—is contingent and, in Mannheim's (1936: 78–81) terms, "relational." As William Sewell puts it, "Enactments of structures imply a particular concept of agency—one that sees agency not as opposed to, but as constituent of, structure. To be an agent means to be capable of exerting some degree of control over the social relations in which one is enmeshed, which in turn implies the ability to transform those social relations to some degree" (1992: 20; see also

Sewell, 1999). The same observation applies to the themes "performed" by academic scholars.

Let me restate my argument: I maintain that for most of the time between 1955 and 1970, Yale political science produced a useful legitimating discourse—pluralism—for the American political regime. Scholarly writings and improvised performances favored the regime. However, after 1965, Yale political scientists increasingly did not "play tunes" that supported the regime.

Am I just stating the obvious, namely, that "the sixties" changed political science at Yale? If so, why all the theory? But just as intellectual themes may fail to reproduce themselves, so also may challenges to such themes—as represented by "the 1960s"—not necessarily succeed (e.g., Wolin, 1997). After all, performers may choose to play the same old tunes in the same old ways. Only the complex, undetermined but probabilistic interplay between scholarly theme and experiential improvisation—idea and action—decides whether political scientists produce a legitimating discourse for the American regime, or whether they reformulate, weaken, or ultimately abandon that discourse.

Of course, a single case study has limitations. By choosing depth, I sacrifice breadth. I do not compare the Yale department to other departments and can therefore not definitively generalize my interpretation of Yale to other settings. But how serious is this weakness? A comparison might reveal that Yale resembled many other departments. If so, this finding would vindicate my concentration on Yale. Indeed, I have already argued that Yale was part of a national movement toward pluralism and behavioralism. In addition, I have argued in chapter 1 that all academics are predisposed—but not fated— to create legitimating discourses. Therefore, complementary findings would validate my concentration on Yale.

The more threatening possibility is that Yale was different from other departments. Perhaps other departments created some pluralist writings but lacked pluralist improvisations. Or perhaps other departments operated in a pluralist fashion but produced few pluralist texts. However, this finding would show only that the congruence of texts and improvisations is not a *given* but, rather, an *achievement*, as Sewell's comment suggests. Still, once achieved, congruence produces a legitimating discourse of real significance, such as pluralism at Yale.

In any case, the concern with comparison and breadth misunderstands the logic of this research. Only an in-depth case study can add a performative element to the study of academic discourse. Only an in-depth case study can illuminate an entire department as a community of experience. Only an in-depth case study can apply my particular approach to academic legitimation, which requires consideration both of writings and actions. To be sure, were I to have had unlimited time and money, I would have explored other cases. I had no such resources; nevertheless, the distinctive importance of Yale, the specific approach I take to academic legitimation, and this case study's actual findings—which do yield some tentative generalizations—justify the method I have chosen.

To summarize: as I hope to demonstrate, through the medium of pluralism Yale faculty acted both as scholars and as department members in accordance with the political system their works described. Partly for this reason, the department—and, by extension, the political system—appeared to work reasonably well. To support this point, I return to the four major pluralist premises and examine each one through the eyes of faculty members.

THE PLURALIST PREMISE IN PERFORMANCE

My interviews reveal that, for the most part, Yale faculty recall the department in pluralist terms. Although they rarely explicitly introduce the term *pluralist*, their descriptions of the department embody the pluralist premise; that is, they portray the department as peacefully competing, sometimes conflictive but accessible, and flexible groups of colleagues. Although some few faculty dissent from this characterization, on balance, the department "performed" the pluralist premise in most of its activities.

For example, the pluralist premise contends that power holders gradually offer marginalized groups access to influence. In the Yale departmental context pluralist access did develop. Thus, one traditionally stigmatized and excluded group—Jews, who had suffered restrictive student and faculty quotas at Yale—gained more faculty positions. Although it was true that in the aftermath of World War II, quotas on Jews had become morally insupportable, eliminating these quotas was also a *political* performance of pluralism. The department also opened doors to Jewish students in the graduate program (see Oren, 1985).

Members of the faculty are quite articulate on this subject. Richard Merritt, for example, explicitly mentions the recruitment (for scholarly purposes) of Jewish faculty to the university. Speaking about the growth of innovative departmental scholarship in the persons of Almond and Deutsch, he notes: "Yale University was willing to support this [innovative] kind of project. Yale had been under fire for anti-Semitism and other things, particularly in the sociology department, and people like Almond and Deutsch served a useful purpose for the university" (interview, January 12, 1998).

Herbert Kaufman reports that although he was among a mere handful of Jewish department chairs at Yale, "at no point did I personally ever encounter any difficulty" (interview, November 29, 1997). Indeed, he remarks that the university had actually become *philo*-Semitic in an effort to overcome the anti-Semitic reputation of the sociology department. Finally, Fred Greenstein remarks that ethnicity had ceased to be salient among graduate students by the late 1950s. Nor did it become visible during his time on the faculty (interview, July 23, 1997).

Of course, Yale was not unique in opening doors to Jews. American higher education in general became more accessible to Jews following World War II. But universities varied in their receptiveness to Jews. David Hollinger notes, for example, that Columbia—historically a bastion of anti-Semitism—reversed course completely. By contrast, other universities, such as Michigan—whose Institute for Social Relations and political science department competed for prominence with Yale's in the 1950s and 1960s—was something of a laggard. Indeed, Hollinger observes that Jewish refugee scholars from Europe did not make their way to Michigan (1996: 136). Hollinger commends Yale for moving more rapidly than Michigan toward the absorption of Jews (9).

Another form of pluralist access is informality and flexibility in recruitment practices. Here again the Yale department performed the pluralist premise. Consider, for example, the recruitment of three junior faculty. In the recruitment of Herbert Kaufman we see the crucial role of informal social networks; in the case of David Danelski we observe the role of department customs; and in the case of Peter Lupsha we encounter the department's capacity to capitalize on pure serendipity. In each case, we see how informal aspects of recruitment performed the pluralist premise.

Informal social networks brought Herbert Kaufman rapidly to the attention of the Yale department. Kaufman originally became associated with Harold Stein, a Yale graduate who edited a case book series in public administration for the Committee on Public Administration Studies. Kaufman published a study of New York airport politics in the series and also authored two additional case studies. He then embarked with Wallace Sayre on the research that became *Governing New York City* (1960). At the same time, Yale was searching for someone to teach state and local government; the department consulted Stein, the Yale alumnus, for advice. Stein recommended Kaufman, whom Yale hired. As Kaufman put it in his interview, it was "sheer chance" that he had "published a study in a public administration case book series whose director happened to have the Yale connection. Otherwise, they wouldn't have known who I was."

Certainly informal social connections often sustain "old boy networks"—exclusive oligarchies rather than pluralist openness. However, in the case of Kaufman—a Jew whose scholarship advanced a pluralist theory of American politics, who had graduated from the unprestigious City College of New York, and who joined a department already tilted toward pluralism—the network's informality constituted a form of pluralist performance.

In David Danelski's case, departmental custom facilitated rapid, informal access via recruitment. Danelski describes his first impressions of the Yale department on his recruitment visit as "just absolutely wonderful."

> They took me to Morey's [the well-known Yale private club], and I had some chowder or whatever that special soup is at Morey's, and we had a lovely conversation around the table. There were a few questions about my work; there was a general discussion about the field. Then I went up to the office, and James Fesler was the chair then, and he made an offer at that time. There was no presentation. . . . I think there was a department meeting between lunch and my meeting, but within an hour or so of the lunch I had an offer to join the department. This is one reason I felt so good. You come there and they take you to lunch, they . . . treat you as one of their own, nothing like you are going to have to work for this or anything like that. They embraced me with style. (Interview, August 28, 1997)

For Danelski, who came from a Polish American working-class neighborhood in Green Bay, Wisconsin, this treatment may well have been heady stuff.

In the case of Peter Lupsha we observe a combination of Yale social networks, informality, and pure serendipity. As a graduate student at Stanford, Lupsha accidentally encountered Nelson Polsby (a Yale Ph.D.) in Palo Alto. According to Lupsha, Polsby phoned Fred Greenstein—his Yale classmate—at Wesleyan University in Middletown, Connecticut, to suggest that Greenstein consider Lupsha for a position at Wesleyan. Greenstein agreed to do so. But on his way to the interview at Wesleyan, Lupsha dropped in on his friend Sidney Tarrow, then teaching at Yale. Lupsha recounts what then occurred:

> The next day Sid took me into the campus and introduced me to Herb Kaufman, who was chair at that time. . . . Sid had a class, so Herb walked me around and showed me the campus. . . . [The campus] was really impressive to me because I had never been there. I grew up in kind of a European family that didn't have a lot of education, an immigrant family. . . . I had never been at a place like Yale. (Interview, June 25, 1998)

As it happened, the monthly faculty lunch at Morey's was scheduled for that day, and Lupsha found himself invited. A scheduled speaker did not show up, Lupsha recounts, and "I was sitting next to Harold Lasswell, and Lasswell said to Kaufman, 'Well, we need a speaker. The guy [Lupsha] was going to do it tomorrow [at Wesleyan]. Let him give his talk to us today.'" Lupsha then spoke at the luncheon; "basically, it turned out to be a bit of questioning of *Who Governs?* . . . I was totally relaxed. I just gave it. You know, what the hell, and answered questions and went on and did the same thing at Wesleyan." Three days later Greenstein called to say that Yale wanted to hire him. So Lupsha found himself at Yale, not Wesleyan.

However, pluralist access did not entirely dominate the Yale department. The relationship between junior and senior faculty provides a case in point. These relations were often distant and tense. But even here there was some pluralism. For example, Hayward Alker, who is quite critical of the department, singles out his easy relationship with Robert Dahl as a highlight of his time at Yale. When Alker remarked to Dahl that there was a "huge social gap" between junior and senior faculty, Dahl "said why don't we play squash so we would have more social interactions. So we did play squash. It was fabulous; that was very decent of him, and that is one reason why I felt so bad when I left" (interview, January 10, 1998). Though Alker thinks junior-senior tensions were chronic at Yale, he also concedes that the senior faculty attempted to alleviate these tensions.

In its relationship to graduate students the department did a somewhat better job of providing access. In fact, during the crises of the late 1960s and early 1970s, graduate students brought about changes in department practice and policy. As a result, relations between graduate students and the department did not become wholly polarized; in adapting to student concerns, the department again performed the politics of pluralist access.

Both archival and interview evidence supports this conclusion. For example, David Mayhew describes the department as "very cool" and "dispassionate" in responding to student demands in the late 1960s. As he puts it, "[Senior faculty] did not get caught up in revolutionary fervor; on the other hand, they did not get caught up in counterrevolutionary fervor" (interview, August 26, 1997). To Mayhew, graduate student activism in the department climaxed during the Black Panther trial in New Haven in April 1970. As Mayhew recalls:

> There was a meeting between graduate students and senior faculty at which there was a call by students to "get rid of distinctions . . . and have just a meeting between the graduate students and faculty." Now the senior faculty, of whom I was not one at the time, made it clear that this is not a department meeting. This is something else. Nonetheless, a vote was taken; somebody made a motion that the university administration be called on to give . . . half a million dollars to the cause of the Black Panthers, and it was voted . . . that was the peak of things, but the department was not criticized.

In Mayhew's reconstruction, the department apparently struck a typical pluralist bargain with graduate students. The department agreed to support student demands addressed to the university; in return, the department retained its formal autonomy and escaped student criticism. Perhaps the department calculated that it would never need to deliver its part of the bargain and considered the commitment simply a symbolic gesture to defuse tension. Yet the department could not be sure; meanwhile, it provided meaningful access and influence to students without jeopardizing its hold on authority and status.

Individual department members also reached out to politically disaffected students. Phillips Shively recalls that Joseph LaPalombara, a comparativist, "got quite engaged having a twenty-four-hour hotline to the students . . . trying to channel this energy into productive directions" (interview, June 4, 1998). Indeed, LaPalombara significantly altered his own political stance. According to several graduate students, LaPalombara originally tended toward hawkishness on the Vietnam War. Nevertheless, perhaps in response to student pressure, LaPalombara softened his political views. Ultimately, according to Shively, he served as a political broker between students and faculty. Thus, LaPalombara practiced the pluralist tactic of extending informal access in order to protect an institution. Shively judges this tactic "a very good reaction."

Graduate student access and influence was not confined to national political issues but also extended to departmental practices. For example, Charles Lindblom recalls that in the late 1960s and early 1970s graduate students began to serve on department committees. For the first time, women graduate students organized; by the early 1970s women pressed for more representation in the graduate program. According to Lindblom, the department responded in typical pluralist fashion: it struck a compromise between conflicting groups. The department appointed a woman graduate student to the admissions committee. Her task was specifically to promote individual women applicants. According to Lindblom, this change worked effectively.

Jessica Wolf, the first graduate student to serve on the admissions committee, confirms Lindblom's account. Wolf, who is otherwise critical of Yale pluralism, speaks warmly of the committee:

> I thought that it was helpful to the process to have some people who were explicitly looking to see whether women candidates were as good as or close to as good as or better than equivalent male candidates. Doing that raised the consciousness of everyone on the committee. And more women were admitted probably than would have been otherwise. And a different perspective was provided about what it was that the institution or the department might be thinking about, or what to think about, in terms of candidates. (Interview, May 19, 1998)

Inevitably, one focus of graduate student concerns is the structure of examinations; after all, these are the gateway to dissertations and first jobs. The ability of graduate students to influence the exam format, therefore, is a significant test of access. By this standard, graduate students at Yale in the late 1960s did perform pluralism effectively. In the 1969–70 academic year, at student urging, the department introduced "Program B" to the traditional Ph.D. program. This new alternative reduced the required graduate courses from sixteen to twelve. Instead of having to pass the usual three exams, students could choose to write three papers under the tutelage of individual advisers. One paper was a field survey; one was "an analysis of a theoretical or empirical problem important to some area of political science"; and one was a paper of the student's own choosing. Students were required to complete these papers by the end of their second year ("Program B," box 3, folder 35, YUDPS). The program stipulated that the papers were to be of "journal quality." According to the Department of Political Science Annual Report of 1968–69, student support for the change was high (4).

Faculty reactions to the new program varied. In a letter to graduate student Richard Simeon, dated December 4, 1969, David Danelski praised the new program because "it brings students and members of the faculty into close intellectual relationships." By contrast, in a memo to Chair Robert Lane a year before the reform, William Foltz responded guardedly to the proposed changes: "If I understand the intellectual (as opposed to the Oedipal) thrust behind the graduate student demands, they seem fundamentally concerned about broadening the range of theoretical perspectives to which they are exposed" (Box 12, folder 22, p. 2, YUDPS). Despite his somewhat jaundiced observation, Foltz displays sympathy for the proposal, especially for the students' interest in nonmathematical approaches to political science.

Also, in the 1968–69 academic year the department provided graduate students more access to a range of department activities. For example, graduate students joined the Student-Faculty Course of Study Committee to discuss curricula. In addition, the department opened faculty meetings to graduate students and allowed students to speak and listen to debate. However, following discussion, students were required to leave the meeting and did not observe the casting of votes ("Program B," box 3, folder 35, p. 5, YUDPS). The report recommending these changes was signed by Chair Lane.

Graduate students did have to struggle for access. As early as the spring of 1965, the Yale International Relations and Political Science Association (YIRPSA), the organization that represented graduate students, had forwarded a proposal to Chair Herbert Kaufman requesting changes in the graduate program and petitioning for further discussions. It took three years and much student pressure both inside and outside the department before the students finally succeeded (Memo to Kaufman from YIRPSA, box 8, folder 89, YUDPS). But, of course, group pressure is central to the pluralist paradigm.

Moreover, the conflict did not end; in fact, ultimately, the change in exam structure did not survive. However, at least temporarily, graduate students did enjoy considerable access and influence. As the faculty committee set up by the department to respond to student concerns commented: "These meetings had the useful effect of increasing our awareness of the students' requests and the rationale for them. . . . Following the meetings with the graduate students, the members of the committee . . . became aware of their shared inclination to propose certain radical departures from past practices" (cited in Bennett et al., 1969: 635).

I don't mean to overemphasize the Yale response to graduate student pressures for reform in the late 1960s. Other universities experienced similar pressures, and many responded in similar ways. However, Yale did depart considerably from its traditional procedures; thus, its reforms performed the pluralist premise.

The department also recruited new thinkers who would add to its evolving pluralist arguments. Moreover, it fought vigorously against administrative opposition to promotions the department favored. These recruitment and promotion initiatives epitomize the pluralist argument that successful power holders must be persistent, flexible, and resourceful in advancing their claims.

Consider, for example, the recruitment of Harold Lasswell and Charles Lindblom to the department. Lasswell initially joined the Law School at Yale, where he retained an office and a position until his retirement. For some time his contacts with the political science department were limited. This detachment ended in the early 1950s, when James Fesler came to the political science department as chair. According to Fesler: "When I came here I was shocked to discover that the most distinguished political scientist was not in the department, and so I had lunch with Lasswell and talked to the Law School. He got his title changed to political science . . . previously he had no connection, which is kind of amazing" (interview, August 26, 1997).

By bringing Lasswell into the department, Fesler practiced what pluralism preached; that is, he forged a coalition to advance the power of his particular group, namely, the political science department. Although Lasswell remained somewhat tangential to the department, he did attract a cadre of students who still consider themselves as "Lasswellian" policy scientists (e.g., Ascher, 1978: 1). Thus, through Lasswell, the department extended its influence to a distinctive segment of graduate students.

Charles Lindblom also began his Yale career outside the political science department. But when his progress in the economics department faltered, political science reached out to him. According to Fred Greenstein:

> Lindblom was probably stymied at associate professor by the economics department, which saw no merit in what he was doing. . . . Then he and Dahl wrote that book (*Politics, Economics, and Welfare*) in a kind of golden Hawthorne effect. You know, they lived two houses apart as part of a housing group with a whole collection of war veterans set up on a hill in the forties, early fifties, cinder block ranch houses. . . . It was a place famous for its parties, and for its cheerful good drinking, as people did in that era. Dahl and Lindblom—this was Lindblom's description—wrote the book in a year when they were both on leave. I think they both taught in one of the Yale upper-class disciplinary programs, and they wrote with one person at the typewriter keyboard, and the two of them composing it. It was like a studio in Hollywood.

Via his connection to Dahl, Lindblom became informally associated with the political science department. Ultimately, Lindblom formally left economics and joined political science in 1965, adding to the department's pluralist perspective. In fact, in 1965 Lindblom published *The Intelligence of Democracy*, which added "partisan mutual adjustment" to the vocabulary of Yale pluralism. By recruiting Lindblom, the department displayed the flexibility that a powerful pluralist coalition requires in order to replenish its ranks.

The department also fought hard to control the recruitment and promotion of junior faculty members. For example, according to one faculty member, the department confronted Yale president Kingman

Brewster himself, who disliked behavioralism and the idea of a science of politics. A fight emerged with Brewster over the proposed promotion of Bruce Russett, an international relations protégée of Karl Deutsch. Ultimately, the department prevailed in the struggle. According to the same faculty member, the department overcame Law School objections to the appointment of David Danelski, who was known for his psychological approach to the Supreme Court. When the department prevailed, Danelski augmented the political psychology aspects of the behavioral approach. More important, the Russett and Danelski struggles performed pluralist politics successfully.

In this section I emphasize access as part of the pluralist premise of multiple, competing political groups. Later I discuss access in connection with the *reactivity* premise. In this latter guise my focus is on the *informal* access of nonleaders to leaders. In the present, pluralist case, students, Jews, and new faculty achieved *formal* positions and powers. They therefore expanded a pluralist system of multiple, competing groups.

However, certain types of access sometimes strained pluralism. After all, if access grants too much power, it threatens the pluralist premise of balanced power centers. The limits of pluralism manifested themselves in the case of Karl Deutsch, who still elicits ambivalent feelings among department faculty. On the one hand, many admire Deutsch's scholarship and pluralist political entrepreneurship. On the other hand, Deutsch strained both personal and collegial relations in the department. His eventful departure from Yale illustrates the limits of Yale pluralism.

Several members of the department comment favorably on Deutsch's role in the department. For example, Sidney Tarrow, a Europeanist, states that his own work on social mobilization "resonated" strongly with the work of Deutsch. Deutsch was not only a "tremendous influence" but also a successful political operator:

> I don't need to remind you that Deutsch was much more aggressive and much more successful at getting his students hired at Yale than Dahl was. When you think of Dahl's famous students, all of them left, went on to other places. Same is true of Lindblom's students. I think Barber was the only one who stayed, and he was a Lane student. Whereas Karl was a classical European imperialist. He hired . . . the department hired at least three of his students. (Interview, January 9, 1998)

41

Tarrow identifies these three students (Richard Merritt, Bruce Russett, and William Foltz) as "acolytes" of Deutsch's. This observation suggests a self-conscious, personal coterie. Robert Dix confirms this aspect of Deutsch's influence: "Karl Deutsch had sort of a following, and people that actually trailed him around and carried his stuff, and things of that sort. If there was any sort of "school" [of thought] that I noted it was that . . . he had his own little empire, his own secretary" (interview, January 8, 1998).

To Tarrow and Dix, Deutsch was aggressive but still only a minor irritant in department life. Significantly, both Gabriel Almond and Robert Dahl refer to Deutsch in precisely this fashion. I inquired of Almond whether, as some I interviewed suggested, friction and rivalry with Deutsch influenced his own decision to leave Yale. He unequivocally denied this account: "No. Karl could be a pain in the neck. He used to make demands for unlimited resources, and I was sorry for Bob Dahl [then chair of the department] because of the experience, but it was not Karl Deutsch. We were friends" (interview, October 2, 1997). Dahl acknowledges that Deutsch was difficult, but he also leaps to Deutsch's defense: "Karl Deutsch was to some extent a difficult person, but he was difficult mainly for a chair, because he had no administrative sense at all. But he was not . . . he wasn't a bad colleague, and he was not in any sense an evil person" (interview, August 27, 1997).

According to these department members, the department's pluralism could accommodate Deutsch. But as Tarrow's comments demonstrate, Deutsch's success had its dark side. Tarrow initially asserts that Deutsch hired his own students; however, Tarrow then quickly corrects himself, and attributes the hiring to the department, not to Deutsch. Tarrow's conflation of Deutsch and the department reveals the chief danger Deutsch posed to pluralist practice: namely, that conflicting factions might place their own interests ahead of the department's, and one faction might become dominant. Pluralism requires multiple, balanced centers of power and strong, unselfish leadership, not a preeminent leader who subordinates the department to his personal interests.

Some members of the department assert that Deutsch did not respect these pluralist rules. The result was chronic friction in the department. For example, contrary to Almond, Bruce Russett observes that: "[Deutsch] and Gabriel Almond didn't get along terribly well. And that relationship, which started out quite hopefully—maybe because they were both basically makers of the behavioral revolution—something went wrong rather quickly" (interview, August 25, 1997).

Russett believes the Almond-Deutsch rivalry hurt the department. According to him, graduate students felt they had to choose between Deutsch and Almond. Russett believes that Almond left the department in part because of Deutsch.

Fred Greenstein extends the criticism of Deutsch. He describes a fraught relationship between Deutsch and Herbert Kaufman during the latter's chairmanship, a conflict Greenstein admits he knows about only "secondhand." According to Greenstein: "Some of it was Deutsch's sheer irresponsibility. I mean some of the Deutsch issues appear in *Tell the Time to None* [a novel by Helen Lane, Robert Lane's wife]. He is the figure whose student commits suicide when someone lost his exam."

Kaufman forcefully confirms Deutsch's refusal to play pluralist politics. Kaufman first supports Greenstein's account of the administrative difficulties Deutsch posed for him as chair: "I had run-ins with Karl even though I had known him for years. I found it impossible to live with him. He was the kind of person you never gave an administrative assignment to because you didn't have confidence that he'd carry it out." According to Kaufman, other members of the department had to do "KP"—that is, extra work—to compensate for Deutsch's administrative lapses.

Kaufman then widens his criticism of Deutsch to embrace personnel, budget, and even department membership. As he puts it:

> In [department] meetings Karl was always vociferous. There was some tensions when Karl wanted to start a center. Then he would try to go and raise money for it. And people began to see that he would use it to staff the department. He would bring people in on his research project and say, "Well, they are doing research, and they are competent people. Why don't we let them teach a course?" And they would teach a course. Suddenly they had a vote in the department on people of their rank. So there was great concern. Moreover, he became very slipshod on his administrative operations—budgetary. So there was real concern about that. And finally there was a time he was flying out to

43

Michigan to teach a course while he was faculty here. Nobody objected to that until Michigan put his name in their department . . . as a member of that department. That really blew the roof off.

These accounts suggest that Deutsch upset the balance of pluralistic power in the department. Deutsch did not navigate flexibly between conflict and cooperation. Most important, Deutsch's drive to amass personal power violated the "plural power centers" norm of pluralism. Thus, when Helen Lane satirized Deutsch in *Tell the Time to None* (1966), she provided an unforeseen, but decisive, denouement to the departmental dilemma Deutsch presented. Extremely angered by the unflattering portrayal, Deutsch chose to leave the department.

In *Tell the Time to None* Helen Lane presents thinly disguised, critical portraits of many department members. But her portrait of Deutsch ("Werner Wolf") is certainly the most biting. Dahl—himself portrayed as so career-centered that he accidentally leaves his wife at a gas station on their honeymoon—contrasts his own and Deutsch's reaction to the novel: "There was a figure I could sort of identify as Helen's using something like me for the purpose of fiction. I didn't feel hurt by that. We continued to be very good friends. But Karl and Ruth [Deutsch] were badly hurt. Helen didn't talk to her about it . . . strange that she didn't foresee that . . . [the Deutsches would be hurt]."

Bruce Russett—also portrayed caustically in the book—is more direct about Deutsch's reaction:

> Karl was definitely hurt. I think it was certainly a factor—I would not call it the . . . principal factor—in his going to Harvard. I think the gold cord [of Harvard] pulled him back. On the other hand, he didn't need it. Karl was always a bargainer; he would try to bargain. He just went and announced that he was going. So I think he was hurt. It was not very flattering—not totally inaccurate, but not really fair. As he said—I was still junior—he did not talk much about this. But I do remember his saying that "I have my faults, but I never drove anybody to suicide."

What does the Deutsch affair tell us about the department's pluralism? In Deutsch's case the normal practices of pluralism—respect for procedures, willingness to compromise, coalition formation, decentralized decision making—had failed. But the department neither wanted Deutsch to leave nor possessed the authority to cut him loose. After all, he was an important, internationally respected scholar. Thus, Helen Lane's book served as a kind of deus ex machina, a fortuitous intervention that helped to resolve the problem Deutsch posed. Moreover, since she was not a member of the department, the department bore no responsibility for the depiction. Despite the pain the book caused some faculty, *Tell the Time to None* actually protected pluralist performance in the department.

In a pluralist system decentralized holders of power forge coalitions with each other on issues of common concern. They also unite to protect the system from external attacks. Therefore, maintaining good relations among faculty was of primary importance. A substantial number of faculty members describe the department in just these pluralist terms.

An example is provided by William Foltz. According to Foltz, the department was mainly collegial when he entered it in 1957. One contributing factor was the Thursday department luncheon at Morey's, which Foltz believes produced informal exchange and comradeship (interview, November 30, 1997).

Douglas Rae agrees. Like Foltz, he joined the department as a junior member, but at a much later and more conflictive point, 1967. Yet Rae characterizes the department during the late 1960s in terms similar to Foltz's, the department, "was an extremely civil place . . . the rules of comity and civility were almost uniformly observed, and where breeched there was a sort of clear, normative response. And I think that hasn't broken down. . . . I think that is still true" (Interview, August 26, 1997).

According to faculty, several factors facilitated pluralist accommodation in the department. One junior member, for example, observes that during his years at Yale the department consisted of three distinct subgroups: a group surrounding Robert Dahl; a group surrounding Robert Lane; and a group of international relations scholars led by Deutsch. These three groups did not interact very much; nevertheless, they were able to cooperate. This member surmises that a unifying factor was social estrangement from the city of New Haven. Like a military unit, department members turned to each other for mutual protection. He believes the social isolation and department solidarity stimulated the scholarship the department produced (interview, January 12, 1998).

Irwin Gertzog, a junior member of the department in the late 1960s, essentially echoes this account. However, Gertzog is more reserved. As he puts it, "The divisions on intellectual grounds that existed I cannot recall very well. I don't think they were particularly evident . . . [but] there was personal animosity" (interview, October 16, 1997). Gertzog found departmental meetings impressive, especially when they concerned "how the department should be run and decisions [that] had to be made." In Gertzog's view, the intellectual strengths of the department mitigated personal rivalries and allowed the department to operate pluralistically.

The personal strains that Gertzog discerned in the late 1960s no doubt owed something to the department's expansion. To Fred Greenstein the smaller department of the late 1950s and early 1960s was "self-effacing, very genteel, and utterly democratic," an observation he repeats at another point. But departmental expansion in the late 1960s disrupted this pattern. Still, even in the late 1960s easy relations remained common, including regular junior-senior contacts. According to Isaac Kramnick, "There was this whole culture of dinner parties . . . and all the senior faculty, I mean, their sense of interacting with junior faculty . . . in my memories, was dinner parties where junior faculty were invited" (interview, October 14, 1999).

At the same time, relaxed socializing and comparatively egalitarian decision making did not compromise another pluralist improvisation—that is, rewarding the most promising scholars. Charles Lindblom remarks:

> I had always seen the department as remarkably harmonious in their dealings with each other. Looking back, I see more than I appreciated at the time, that that was because certain people in the department were being deferred to by others, recognizing that they were on the fast track. . . . Jim [Fesler] tended to say to people like Lane and Dahl, that you guys really are the hotshots here. We will go along with you. (Interview, August 26, 1997)

A further improvisation of the pluralist premise involves leadership. Pluralist political leaders usually function as consensus builders, and they unite competing factions. Though under great strain in the late 1960s, the department struggled to maintain a pluralist, consensus-building leadership. For example, in 1970, it chose as chair H. Bradford Westerfield, who was a self-professed hawk on Vietnam but perceived himself as a moderate consensus builder in department matters. In fact, he attributes his selection as chair to precisely this characteristic:

> The reason I was made chair is—I was in my own mind, nobody ever told me so—was that Bob Lane, who was the chair before me, was particularly anxious that what he had been building in terms of trying to keep the graduate students pacified by endless rapping with them would continue at least a couple more years. I had a certain constitution, because that is just my way under crisis situations. . . . I am an instinctive centrist when you set up any kind of a conflict situation. That makes me very liable to shift my own view over time, because if the center shifts, then I shift. (Interview, August 29, 1997)

Of eighteen faculty members whom I asked explicitly to address the matter of pluralist practice in the department, twelve characterized the department in pluralist terms, and only six demurred. On balance, in its self-conception the department performed the pluralist premise during its most productive period.

What about the teaching of pluralist texts at Yale? Lest there be any doubt, the department certainly did emphasize pluralist theory. Indeed, it taught pluralism almost exclusively. For example, a "Recent Democratic Theories" graduate course in 1964 required students to read Schumpeter, Dahl, Sartori, Downs, Kornhauser, Almond and Verba, and Lipset, Trow and Coleman, scholars who to varying degrees propounded pluralist approaches to democracy. More important, no texts on the syllabus challenged these pluralist arguments. In May of 1964, the Political Science Research Library at Yale provided graduate students with "A List of Some Outstanding Books in Political Science (1940–63)." The list included works by Braybrooke and Lindblom; James Coleman's *Community Conflict;* Dahl; Dahl and Lindblom; Lane; Lipset's *Political Man;* Polsby; March and Simon; David Reisman; Sayre and Kaufman; Schumpeter; and Truman. All of these writers were staples of the pluralist tradition. By contrast, the only works explicitly critical of pluralism were Mills's *The Power Elite* (1956), Christian Bay's *The Structure of Freedom* (1958), and Sheldon Wolin's *Politics and Vision* (1960).

Or consider examinations. The first question on the graduate Political Institutions and Behavior section of the Modern State General

Examination in September 1967 required the student to review the pluralist approach to community power. It also asked students to discuss critics of the pluralist approach. Clearly, Yale political science did teach pluralism to many of its students until the very end of the 1960s.

A useful test of the argument in this section involves Charles Lindblom's ruminations on governance at Yale. In a 1971 *Yale Alumni Magazine* article, Lindblom described "Yale as a Political System." Did Lindblom see Yale in pluralist terms? And, in so doing, did he improvise pluralism?

For the most part, Lindblom does ascribe pluralist features to Yale. First, he argues, policymaking takes place primarily through persuasion rather than through formal centralized authority. Second, protecting the university (and, presumably, its "rules of the game") is more important than the pursuit of individual or group goals. Third, professional and disciplinary (group) interests "actually subvert to a degree the University as an educational institution" (11). Fourth, because "these conflicting commitments and loyalties are out in the open" (12), there is trust among political actors. Fifth, as in pluralism, there is much decentralization and informal delegation of authority: "Neither faculty nor administration see it necessary to concentrate responsibility in the hands of any one conspicuous committee or cabinet" (12). Sixth, and finally, budgetary allocations usually take place "at the margin—that is incrementally, rather than in conspicuous large moves" (16).

However, according to Lindblom, other aspects of the university depart from pluralism. Yale enjoys a substantive as well as procedural consensus, something a pluralist system never achieves. Moreover, there have not been power struggles at Yale. There is also more candor at Yale than is typical in most political systems, pluralism included. Also, participants at Yale think of themselves not as citizens but as trustees. Finally, Yale's leaders do not attempt to claim personal credit for decisive wins in issue controversies.

While not entirely pluralist, Yale resembles a pluralist democracy more than it does a system of centralized authority, participatory democracy, or social democracy. In Lindblom's view, Yale embodies ideals—such as agreement on goals—that support pluralism, but that pluralism never itself achieves.

THE REACTIVE PREMISE IN PERFORMANCE

At the outset of my interview with Herbert Kaufman, without my prompting, Kaufman spells out the reactive premise of pluralist theory: "My impression, anyway, is that academics generally chase after what's happening in the world and offer explanations for what has happened. . . . Maybe I'm wrong, but seldom did they have—somebody like Marx—an influence on events." In short, according to Kaufman, academic behavior resembles that of the American political regime, which also responds to events and does not control the future. To substantiate his point, Kaufman cites Harold Laski, an early twentieth-century British political scientist. "Does anybody know where Laski is today? In my day as an undergraduate, even when I was a graduate student, he was a giant." In Kaufman's view, most academics, even the Laskis, are "chroniclers," not "fashioners" of politics.

Later Kaufman situates the reactive premise in relation to World War II. Speaking of public administration, he states:

> What changed perceptions in my field and I think in the rest of political science was World War II, because a lot of political scientists were drawn into government . . . they got into the political scene, and the government didn't look like what they had been portraying it. . . . It wasn't a matter of a bunch of economic masters cracking a whip . . . it was a great buzzing confusion, and different people had different segments of it.

Thus, pluralist analysis was a reaction to experience. Kaufman even applies the reactive premise to his own research:

> I didn't get into Washington until 1946 as an intern, and there were a group of us who fanned out through the government. . . . I would talk to the kids working on the Hill and say, "Who was calling the shots?" Taft was the leader of the conservatives, and where does he get his instructions from? That's what he believes. Nobody has to tell him. It's a matter of conviction, of deep conviction.
>
> I worked in the administrative management division of the department, and I was trying to get a feel for the bureaucracy. That is when I came to the realization that the bureaucracy, the government, is not a cohesive entity. It's really a lot of people in business for themselves once the money is made available.

In essence, Kaufman concluded that government was a pluralist enterprise, a view he carried to his study of New York City: "You start looking around, and you discover big chunks of a system have virtually no connection with other chunks of the system . . . a whole different set of actors. Occasionally somebody would come in and would clearly have an impact elsewhere, like Robert Moses, [but] most of them work without reference to one another." Kaufman, who states that, "When I was an undergraduate, we were all some form of Marxist," became a pluralist as a result of his experience. Thus, he improvised the reactive premise contained in his pluralist texts.

Another version of the reactive premise emerges in Hayward Alker's account of Yale pluralism. Alker, who taught methods and international relations at Yale in the early and mid-1960s, was much influenced by Harold Lasswell at Yale. Indeed, Alker considers Lasswell a key figure in the origin of Yale pluralism. More important, through Lasswell the Cold War indirectly influenced Yale pluralism. As Alker puts it:

> Lasswell is very much a Cold War figure in this regard. Lasswell shifts from his Pareto kind of elitism stuff of the thirties to policy science for democracies and training Yale elite lawyers to run the world, in the sense that Yale was running the world, or America was running the world . . . so that kind of elitist training for democracy, I think, was very important in Lasswell's redefinition of himself.

In Alker's view the Cold War made the United States the leader of liberal democracies. In reaction to this new situation, Lasswell jettisoned his earlier, pessimistic elitism (e.g., 1930) in favor of democratic elitism, labeled the policy sciences of democracy. In turn, Lasswell's reaction influenced other Yale scholars. Indeed, according to Alker, Dahl's original title for *Who Governs?* was *Power and Democracy*, a gloss upon Lasswell and Kaplan's *Power and Society* (1950). The phrase "Democracy and Power" did survive, forming the subtitle of *Who Governs?*

Another variation of the reactivity premise emerges in the observations of Douglas Rae, who joined the Yale department in 1967 and who is now a member of the Yale School of Management. Rae states that Dahl's *Preface* and *Who Governs?*

> portrayed capitalist democracy in a favorable light and gave it a little theoretical apparatus which discriminated nicely between this system

and other systems with which we as a nation were in rivalrous relations. His intuitions corresponded closely to those of national political elites, and I think that had something to do with the Cold War and with Bob's fleshing out of a kind of open society story . . . Karl Popper's story, in a way which appeared to blend it with science and to give it a degree of scientific rigor.

Thus, Dahl's pluralism reacted to ("corresponded to") the Cold War competition between the United States and the Soviet Union.

Rae's observation reveals both the strengths and the limitations of my argument about the reactive premise. First, department members rarely assert the reactive premise decisively or coherently; certainly, Rae's "correspond" or "something to do with the Cold War" does not claim that the Cold War or political elites actually *caused* pluralism. Nor does Rae state that political events or economic systems ("capitalist democracy") *determined* pluralist thought. But pluralism *is* a legitimating discourse, for it "portrayed capitalist democracy in a favorable light."

Second, Rae, never reduces the reactive premise to single phenomena. To the contrary, he combines the reactive premise with Karl Popper's ideas (1950); thus, pluralism is a reaction both to political conditions and to influential ideas.

Finally, Rae's version of the reactive premise is different from that of Kaufman. Where Kaufman emphasizes his personal experiences in explaining pluralism, Rae omits reference to Dahl's personal experiences. In fact, the closer the reactive premise approaches personal experience, the more powerful the influence it describes. However, as impersonal factors become more important (e.g., the Cold War), the less powerful is the reactive premise. In sum, personal experience is a powerful mediator between political events and scholarship.

Of the three Yale political scientists whose pluralist scholarship in the 1955–70 period became especially influential—Robert Lane, Robert Dahl, and Charles Lindblom—only Dahl improvises upon the reactivity premise. In a published interview with Nelson Polsby, Dahl discussed his experience at the National Labor Relations Board during the New Deal, an experience that gradually moved him away from socialism. Dahl's observations of factional infighting at the board brought him into sharp conflict with Stalinists. "I came to hold a view about the Soviet Union, which pretty much has been my view since then, that maybe it was socialist but it certainly wasn't democratic, and it certainly wasn't the wave of the future, as far as I was concerned. This view brought me constantly into friction with Stalinists" (in Baer, Jewell, and Sigelman, 1991: 171; see also Dahl, 1997: 69). Eventually, again partly in reaction to political events, Dahl began to question socialism itself.

> I had come to the conclusion that the nationalization of industry was not a satisfactory solution. . . . When France fell, I realized that the isolationist or semi-isolationist position I had shared with the Socialists had depended . . . on the implicit assumption that France and Britain would never fall, and, when it became clear that one of those two had fallen, for me, it was obvious that the United States had to get into the war.

Yet these events do not explain why Dahl's rejection of socialism should have produced *pluralism*. After all, there are many versions of democracy, of which pluralism is only a variant. In my interview, Dahl traced his evolution toward pluralism back to his experience at the National Labor Relations Board in 1937 and 1938:

> In the National Labor Relations Board in 1937, 1938, again I saw executive leadership mobilizing a coalition. It was coalition politics under the leadership of a master, who couldn't carry that on from 1937. So where some people on the Left saw some sort of unified elite at work, what I saw was coalition politics with very strong central leadership. Of course, this shows up in *Who Governs?*

Indeed, as he writes in chapter 17 of that book, New Haven was "an executive centered coalition."

Of the four premises in Yale pluralism, the reactive premise appears less frequently than the other three. Of the twenty-seven members of the department I interviewed, fifteen asserted the premise— either in relation to their own scholarship or to academic scholarship as a whole. Of this fifteen, however, ten (Dahl, Almond, Danelski, Greenstein, Kramnick, Kaufman, Mayhew, Rae, Shively, Lupsha) were primarily Americanists or at least wrote substantially about the United States. Still, neither Lane nor Lindblom attributed their scholarship to political events. Moreover, no member of the department introduced the reactive premise as the sole explanation for scholarship.

Nevertheless, a reactive account of scholarship was clearly more common than a *pro*active, much less a critical, view. For example, only eleven of those I interviewed claimed that Yale pluralism or scholarship in general had much impact on American politics. Moreover, only Charles Lindblom volunteered that academics and universities have an obligation to *criticize* government. Yale scholars are more likely to see their scholarship as a legitimating *reaction* to events / than as a *de*legitimating discourse.

It is worth quoting Lindblom at some length, since his critical position deviates sharply from the reactive views of many others whom I interviewed:

> The universities . . . we have institutions that are afraid of this powerful dyad [business, government]. . . . Our public schools plus university education [are] full of an endorsement of hierarchy, inequality, difference, and the efforts of the American public school system is to teach kids to be good citizens. What I mean by that, don't rock the boat but otherwise keep your mouth shut, do not organize, do not parade, do not agitate. These ideas have turned out to be partially effective instruments in the hands of women and gays and blacks.

Speaking specifically of Yale pluralism between 1955 and 1970, Lindblom remarks: "I think generally, as I suggested before, I don't think in that period or any other period political science has been critical enough; it has been too benign."

Not surprisingly, the department improvised upon the reactive premise programmatically. As New Haven's racial conflicts escalated in the late 1960s, the department envisaged a Center for Urban Studies at Yale (for a portrait of New Haven's changing urban structure at the time, see Birch et al., 1974). Goaded by the provost and the associate provost for urban studies, Joel Fleischman, himself a political scientist, the department established the Office for Advanced Political Studies in May 1967 (Lane letter to Brewster, May 3, 1967, box 9, folder 102, YUDPS). David Barber chaired a committee within the office to design an expanded program in urban studies. On October 10, 1967, the office held a meeting of interested faculty to speed the program along. Among those in attendance, in addition to Barber, were Irwin Gertzog, Robert Lane, and Peter Lupsha. Lupsha made an especially strong plea for political science to take a leading role in an expanded urban program ("Meeting Minutes of Office for Advanced Political Studies," box 9, folder 97, YUDPS). The committee pursued several avenues. Barber organized seminars that included officials from the federal Office of Economic Opportunity (OEO) and local poverty agencies in New Haven (box 6, folder 75. YUDPS). Barber hoped that a Yale contact at OEO would give Yale an entrée to support from the agency (memo, July 21, 1967, YUDPS). Borrowing the language of his colleague Charles Lindblom, Barber proposed to "proceed by disjointed incrementalism" (memo box 9, folder 102, YUDPS). Meanwhile, in a letter to Chairman Lane dated May 17, 1967, Irwin Gertzog proposed a master's degree program in urban studies (box 9, folder 102, YUDPS). Finally, in a letter to Barber dated May 26, 1967, Lane expressed an interest in recruiting to the department the noted urbanist and Lyndon Johnson administration official Robert Wood (box 9, folder 102, YUDPS).

The department also created an undergraduate program called "The Study of the City" in November 1968 (program description, box 9, folder 102, YUDPS). In reaction to demands from the Black Student Alliance at Yale, Robert Dahl endorsed a divisional major in Afro-American Studies (May 11, 1968, box 1, folder 1, YUDPS). Lane wrote Joel Fleischman early in 1968, again urging an expanded political science effort in urban affairs. Not surprisingly, Lane requested additional faculty positions to staff the effort (letter from Lane to Fleischman, February 26, 1968, box 9, Folder 98, YUDPS). Finally, thanks to pressure from the Office for Advanced Political Studies, Kingman Brewster, president of Yale, forwarded to the Carnegie Foundation a grant application for the establishment of an Urban Studies Center. The grant requested $867,650 for the initial phase.

Thus, the department improvised upon the reactive premise in its programs. These performances embodied the reactive premise embedded in Yale scholarship describing the American political system. In short, the department's improvisations helped reproduce the regime its works described.

THE ELITE TOLERANCE PREMISE
IN PERFORMANCE

The elite tolerance premise states that policymakers respect conflicting views and forge coalitions and compromises among contesting groups. Dissenting views are accommodated, and dissenters are included so long as they, too, practice tolerance. Did a culture of intel-lectual tolerance emerge at Yale? Did faculty improvise within the department upon the tolerance premise in their work on American politics? As seen by faculty, the answer is mostly yes. However, toler-ance was not universal.

A particularly interesting improvisation of intellectual tolerance concerns Peter Lupsha. Lupsha recounts the following story that took place at an informal gathering prior to his unplanned appearance at Morey's:

> Tarrow . . . had LaPalombara and Dahl and a few other faculty and other assistants, so we sat around and bullshitted around his place, and I got into some arguments with Dahl about *Who Governs?* But nothing big time, and differences from my research. See, I had just researched a hundred California cities . . . and the results were very different in many respects than *Who Governs?*

I asked Lupsha how Dahl and his colleagues responded to his criti-cisms. Lupsha strongly affirmed the tolerance premise: "Good na-tured. I had only seen one ugly incident regarding their work, and that was with a graduate student who wrote a highly critical dissertation of Lindblom, and they didn't let that out."

At Yale Lupsha became deeply immersed in campus and national protest politics. Indeed, he once brought some Black Panthers into his Pierson College office at Yale. Certainly, he provided the depart-ment with opportunities to retaliate against his political views. But he denies any retaliation. I asked him if activist junior faculty such as himself suffered in competition for department promotions. He responded: "No, no. In fact, if anything, they were very good to me. They went the other way."

From a political perspective opposite to that of Lupsha, David Calleo—who taught in the department between 1960 and 1967—reports a similar pattern of tolerance. Unlike Lupsha, Calleo criti-cized Yale pluralism from the political right. Calleo faults pluralism for legitimizing "the pursuit of interest for its own sake, the very indi-vidual definition of interest all the time without a countervailing sense of general interest," a point of view he labels "ignoble." "I think if you were going to criticize people like Dahl and so on, then you could say they underestimated the importance of leadership . . . you know, our history is sort of an alternation between flying apart, then somebody coming and trying to pull it back together again" (interview, January 27, 1998). In short, Calleo was more interested and impressed by the high politics of Charles de Gaulle, a hero of his, than in the politics of Richard Lee (the mayor of New Haven described in *Who Governs?*).

As a Yale graduate student (and undergraduate) in the 1950s, Calleo had often raised his basic philosophical and epistemological differences with Dahl.

> Dahl in particular, was immensely sympathetic to this kind of debating. He didn't agree with me, it was perfectly obvious. He had quite different basic views about things. But he was patient, encouraging, a bit long-suffering. I enjoyed his class thoroughly, and he was very pleased with what I did. . . . I did very well in nearly all my graduate classes, including his . . . more or less straight A's.

The intellectual tolerance Calleo describes carried over to Calleo's period as a faculty member. In speaking of how the department operated, Calleo recalls: "I don't remember any ferocious conflicts. I think Almond was a bit more cantankerous. . . . I suppose the fights were over personnel questions. But Yale seemed to have evolved a kind of system where nobody junior ever stayed on. That simplified things. If nobody junior stayed on, there was much less to fight about."

While Calleo's wry observation about junior faculty termination is not a ringing endorsement of Yale's personnel practices, he does observe that these practices permitted intellectual tolerance. Unlike many junior faculty, Calleo did not resent Yale's draconian policy toward retention: "It didn't [produce friction] in my case. My own interests were settling on European and international politics, where Yale did not have much to offer. As I say, I don't have the impression that there was a great deal of friction. Of course, I wasn't participating in the senior discussions, where the stakes were higher."

Another improvisation of the tolerance premise concerns Robert Lane, whose innovative political psychology research caused conflict with the president of Yale, Kingman Brewster. However, Lane experienced little opposition from traditionalists within the department. He observes:

> It was a department that everybody could—I am going to avoid that sixties phrase—everybody could pursue that vision of what they felt was important. . . . Fesler [James Fesler, chair of the department from

1962 to 1964] represented the most orthodox way of looking at things. And yet it was extremely tolerant. One never felt that one would lose out because one said something that was unorthodox. (Interview, November 30, 1997)

The intellectual tolerance Lane perceives extended to disagreements over the Vietnam War. Despite different views of the war, Lane argues that the department remained cohesive. For example, although Joseph LaPalombara and H. Bradford Westerfield generally supported the war, "I don't think there was conflict. It was probably that you might not talk about it." Thus, mutual avoidance preserved tolerance.

Another improvisation of the tolerance premise involved the publication of Helen Lane's *Tell the Time to None*. As previously mentioned, this roman à clef sharply criticized the political science department at Yale. The author was the spouse of one of the department's prominent senior members, and many of the characters were thinly disguised versions of department faculty. I asked Dahl about the department's overall reaction to the book. He responded: "The department surmounted it because Karl and Ruth [Deutsch] left. There was a figure I could sort of identify as Helen's using something like me for the purpose of fiction. I didn't feel hurt by that. We continued to be good friends."

Not every member of the department is as tolerant of Helen Lane as Robert Dahl. For example, James Fesler remarked that in an earlier short story Helen Lane had betrayed a friendship with a department member's spouse. Fesler himself felt misused by the story's publication. He had consulted Robert Lane as an adviser and lunched with him regularly when Lane had been an assistant professor. Moreover, he charges that Helen Lane established opportunistic friendships within the department and then cavalierly destroyed these relationships. Nevertheless, Fesler emphasizes that Lane's career at Yale did not suffer from *Tell the Time to None*. Only a tiny minority of department faculty stated that Helen Lane's novel caused friction in the department.

The tolerance premise also appears in the recollections of David Danelski, who joined the department in 1964 and left in 1970 for Cornell. According to Danelski, an atmosphere of informal, tolerant collegiality persisted despite the conflicts of the 1960s. "I am a good one to talk to about this, because I have been to so many departments in Illinois, and Washington, Yale, Cornell, and Stanford. It was in terms of collegial relationships, the best department I had ever been in. It was the exception to the rule" (on Cornell at the time, see Downs, 1999). Speaking of the effects of local Vietnam War protests, Danelski reiterates the tolerance premise: "There was some discussion, and there was some disagreement, but it was not uncivil."

Yet, some members of the department deny that the tolerance premise weathered the late 1960s. During his graduate years in the late 1950s and early 1960s, Fred Greenstein recalls, "The department was very small and very democratic. Very easy going." According to Greenstein, "There was a lot of room for relaxed and comfortable personal bonding." The department, Greenstein states, was "remarkably open and conflict-free in that period."

However, Greenstein believes that the atmosphere of tolerance vanished in the late 1960s. He argues that internal stresses destroyed the collegiality of the department. For our purposes the contrasting memories of Danelski and Greenstein are significant. After all, in many ways, the two men were similar; each had substantial association with Yale prior to the late 1960s, and neither was insecure at Yale. Greenstein's faculty appointment was at Wesleyan University, and Danelski's decision to depart Yale in 1970 was voluntary. Yet Greenstein sees the department as divided during the late 1960s, and Danelski disagrees. Their opposed impressions suggest that, by the late 1960s, the department found it difficult to enforce the tolerance premise. We revisit this subject in chapter 3.

Of the twenty-seven faculty members I interviewed, twenty affirmed that the department did, for the most part, practice intellectual tolerance in its collegial relationships. Still, as the case of Willmoore Kendall will demonstrate, the tolerance premise was not without limits. Nor did the department extend the tolerance premise as fully to graduate students as it did to faculty, especially in the late 1960s. For example, Robert Dahl recalls that at one point graduate students demanded to take part in personnel decisions. Dahl recalls "a very testy meeting with graduate students in which, one who was sort of the leader of the demand for greater participation. . . . Anyway, he said, 'We are the niggers of the academic world.' And I as a teacher was deeply offended that thinking the life of a graduate student at Yale had anything comparable to that of an American black. And I think I may have said so."

Thus, intellectual tolerance was limited. The tolerance premise extended to rhetorical transgressions by faculty, including Helen Lane's book. It also encompassed differences of political opinion. But as evidenced by Dahl's exchange with the graduate student, inflammatory rhetoric by graduate students was not acceptable.

THE REFORM PREMISE IN PERFORMANCE

The reform premise asserts that creative political leadership forges coalitions of incremental, progressive change. Reform is opposed both to revolution, which disavows the past, and to conservatism, which resists the future. Reform preserves continuity; it adapts the past to the future. In national politics the reform premise is typified by the liberal wing of the Democratic Party, by presidents such as Roosevelt, Truman, Kennedy, and Johnson, and by the policies of the New Deal, the Fair Deal, and the Great Society.

Did the Yale political science department improvise upon the theme of reform? Was the Yale department a stage upon which the faculty successfully performed the theme of reform? Certainly academic reform is by no means easy. As F. G. Bailey wryly observes in his discussion of academic politics, "The horse of innovation runs with a heavy handicap. Even if it wins, the followers of racing form are going to look for reasons other than its intrinsic abilities, for they are unwilling to give up their conviction that it should not have won" (1977: 183). If Bailey is right, the odds are stacked against reform.

Yet the Yale department did improvise upon the reform theme. Indeed, reform achieved the status of a department norm. Certainly Yale political scientists retrospectively characterize their scholarship as reformist. They consistently tie their writings to earlier schools of thought. Indeed, they deny that a behavioral or pluralist "revolution" ever actually occurred at Yale. Instead, they assert that their work respected and incorporated past scholarship, even as they looked toward the future.

Consider, for example, Gabriel Almond's comparison of Yale scholarship to contemporary rational choice theory:

> I don't think at any time, from Merriam right onto Dahl, did we ever really draw a sharp line, and say, "OK, on this line there is science, and

59

on the other line there is a bunch of amateur stuff." On the contrary, we had a very deep respect for good political theory, or good constitutional law, good lawyers, or good historians. . . . And I think we read that literature, and we respected those people, and we could be equal collegially. But I think the rational choice people draw a sharper line. I think there is that, and, I mean, you have to do it their way.

Almond's comment improvises the reform theme in three respects. First, by referencing Charles Merriam—an early-twentieth-century pioneer of behavioralism (Karl, 1974)—he explicitly asserts continuity in Dahl's novel scholarship. Second, he states that the Yale department welcomed normative theorists, legalists, and historians—the traditionalists of political science. Third, his reference to rational choice theory permits him to portray pluralism and behavioralism as reformist rather than revolutionary.

In his analysis of Yale scholarship, David Mayhew also asserts the reformist premise:

> In the fifties and sixties they showed in the Yale department that to some degree "scientizing" the study of politics can be very successful, very fruitful, very influential, evocative. I think the scientific component of what they are doing is very important with these writers, all of them. On the other hand, I do think that in the fifties and sixties the real politics—its possibilities and problems—is very much at the center of what they were doing, and supplied by the real political world.

Unlike Almond, Mayhew places the reform premise within a political context. To Mayhew, Yale scholarship applied pathbreaking science to actual political events. In fact, according to Mayhew, its direct connection to the political world enhanced the scholarship's scientific qualities. At the same time, retaining their ties to "real politics," Yale scholars produced a reformist, not a revolutionary, political science.

Mayhew also observes that Yale political scientists reached a general audience, not just professional social scientists. As he puts it, "The books that were written in the fifties and sixties could sell in the book stores. *Who Governs?* is not going to make the Reader's Digest Condensed Book Club, but it is accessible. Many people could read it and appreciate it. You didn't have to be scientifically trained in order to appreciate it, as much political science today." By contrast, now "Scholasticism is afflicting us, and we are suffering from it as a consequence."

For Mayhew, Yale scholarship falls somewhere between Russell Jacoby's (1987) engaged New York intellectuals outside the academy and today's insular, bloodless, thoroughly professional political scientists, who speak only to each other (but see Robbins, 1993). The Yale approach eschewed the older, normative radicalism of the New York intellectuals, but it retained the latter's dedication to engaging the lay public. Indeed, an engaging, jargon-free style and an appreciation for concrete political events kept the "science" of the Yale approach from mutating into today's scholasticism. Thus, Yale scholarship took the middle way of reform.

Archival evidence reveals that the Yale department consciously constructed a reformist identity. For example, in 1958 Robert Dahl wrote to the Executive Committee of the Faculty of Arts and Sciences at Yale proposing a program of training in political *theory,* not political *behavior.* In the proposal Dahl laments the emerging split between empirical political science and political theory. He proposes a seven-year program to bridge the gap between political theory and empirical social science. In doing so, he compares Yale favorably to other universities: "To a much greater degree than elsewhere, the gap seems to be closed at Yale" ("Future Needs of the Department of Political Science," appendix A, October 15, 1958, box 3, folder 32, YUDPS). Thus, no matter how innovative, Yale should remain connected to the past.

Ten years later, in a letter to John Gardner at the National Endowment for the Humanities, David Barber made a similar argument, lamenting the false and unnecessary divide between behavioralism and traditionalism and urging NEH to address this problem in its programs (letter, August 22, 1967, box 14, folder 40, YUDPS). As these two cases illustrate, the reform theme took hold in the department's identity.

The reform premise also appears in accounts of specific department practices. Take, for example, the all-important question of faculty recruitment. In 1968 the department hired the political theorist Roger Masters. Masters had studied at Chicago with Leo Strauss, perhaps the most powerful critic of Yale behavioralism and pluralism. In our interview, Masters acknowledged his strong attachment to

Strauss ("you encounter one teacher of that caliber in your life"). Why did Yale hire Masters? Because Masters was also conversant with, and sympathetic to, the Yale approach to American politics. As he puts it:

> I got along fine with all the people in the behavioral sciences, partly because I was a very eccentric Straussian. . . . I was a research assistant for Duncan Macrae. I remember computing regression coefficients . . . for Duncan. It was really interesting stuff. And then I worked for Easton on his political socialization stuff. So while I went to Yale as a theorist . . . the reason was that Mort Kaplan had talked to Bob Dahl about it. . . . Dahl says, "You know, we need someone in theory," and Mort saw, "Well, why not get this kid." . . . I was a funny Straussian. I didn't hate these other people. I could actually talk to them and work with them from the inside. (Interview, June 4, 1998)

By hiring an "eccentric" Straussian, Yale improvised upon its reform theme. Through Strauss, Masters connected Yale to classical political theory; yet Masters did not want to torpedo behavioralism or pluralism, as did the reactionary Strauss. Masters's contribution was to bring the old and new together; his very presence embodied the reform theme.

But Roger Masters's successor in the department—Isaac Kramnick—interprets the role of political theory at Yale somewhat less benignly than Masters. Kramnick initially places political theory within the tolerance theme, not the reform premise. But he gives tolerance a different twist than Masters gives reform: "They were very tolerant of political theorists. 'Let them do their own thing,' partly because they thought, I think, they assumed you were irrelevant to the discipline."

Kramnick charges that Yale deliberately recruited theorists who would not be "saying relevant things about politics." He believes this practice served two purposes: it insulated the department from claims that it was biased against traditional, textually based theory, and it permitted the department to pursue unhindered its path of pluralist, behavioral political science.

In fact, the Yale department did not condone activities or behavior that impeded reform. Beginning in the early 1950s there occurred an internal "clearing of the decks" that removed impediments to pluralism and behavioralism. These events—partly serendipitous, partly planned—improvised upon the reformist premise.

One such event was the departure of the Institute of International Studies from Yale. The institute included six prominent foreign affairs scholars (Arnold Wolfers, Klauss Knorr, Percy Corbett, William Kaufman, Bernard Cohen, and Gabriel Almond) who, according to James Fesler, chair of the political science department in 1951, had for some time dominated the department. Yale president A. Whitney Griswold charged the institute with a lack of scholarly productivity and too much involvement in national politics. Fesler recounts that when the institute applied to the university for new money, Griswold refused his support. Five members of the institute immediately decamped to Princeton, and a sixth—Arnold Wolfers—departed several years later for Johns Hopkins.

Conflict between the university and the institute proved a blessing in disguise for the reform of the department. Fesler asserts that the institute had stifled new directions for the Yale department. Almond agrees that the institute created chronic tension and impeded change. The departure of the institute opened a space for reform.

True, in the short run, the affair took a toll on reform in the department. V. O. Key, a leading proponent of behavioralism and chair of the Yale department prior to Fesler's arrival, chose to leave Yale. James Fesler believes the institute debacle put the department "in shambles" in the early 1950s. So much was this the case, in fact, that the university turned to Fesler, an outsider, to assume the chairmanship. Nevertheless, once the institute had left, there emerged an opportunity for departmental reform. Fesler, whose first tour of duty as chair ended in 1955, and who again occupied the chairmanship from 1962–64, seized this opportunity. Ultimately, his recruitment, combined with the loss of the institute, spurred reform.

Another improvisation of reform was the engineered departure of the conservative political theorist Willmoore Kendall from the department. Kendall had a stormy relationship with his colleagues. The problem was partly political; Kendall's extremely conservative politics and his collaboration with one of his undergraduate students—William Buckley—in establishing the right-wing *National Review* placed him outside the dominant liberalism of the department. (For Buckley's famous attack on Yale at the time, see Buckley, 1951.) Still, there were other conservatives in the department, such as David Rowe, a China specialist and former Office of Strategic Services operative in World War II (Winks, 1987: 104), and Walter Sharp, an international relations scholar. Yet these conservatives did not encounter the difficulties Kendall experienced. Why? Rowe and Sharp were conspicuously inconspicuous in the daily life of the department; by contrast, Kendall disrupted the department regularly. Ultimately, Kendall's personal behavior hindered reform. Therefore, removing him became necessary to promote reform.

According to Fesler, in the 1956–57 academic year Kendall, a tenured associate professor, requested promotion to full professor. All the full professors, save Rowe, voted against the request. Angered, Kendall threatened legal retaliation, claiming he was being punished for his political views. Not surprisingly, Fesler disputes Kendall's characterization, describing the department's decision as based on Kendall's lack of scholarly publications. But Kendall's personal relationship to the department had also deteriorated. His feud with Cecil Driver, another political theorist, paralyzed graduate training in political theory (Dahl interview, August 27, 1997). Students felt they had to choose between Driver and Kendall; the two men simply did not cooperate. In addition, Kendall's conduct was erratic and unpredictable. He was by turns acerbic and witty, confrontational and thoughtful. According to Charles Lindblom, Kendall was "most stimulating," but also divisive. Robert Lane continued to befriend Kendall, even as he decried Kendall's "impossible politics."

Smarting from the rejection of his promotion request, Kendall wrote then-chairman Robert Dahl, stating that, in view of the unhappiness he caused at Yale, perhaps he ought to leave the university (Fesler interview, August 26, 1997). Dahl chose to treat the letter as a tacit resignation offer. The university also regarded it as such and ultimately worked out a severance package with Kendall. Kendall formally left Yale in 1961, removing himself as an obstacle to pluralism and behavioralism at Yale.

Significantly, most Yale faculty regard the Kendall case as a legitimate improvisation of departmental reform, not as political or personal retaliation. Indeed, members of the department construe the Kendall case in terms of three pluralist themes. Dismissing Kendall was a necessary *reaction* to chronically disruptive behavior that violated the norm of elite *tolerance*. Ultimately, they claim, the Kendall affair was a performance of *reform*.

Consider the recollections of Fesler, Dahl, and Kaufman. As we have seen, Fesler describes the reasons for denying Kendall's promotion as a "paucity of publication of scholarly work" (1997: 196). However, in his conversation with me, Fesler focused mainly on Kendall's conduct, not his productivity. Moreover, he explicitly introduces the reform premise. Kendall, says Fesler,

> was just his own worst enemy. He could be charming and had great linguistic ability. But here's one example. The first lunch I invited him to—I [as chair] regarded lunch as a social function—he said, "What do you mean by a democracy?" I responded that I thought it was government by a majority of the people. He said, "Then you think the Greeks were right to kill Socrates?" That was one of his favorite ploys. . . . I was assured when I was to be appointed here that I would not have to deal with Kendall and was promised that if there were any problems . . . that the administration would support me even if the faculty of the department did not in my reforms.

Kendall's destructive effect on graduate training is the central issue for Robert Dahl. Dahl explains that Kendall and Cecil Driver detested each other: "It was basically personal, but it also involved whole different views of the world. . . . Basically, I think there was a fundamental difference in temperament. That was very corrosive. Graduate students would get pulled in one way or another. We still had oral exams for the Ph.D., and those would sometimes be embarrassing."

Herbert Kaufman expands on Dahl's version of the Kendall case:

> Most of the tension came from Willmoore Kendall. . . . Kendall and Driver had a feud that was known nationally in the profession. . . . Students at the time told me that it got so bad, the tension got so bad between them, that they called all the graduate students together to assure them that they were not torpedoing each other's students. In fact, that was one reason they introduced written generals that could be judged by independent parties. . . . Kendall was a self-destructive man. He was very bright, but he was a psychological mess. And he said to me, "You know, you could say I hate Driver, but I married one of his students." And he did for a time, but she divorced him. . . . Kendall was tough on everybody, but I found him amusing.

For Kaufman, as for Dahl, the upshot of the Kendall case was reform in the graduate program: "written generals that could be judged by independent parties."

A more complicated, though still reformist, interpretation of the

Kendall affair is provided by Bradford Westerfield. According to Westerfield, Kendall did not "pull his full weight in the department"; moreover, he had a dangerously charismatic impact on some undergraduates, for whom he was a mentor. Westerfield then places these factors within a political context, unlike the then-senior members of the department: "Kendall . . . was chiefly seen in that period as a right-wing political theorist . . . no, a right-wing populist political theorist, a right-wing populist slant on American political theory and in a very intolerant way, would like to say McCarthyite, political connected mode. And this was just beyond the pale of the Hartzian consensus."

Westerfield's political construction of the Kendall affair differs from the reform interpretation offered by others. The latter's improvisations embrace only the department's internal operations, ignoring the political views of faculty. Reform clears the way for *departmental* advance; it is not a *political* stance. But Westerfield asserts that in the Kendall case departmental reform is inseparable from national politics, citing Louis Hartz's version of pluralist legitimation. The problem, for Westerfield, is that Kendall's politics as well as his personal conduct disrupted the department.

This construction of the case presents Westerfield with a dilemma. Pluralist reform in the department required that Kendall be controlled. Yet controlling him endangered another pluralist premise—that of political tolerance. Westerfield must find a way out of this dilemma. How does he proceed? His solution is to treat the "Hartzian consensus" (Hartz, 1955) as a form of tolerance. Thus, Kendall, not the department, becomes "very intolerant." This reasoning not only protects but also improvises the departmental tolerance theme. Further, Kendall's departure created "an absolutely traumatized, implanted, imprinted live-and-let-live approach to collegial relationships." In sum, to Westerfield, the Kendall affair strengthened both reform and tolerance in the department.

Reform also took place in thoroughly mundane ways. Take, for example, the recruitment of second-generation reformers. At the national level, of course, Franklin Roosevelt had his "whiz kids," and John Kennedy and Lyndon Johnson had their "new generations" of activist lawyers, academics, and planners. At Yale, the department recruited a second generation of young reformers. Beginning in the mid-1950s, innovative, energetic graduate students streamed into the department. Between 1963 and 1968 alone the number of graduate students increased from fifty-two to one hundred (Lane letter, September 27, 1968, box 13, folder 23, YUDPS). Department faculty remember these graduate students as key players in departmental reform, and as stimulants to pluralist scholarship within the department.

Two of my interviews illustrate this point. One comes from the early part of the period, the other from the end. Observing Yale in the mid-1950s, Gabriel Almond remarks that the department recruited "unusually talented graduates. They got this grant, and they were able . . . they brought that whole first generation of graduate students—Wildavsky, Polsby, Greenstein, and several others."

The grant to which Almond alludes came from the Falk Foundation in 1953. Falk, a Yale alumnus, gave the department $20–30,000 per year from 1953 to 1959, a grant that was subsequently renewed. Although Falk designated that his grant be used "to improve the teaching of politics at the undergraduate level" ("Memo to all Falk Fellows," October 12, 1959, box 3, folder 32 and box 2, folder 18, YUDPS), the department used the Falk money to bring promising graduate student researchers in American politics to Yale. This infusion of outside money improvised the reform in national politics then taking place and described in pluralist scholarship. In the 1960s, for example, the Ford Foundation injected money into innovative policy experiments, such as the War on Poverty. In fact, Ford pioneered New Haven's urban renewal and anti-poverty programs during the 1950s and 1960s (Powledge, 1970: 21, 66). Thus, again, textual theme and department improvisation together reproduced the reform premise.

Successful graduate student recruitment became part of the department's collective memory of reform. Consider Peter Lupsha's characterization of the department in the late 1960s:

> Yale happened to have the unique phenomena that I saw at Stanford, but was certainly there at Yale before I was there. And that was a unique group of graduate students, who all arrived at roughly the same set of years overlapping each other a bit . . . the whole network of people as graduate students who were rich fertile minds themselves, and very creative, dynamic, in the sense of learning. I think that . . . helped fuel the professors. Dahl could rely on a coterie of graduate students.

Lupsha's observation contains three interrelated reform assertions. First, promising graduate students regularly exchanged ideas with each other, stimulating new pluralist scholarship. Second, graduate students forced faculty to develop and refine their ideas. Indeed, Lupsha believes graduate students provided "the intellectual energy to push [Dahl] from *Preface* to *Who Governs?*" Third, by using the term *coterie*, Lupsha implies that second-generation Yale scholars intended to reproduce pluralism and behavioralism. Thus, graduate student recruitment indeed supported, and improvised upon, the reform premise.

Another aspect of reform is leadership. In pluralism, political leaders forge winning reformist coalitions. The practice of reform at Yale required such leaders. In the accounts of my interviewees, two such leaders emerged: James Fesler and Robert Dahl.

Fesler looms large both among those faculty who were present at Yale in the early 1950s, when he became chair for the first time, and among those who arrived later. A quiet, soft-spoken man with no background in the Ivy League, Fesler repaired the fortunes of a department badly hurt by the Institute of International Studies struggle, starved of funds, and lacking national stature. Fesler hired new faculty and made the department more visible nationally. As he explained in a letter to Robert Lane in 1958—Lane was then chairing a "Committee on the Department's Needs"—Yale required strong recruitment to become "the most exciting and constructive center of political science in the country" (box 3, folder 32, YUDPS). In his written memoir, Fesler notes that in the late 1950s many members of the department did not even attend meetings of the American Political Science Association; he therefore "encouraged them to do some of that." Improving the visibility and reputation of the department preoccupied Fesler throughout his career. In his memoirs he records that the "most gratifying event of this period" was the fact that by 1964 the Yale department ranked first in the country, as compared to 1957, when it ranked seventh (1997: 201).

Herbert Kaufman states that Fesler's low-key style, his flexibility, and his determination promoted the initial reform surge of the department. "Jim Fesler came in . . . and he was instrumental in rebuilding the department very quietly and carefully." Reflecting on the department in the mid-1960s, William Muir concurs in this assessment. His comment reveals how deeply embedded is Fesler's chairmanship in the department's cultural memory:

Jim Fesler is probably the critical person. As I understand it, the department was reviewed in early 1950s, and it got a failing grade. Whether that review was internal or whether it came from the political science end, I am not sure. . . . What Fesler told me, it was just not a very good department, and I think Yale went to Fesler . . . and said, well, "Here is a blank check. Draw it, and get good people into the department," and I think he chose well. (Interview, January 19, 1998)

Of course, Fesler's efforts would have gone for naught had the department not produced exciting scholarship. Here the key figure is Robert Dahl. But Dahl's importance to the department resides not only in his scholarship but also in the relationship between his texts and departmental practice. Faculty who observed the department at the beginning, middle, and end of the period all concur in Dahl's pivotal role. Recalling the beginning of the period, Bradford Westerfield states:

One more thing that seems central . . . is the ascendancy of Robert Dahl. He took over the chairmanship around '62. He took it over from Fesler, who was . . . more sensitive to kind of get the Yale political science department . . . integrated into the profession at large. But he was providing leadership and sort of opening up Yale to the outer world regarding American political science. Inside Yale he wasn't providing any leadership, except that I suppose he was implicitly . . . providing room for Dahl and Lane and Deutsch to get their feet on the ground.

But Dahl took over as chair in the early sixties . . . as I came to senior faculty meetings around 1964 his presence was just totally, quietly—always quietly—but totally commanding. Anything that Dahl wanted happened. Nothing that he didn't want would happen.

Westerfield concludes that Dahl "was a guru almost to a magic level."

I asked William Foltz, who came to Yale first as a graduate student in 1957 and then joined the department in 1962, about the influences that shaped Yale scholarship. Immediately Foltz identifies Dahl: "There were lots of little elements which I haven't really sorted out. One of them without doubt was just the personality and the role of Bob Dahl. . . . He just had a terrific, tremendous intellectual power and influence, very subtle influence on the way people talk about things." Note that Foltz refers to Dahl's contribution to the internal life of the department, not his scholarship ("personality," "role," "the way people talk about things"). Foltz implies that Dahl's intellectual power allowed him to dominate the department.

A final characterization of Dahl's reform role emerges from Douglas Rae. His comment perhaps reflects the critical consciousness of the late 1960s (Rae joined the department in 1967). According to Rae:

> I was . . . we all lived in considerable awe of Dahl and Lindblom. . . . Dahl was the pope of American political science at the end of that period and was the arbiter of taste in many, many matters. He was also, I think probably less than half-consciously, an important ideological figure in the country.
>
> I think the two books, *Preface* and *Who Governs?*, both of which— American hybrid in *Preface,* and New Haven pluralism in *Who Governs?*—portrayed capitalist democracy in a favorable light and gave it a little theoretical apparatus which discriminated nicely between this system and other systems with which we as a nation were in rivalrous relations.

Unlike Westerfield and Foltz, Rae assigns to Dahl a hyperbolic, quasi-religious role ("the pope of American political science"). Also, unlike Westerfield and Foltz, Rae ascribes to Dahl an ideological function. Some may ascribe Rae's observations entirely to the turmoil of the late 1960s. But so deterministic an analysis does not reveal how events make their mark on people. Nor does it capture the irony in Rae's constructing a "heroic" narrative of Dahl, then, by ascribing to this hero a "papal" function, undermining the narrative. For these purposes, the nuanced concept of a legitimating discourse is well suited.

Dahl vigorously defended the department's reformist agenda. While he was chair the department unanimously recommended Robert Lane for tenure. However, recalls Dahl, Yale president Griswold, who "was never particularly sympathetic to behavioral political science," baulked at granting tenure to Lane. Lane's psychological approach to politics apparently alienated Griswold. Griswold even wondered, according to Dahl, whether "this was political science." Dahl responded by sending Griswold a memo on "Political Behavior as a Field of Political Science" (n.d., box 3, folder 77, YUDPS). In the memo he defended Lane. Dahl asserted that "the national and international reputation gained by the department over the past decade rests in part on the extent to which members of the Yale department have emphasized the 'behavioral approach' to the study of politics" (3). Dahl pointed out that there was no comparable concentration of behavioral political scientists elsewhere at other universities. But, he was also careful to argue that the behavioral approach "builds on the enormous strengths of the traditional approaches." Thus, Dahl behaved as pluralist theory suggested a reformist coalition leader ought to behave; he marshaled his forces, and not only assured Lane's promotion but also improvised upon the reform premise.

Dahl's authority as chair was not equaled by Robert Lane and Bradford Westerfield, his successors in the late 1960s and early 1970s. Indeed, during those years the department weakened its four pluralist premises. The result was increased conflict and the decline of pluralism both as textual theme and department improvisation. An example of this change involves the policy of junior faculty promotions. Recalling the Yale department when he was an assistant professor in 1962, Robert Dix, a Latin Americanist, reflects: "It was made very clear to us—I think it was Fesler [who] got all the half a dozen first-year people; he got us all together and he said, 'Most of you will not stay at Yale.' He put it very directly."

I asked Dix whether he and his peers found this statement demoralizing. He replied, "Well, it sure must have been. There was no big resentment . . . maybe we half expected it." Thus, though perhaps angry, junior faculty apparently accepted their painful lot with resignation. As a result, the department proceeded in comparative peace.

By contrast, in the late 1960s junior faculty would no longer accept so quietly Yale's practice of dismissing most of its junior faculty. Some not only resented their treatment but also articulated their anger. Consider the comments of two anonymous former junior faculty members who were at Yale from 1968 to 1972. Speaking of Robert Lane, then the chair, one states:

> When he was chair of the department and teaching there, he was the one who hired me. He was an inveterate liar, I thought. He was just someone who would tell you whatever you would want to hear without the intention of doing it. . . . I didn't have a lot of respect for the way the department was run as a sort of human organization. And there was nothing I could do about that.
>
> Q.: When you say as a human organization, that refers to what, patterns of communication?
>
> A.: Or patterns of participation. What I said in the beginning of being seen and not heard, that was very stratified. . . . It wasn't far from the "Old Blue" pattern, and I didn't like that at all.
>
> Q.: Did you express that when you were there? Did you show that irritation?
>
> A.: Not in public, no. With my colleagues and friends.

71

The second junior faculty member begins with promotions and then turns his ire on leadership:

> We used to talk about the metaphor of dogs, you know . . . that they just threw all these dogs in an arena, and they fought with each other, and then whoever survives will get promoted.
>
> There was bitterness that it didn't have to be this way. But of course this was always counterbalanced by the sense that, after all, we were at Yale. And we were constantly being told that Yale was number one.

Of Robert Lane and Bradford Westerfield, this faculty member observes:

> I thought [Lane] was fair, and I had no problems with him. I mean, off the record now, not for attribution, the junior faculty, of course, felt that the transition from Lane to Westerfield was an incredible one, in the sense of, we were being led by somebody, initially Lane, who we all felt was a very distinguished scholar and an important scholar. And then we were suddenly being led by Brad Westerfield, who very few of us had any respect for as a scholar.

As this exchange intimates, by the late 1960s the Yale department no longer improvised as effectively upon certain of its pluralist themes. Indeed, a subculture of seething resentment built up within the department. Not only did this subculture disturb the department, but it also indirectly challenged pluralist writings on American politics. Soon Yale ceased to produce a legitimating discourse for the American political regime.

CONCLUSION

In this chapter I have argued that the Yale political science department performed multiple improvisations on the four theoretical premises of pluralism. With some exceptions, pluralism both as theme and improvisation constituted the core of the department's culture between 1955 and 1970. The question to which I turn next is how challenges to pluralism appeared among faculty, and how these challenges diminished the legitimating power of pluralism at Yale.

3

Challenging Pluralism

INTRODUCTION: YALE'S "SIXTIES"

The "sixties" mean different things to different people. Not surprisingly, conservatives and (former or present) radicals conceive of the period in diametrically opposed ways. Many who were on the Left, such as Sheldon Wolin and Alan Wolfe, consider that the 1960s were ✓ a time of failed academic revolution against, among other things, the pluralism, behavioralism, and liberal democratic politics propounded at Yale. For Wolin, the academic revolution at Berkeley ended abruptly in 1970, when the faculty rejected a campus version of participatory democracy as "inconsistent with the requirements of a high-powered research university" (1997: 151). For Wolfe, popular radical politics mutated into an academic Leftist establishment that virtually marinates in inaccessible professional jargon. Today Leftist academics "pride themselves on their ability to write in ways that few can understand" (Wolfe, 1997: 198). For Wolfe, the Left jettisoned the disempowered in quest of academic respectability. And, for Wolin, the Left never gained academic power at all.

If the Left envisages the 1960s as an academic 1848, the Right castigates the 1960s as a kind of academic Terror. To Harvey Mansfield, the period was disastrous both for America and for his university, Harvard. As he laments, "I suffered through the sixties and now live with their legacy at a university I once admired" (1997: 21). Walter Berns is no less condemnatory. Berns sees a direct line between "the assault on the universities" of the 1960s and today's academy, which "offers a politicized curriculum, the core of which is antirationalist, antihumanist, and antiliberal" (1997: 180).

If Wolfe and Wolin are correct, Yale pluralism should have come through the 1960s triumphant and intact. But if one believes Mans-

field and Berns, the academic Left should have swept away the tolerance, the incremental reformism, and the multiple centers of power
characteristic of pluralism (see also Glazer, 1997). Yet, an examination
of the Yale political science department supports neither the Left nor
the Right. In the late 1960s there did emerge a gap between pluralism
as literary theme and departmental improvisations. However, the result was neither pluralist reaction nor anti-pluralist revolution; instead, there occurred complex rethinking that distanced many faculty
members from pluralism and propelled some to leave Yale. The fissures that emerged resemble Bourdieu's characterization of French
universities, where academics possess multiple forms of "cultural capital" that occasionally estrange people from each other (Swartz, 1997:
242). Pluralism became *fragmented;* it did not vanish, nor did it survive intact.

ENGAGING THE SIXTIES: THE EXPERIENCE OF JUNIOR FACULTY

Close examination reveals generational splits in the way Yale political
scientists experienced the 1960s. Several younger faculty members
did not improvise successfully upon pluralist themes. Instead, they
invented new improvisations that led them either to question pluralist
theory or to leave Yale, or sometimes both. For a few junior academics, however, the 1960s did not matter at all; these scholars had *never*
embraced pluralist themes. Significantly, the most successful junior
faculty "alumnus" of the late 1960s who actually remained at Yale—
David Mayhew—experienced no tension at all between pluralist
themes and department improvisations. In fact, Mayhew describes
his breakthrough study, *Congress: The Electoral Connection* (1974),
as a book he could not have written other than at Yale; the work, he
claims, is marked by the influences of Charles Lindblom, Douglas
Rae, and Robert Dahl. Of the junior faculty I discuss, only Mayhew
remains securely ensconced today within the Yale political science
department.

The impact of 1960s improvisations on pluralist thinking reveals
itself among seven faculty members. These scholars characterize
themselves as critical either of pluralism, of the behavioral approach
to the study of politics, or both. Political events, such as urban rioting

and Vietnam War protests, both of which occurred in New Haven, contributed to these scholars' criticism of pluralism. But departmental improvisations also made a great difference. Only one of these seven (Douglas Rae) remained at Yale. These seven cases reveal how strain between pluralism as theme and nonpluralist improvisation at Yale began to fragment pluralism itself.

Hayward Alker, Isaac Kramnick, Douglas Rae, Sidney Tarrow, and one anonymous junior faculty member sharply criticize the way the department functioned in the late 1960s; significantly, all five also were critics of pluralist theory. To be sure, their criticism sometimes predated their arrival at Yale. Yet their experiences in the department clearly reinforced their dissatisfaction with pluralism.

Consider first Hayward Alker, Sidney Tarrow, and Isaac Kramnick. Although Alker is mainly an international relations scholar, he is unusually eclectic (e.g., Alker, 1996). Today he characterizes his work as a hermeneutical alternative devised to challenge the positivistic behavioralism he learned at Yale. He is also keenly conscious of pluralism as a legitimating discourse. Yale was, he says, "a place that had sort of given me the pluralist, anti-Marxist kind of argument which legitimated American democracy during the Cold War" (interview, January 10, 1998). Although Alker's departure from Yale was not personally bitter, he is a critic of how the department functioned. As he puts it, "There was a huge social gap between junior faculty and tenured faculty at Yale when I was a junior faculty there." Dahl and others attempted to bridge the gap, but they did not succeed. "There was nothing malevolent about it. I think it is the structure of the university, and it's sort of an elite university, Yale, and there was this social relation to American society. The Ivy League universities especially . . . a kind of status hierarchy." Alker clearly perceived a gap between the pluralist premise of modest egalitarian reform and the department's status hierarchy.

The Vietnam War also encouraged Alker to leave Yale. Although he, like most members of the political science department, opposed the war, he states that the department provided "an incomplete presentation of what they were doing, because they were making political arguments on the legitimization of the pluralistic conception of democracy." For Alker, there was tension between pluralism and opposition to the war. His reflections on this conflict, and on the conflict between pluralist themes and departmental improvisations, motivated his defection from pluralist theory and, ultimately, from Yale itself.

Sidney Tarrow also perceived tension between pluralist theory and department improvisation. Tarrow already held anti-pluralist views before arriving at Yale in 1965. Indeed, he describes his dissertation as a conscious attack on Gabriel Almond's version of Italy in *The Civic Culture*. Tarrow believed "that if you really were progressive you couldn't be a behavioralist" (interview, January 9, 1998). And Tarrow certainly did view himself as a progressive. Interestingly, Tarrow reconsidered his view of pluralism at Yale; by the time he arrived, Dahl "had evolved" and had become more interested in political conflict. Moreover, the comparatively collegial political atmosphere he experienced at Yale agreed with him, particularly after his alienating graduate experience at Berkeley. He describes himself as "opened up" by Lane and Dahl and especially by Karl Deutsch's approach to social mobilization, a subject that became the center of Tarrow's scholarship (e.g., Tarrow, 1994).

Nevertheless, for Tarrow, Yale was not "a particularly happy time. . . . I did have the feeling that junior faculty were not valued. . . . It was institutional, not personal, and there was a real feeling of being thrown in the cockpit to compete. . . . There were three of us who had come in more or less at the same time, and we were essentially told all three of us weren't going to make it, and we had to compete. And I remember feeling that this was most unjust because our fields were completely different." Tarrow remarks that junior faculty ranked even lower in the informal status hierarchy than graduate students. Like Alker, he believes that junior and senior faculty did not really interact very much socially. Ultimately, Tarrow says he left Yale because he received offers elsewhere; in addition, however, "It seemed, given the lack of warmth for our careers at New Haven," that leaving was a prudent thing to do. For Tarrow, the department was too hierarchical, competitive, and inaccessible socially—and non-pluralist.

Isaac Kramnick, who came to Yale in 1968 and left in 1972, shares Tarrow's criticism of the department. But unlike Tarrow, Kramnick feels the department punished him for his visible Leftist politics. He also claims that the department, especially Chairman Westerfield, misled him about his promotion prospects. In addition, he also alleges that his support for graduate student protesters within the department harmed him at Yale. Finally, he reports an instance of anti-Semitism that a senior department member directed against him. However, he points out that the department did offer him an associate professor position without tenure. Moreover, Westerfield assured him that a second book "more in the mold of Yale political science" would get him tenure. Nevertheless, Kramnick, angered by the department, left Yale for Cornell (interview, October 14, 1999).

Kramnick agrees with Tarrow that there was an "unbelievable hierarchical quality of the department." Moreover, like Tarrow, Kramnick is clear about his rejection of pluralist theory. In fact, his alienation from Yale and pluralism took a particularly visible public form. In a long article about Yale in the *New York Times Magazine* (February 7, 1971), Kramnick was quoted in criticism of Charles Reich, a prominent New Left law professor. As he described his remarks to me, he had stated, "What difference does it make if the very top of the Establishment's kids give up material goods; we've got to worry about people who don't have material goods." This language caused the article's author to describe Kramnick as an "angry, young card-carrying leftist . . . with bushy hair." Kramnick complained about this characterization in a letter to the *Times,* but the letter only drew further public attention to him.

According to Kramnick, prior to the *Times* article, Chairman Westerfield had assured him that he would soon be considered for tenure and told him that "I [Westerfield] assume all is going to go well." However, after the *Times* article appeared, Kramnick heard nothing for some time about promotion. Finally, he received a letter from Westerfield stating that many faculty had not actually read Kramnick's first book at the time Westerfield made his original statement. Having now read the book, the department decided it was not yet ready to offer him tenure. Westerfield read Kramnick the letter by phone (Kramnick was then in London) before sending it. Westerfield explained that he did not want Kramnick to "go off and do something irresponsible, . . . which introduced the whole political thing." Kramnick also alludes to a Theories of Revolution undergraduate course he taught to three hundred students. As he sums up his analysis of the events: "Here's the guy who's been called a card-carrying Leftist and then intemperately wrote this letter back to the *Times.* . . . And

I'm sort of the graduate student symp [for his support of graduate student demands]. I'm teaching a course on revolution. In addition to which I was self-consciously Jewish."

As his final remark implies, Kramnick believes he experienced anti-Semitism at Yale. He recounts the following incident:

> At a department picnic, playing volleyball with a mix of junior faculty/ senior faculty, a senior faculty member turned to me at some point and said, "It's your turn, Rabbi." And I actually was not terribly struck by that, but later in conversations with my wife and with Doug Rae and Jay Casper, I said, "Do you think that's anti-Semitic?" And they said, "Well, I don't know, but it sounds that way to me."

Kramnick obviously perceived a significant discrepancy between pluralist themes and departmental improvisations. His departure from Yale seems a response both to his own anti-pluralist theoretical stance and to the department's treatment of him.

To be sure, one did not need to criticize department improvisations in order to embrace a skeptical position toward pluralism. The cases of David Calleo and William Muir demonstrate this point. Neither Calleo nor Muir objected to the department's operations; yet by 1970 both were critical of pluralist theory. Notably, their criticism took politically conservative rather than radical forms. Improvisational failures, on the other hand, typically moved people to the left, not to the right, in their critiques of pluralism.

As already mentioned, as an undergraduate student Calleo was a critic of pluralist theory. His anti-pluralist views were so strong that neither exposure to pluralist scholarship during his faculty years at Yale nor departmental improvisations mattered very much to him.

But Muir's case is different. Unlike Calleo, Muir characterizes himself as very much a pluralist well into the 1960s; indeed, I have used his 1967 book to illustrate the reform premise of pluralism. However, after leaving Yale in 1968, Muir became critical of pluralism: "It struck me that the questions that weren't being asked at Yale were questions . . . worth exploring. Because the Yale pattern didn't seem to be so thoughtful. . . . Then I asked the question, what did we ignore. . . . Yale has affected me but in a kind of reverse way. What was incomplete or what was fallacious about it" (interview, January 19, 1998).

Muir's comment about Yale's omissions hints at his turn toward conservatism. He explains his growing reservations about pluralism in the following passage:

> Everything was a resource, and that was the effect of Harold Lasswell
> . . . an exchange metaphor. You do this, and I will do that. Here is the
> resource, and you want it; now you have a resource, and I want it, and
> we'll exchange it. And it overlooked coercion. That is when a person
> has a lot of resources, that makes you a victim—vulnerable—puts you
> on the deficit side of coercion. And I think we have so underemphasized
> coercion . . . that we were surprised by it when it took place, because
> suddenly the have-nots were the powerful people. . . . I think we missed
> the boat.

Muir believes pluralism overlooked the coercion that perennial "have-nots"—the poor, racial minorities—who are suddenly propelled to power would exert against their traditional foes. This coercion destroyed pluralism. Attributing coercion to have-nots rather than haves, of course, is a strong stimulant to conservativism. Not surprisingly, Muir also criticizes the idea of cultural diversity in today's politics. "We have bought into cultural diversity without emphasizing the unity side of things." Finally, Muir argues that political science should play a conservative role, emphasize the valuable autonomy of politics, and fortify the unifying role of law. Unfortunately, for Muir, pluralism is simply not up to this task.

How did Muir evolve from being a fairly convinced pluralist to a conservative critic of pluralism? The answer does not lie in his Yale experience. To the contrary, where Calleo is wryly neutral about the department's improvisations, Muir is an enthusiast: "There was a tolerance and a variety of approach at Yale which I really loved. . . . I think the catholicity or the 'eclecticness' of the department has affected me. . . . I loved the gentleness of the Yale department."

Instead, very different improvisations triggered Muir's evolution. For Muir the events of the 1960s still have a raw immediacy absent from the accounts of other scholars. Indeed, of the faculty so far discussed, Muir most directly connects his scholarship to the 1960s: "The major thing that affected my own work was the disruption of the country. The sixties were just a big factor." To Muir, the 1960s seem to have demonstrated the emptiness of pluralism.

How to sum up the complex development of anti-pluralist criticism among younger Yale faculty during the late 1960s? For five of

79

the seven, criticisms of departmental improvisations reinforced criticisms of pluralist themes. For a sixth, Muir—who had left Yale for Berkeley in the mid-1960s—the urban riots shattered the pluralist spell. Nothing he learned at Yale could shield him from these events. For only the seventh person—David Calleo—did neither departmental improvisations nor outside events matter.

By the late 1960s the department's treatment of junior faculty also created unhappiness among some friends of pluralism. Part of the reason for this development was the rapid expansion of the department. Between 1963 and 1968 eight new faculty members joined the department; in fact, in 1968 Robert Lane requested *ten* new hires, citing the growth in graduate numbers from fifty-two in 1963 to one hundred in 1968 (Lane letter, September 27, 1968, box 13, folder 23, YUDPS). Inevitably, expansion reduced junior-senior and junior-junior interactions, thereby challenging longstanding pluralist patterns.

Three young pluralist scholars—Irwin Gertzog, Peter Lupsha, and Phillips Shively—illustrate the detrimental impact of these nonpluralist improvisations. These three also demonstrate how unhappiness at Yale became a medium through which the events of the 1960s caused further stress within the department. Though the three scholars never wholly rejected pluralism, their reactions to political events—and their criticisms of the Yale department—caused strife. All three left New Haven.

The immediate pressure placed on the department's junior faculty in the late 1960s stemmed from the hiring of *twelve*, not ten, new faculty members in 1968. According to Phillips Shively, Robert Lane, then chair of the department, "was very concerned about Yale's 1984 problem" (1984 being the retirement year for Dahl and Lindblom). No doubt this concern, coupled with the strong financial support of the administration and the great national reputation of the department, explains this massive burst of hiring. However, Lane's bold effort to secure the department's future failed. By 1970, the administration had to cut back financially, partly because of financial losses, and partly because of negative alumni reactions to Kingman Brewster's management of student protests against the Black Panther trial (Kernan, 1999: 148, 172). Lane characterizes the decisions the department then made—to fire five junior people of ten—as quite difficult, but defensible. However, the "bloodbath," as one junior faculty

person dubs it, demonstrated that a practice previously accepted—
namely, competition among and dismissal of junior faculty—would
no longer operate as in the past. Instead, especially heightened competition for promotion brought to the surface long-standing resent-
ments that challenged pluralist themes.

Phillips Shively's unhappiness with the department emerged soon
after his arrival in 1968.

> It was difficult for the department to absorb that many assistant profes-
> sors at once, so there was some unhappiness among the assistant profes-
> sors. Maybe there always is. I myself decided in that year I was ready
> to play a more responsible role someplace than which I was playing
> there. . . . In fact, I told Bob Lane in my first year . . . I was going to
> look around and in fact I left in three years. (Interview, June 4, 1998)

Shively cites several influences on his decision to leave Yale early.
One was his desire "to be a grown-up political scientist," rather than
to fight against his peers for an uncertain tenure years away. He also
found the department less intellectually stimulating than he had
imagined. In addition, Shively remarks that he took a cut in pay to
go to Yale. There he lived in a suburb overlooking a shopping center,
which displeased his family. Peter Lupsha recalls that Shively did not
keep his unhappiness to himself. Lupsha recounts a "meeting which
kind of expressed the junior faculty opinion versus the senior faculty
opinion, and that was with Shively, Rae, myself, Dave Price, bunch
of other juniors, Hawley, I think was there, and Bob Lane in which
we were asking for raises. The salary was lousy. I took a cut in pay
from what I was getting as a graduate student in Stanford" (interview,
June 25, 1998). At the meeting, "Lane finally turned to Shively and
said, 'Phil, you know you might be better off someplace else,' because
'Phil, you have a trade union mentality.' I'll never forget those words."
Obviously, Lane's remarks are inconsistent with pluralist premises of
tolerance and multiple, competing centers of power that compromise
differences.

External political events may also have influenced Shively's view
of the department. In his youth Shively was "a born-again, flying sau-
cer–believing, Goldwater Republican." But 1968 was a "watershed
year." "For me personally the race riots in '68, which were totally
unpredicted by political science, was a momentous event intellectually." Shively's sense of pluralism's incapacity to explain racial unrest

clearly paralleled his personal dissatisfaction with the Yale department. The two factors make Shively critical of the department, even though he never wholly abandoned pluralism.

Like Shively, an anonymous junior faculty member also strongly criticizes the department's internal workings, especially the chairmanship of Robert Lane. "Generally speaking, it was during his reign that the department was decimated. . . . I would say a minimum of ten were forced out. Lane was blamed. Of course, it was a period of some austerity. I believe that many of these people . . . hold a considerable grudge" (interview, October 16, 1997). This member believes that Lane singled him out for punishment. "My problem arose earlier, and I resigned even though I didn't have a job yet. I was so upset with him. I felt the right thing to do was to submit a letter of resignation." He states that Lane never liked him personally; in addition, he charges that the department overlooked his sterling teaching reputation, which was widely acclaimed. When in his fifth year he requested promotion to associate professor without tenure, the department turned him down. He resigned immediately.

Also like Shively, this scholar's experience of the Vietnam War at Yale affected his view of the department. As he puts it, "It became evident that our own students were very unhappy with both the war and the institutional response to it." Hoping to disarm this discontent, he formed a group of undergraduate political science majors. "I thought this was a way of taking some of the heat out of the emotion, giving people a chance to participate." Further, he agreed to facilitate the group's communication with the department on questions of curricula. His self-created role as a conduit of student discontent did not succeed, however. Although he did not abandon pluralist theory, he did increasingly question the department's improvisations. For example, of his promotion debacle this scholar comments, "I don't know what the committee [on promotion] recommended. I never did find out." This failure of communication contradicts pluralism's reactive premise, which states that leaders are accessible to followers. Clearly, this case illustrates pluralism's weakening hold on department operations.

A combination of political events and departmental actions also alienated Peter Lupsha from the department. Although Lupsha acknowledges the weakness of his publication record, he is critical of the department on nonscholarly grounds. He, too, found Chairman

Lane off-putting, suggesting that Lane did not implement the toler-ance theme of pluralism. "His goal as chairman was to push the be-havioral revolution to its ultimate conclusion, and we went through two years, I think it was '69 and '70, in which no graduate student was admitted that didn't have a biology or math background." This narrowing of recruitment clearly is at odds with pluralist eclecticism.

Lupsha, like Shively, resented the low pay at Yale. Unlike Shively, he connected his low income to Yale's elite, old-money status. As Lupsha puts it, "There was the assumption that Westerfield and oth-ers had that you shouldn't be here unless you were independently wealthy, and there was tension at that time" (see White, 1966). Also, Lupsha detected traces of anti-Semitism in the undergraduate college system. Clearly, for Lupsha, social inequality eclipsed the depart-ment's attempts to improvise pluralism.

Most important, Lupsha felt that he did not fit in personally at Yale. He refused to "kowtow" to senior faculty and to keep quiet at meetings. No doubt the strongest symptom of not "fitting in" was Lupsha's affair with a graduate student in the department, which he admits "didn't sit too well." Lupsha believes that some faculty mem-bers at Yale deliberately prevented his getting other academic jobs. Eventually, he recounts, "They gave me a junior social science fellow-ship for a year to get me off campus. . . . They bent over backwards and opened their purses provided I didn't come around in '70, '71. Basically, I was paid not to be there."

Racial politics in New Haven also alienated Lupsha from the de-partment. Lupsha was "kind of active in the Panther trial business and what was going on in the street." He claims that the department designated two members "basically to cool me out on Vietnam marches and activities and things. . . . If you are going to get along here, these are things you have to do." While Lupsha does not believe that his political views destroyed his prospects in the department, he points out that those who "fit in" and stayed at Yale—chiefly David Mayhew and Douglas Rae—spent their time writing and publishing successfully, rather than being political activists.

As these cases reveal, unusually severe competition for tenure in-teracted with political events to weaken junior faculty attachments to the department and to pluralism. Had the department effectively improvised upon its own pluralist texts, however, it might have fore-stalled some junior faculty discontent. After all, pluralist theory celebrates flexible, accommodating political leaders able to co-opt dissenters. But the department did not improvise upon this pluralist theme; it did not relax its tenure requirements, nor did it handle junior members gracefully. Instead, its inflexible promotion policies exacerbated anti-pluralist political sentiments among junior faculty.

As we have observed, Chairs Lane and Westerfield receive much of the criticism for the breakdown in the department's pluralist improvisations. Archival materials support some of these criticisms; however, Lane did attempt to play the reform-leadership role of his pluralist predecessors, albeit with limited success.

It is true that Lane wished to increase the role of mathematics and politics in the department. Indeed, as early as June 1963, he expressed to Chairman Fesler a desire to develop a program in political science and mathematics at Yale (Lane letter to Fesler, June 24, 1963, box 8, folder 89, YUDPS). In 1967, as chairman, Lane asked Hayward Alker to evaluate five young scholars for a new mathematics and politics position in the department, a position that Gerry Kramer eventually filled (September 13, 1967, box 9, folder 101, YUDPS). Finally, in 1969, the department submitted an ambitious $1,147,600 grant proposal to the Ford Foundation for a Program in the Mathematical Study of Politics. The proposal envisaged a center headed by Kramer, four new young scholars to be hired, three designated graduate fellowships, and a total of fifteen Yale graduate students in mathematics and politics ("Proposal for a Program in the Mathematical Study of Politics—1968," box 11, folder 10, YUDPS; also box 11, folder 18). But despite the department's strenuous lobbying efforts (including a conference), the Ford Foundation turned down the proposal.

However, Lane did not focus reform exclusively on mathematics and politics. True to pluralism, he pursued a variety of scholarly perspectives. For example, in 1968 the National Institute of Mental Health funded a program in psychology and politics at Yale. This program, though small, provided a faculty position for John McConahay. Thus, Lane attempted to improvise a pluralist reform agenda, but unlike his reform predecessors, he failed to win over the junior faculty.

Nor was Lane insensitive to the low pay of junior faculty. For example, in a statement on "Core Research and Educational Functions in Political Science at Yale University" in January 1968, the department requested more salary support, noting that Yale ranked nineteenth in the country in faculty compensation (box 1, folder 11, YUDPS). Again, however, this effort failed to provide satisfaction to junior faculty.

Of the junior faculty in the late 1960s, only David Mayhew and Douglas Rae remained at Yale with tenure. Only Mayhew remains in the department today. Significantly, Mayhew treats both pluralist theory and departmental improvisations more gently than do those faculty members who left. Consider, for example, his estimation of intellectual life in the department. As compared with Shively, who found intellectual life at Yale disappointing, Mayhew "was impressed with it" (interview, August 26, 1997). He contrasts it favorably with Harvard and the University of Massachusetts, where he had taught earlier. As he sums it up, "Intellectually, it was very satisfying."

Mayhew also agrees that pluralism's reform theme is part of a legitimating discourse. Indeed, he connects it to the New Deal. As he puts it: "The Yale behavioral revolution . . . is New Dealish. . . . Pluralism is a New Dealish philosophy. It's . . . let's have a lot of parties to the table, unions, and all that. It's in one sense a rationalization of what they were doing or what they thought they were doing in the New Deal, farmers and workers." In short, for Mayhew, political reform and Yale pluralism were part of the same process (cf. Purcell, 1973: 240).

Although it may seem that Mayhew's use of the term "rationalization" places him among pluralism's critics, this is not so. For Mayhew, rationalization is necessary to progress. He asserts that there is a necessary linkage between academic scholarship and the general public. A strong tie between academia and laypersons promotes both intellectual and political reform. Pluralism forged such a link, as we saw earlier. As opposed, say, to David Calleo or William Muir, who regret pluralism's impact on the public, Mayhew celebrates pluralism's success. And where Hayward Alker blames pluralism for legitimizing the Vietnam War, Mayhew commends pluralism for legitimizing domestic political reform.

Significantly, Mayhew is also less critical of departmental improvisations than, for example, Peter Lupsha or Sidney Tarrow. Mayhew agrees with Tarrow that the department treated junior faculty in an authoritarian fashion. However, his reaction to this treatment is dramatically different from Tarrow's:

I was treated well. Certainly, I was treated like a junior faculty member, which meant that I was treated well, but there was hierarchy. There was intellectual and, I wouldn't say so much, social hierarchy—not quite that. . . . The senior people at the time . . . are in some respects very democratic. They are about as democratic as I think you could be in the Yale culture. My guess is that the Yale department was more democratic in relationships among people than was, let's say, the English department or the history department.

As we can see, Mayhew separates intellectual hierarchy from social hierarchy. Moreover, he believes Yale circumvented hierarchy somewhat through democratic practice. Whereas Tarrow and Shively complain about the department's hierarchical qualities, Mayhew does not chafe, at least outwardly. Unlike Shively and Tarrow, Mayhew softens his judgment by comparing the department favorably with other Yale departments. Lastly, where many junior faculty focus their anger on Robert Lane, Mayhew does not mention Lane at all. For Mayhew, the department's improvisations did not contradict its pluralist themes.

Not surprisingly, Mayhew's account of the 1960s at Yale is also different from that of Alker or Muir or Shively. The latter three believe the period affected both their own thinking about pluralism and their reaction to the department. Mayhew, however, does not. In addition, unlike Lupsha, Mayhew mentions no personal involvement in student anti-war politics.

In fact, Mayhew argues that the protests of the 1960s had little effect on the department, which he describes at the time as "very cool. The senior people in particular were very, very cool and dispassionate about what was going on." Moreover, according to Mayhew, no personal animosities developed during this period. Nor does Mayhew report any personal unhappiness among his fellow junior faculty. There is, for example, no mention of confrontations over salary or promotions. True, the department was "hierarchical," even "threatening." He also concedes that, "intellectual standards were out of sight." Yet, he was unbothered; "that is just the way it was." Obviously, competition at Yale did not irritate Mayhew as, for example, it did irritate Tarrow. Finally, Mayhew balances the hierarchy of Yale against something overlooked by other junior faculty: the department's provision of upward social mobility for young scholars: "I think [the behavioral revolution] also was a social revolution. . . . You won't find in the Yale department very many people who are socially pedigreed, who thought of themselves as socially pedigreed." These observations certainly differ from those of Lupsha or Isaac Kramnick, who detected lingering anti-Semitism at Yale.

Mayhew's snug fit at Yale illustrates how departmental improvisations helped pluralist themes to survive. Consider Mayhew's view of rational choice theory in relation both to pluralism and to his own early version of rational choice propounded in *Congress: The Electoral Connection*. Mayhew believes the theory of rational choice is consistent both in style and substance with Dahl's work on democratic theory. But he distinguishes between his book on Congress and contemporary rational choice studies of Congress. He criticizes the latter for excessive formality and insufficient appreciation for Congress as an institution. He thus places his congressional scholarship within a Yale pluralist tradition that, while it encompasses rational choice, does not elevate "science over politics" (see also Shapiro and Green, 1994).

The only junior faculty member I interviewed who neither rejected pluralism nor became alienated from the department, but who nevertheless left Yale, is David Price. Like Mayhew, Price was a congressional politics scholar at Yale. Indeed, Price had been a graduate student in the Yale department. Significantly, however, Price had migrated to political science from the Yale Divinity School, from civil rights politics in North Carolina, and from five years as a legislative assistant in Washington. In fact, Price now serves as a member of the House of Representatives from North Carolina. His case illustrates how deeply held normative values sometimes may trump both pluralist theory and successful pluralist improvisations.

Price's civil rights experience, his Divinity School education, and his interest in American political theory, especially in the Progressive tradition and ethicists such as Reinhold Niebhur, set him apart from his fellow junior faculty. Even as a graduate student, he had reservations about pluralism. As he puts it, "The theories underlining the pluralist approach—especially some of the more, I guess, optimistic assumptions about the political outcomes of pluralism, I was somewhat skeptical about that" (interview, April 28, 1998). The events of the late 1960s reinforced his reservations. Indeed, in the early 1970s he wrote that Dahl had overlooked important ethical questions in *After the Revolution?* (Price, 1974). Today he describes his political philosophy as more communitarian than pluralist, and he commends recent communitarian writing, such as that of Michael Sandel (see a useful overview in Fowler, 1991).

Yet, in contrast to Alker, Muir, or Tarrow, Price does not entirely reject pluralism either as theme or as improvisations. Unlike Alker and Tarrow, he doesn't criticize departmental practices; indeed, he notes that when he was a student, "Dahl and Lane and Lindblom were supremely tolerant and open people. . . . They didn't necessarily think these criticisms [of pluralism] had too much weight, but they were certainly willing to listen." True, Price's graduate seminars were not "searching discussions" of pluralism; however, he does commend the department for its responsiveness to student complaints. For example, he recalls that when he and a few other graduate students lobbied Herbert Kaufman about providing a course on Congress or the presidency, Kaufman, then chair, responded immediately, hiring William Muir to teach a year-long course on these two subjects.

Nor did Price completely abandon pluralist theory. As he puts it:

> The climate of protests in the country did influence our politics, and the study of politics, and raised certain questions about the relevance of political science, and also perhaps some of assumptions underlying the Yale brand of political science. I wouldn't call myself one of these who was. . . . I was never particularly attracted to the Caucus for a New Political Science and some of the groups that were very quick to denounce mainstream political science. I like to think that I took the criticisms with a grain of salt. The kind of communitarian critique of liberalism and of pluralist political science—that was more my cup of tea, not so much the New Left.

Critique and reform sum up Price's stance toward pluralism. In fact, Price believes that pluralism still provides an accurate account of congressional behavior. He characterizes Braybrooke and Lindblom's *A Strategy of Decision* (1963) as "on the money" regarding Congress. His objections to pluralism are normative, not empirical. Pluralism simply needs to supplement interest group competition with communitarian values.

Thus, the chief difference between Mayhew, who stayed at Yale, and Price, who left, is that normative issues influenced Price more strongly than Mayhew. Price's value commitments eventually impelled him to run for Congress. Ultimately, Price's movement from academia to Congress was an expression of, rather than a repudiation of, the ethically expanded concept of pluralism he developed at Yale.

To summarize: many junior faculty at Yale in the late 1960s encountered stress in their relations to the department or in their evaluations of pluralist theory. Most of these departed Yale, reevaluated pluralism, and reconstructed their scholarship. In short, the sixties did weaken the reproduction of pluralism at Yale. But this development was not a simple reflection of a changing external political climate. Instead, like the original *generation* of pluralism, it was composed of multiple connections between pluralist themes and departmental improvisations.

DISTANCING THE SIXTIES: THE EXPERIENCE OF SENIOR FACULTY

In contrast to junior faculty, senior faculty say little about changed departmental improvisations in the late 1960s and doubt that the 1960s had much impact on the department. Also, they see few connections between departmental improvisations and their writings on pluralism in the late 1960s and 1970s. This unconsciousness compares vividly to senior faculty accounts of their *earlier* scholarship, which vividly connect their writing to personal experience. As a result of this distancing, I believe, faculty could not shape departmental improvisations to protect pluralism against an increasingly hostile political world. In short, senior faculty unwittingly abandoned the experiential foundations of pluralism.

Certainly many departmental practices did change during the late 1960s. Moreover, traditional practices no longer enjoyed easy acceptance. By any objective standard the department experienced serious internal stress in the late 1960s. These stresses involved, inter alia, the emergence of women's issues among graduate students, the adoption of a new graduate examination system, the denial of tenure to many junior faculty, unprecedented graduate student demands for representation on department committees, and sporadic challenges to pluralism by graduate students in and out of classes.

Yet most senior faculty do not incorporate either their personal experience or these changing departmental improvisations into accounts of their scholarship. Instead, a curious pattern emerges: senior members report that the 1960s influenced *other* faculty but deny that they themselves were affected. I believe that this pattern of pluralistic ignorance (no pun intended) both symptomizes and contributed to the weakening of Yale pluralism.

Two prominent examples of this pattern appear in my interviews with Robert Lane and Robert Dahl. According to other faculty, political events deeply affected both men. And both acknowledge that the department did change improvisationally in reaction to the strains of the 1960s. Yet neither connects personal experiences or department improvisations to scholarship. By contrast, both men consciously connected their personal experiences to their earlier production of pluralism. But in the late 1960s, their scholarship drifted free of their conscious experience.

According to other informants, both the Vietnam War and the Black Panther trial in New Haven had a deep impact on Lane. For example, I had asked John McConahay if the late 1960s had influenced his own work and he responded:

> It is probably hard to say directly. I know Lane had a major influence on me. As I say, we ate lunch almost once a week, and we talked about things.
>
> *Q:* Did you ever talk about the political events that were going on?
> *A:* Oh yeah, sure.
> *Q:* Do you have any sense of what his view might have been?
> *A:* He put his house up for bail for Bobby Seale. (Interview, March 10, 1998)

According to McConahay, everyone in the department knew Lane had made a great financial sacrifice on behalf of Seale. Nor was this the full extent of Lane's support for radical politics during those years. According to Douglas Bennett, a graduate student in the department, Lane and Dahl posted his bail after New Haven police arrested him in an anti-war protest. Moreover, in a Seminar on the Future (March 5, 1968) Lane even discussed developing individualism and consciousness via "a kind of psychedelic experience(s)." He observes that such experiences could lead to the questioning of established value premises and a greater appreciation for subjectivity in social science (Yale University Library transcript, box 6, folder 75, YUDPS, p. 18). Thus, there is indirect evidence that Lane did react strongly to the 1960s. Moreover, his current research is quite critical of American politics and society (1991, 2000).

Yet Lane mentions none of these things in his interview with me. I asked him about the civil rights movement as a possible influence on the department in that period. His response displays more personal detachment than McConahay's or Bennett's accounts would lead us to expect:

> Well, I would like to say that it did . . . and, in a way, I mean, I wrote a piece for some Yale science journal on McCarthyism at Yale. . . . I felt at the time, if we don't say this, who will? And a little bit of bravado. So in some sense, it was reactive, yes. But how did that affect the core of what I was trying to do then was make a pattern of how people behaved the way they did. And it was almost humanistic, but neutral, left-right. And on the Vietnam War, I was greatly influenced by Helen, my wife. She was bitterly opposed; she was extremely opposed. And I was less opposed, and I kept thinking—maybe this is retrospective— but in Korea, the northern Koreans are a pretty repulsive lot, and south- ern Koreans aren't a lot better, but they are not so repressive. And I kept thinking it is not impossible to draw a line across Vietnam and have an experiment. (Interview, November 30, 1997)

Notice that Lane acknowledges a reaction to McCarthyism in his writing. But he does not even mention any comparable reaction to Vietnam. In fact, he characterizes himself as more moderate than his wife; and he says nothing about helping Seale or Doug Bennett. Thus, in the late 1960s Lane appears to have alienated his connections to political and departmental improvisations.

Compare this detachment with the way Lane comes alive in de- scribing the way events affected his earlier political thinking. He pro- vides the following passionate account of his youthful break with com- munism:

> I won't say I was a fellow traveler. I was . . . throughout my college years I was dedicated first to organizing the rubber workers in the neighboring town of Watertown. I organized peace movements; I was the head of the Harvard Student Union, the American Student Union, the American Youth Congress, a front for various other groups. . . . My best friends were a combination of communists and socialists. We got ambulances, raised money for ambulances, sent them to Spain, the civil war there. But I don't think the ambulances ever got there. Last we heard they were being used for communist front activities in Houston or Dallas. One kept being hijacked by communist cells. I was working with Mrs. Roosevelt on a student work camp project; organized it, got

refugee students. I had a little office in New York when I got out—
this would be '39 or '40—I got out of Harvard and hired a secretary.
Then suddenly everything I had said appeared in the communist news
program. The secretary was a plant by the communists. So, you know,
by the time I got to Yale I was shy of communists.

Lane clearly responded strongly to these political events, in effect
improvising upon pluralism's reactive premise. The personal roots of
both his pluralism and his devotion to an objective political science
are apparent. By contrast, his self-reported detachment from the
1960s weakened the link between his scholarship and his experience.
He therefore denies himself the opportunity either to *improvise* pluralism in experience or to discard pluralist theory in the face of *contradictory* improvisations. Perhaps it is therefore understandable that
his influential 1962 book (*Political Ideology*) was not equaled by his
1969 *Political Thinking and Consciousness.* The former incorporated
more of his experience.

A similar disjunction between experience and scholarship
emerges in the case of Robert Dahl. Dahl's *After the Revolution?*
(1970) and the preface to the second edition of *Politics, Economics,
and Welfare* (1976) moved him away from his earlier pluralism. For
example, in 1976 he and Lindblom observe that consensus among
pluralist leaders does not entirely support democracy: "Consensus
also constitutes a restriction on the range of alternative policies that
will be debated in polyarchal politics." (1976, xxxviii) In addition, in
1976 Dahl and Lindblom lament the absence of serious debate about
the anti-democratic power of corporations in American politics.
These positions certainly represent a shift in emphasis from his earlier
pluralism.

We have already seen that Dahl connects his personal experience
closely to his original pluralism. Yet he says little about personal experience in relation to his writing of the late 1960s and 1970s. Others
report, however, that personal experiences did transform his political
views in the 1960s. For example, Fred Greenstein contrasts Dahl in
the late 1950s with Dahl in the late 1960s. In the late 1950s, according
to Greenstein, "All of the students liked him a lot, but at the same
time there was this kind of detachment which appears in Helen
Lane's *Tell the Time to None*" (interview, July 23, 1997). However,
says Greenstein, "By the end of the 1960s, [the detachment] was going. He had become someone who meditates. He had been influ-

enced by one of his children. He became an anti-war activist by the late sixties. He wrote a fervent letter to the *Times* attacking the war." According to William Muir, by 1964 Dahl had become deeply excited about the War on Poverty, viewing it as a welcome opportunity to democratize American politics. Moreover, Greenstein's observation is supported by the fact that, when Yale chaplain William Sloane Coffin was arrested for anti-war activities in 1968 (*Yale Daily News*, February 23, 1968, box 1, folder 7, YUDPS), Dahl not only contributed to Coffin's defense fund but also signed a statement supporting Coffin in the *New York Times*. (In fact, thirteen members of the department signed the statement in support of Coffin.)

Yet Dahl mentions none of these events in his interview with me. True, I did not ask him directly about his experience of the 1960s; however, neither did he offer any such commentary in response to my questions about the department, graduate students, and the university in the 1960s. With but one notable exception, he distances his personal experience and the department's improvisations from the interview. For example, he states that departmental strains in the 1960s had no lasting effects: "Well, I can't call to mind any. It was a stressful period . . . we must have been seen by some of you guys as a pretty standard group of elders, because we didn't give in much to graduate student demands. We had a fairly solidary front on that" (interview, August 27, 1997).

The only vivid personal experience Dahl reports is his previously cited angry pluralist defense of the department against the challenge of a radical graduate student. In short, by the late 1960s Dahl apparently no longer applies his experiences to the support or renovation of pluralism. Where personal, departmental, and national experience converged to promote Dahl's pluralism into the early 1960s, these three components of a legitimating discourse later diverged, weakening Dahl's pluralism.

Five other senior members of the department manifest similar forms of disengagement between personal experience, departmental improvisations, and scholarship in the 1960s. These members run the gamut from David Danelski, an active participant in civil rights protest (he and Helen Lane attended the march in Selma, Alabama), to the self-proclaimed "hawkish" H. Bradford Westerfield. All five members of the department deny that the 1960s influenced either department improvisations or scholarship. For these members—as for Dahl and Lane—department scholarship did not engage everyday practices; as a result, pluralist theory could fade more easily.

Consider, for example, David Danelski. Danelski states that he was unusually close to undergraduates, to editors of the *Yale Daily News,* and to student protesters. But he has unusually little to say about the department's reaction to graduate student challenges. When I asked him if graduate students had attacked him or Lane and Dahl, he responded, "No . . . no, because our ideas were pretty much the same. LaPalombara at first did not go along with some of this, but he turned around fairly quickly and objected to the Vietnam War. At first, he supported it, as I recall" (interview, August 28, 1997). This account of a comparatively untroubled department is clearly at odds with other memories of the department during the period. Certainly Danelski himself was deeply involved in the political events of the time. Nor does he report any effects of the 1960s on scholarship. True, the department discussed salient issues, but people never became "uncivil." For Danelski, as for Lane and Dahl, there is no connection between personal experience and department life, and scholarship diverged from experience.

At the conservative extreme from Danelski lies H. Bradford Westerfield. Westerfield's undergraduate classes in American foreign policy had long been a favorite of Yale students; however, his scholarship did not engage pluralism or its critics in the late 1960s. Like Danelski, Westerfield denies that the graduate student challenge in the 1960s disturbed the department. Indeed, he cites his position as a hawk in a primarily dovish environment in support for his claim. "I never felt in any way pressured or in any way downgraded. After all, they made me chairman in the middle of all this, knowing perfectly well that I was still relatively hawkish" (interview, August 29, 1997). He also states that, "Compared with the tensions that wrenched other leading departments and other leading universities in that period, Yale was a very quiet place."

Like other senior members of the department, Westerfield detaches scholarship from departmental improvisations and personal experiences in the 1960s. He agrees that Robert Dahl developed a deeper commitment to democracy during the 1960s; however, he does not mention any departmental or personal reasons for Dahl's evolution. Nor does Westerfield believe that his own work responded to the 1960s. For Westerfield, as for Danelski, Lane, and, to a lesser degree, Dahl, experience and scholarship diverged. Pluralism thus lost its vital connection to everyday life (cf. Hamilton, 1999).

William Foltz, an Africanist, displays a similar detachment. In response to my question about the department's reaction to the 1960s, Foltz contrasts the relative harmony of the Yale department then with recent strife in the department. Moreover, like Westerfield, Foltz compares the Yale department positively with more conflictive universities in the 1960s. For example, he observes that the Yale department considered offering refuge to beleaguered members of the Cornell government department, who believed they had been mistreated in Cornell's racial upheavals. According to Foltz:

> Jim Fesler wrote to Cornell, and before you knew it, Mayhew and I— both as junior faculty members—and Fred Watkins were dispatched as a Yale visiting committee to go and look at the situation in Cornell. And by and large we came back saying this is not the Third Reich. There is a lot of turmoil, a lot of upheaval, but some of these guys looking for academic hospitality or refuge are really making asses of themselves and overdramatizing the situation. . . . Their government department had not been singled out for particular persecution. (Interview, November 30, 1997)

Opposing memories of the visit to Cornell illustrate how senior and junior faculty members differed in their reactions to the 1960s. Foltz characterizes the visit quite matter-of-factly. By contrast, Isaac Kramnick recalls the visit with anger, seeing it as revealing Yale's exaggerated self-conception in relation to American political science: "But it was this incredible hubris. 'We are the protectors and the custodians of political science in America. Something has happened to the political science department at Cornell, especially one of our own beloved, former colleagues, Allen Bloom. We must send a team to investigate what happened there!' And they did."

Two senior faculty members whose scholarly interests would naturally have drawn them into a dialogue about pluralism at the end of the 1960s were James Fesler and Herbert Kaufman. Both, after all, were students of American bureaucracy. However, they, too see no influence of the period on scholarship or departmental functioning. I asked Fesler about whether the Vietnam War, the Black Panthers trial in New Haven, and graduate student discontent had created strains in the department. He responded:

My impression is that it didn't, surprisingly, because it did in other areas of the university. We didn't have the experience of Berkeley. But it was a very perilous period. There was a meeting . . . Dahl presided over, Black Panthers and all. . . . For one thing, a lot of us had great confidence in President Brewster. . . . Often over the country the radical on campus is not in the political science department. . . . And so I think political scientists are not that marginalized in terms of their views. (Interview, August 26, 1997)

Fesler reports some guilt and disquiet about his own actions at the time. Still, he concludes that "I was not affected." When I asked him about 1960s effects on scholarship generally in the department, he responded simply, "I really don't know."

Herbert Kaufman manifests a more complex detachment. As we have seen, Kaufman 's early work advanced pluralist arguments about city politics that were deeply influenced by his personal experience. By contrast, although student activism during the late 1960s alienated him, he does not relate this experience to his research nor to department scholarship.

Kaufman observes that:

There was pressure for pass-fail grades [among undergraduates]. I think they adopted it for a while. It was an option which the students were given. . . . The time came for the general exams that they gave undergraduates at the end of the fourth year, and they didn't want to take it. And so the department backed off. And they had what I gather were essentially rap sessions. They would just meet with a group of students, and that would be final exams. So I thought things are going to pieces. I don't know what happened at the graduate level . . . they were beginning to agitate to be represented on various committees, that's the form it took. (Interview, November 29, 1997)

Obviously, Kaufman was disturbed by these developments. Yet in answer to my question about whether scholarship within the department responded to these events, he has little to say: "I just don't have a sense of the literature of the times well enough. And as I say, I was here only for a year in the midst of it. I was away for the Black Panther uprising."

Kaufman's antipathy to the 1960s is unconnected to his views of scholarship during that period. Interestingly, by the late 1960s his own scholarship ceased to engage either pluralists or their critics. He ob-

serves that his 1960 book, *The Forest Ranger*, was an influential contribution to American politics—as, indeed, it was; by contrast, he regrets
that *Time, Chance, and Organizations* (1974) received little attention.
But the latter book, whatever its other merits, does not engage either
pluralism or contemporary political events as deeply as did *The Forest
Ranger*. Arguably, had Kaufman retained a connection between his
personal experience, Yale departmental improvisations, and his scholarship, his later work would have attracted more attention.

Of course, conscious engagement with the 1960s usually did not
support pluralism. Instead, people who sensed inconsistency between
pluralist themes, departmental improvisations, and personal experiences usually *jettisoned* pluralism in favor of new ideas. For Bruce
Russett and Charles Lindblom, personal experience and departmental improvisation weakened pluralism.

Bruce Russett, a student of international relations, agrees with
other senior scholars that the department survived the 1960s well.
Like others, he contrasts Yale's peaceful experience with the strife
other universities suffered. However, unlike fully detached scholars,
Russett argues that the department's position on the Vietnam War
helped to sustain its internal cohesion:

> This was very much a liberal democratic department. So I think the
> . . . mode in the department was very much "We don't like this war
> very much, but we are not out there burning anything down, and how
> do we ride through this? How do we keep our sanity around here? How
> do we keep the integrity of the department and of the university?" At
> the same time, nudging American politics in the direction of getting us
> out of this thing. (Interview, August 25, 1997)

By ascribing a specific political position to the department, Russett differs from his detached colleagues. Moreover, although he does
not describe the department's position as repudiating pluralism, he
does hint at tensions (e.g., "at the same time") between pluralist consensus in the department and the "nudging" of American politics
away from Vietnam. In short, unlike others, Russett did connect departmental improvisations to national politics.

Russett also believes national and departmental politics changed
department scholarship. He remarks:

> Yes, [the 1960s] did affect the way people thought. I think Dahl had
> the book *After the Revolution?*, which was clearly a reflection of that.

97

I had started out with rather systemic interests in international relations in the sixties and decided I really wanted to know what was driving this beast of American foreign policy. So that is where I moved as a conscious reaction; it was a consciousness . . . this was my contribution to hopefully ending the war . . . understanding what was driving it.

Russett's new scholarly emphasis produced his 1972 book, *No Clear and Present Danger*. In this study he provocatively defends the isolationist position on American entrance into World War II. Extrapolating from this analysis, he argues that the Johnson administration could have avoided involvement in Vietnam. Russett is also critical of American foreign policy elites; he writes, "It is fair to insist on a degree of humility in our leaders of all eras" (1972: 21–22). In short, Russett's confrontation with the Vietnam War led him to criticize the American regime, and—indirectly—pluralist theory.

Of the leading pluralist scholars at Yale, the 1960s had the greatest impact on Charles Lindblom. Indeed, when I asked Lindblom whether he had any regrets about his scholarly life, he replied that he and other Yale scholars should have been more critical of the American regime. Most important, Lindblom, like Russett, is especially conscious of how political events affected scholarship.

When I asked Lindblom if the 1960s influenced Yale scholarship about American politics, he responded:

I think so.
    Q: Can you think of any examples?
    A: Look at Bob's *After the Revolution?* He wouldn't have went there except for the troubles in the sixties. . . . He might not have even got interested as much as he did in workers control. But I think it moved him; it moved me. (Interview, August 26, 1997)

Lindblom also claims that the 1960s alerted him to the importance of social class in political life and to the defects of his earlier pluralist arguments. Finally, Lindblom is the only senior member of the department to theorize about the role of legitimating discourses in politics. He remarks:

Look at the evidence of collaboration between church and nobility in medieval Europe to maintain a set of advantages. . . . These were attempts to reach people to be satisfied with what damn little they had. The church's message was that your rewards come in heaven, and that the order of inequality on earth is God-given. The whole history of thought is full of lessons. . . . I think this continues to come down, comes down through the business elite, but it comes down through the school system.

It is not surprising that Lindblom moved far away from pluralism. Lindblom's *Politics and Markets* (1977) treated businesspeople not as a pluralist interest group but, rather, as a set of "public official(s)" performing governmental functions of allocation (172). Therefore, business possesses unique power that no interest group enjoys: government officials *must* cater to its demands. As a result, political power is more unequally distributed than pluralism envisaged.

Lindblom also rethought the role of ideas in pluralist systems. As we have seen, his early pluralist work derogated "big ideas" in politics; politics, he claimed, proceeded through partisan mutual adjustment and incrementalism, not through overarching values, comprehensive programs, or total ideologies. However, in his 1982 presidential address to the American Political Science Association, Lindblom placed ideas—including legitimating discourses—at the very center of pluralist politics. He argued that in pluralist systems political socialization and political education did not produce democratic citizens. In fact, he called for political scientists to analyze the way ideas legitimized political systems, including that of the United States (1982).

Nor did Lindblom exempt social science from his critique of pluralism. In *Inquiry and Change* (1990) he charged that social scientists had given little help to policymakers struggling to implement truly democratic reforms. Most social science, he claimed, merely put an expert gloss on common sense; it did not transform policy perspectives. Although Lindblom leaves open the question of why so deficient an endeavor as social science has managed to thrive, the question begs discussion. A plausible answer Lindblom might offer to this rhetorical question is that, under its veil of objectivity, most social science masks the tyranny of a "common sense" *meant* not to advance democracy. Such pessimism would be a long way from the comparative optimism of earlier Yale scholarship.

CONCLUSION: PLURALISM DETHRONED

By the early 1970s, pluralism had been dethroned at Yale. In this chapter I identified several processes by which this dethronement took place. Contrary to most commentators on the 1960s, I try to show that traumatic political events have no uniform "effect" on the production of ideas. Instead, ideas, events, and experience—themes and improvisations—intertwine in complicated forms. The withdrawal from pluralism was contingent rather than determined, heterogeneous rather than homogeneous, partial rather than total, reversible rather than irremediable. Indeed, though pluralism declined, it remains alive as a legitimating discourse. In fact, as we will see, today it serves to resist identity politics in the United States.

For junior faculty, the dethronement of pluralism at Yale occurred in two ways. First, specific anti-pluralist department practices alienated several junior faculty members who were already skeptical of pluralism. Isaac Kramnick, Sidney Tarrow, Hayward Alker, and, to a lesser extent, Douglas Rae, among others, complemented their objections to pluralism as *text* with their criticisms of department practices (for a related argument, see Sewell, 1996). As these faculty members saw it, new improvisations in the department contradicted pluralist themes. This department experience supported their intellectual reservations about pluralism. Would effective pluralist improvisations in the department have prevented these scholars' rejection of pluralism? We cannot say. But certainly departmental improvisations supported their disenchantment with pluralism.

Second, department improvisations eliminated some junior faculty who generally subscribed to pluralist views, such as, among others, Phillips Shively. He, together with two others, left Yale. Significantly, the three scholars felt deeply the impact of the 1960s. Caught between their support for pluralist themes and their counterpluralist experiences, they did not survive at Yale.

But department improvisations helped *salvage* pluralism for some of its junior defenders. David Price, John McConahay, and David Mayhew perceived the department to be performing its pluralist themes effectively. All three, though touched by the 1960s, maintained pluralism in the face of criticism. Had they become disenchanted with the department, would they have abandoned pluralism? Perhaps not. But certainly their approval of departmental improvisations buttressed their support for pluralist themes.

In only two cases did improvisation within the department have no discernible connection to pluralism. As we have seen, both William Muir and David Calleo were skeptical about pluralism before the late

1960s. But the 1960s convinced Muir that pluralism lacked a crucial normative dimension. Once at Berkeley, a more conflictive department than Yale, Muir no longer experienced pluralist practices that might have overcome his growing disenchantment with pluralist theory. Finally, David Calleo dissented from pluralism even as an undergraduate at Yale. Neither the 1960s nor departmental improvisations altered his entrenched views. If anything, he held pluralism itself responsible for the 1960s.

In sum, for most junior faculty at Yale in the late 1960s pluralist text, department improvisations, and personal experiences were interconnected. Strain among these three factors emerged, with the result that pluralism declined as a legitimating discourse.

Among senior faculty, the story is quite different. Growing detachment from personal and departmental experience provided no fertile ground for pluralism. The improvisational roots of pluralism withered; no wonder pluralism ceased to blossom textually.

For most Yale senior faculty, prior connections between experience, improvisations, and themes became attenuated. Early pluralists such as Dahl, Lane, and Kaufman apparently distanced themselves psychologically from events both within and without the department. In stark contrast to their earlier improvisational immersion, which fueled pluralism, they now withdrew. Because they no longer drew upon improvisations and experience to anchor pluralism, they found it easy to reconsider and modify their earlier positions.

A few senior faculty members, such as Lindblom and Russett, retained their connection to events, but now their engagement undermined pluralist themes. As a result, they modified their scholarship, and Lindblom sharply attacked his earlier pluralism.

These complex interactions between texts, political events, department improvisation, and personal experiences yield some tentative generalizations about how legitimating discourses rise and fall among academics. When the personal experiences of youthful academics confirm the political claims of the state, these academics create legitimating discourses. Later, in positions of academic power, they improvise effectively upon these discourses. Personal experience, department practice, and legitimating texts work together smoothly. In the present case, the result was—to use Robert Putnam's phrase—the "golden age" of Yale pluralism (interview, April 24, 1998).

As time passes, however, these aging academics begin to lose touch with the experiences and improvisations that supported their earlier scholarship. They also distance themselves from new experiences and improvisations that might fortify their theories. Therefore, when regime challenges emerge—as in the late 1960s—they no longer produce legitimating discourses. Instead, they adopt new discourses in reaction to disorienting national events and personal experiences. Also, they sometimes adopt practices that are inconsistent with their earlier scholarship. The result is either a silencing of pluralism—as in the cases of Fesler, Danelski, and Kaufman—or reconsiderations of pluralism—as in the cases of Lindblom, Russett, and Dahl.

As senior scholars slowly abandon a legitimating discourse, their natural successors—younger scholars—never fully adopt the discourse. Unlike senior faculty, junior scholars are unable to detach themselves from experience and events. Personal experiences that disconfirm the discourse drive some younger scholars away from the universities in which the doctrine flourished. In some cases, delegitimizing personal and department improvisations take their toll on the discourse itself. The discourse begins to fragment, to become "normalized" (e.g., Billig, 1995), to make its way piecemeal into specialized research areas and, finally, to be vigorously attacked.

Yet pluralism has not died. Indeed, it remains a useful legitimating discourse for the American political regime. In fact, its survival counterbalances identity politics in the current struggle over American political culture. Though weakened by pluralism's decline, American political institutions still benefit from pluralism's survival.

4

Incorporating Pluralism

INTRODUCTION: PLURALISM'S CHILDREN

As theme (literary texts), Yale pluralism declined after 1970. A contributing factor to this decline was increasing divergence between pluralist theory, on the one hand, and departmental improvisations and personal experience, on the other. As a result, many Yale faculty—Dahl, Lindblom, Tarrow, Alker, for example—found themselves composing new, nonpluralist tunes. Yet Yale pluralism did not die. Instead, as both theme and improvisation, Yale pluralism survived among a majority of those who were graduate students in the department during its pluralist salad years. Though generally less distinguished than their teachers, they have carried pluralism to cultural sites beyond Yale. These younger scholars—pluralism's children—have carried pluralism into our own time.

This chapter inquires not into the *production* but into the *reproduction* (Jenks, 1993a: chapter 6) of Yale pluralism as a legitimating discourse. Pluralism embraces the scholars who encountered it as graduate students between 1955 and 1970 at Yale. Many of these students not only accepted pluralism's premises but also adopted these premises to fit their own themes and improvisations. Their very "ordinariness," as compared with their gifted teachers, normalized pluralism, turning it from a high-profile, contested doctrine into scholarly "common sense." Although they could not prevent pluralism's decline, they did keep pluralism an active participant in contemporary American political science—and in American political culture.

Let me justify my attention to "ordinary" second-generation Yale scholars. Traditional intellectual and cultural histories focus upon seminal works by distinguished thinkers. But virtually by definition, most intellectuals are not eminent, nor are most works seminal. However, this very *lack* of distinction makes its own contribution to political discourse. In order to become influential, an esoteric legitimating discourse must assume mundane terms and forms. "Ordinary" intellectuals accomplish this transformation and diffuse the discourse far from its specific origins. In addition, by applying pluralism to many specialized fields of scholarship and to many different improvisations, ordinary intellectuals model the discourse for others who were not at Yale.

This process of diffusion and reproduction is double-sided, however. On the one hand, pluralism's children adapt pluralism to new challenges, thus revitalizing, embellishing, and refining the discourse. By selectively adapting or modifying pluralism, they improvise upon—and perform anew—the pluralist themes of tolerance, competing power centers, reaction, and reform.

On the other hand, this very process of reproduction takes its toll on pluralism. The strategies necessary to sustain pluralist ideas also compromise the ideas, inevitably revealing both the ideas' limits and, often, their inconsistencies. In addition, the tensions between social context, personal experience, political events, and pluralist ideas that pluralism's progenitors at Yale encountered reappear—with yet greater force—among pluralism's children. After all, male graduate students at Yale in the late 1960s faced possible service in the Vietnam War. Also, changing gender roles and sexual mores offered new opportunities and dangers to female graduate students at Yale. Finally, racial politics not only challenged pluralism but also gave students novel opportunities to engage in the politics of protest. But protest politics commented ironically on pluralism's argument that insurgent groups *already* enjoyed opportunities for effective access to the political system. Many Yale students perceived and responded to this irony.

Today, of course, those who adhered to pluralism have had to cope with the sea changes in American politics since the 1950s and 1960s. The context that favored pluralism during their graduate years no longer exists. Instead, contemporary proponents of market-based approaches to political problems or "identity politics" confront pluralists with powerful, if different, challenges. Moreover, most pluralists recognize that the theory's modest promises of reform were not entirely fulfilled. Yale graduate students who retain pluralism in our own time must engage in continual struggle. "Performing pluralism" remains a constant challenge.

Nevertheless, for many Yale graduate students, pluralism at Yale "took." No doubt socialization processes common to late adolescence and early adulthood (Hahn, 1998) help to explain this fact. In addition, most who accepted and retain pluralism improvised upon pluralist themes at Yale. Repeated improvisations of pluralist themes have reinforced each other, embedding pluralism in the majority of pluralism's children.

To be sure, pluralism enjoyed a natural advantage among Yale graduate students. Regular contact with respected pluralist scholars encouraged students not only to incorporate pluralist ideas but also to see pluralists as "role models." Moreover, acceptance to Yale graduate school was a considerable achievement. To reject pluralism would be tantamount to doubting the wisdom of scholars who had just bolstered the student's pride. Thus, pluralism had a head start in its competition for the hearts and minds of Yale graduate students.

Also, not surprisingly, many graduate students chose Yale *because* of pluralism. Many had encountered pluralism as undergraduates, liked its ideas, and wanted to pursue it at its nerve center. Questioning pluralism, therefore, meant questioning not only Yale but also their own judgment. In short, many students had a deep psychological investment in pluralism. Rejecting the discourse would have been not only an intellectual, but also a personal, wrench.

Yet a substantial minority of students did reject pluralism either permanently or temporarily. These students discovered that neither early experience nor the Yale milieu supported pluralism. Instead, in contrast to the students who incorporated pluralism, this minority remembers Yale negatively. They are critical of classes, of faculty, of their fellow students, and of the gap between pluralist themes and political events. Indeed, differences in personal experience and departmental improvisations are good predictors of a student's stance toward pluralism.

Yet the term *predictor,* by artificially separating ideas from experiences, frames my analysis in inappropriately causal terms. After all, graduate students pursue their ideas in real contexts; in a sense, pluralist theory is a tool (Swidler, 1984) with which students fashioned their identities, expressed their evolving selves, and lived their lives. Ideas and experience—themes and improvisations—are a single ensemble. The complex ensemble of themes and improvisations defies a simple, linear model of causation. It is better to see ideas and experience together forming *interpretations* that students give to Yale pluralism. The adoption or rejection of pluralism lies in these interpretations, not in texts or experiences—themes and improvisations—considered separately.

What do I mean by "being" a pluralist? Being a pluralist refers to two things: the individual's self-professed acceptance of pluralism at Yale and the individual's self-professed employment of pluralism to interpret contemporary American politics. This combination of early internalization and contemporary application takes many forms. Graduate students who became academics have professed pluralism in writings and in teaching. Those who left academia apply pluralism to understand the political world and to conduct their careers (e.g., in dealing with politicians, in making and advising on public policy, and in arriving at consequential decisions). In short, pluralists not only continue to expand the doctrine textually or through improvisation, but they also interpret their actions in pluralist terms. It is through their multifarious pluralist interpretations of theme and improvisation that students have reproduced pluralism as a legitimating discourse.

I used two interview questions in order to classify Yale graduate students as pluralists or nonpluralists. I first asked about each student's initial reception of pluralist ideas at Yale. Did the student find pluralist ideas persuasive? The second question, asked later in each interview, inquired whether the individual believed pluralism was still a useful framework for understanding American politics. Positive responses to both questions qualified the student as a pluralist. Negative responses to one or both questions qualified the student as a "disrupter." I discuss disrupters in chapter 5. Here I concentrate on pluralists.

Is this classificatory process sufficient? I believe so. As subsequent discussion indicates, pluralists identified in this way provide rich, subtle, and complex pluralist interpretations. Most pluralist graduate students did not become "true believers." Instead, they ruminate, discard, combine, modify, and reconstruct pluralism in multiple, nuanced ways. Pluralism is no uniformly understood body of ideas that is absorbed and expressed in an identical fashion. Some pluralist students espouse more comprehensive versions of the discourse than others. Some apply pluralism with greater confidence and fidelity than others. Some are more certain than others about what pluralism entails. Finally, some are more personally devoted to pluralism than others. My analysis of student interviews not only respects these complexities but also reveals the subtlety of pluralism.

Of course, there is a subjective element in my procedure. Yet there are also checks against bias. For one thing, most whom I classify as pluralists offer concrete personal illustrations of the doctrine; I have also collected many examples of their pluralist scholarship. In addition, I analyzed each interview *twice*. First, I examined my handwritten interview notes of each interview, classifying each respondent. Second, months later, after I had in hand full transcripts of the tape-recorded interviews, I read each full transcript blind, that is, without consulting my preliminary classification based on handwritten notes. I then again assigned each transcript to the pluralist or nonpluralist category. Comparing the two classifications yields an 80 percent level of agreement, quite robust given the complexity of the interviews. When my two classifications disagreed, I carefully reread both the handwritten interview notes and the interview transcript and then assigned the interview to a category.

PLURALISM ENCOUNTERED

Although a majority of the Yale students graduating between 1955 and 1970 whom I interviewed embraced *pluralism,* they did not display comparable enthusiasm for *behavioralism*—the methodological approach favored at Yale. Indeed, many students distinguished between pluralism and behavioralism, dismissing the latter while accepting the former. This distinction demonstrates one important way by which young intellectuals begin to absorb a legitimating discourse. By separating research method from theoretical substance, students assure themselves they are not uncritical celebrants of a *Zeitgeist* but are mature critics, able to sort out wheat from chaff. Indeed, for some students, skepticism about behavioralism may have actually encouraged the adoption of pluralism. Rejecting behavioralism may have made accepting pluralism a sign of discernment, not of sycophancy.

Why did some pluralist graduate students find behavioralism unappealing? Answering this question necessitates a brief account of behavioralism. As David Brian Robertson notes, behavioralism approached the study of politics not through history or political institutions or law, but through the scientific study of individuals:

> Behavioralists assumed that there are discoverable regularities in individual political behavior, an assumption which . . . implies that the scientific analysis of contemporary behavior yields adequate insight into political truth. They believed that research should be driven by empirical theories about these regularities, that the validity of these theories must be testable and subject to invalidation, and that rigorous (preferably quantifiable) data analysis be used to test these theories. (Robertson, 1994: 116–17)

As Wilfred McClay has suggested (1994: 192–93), behavioralism strongly advocated the moral neutrality of political research and researchers. In this way, according to McClay, behavioralism tried to respect intellectual debate and to reject stale, polarizing ideological categories. Behavioralism advanced a Deweyian normative relativism; it claimed to oppose all encompassing, ideological frameworks. Behavioralists held ideological commitment responsible for Nazism, for Soviet Communism, and for the reactionary politics of Joseph McCarthy. Behavioralism's concentration on individuals rather than institutions and structures also complemented American values, especially personal freedom, voter choice, and entrepreneurship. Thus, adherence to behavioralism served to legitimate the "free world," especially the United States, in its competition against its chief political opponents.

Indeed, Gabriel Almond expressly enunciated this position as early as 1954, in *The Appeals of Communism,* where he wrote: "Once involved in the struggle for political power, the ethical absolutist is confronted by the most serious temptation" (quoted in Purcell, 1973: 138). The "temptation" Almond referred to was, of course, totalitarianism as practiced in the Soviet Union. Behavioralism, by contrast, was meant to be anti-absolutist. As method, it claimed to promote intellectual pluralism, just as, substantively, pluralist theory promoted American liberal democracy.

However, behavioralism paid a price for its ethical relativism; it abandoned the idea that, explicitly at least, the study of politics could reveal any universal political values. This feature of behavioralism antagonized some graduate student pluralists. Though persuaded by *empirical* pluralism, they yearned for an *explicitly normative* pluralist theory. But the behavioral method deprived pluralism of the desired normative argument. A typical statement appears in the observations of Robert Lyke, who studied American politics at Yale from 1963 to 1966, taught at Princeton, and then left academic life to join the Congressional Research Service. Citing his "aversion to behavioralism," Lyke took a year off from Yale to attend Oxford University. As he puts it:

> I developed a sense across the years that I was at Yale that there was a shallowness to behavioralism. . . . I really suspected that there weren't any philosophical ideas that underpinned it. And so I went out to Oxford . . . with an attempt to see whether that would be kind of my true area of interest . . . to develop a critique of behavioralism from a more substantial philosophical perspective. (Interview, March 6, 1998)

Lyke regrets that there was little interest at Yale in philosophical issues. Nevertheless, despite his objections to behavioralism he embraced pluralism. In fact, he describes himself as a "split personality," whose philosophical rejection of behavioralism did not prevent his writing a pluralist dissertation on suburban politics.

Other pluralist students objected to behavioralism on the grounds that it did not deliver on its scientific pretensions. For example, Patrick Morgan, now a well-known international relations scholar, resisted behavioralism in a class with Karl Deutsch: "I wasn't overly thrilled by the behavioral approach. . . . It was excessively confident about the ability to put precise measures on things. Even though it then claimed that it was fully aware that this was a tricky thing to do, people lived and died by the measures. . . . And that to me tended to distort the understanding you could get about important political phenomena" (interview, March 23, 1998).

However, Morgan did not reject pluralism, although as an international relations specialist, pluralist theory was clearly peripheral. For Morgan, domestic American politics became important when it had an impact on foreign policy. Therefore, pluralism had little salience for him.

But if behavioralism did not help students to endorse pluralism, how did pluralism take hold? For some students, merely being at Yale did the trick. Validated by their acceptance in so prestigious an institution as Yale, they gravitated to the pluralism of their instructors. For example, Herbert Alexander, an influential scholar of campaign finance (see, e.g., Alexander and Shiratori, 1994), recounts his awe at Yale and his veneration of Robert Dahl. As Alexander puts it: "I was from Waterbury, Connecticut, and, you know, I was just over-whelmed with the thought that, 'Gee, little me got accepted at Yale University.' . . . I was in awe at a number of people there. I still to this day maintain that Bob Dahl is at the top of the list for just sheer intellectual ability" (interview, September 18, 1997). Alexander states that Dahl "made a pluralist out of me, and I still am to this day."

Students who came to Yale from small schools or from universities outside the Ivy League were especially prone to this reaction. For example, John Fitch came to Yale in 1965 from Randolph-Macon College in Virginia. Fitch—now director of an environmental policy program at the University of Colorado and a much-published writer on Latin America—accepted pluralism at Yale. Fitch remembers the power of his initial Yale experience. "For somebody that comes from this very small school, ah, this sort of parochial, Virginia background, it was totally mind-boggling" (interview, March 3, 1998). Fitch also was so immersed in trying to survive intellectually that he had little time to reflect on pluralism. The combination of awe, intimidation, and overwork may have favored a naive absorption of pluralism not only for Fitch but also for other Yale students.

Youthful inexperience also promoted pluralism. Many pluralists I interviewed reflected wryly or regretfully on their lack of sophis-tication at Yale. These students lacked enough self-confidence or knowledge to scrutinize pluralism skeptically. For example, Laurel Files characterizes herself as "a bright person" but concedes that she was "a very different learner then than I am now. I didn't question anything" (interview, February 25, 1998). Files attributes her attitude to limited self-confidence, to not being innately an "intellectual," and to being "more like my mother's generation" (in her lack of feminist consciousness).

Awe, inexperience, self-doubt, intimidation, parochialism—these are the stuff of ordinary graduate life and hardly, it would seem, worth mentioning. Yet legitimating discourses enjoy an advantage over other discourses in exploiting these psychological qualities. Unlike *oppositional* discourses, which, by criticizing a regime, imply to stu-dents that they ought *not* be intimidated or awestruck by authority, legitimating discourses play upon the most commonplace and taken-for-granted feelings. It is precisely through mundane, unremarked

improvisations of the ordinary that a legitimating discourse is reproduced (cf. Billig, 1998).

Elite institutions—such as Ivy League universities containing nationally known scholars—are especially likely sites for the creation
and transmission of legitimating discourses. Not only are dominant
groups overrepresented in such places, but also attending these institutions constitutes a valuable form of cultural capital. Attending such
an institution gives instant prestige to the provincial, the outsider, the
impressionable. To reject the ideas the institution purveys threatens
the social "promotion"—the instant social mobility—that the institution extends. Charles McCall, who taught at a California State University and who was at Yale from 1958 to 1962, captures this reaction
well: "Look . . . I'm a small-town boy. My folks were both working
class, and all of a sudden I was at Yale . . . and so I would be walking
back to my apartment, and, you know, just the look of the place. . . .
I would sometimes just burst out laughing. What am I doing here?"
(interview, March 31, 1998).

Another factor that favored pluralism was its verisimilitude. Pluralism made so few controversial or complicated claims. For example,
William Ascher, who was at Yale from 1968 to 1971 during the height
of student activism, explains his receptivity to pluralism this way: "I
think at the time it was persuasive. . . . It seemed, not tautological,
but it seemed quite obvious. . . . It wasn't until somewhat later that
I was actually exposed to some of the critiques of pluralism. . . . I
don't recall that much that was really questioning the fundamental
premises of pluralism" (interview, May 20, 1998).

Ascher's use of "obvious" to describe pluralism construes the discourse as an objective, transparent, and self-evident portrait of the
American political regime. His interview makes pluralism seem natural and normal; thus, any competing discourse immediately appears
abnormal, artificial, and immediately suspect.

I do not imply that most pluralist students adopted pluralism for
irrational reasons. Indeed, the overwhelming majority of students reflected upon pluralism coolly and dispassionately. Many students selected some features of pluralism and rejected others. In fact, pluralist theory recommended itself precisely because it did not claim to
explain *everything;* it simply claimed to solve some specific puzzles
better than did other theories. The very modesty of pluralism—its
deliberate avoidance of sweeping explanations, the tentativeness of

its language—encouraged thoughtful students to engage in pluralist improvisations. Ultimately, students who made judicious, cautious, careful selections among pluralist themes were doing precisely what pluralism claimed the American political system regularly did. Both the political system and youthful pluralists proceeded incrementally to cope with immediate problems. Both weighed evidence and respected alternative points of view. In summary, in the very act of choosing pluralist theory judiciously, students improvised upon pluralist themes.

Pluralism also offered multiple arguments to its youthful adherents. In fact, different students adopted pluralism for quite contradictory reasons. For example, some students initially chose pluralism on methodological grounds. Consider, for example, Robert Axelrod, a leading scholar of rational choice and international relations, who studied at Yale between 1964 and 1968. Axelrod's influential theory of evolving political norms incorporates the incrementalism and reactivity of Yale pluralism (1986: 1095–111). To Axelrod,

> There was a lot of enthusiasm for that set of ideas [pluralism]. Methodologically we were—I think the whole class was—looking for ways of doing research that would be empirically based and justifiable. And also, I think the concern with what makes democracy work and the competition among elites was interesting and congenial. . . . Now, later, years later, there was criticism along the lines of, well, where were the blacks, for example. (Interview, February 3, 1998)

Axelrod particularly admired the methodology of *Who Governs?*, which he thought "an excellent model for how to do social science research." For Axelrod, the behavioral approach and pluralist theory fortified each other; the former provided the necessary empirical and methodological foundation for the latter.

By contrast, Elinor Bowen, who was at Yale in the mid-1960s, gravitated to pluralism mainly "as normative political theory." Before coming to Yale she had avoided normative theory, but at Yale she suddenly found normative theory attractive. According to Bowen, normatively pluralism argued that, "If you want a government which is non-exploitative of its own population, then the best shot is pluralism of the particular kind that the Yale School, or Madison, or whoever would have written about" (interview, June 5, 1998.) Bowen found this quite modest normative statement persuasive.

112

Bowen's and Axelrod's constructions of pluralism obviously diverge considerably. To Axelrod, pluralism's failure to encompass the black experience is, first and foremost, an empirical problem. In fact, Axelrod adheres to pluralism today only by rationalizing the empirical damage the civil rights movement caused pluralism. He acknowledges that pluralism "did minimize serious and enduring conflict, especially racial conflict." But then he rescues pluralism from this criticism: "However, I don't see that's sort of outside of what they could have studied, and what the methods and approaches are relevant to. So I don't see that kind of . . . that they're out of date or something like that." In short, Axelrod's original embrace of pluralism on empirical grounds serves as the lens through which he evaluates—and defends—pluralist discourse today.

By contrast, Bowen tries to repair pluralism's weaknesses *normatively*. Unlike Axelrod, Bowen argues that pluralism cannot comprehend contemporary identity politics empirically. As she puts it with characteristic directness, "I don't think that pluralism can explain them." However, this failure does not dissuade her from pluralism; in fact, the contrary is true. As she puts it, "Maybe that's why . . . initially I was saying that I've thought of it as normative theory. Pluralism comes in to tell you what's wrong with it, to tell you how to react if you care about a decent political system. But I don't believe it explains why these things arose." For Bowen, pluralism's normative superiority to identity politics exempts it from the empirical failures that Axelrod addresses. The point is that these two pluralists have fashioned quite differing ways to remain pluralist today.

To summarize: pluralism appealed to Yale graduate students for many personal, political, and intellectual reasons. As a result, each pluralist student developed his or her own particular version of the discourse. This heterogeneity should not surprise us. As Paul Simpson (1993) has demonstrated, subtle syntactical alterations in even apparently straightforward texts, such as newspaper stories, convey quite different messages. Far greater multiplicity characterizes more complex discourses about politics—such as pluralist theory. As a result, multiple versions of—and improvisations on—pluralism have helped to reproduce the discourse over time.

This microanalytic analysis needs to be placed in a larger theoretical context. Because legitimating discourses favor politically dominant groups, dominants naturally strive to present them in multiple forms, from the classroom to the computer screen to the advertisement to the patriotic celebration (see, e.g., Levin, 1999; Berezin, 1997; Spillman, 1997; Zerubavel, 1995). Pluralism, too, appeared in multiple incarnations. By contrast, challenging or oppositional discourses—such as Marxism or elite theory—do not penetrate as many sites as dominant discourses. Therefore, discourses of resistance appear in fewer and more inflexible forms. They therefore attract fewer adherents. In short, distinct advantages have helped pluralism to survive over time.

PLURALISM AFFIRMED

The Yale graduate students whom I have classified as pluralists not only embraced pluralism at Yale but also affirm pluralist ideas today. This affirmation, however, is more complex and nuanced than the original embrace; after all, the last thirty years have produced many challenges to pluralism. Therefore, pluralists have continuously improvised and reflected upon pluralist themes. In this section I first describe a few basic styles of contemporary pluralism and then examine the way pluralists use the discourse to interpret the contemporary political world.

One style of current pluralism is to argue that potentially challenging political events, such as the Vietnam War, the eruption of religious fundamentalism, and the emergence of identity politics, are caused by nonpluralist theories. For example, Nan Keohane, a political theorist who is now president of Duke University, points out that theories that have emerged since pluralism's high tide have strongly influenced recent political events. Because there is no "causal link" (interview, March 18, 1998) between pluralism and these events, pluralism is not compromised. In effect, for Keohane, because pluralism isn't *responsible* for recent challenges, the challenges don't undermine pluralism. As a result, Keohane responds to my question about whether pluralism is still persuasive with a simple, "In large part, sure."

Where Keohane is unusually direct, terse, and narrow in her affirmation of pluralism, other pluralists are voluble and personal. Richard Ayres, who took courses in political science as part of his Yale law school education between 1965 and 1969, provides a good example of this expansive style. He believes that pluralism has stood up "pretty well" over time. He admits, however, that in the last ten or fifteen years the issue of money in politics has challenged his pluralist views. And, like most others of his generation, he was touched by the "revolutionary rhetoric" of the 1960s. Nevertheless, his pluralism remains strong for several practical, personal reasons:

> You know, I've been here in Washington almost twenty-five years and for most of that time engaged in the public policy process, and I feel that the understanding that I got in college and graduate school has been tremendously helpful. . . . None of those things [i.e., the corrupting power of money in politics recently] are fundamentally at odds with the things that I read, and I think they're the things that, if Dahl were writing now, he would be writing about too. [Moreover], I always felt like I understood too much, thanks to those guys, of how the system worked, to be a revolutionary. (Interview, October 14, 1997)

Between Keohane's impersonal terseness and Ayer's highly personal volubility, there exist many intermediate styles of pluralist affirmation. Two forms of this stylistic middle ground deserve discussion. First, some former students assert pluralism strongly but then quickly admit that pluralism has not solved all the political problems the speaker has considered. The speaker then attempts to *supplement* pluralism. Walton Francis, who spent only one year (1963–64) at Yale, exemplifies this style. After leaving Yale, Francis took a job at the Office of Management and Budget, where he made his career. Although he found pluralism persuasive at Yale, today he sees pluralism in the context of his OMB policy recommendations to presidents. He declares that pluralist ideas "accurately describe the political system in which we operate" (cf. Wildavsky, 1964b). However, "What they didn't do, and what I didn't get from that year at Yale, was the tools I subsequently decided I needed" (interview, February 13, 1998). These are the "tools that help me prescribe public policy." To acquire these tools, Francis returned to school at Harvard to study economics. Today he thinks of himself mainly as an economist, not a political scientist. Francis's supplementation of pluralism with economics, however, does allow him to affirm pluralism as an accurate description of the American political system.

Francis does not criticize pluralism for its incompleteness; to the contrary, he believes pluralism performs a necessary legitimating

function in American politics. Pluralism, he says, "tended to legitimize decisions, and in one sense they should be legitimized. . . . These
were decisions reached by the duly anointed political process operating through, you know, polyarchy." Supplementing pluralism with
economics does not weaken pluralism's legitimizing role. However,
owing in part to economics and in part to personal experience, Francis has rejected the liberal politics he associates with pluralism. The
welfare policies to which his expertise contributed have disillusioned
him. As he puts it, "I was a liberal, and I knew that welfare wasn't
working, okay? Thirty years ago. Because I dealt in the stuff, I mean
I knew all about it. And we had programs that failed. And we were
leaving people in the lurch." Francis praises pluralism as a legitimating discourse; yet he objects to pluralism's lack of policy guidance and
its endorsement of liberal politics. He has therefore supplemented
pluralism with economics and with a dose of welfare reform.

A second stylistic middle ground is to *exempt* pluralism from challenges. An example is provided by Stephen Hintz, who was at Yale
from 1967 to 1971, where he mainly studied comparative politics.
Today, he is an associate professor of public affairs and an administrator at the University of Wisconsin–Oshkosh, where he concentrates
on American state and local government. He encountered pluralism
in his American politics courses at Yale and asserts that "the Yale
conceptions of American government in state and local . . . I would
say, hold true today" (interview, March 9, 1998).

Hintz admits that some of what he believed at Yale was mis-
leading. Even at Yale he recognized that urban renewal did little for
blacks in New Haven. He recalls that during his doctoral fieldwork
in Rhodesia, he gave a talk that described American politics as con-
sensual, only to be rapidly contradicted by events at home.

How then does Hintz maintain his pluralism? By practicing exemption. First, he notes that pluralism was "work being written at a
particular moment in time." Second, he observes that when challenges to pluralism emerged, he no longer at Yale. Third, not
only does pluralism still apply to state and local government in
America, but also, "I find the approach to be methodologically sound
from my perspective." In short, pluralism ought to be excused from
its failures and commended for its successes, a cognitive strategy that
exempts pluralism from crippling criticism.

Do different styles of affirming pluralism matter politically? I believe so. For one thing, these styles allow individuals to adapt pluralism both to their discursive proclivities and to their political experiences. Pluralism can thus blend subtly into the larger fabric of a person's political thinking. Moreover, multiple styles of affirmation favor pluralism's continuing legitimating role. Compare pluralism, for example, with a more terminologically rigid discourse—such as Marxism-Leninism in the former Soviet Union. Marxism-Leninism provided its adherents little flexibility or adaptability; only one "party line" could be correct. Therefore, when subjected to prolonged, multiple challenges, Marxist discourse shattered. By contrast, pluralism's flexibility, adaptability, terminological simplicity, and variable cognitive styles permit the discourse to survive and continue—quite unremarkably—to play its legitimating role (see, for a foreign example, Barnard, 1991).

For most students, encountering pluralism at Yale left a powerful impression. Less than one-fifth (13 of 69) of those who embraced pluralism at Yale subsequently rejected it completely. By contrast, of those who were unpersuaded by pluralism while at Yale, 28 percent (9 of 33) actually recovered the discourse later. Only 23 percent (24 of 102) students resisted pluralism at Yale and continue to do so today. By contrast, 55 percent (56 of 102) of the Yale graduate students I interviewed have consistently avowed pluralism throughout most of their careers. As a legitimating discourse, therefore, Yale pluralism has indeed survived.

Some pluralists apply the discourse broadly to contemporary political issues. For example, Charles McCall believes that pluralism effectively explains every form of contemporary identity politics except black politics. McCall explains that black identity is *total* and is therefore inconsistent with pluralism's theory of cross-cutting social cleavages. Race is a *master* identity for blacks; therefore, blacks cannot be just another pluralist interest group (cf. Jacobson, 1998). McCall laments the fact that "social tyranny" forces blacks into this unique condition. He also believes that blacks suffer "continued economic discrimination." Yet McCall does not conclude from the case of blacks that pluralism fails, for pluralism covers a wide range of other identity politics. An example is the Christian Right, which McCall characterizes as simply another pluralist interest group. He notes, in fact, that fundamentalist Christians are divided politically; therefore, Christian political leaders cannot mobilize their followers effectively. In short, fundamentalist Christians suffer from precisely the same coalitional problems pluralists analyzed.

Other pluralists apply the discourse less broadly than McCall. An example is Douglas Rosenthal, who received both a Yale law degree and a Ph.D. in political science in 1970. Rosenthal, now a Washington attorney, was lead counsel in the Pam Am 103 suit against the government of Libya. Rosenthal was strongly influenced by anti-war protests during his years in graduate school; in fact, in 1970, having concluded that Bobby Seale could not get a fair trial in New Haven, he considered emigrating to Europe.

Yet Rosenthal still adheres to pluralism. Why? Because he improvises upon the discourse so dexterously. For example, despite his opposition to the Vietnam War, he reasoned that a majority of Americans supported the war. Therefore, the war, no matter how objectionable, was a legitimate expression of pluralist democracy. True, pluralism states that "*minorities* rule" (Dahl, 1956: 132; emphasis added), but minorities are responsive to nonleaders. Therefore, the war conformed to pluralism. Perhaps American political culture should be blamed for the war, but certainly not democracy or pluralism. Moreover, Rosenthal believes that Kingman Brewster—president of Yale at the time—adroitly managed the Seale affair and transformed Yale's political culture. Therefore, Brewster at least brought Yale closer to pluralist discourse.

Rosenthal is contemptuous of contemporary identity politics, singling out for particular disdain Lani Guinier's theory of race-based political representation. Rosenthal considers Guinier's proposals "an assault on the view of democracy that I did learn and did come to believe in my studies at Yale" (interview, May 1, 1998). In fact, again improvising deftly, Rosenthal turns Guinier's specific argument and identity politics in general to pluralist advantage. He describes himself as "tolerant [of identity politics] in the same sort of pluralistic way one would expect to be." Rosenthal also mobilizes pluralism's arguments against single-issue identity groups; he notes with satisfaction that Guinier's proposals have not gotten far. Nevertheless, he admits that, "I am . . . concerned, and I think the Yale approach was concerned, about one-issue constituencies."

Rosenthal improvises upon pluralism with great dexterity. He calls upon pluralism's democratic elements, its premise of elite tolerance, its predictions of single-issue interest group failure, and, above all, its normative aspects. At the same time, he believes that pluralism must respond to its contemporary opponents. He agrees that conservative, market-based critiques of government programs have merit, just as did anti-war protests at Yale. Nevertheless, "I still believe in government, in the role of government." And he improvises a pluralist response to free-market advocates; he claims that pluralism's receptivity to multiple values opened the way for privatization alternatives in the United States. Thus, the turn to the market—like Yale's response to the Bobby Seale case—also vindicates pluralism.

Of course, the main arena where academics have improvised pluralist discourse is the classroom. A case in point is William Flanigan, who as a graduate student assisted Dahl's fieldwork for *Who Governs?* Flanigan believes that pluralism "has really held up under lots of different kinds of criticism with no fundamental change, I think" (interview, February 13, 1998). Flanigan has rebuffed many uninformed criticisms of pluralism in his classes at the University of Minnesota. Flanigan regrets that the many pluralist students at Yale have produced no good textbooks that could clarify pluralism for undergraduates. (Flanigan overlooks Prentice-Hall's Foundations of Modern Political Science series of short paperback texts written in the 1960s by, among others, Polsby, Danelski, Kaufman, Lane, Fesler, Greenstein, Lindblom, Deutsch, and Dahl. These texts went through several editions.) Flanigan believes that had the department at Yale produced an excellent pluralist text, "It would have made a hell of a difference." Better textbooks would have highlighted pluralism's reform premise and thus met the criticism that pluralism was conservative. Ironically, Flanigan's conviction that critics have misunderstood pluralism actually permits him to expound the discourse more easily. After all, it falls to him to defend the discourse. Certainly his own excellent text on American elections fits pluralist theory neatly (Flanigan and Zingale, 1998).

As we can see, improvisational applications of pluralism to contemporary politics include several distinct rhetorical devices, including breadth, exemption, supplementation, and flexibility. The most common and powerful rhetorical form of affirming pluralism, however, is *segmentation*, by which I refer to the division of pluralism into several unequally effective parts. According to the segmentation argument, when examined carefully, enough of pluralism *does* apply effectively to contemporary events. On this narrowed ground pluralism gains affirmation.

Because segmentation takes many forms, to review the device exhaustively is impossible. However, presenting some examples is necessary in order to reveal the pluralist search for the "one best idea" that maintains continuity between the pluralism they learned at Yale and the pluralism they now affirm.

The reflections of Arthur Goldberg are especially illuminating in this regard. Goldberg, like Flanigan, was a research assistant on Dahl's *Who Governs?* study. He then taught for many years at the University of Rochester (where he combined rational choice theory with pluralism). He now operates a consulting business in Washington. Although Goldberg describes himself as sympathetic to pluralism at Yale, he sensed pluralism's limitations. For instance, he recounts that during the fieldwork for *Who Governs?* researchers conducted many in-depth interviews with ordinary New Haven citizens. One interview continues to stick in his mind. After trying unsuccessfully to get an elderly black man to talk about politics in New Haven, the frustrated interviewer—a light-skinned black—protested that the elderly man was not being responsive. The man shot back that his grandfather had been a slave, so no white interviewer should reproach him. The interviewer then identified himself as black. Immediately the man opened up, revealing a nuanced understanding of New Haven politics. Goldberg admits that, "Right there was this little hint that there was this vast untapped vein" of experience that *Who Governs?* missed.

Yet Goldberg accepted pluralism at Yale and affirms the discourse today. To do so, he searches for the "one best idea" in pluralism, in his case coalition building and political compromise. As he sees it, anti–Vietnam War protests, the civil rights movement, and the McGovern and Goldwater candidacies all vindicate pluralism's arguments about the necessity for coalition formation and compromise. These events "gave me an opportunity to see coalitions forming and coming apart, and multiple power centers, and what happens when people move out to the extremes, the McGovern case . . . a great remove from the median voter, and they sank themselves basically" (interview, February 25, 1998). In short, according to Goldberg, these movements floundered because they violated pluralism (see Goldberg and Wright, 1985: 704–18).

A narrower segmentation of pluralism emerges from the observations of Gary Jacobson. Jacobson was at Yale in the late 1960s and is today a leading student of congressional elections and fund-raising. His research (e.g., Jacobson, 1985–86: 603–25) has applied rational choice theory to these subjects in ways consistent with pluralism. He has been a Fellow of the American Academy of Arts and Sciences since 1991. By any standard, Jacobson is a jewel in the crown of Yale political science.

Jacobson admits that even a "starry-eyed pluralist" would have to confront persistent problems of race and poverty. These issues continue to challenge the pluralist argument that every group in America can have its preferences taken seriously in the political process. Moreover, he admits he was naive in believing that the pluralist incorporation of blacks would take place quickly. In short, Jacobson would seem to have ample reason to discard pluralism.

Yet he does not do so. Instead, as he puts it, "I have never really matched those two things [pluralism and continuing racial conflict] up." Why? "Because I am not sure that you could come up with something out of the Yale School which would tell you one way or the other how fast to expect this kind of change to take place." Further, "I was taught in the behavioral world that mass attitudes are not easy to change . . . from that perspective, one could anticipate that they would be hard to change" (interview, March 10, 1998). Thus, Jacobson segments pluralism. By singling out pluralism's behavioral component, he rationalizes the slowness of change in racial attitude. Also, he cites pluralism's own vagueness about the pace of change in American racial politics. This last argument is a particularly good example of segmentation. After all, Jacobson could as reasonably have chosen to *attack* pluralism for not exploring the rate of change and, therefore, for blurring the distinction between political reform and political stagnation. But he chooses not to do so; instead, pluralism's absence of specificity becomes a theoretical virtue.

A last improvisational defense of pluralism is *foundationalism*—that is, the assertion that pluralism provides a strong foundation for understanding American politics. An anonymous ex-student's struggle to reconcile the religious Right with her continuing support for pluralism provides a good case in point. This ex-student, who was at Yale from 1962 to 1968, believes that the power achieved by the contemporary religious Right in Iowa is inconsistent with the pluralism she learned at Yale. At the same time, the Christian Right illustrates how open the American political system is; this aspect of the Christian Right *is* consistent with pluralism. According to her, with the Christian Right, "You take the Yale model to its extreme, and not realizing that the model itself says you shouldn't be doing that" (interview, March 31, 1998). She argues that pluralism at Yale assumed a normal distribution of political attitudes; the Christian Right is simply at one extreme end of this normal distribution. She implies that extreme positions eventually fail; after all, pluralism warns against extremism. Thus, the Christian Right ought not to—and ultimately won't—succeed. The foundations of pluralism remain strong.

Such rhetorical strategies as breadth, exemption, foundationalism, supplementation, and segmentation do not do full justice to the many ways pluralists improvise the discourse today. Two brief illustrations support this point. Arnold Kanter, a student of international relations who encountered pluralism at Yale between 1966 and 1969, admits that contemporary identity politics demonstrates pluralism's limitations. Nevertheless, he continues to value pluralism for its realism and methodological rigor. Moreover, his long experience in the Washington bureaucracy is full of the bargaining and coalition building he learned about at Yale. Thus, for Kanter, the empirical assertions of pluralism survive quite well (interview, March 24, 1998).

By contrast, Sarah McCally Morehouse—one of only three women to come to Yale in 1955—adheres to pluralism more for normative than empirical reasons. Although Morehouse's recent book on state governors (1998) fits easily into a pluralist framework, she worries that the increasingly dominant role of money in politics and the decline of political parties are harming pluralism. Indeed, Morehouse has attacked this phenomenon in print (Jewell and Morehouse, 1996: 338–62). Nevertheless, she holds fast to pluralism as an ideal. As she puts it, "I think now that we can't assume that pluralism will work unless we keep a careful eye on it. . . . I don't think it's necessarily a natural order. I think you have to work at it" (interview, March 12, 1998). Both Kanter and Morehouse remain pluralists; yet Kanter's pluralism is empirical, while Morehouse's is normative.

To summarize: though diminished in power, pluralism retains its centrality for most of those who embraced it at Yale. Pluralism thus continues to function as a legitimating discourse. The discourse survives because it lends itself to multiple interpretations and to both broad and narrow readings, because it contains both normative and empirical arguments, and because it can be extended, segmented, supplemented, and grounded. As pluralists continually use the discourse to scrutinize the contemporary political world, they keep pluralism alive—if largely unremarked—as a stabilizing force in the American political system.

PLURALISM INCORPORATED

My principal contention, to repeat, is that pluralism is not only a theory but also a combination of literary themes and mundane improvisations. The power of a political discourse depends on complementarity between themes and variations, texts and practices. When complementarity declines, the discourse suffers. I attempted to demonstrate this argument in my discussion of Yale faculty. But what of graduate students? In particular, did pluralist graduate students improvise upon pluralist themes while at Yale? Put differently, did pluralist students incorporate pluralism? As the term *incorporation* denotes, there is a bodily component to any political discourse. As we will see, pluralists did complement intellectual themes with embodied improvisations. For most, the pluralist "word" did indeed become flesh.

Pluralist students improvised upon pluralist texts in at least six ways. First, as socialization research would lead us to predict (Sears, 1990), many pluralists construe their pre-Yale family, political, and educational experiences in pluralistic ways. Second, many pluralists experienced Yale graduate school positively; moreover, the positive experiences they mention are, for the most part, improvisations upon pluralism. Third, pluralists describe more favorable relationships with fellow graduate students than do nonpluralists. Fourth, pluralists enjoyed their classes more than did nonpluralists. Fifth, most pluralists perceive their political activities at Yale as consistent with pluralism. Sixth and finally, many pluralists had begun to internalize pluralist discourse before coming to Yale. Not surprisingly, these students found it easy to improvise upon pluralism at Yale.

However, a minority of pluralist students did not improvise upon pluralism at Yale. Some, for example, complained that faculty did not practice pluralism in teacher-student relations. Others simply disliked Yale itself. Still others were unhappy in classes or were disappointed by particular instructors. Many female students felt that the entirely male faculty did not treat them fairly. And almost all pluralist students have at least a few negative as well as many positive things to say about their experience at Yale. Importantly, however, pluralist student improvisations complemented pluralist themes more than did the improvisations of students who did not adopt pluralism.

For some pluralists, parental political beliefs paved the way. Some parents were political activists who demonstrated to their children that working within the political system bore fruit. In a sense, pluralism helped these students to understand how their parents had succeeded politically. Thus, pluralism not only supported the parents' political activity but also, indirectly, connected parents to children. No wonder these students gravitated to pluralism. In other cases, parental political influence was more diffuse, manifesting itself not in concrete political actions but in ways of life that incorporated the pluralist understanding of American politics.

For other students, ethnic identity supported pluralism. There is, after all, a thematic affinity between ethnic politics and pluralism. *Who Governs?*, for example, narrates the story of how politically adroit Italians and Irish achieved power in New Haven, a pattern Fox describes for urban white ethnics nationally (1986: 122–23). In addition, as previously mentioned, the relatively many Jews among Yale graduate students in the late 1950s and 1960s were themselves demonstrations of pluralism in academia. Yale—previously an elite WASP institution—had finally responded to the justified, meritorious demand of non-WASPSs for entrance to prestigious academic institutions. Not surprisingly, a number of Jewish graduate students commented positively on the ethnic aspect of their Yale experience.

An example is Nelson Polsby's recollections of himself and Fred Greenstein—both Jewish students—in a first-semester seminar with James Fesler during the mid-1950s. Polsby notes that his graduate class was really the first at Yale to contain a significant Jewish presence. Polsby recalls Fesler's presenting one of his own papers to the six graduate students. Starting with Fred Greenstein, the two Jewish students savaged the paper. Polsby remembers, "I picked up what I thought was a logical gap or fallacy in it and sat there thinking as follows. 'Are the norms such that if you bring this up you'll be sent to hell? Is Fesler the sort of person who would be threatened by such a comment?'" (interview, July 7, 1998). Polsby breathed a "sigh of relief" when Fesler responded in a gentlemanly way to the criticism.

Wildavsky seconds Polsby's commendation of Fesler. According to Wildavsky, Fesler "possessed an unerring sense of the critical problem. Whatever insight, clarity of mind, and a sense of proportion could do for his students, he did" (1989: 148–49). In addition, Wildavsky describes his seminar with Lindblom as "the best seminar I have known" (149). He also writes that, "Those who did not come from immigrant families cannot imagine the importance of being socialized into a profession," and praises Yale for this experience. Finally, he states that Yale faculty, including Frederich Barghoorn, Dahl, Fesler, Kaufman, Lane, and Alan Sindler, taught him "how political scientists ought to comport themselves."

Unlike Wildavsky, Polsby observes that he was not a "typical" Jew. He grew up in "Yankee land"—eastern Connecticut—and in majority Gentile environments. Also, he stresses that his parents were well-to-do and did not live in a Jewish ghetto. Therefore, he implies, his upper-middle-class background eased his career at Yale. This observation is consistent with pluralism, which sponsors *gradual*, incremental reform, not wholesale change. Perhaps it is not surprising, therefore, that Polsby spontaneously remarks on his support for incrementalism: "I want to clear up one thing. . . . Incrementalism. I've been an incrementalist since birth. . . . When people would say, 'What is your grand plan?' I would . . . say I can tell you what I want to do next. That's all I could say. So that when, in effect, Lindblom sprang incrementalism on us and put it into some kind of an intellectual context, I had already decided that that was the way to go."

For some pluralists it was *anomalies* of ethnicity that dovetailed nicely with pluralism. James Toscano, for example, grew up in an East Coast, Italian, Republican family, where, as he puts it, "Certain of the predictors didn't work. I mean Italian New York being Republicans, and, you know, the things that didn't make sense from a . . . socialist, Marxist point of view" (interview, May 4, 1998). Toscano's ethnic history presented him with a puzzle. "Now what would make an immigrant family of two generations before that into Taft Republicans? . . . The other point here is the pluralism, I think." For Toscano, pluralism solves the puzzle of Italian Republicanism. Pluralism explains how, thanks to the access the American political system offered ethnic minorities, ethnic identity could mutate from radical to conservative.

Toscano and Polsby found that pluralism confirmed their personal experience of ethnicity. To other students, however, pluralism offered an *escape* from ethnicity and, perhaps, from family conflicts. A particularly good illustration of this pattern is Oliver Woshinsky, now at the University of Maine. Although Woshinsky studied at Yale in the late 1960s, he proclaims himself very much a pluralist—"an instant convert"—relatively untouched by the radical challenges to pluralism at the time. His pluralism comes out in a 1972 article, where he treats political participation as a response to personal motives, rather than political ideologies (Payne and Woshinsky, 1972: 518–46). Woshinsky traces his attraction to pluralism all the way back to his early life:

> I grew up in a family that was . . . what I always thought of as pretty marginal, and I think I've always sort of wanted to be a center part of the culture and really wasn't. . . . My father was a Russian immigrant from Odessa. He was basically a fellow traveler. In the forties he was never a Communist, but he was clearly further left than you normally get in the forties. And we grew up in Vermont, of all places . . . even more crazy. I always wanted to move more centrist than the family was. (Interview, May 27, 1998)

Woshinsky states that pluralism suited his aspirations for change. In fact, pluralism provided "a justification of the broader culture" he yearned to enter. In short, pluralism legitimated both the American political regime and Woshinsky's personal aspirations.

Although youthful influence propelled some students toward pluralism, early adult experience persuaded others. Some pluralists discovered either in political activity or in jobs that pluralism seemed to work. Others liked pluralism because it represented *professionalization;* for personal reasons, these students wanted political science to become a profession, rather than a traditional academic discipline.

The range of early adult improvisations that prepared the way for pluralism is broad. For example, a female ex-student, who was at Yale between 1963 and 1968 but never received her doctorate, is actually critical of Yale. She faults the department for its "otherworldly" quality and its inability to bridge the gap between academic theory and practical politics. Nevertheless, her political experience before coming to Yale supported pluralist theory. She describes herself as having been politically active from the age of ten. Before attending Yale, she had worked in political campaigns and had spent two summers on Capitol Hill. She believes that pluralism and incrementalism effectively captured the Capitol Hill politics of those years, when there were "shifting majorities, expedience, deal-making system with very little ideology" (interview, April 4, 1998). Although Yale itself disdained practical politics, pluralism won her adherence.

A more intense early adult improvisation of pluralism was that of Russell Murphy. Murphy's *Political Entrepreneurs and Urban Poverty* (1971) was part of pluralism's second generation at Yale. Interestingly, Murphy had not studied political science before coming to Yale. In fact, he had prepared for the priesthood at Boston College but changed his vocation. He then served in the U.S. Navy and found this experience supported pluralism. Contrary to his expectations, the Navy proved to be not a hierarchical command system but a congeries of multiple, competing groups, each with some power. He served in naval security as a cryptographer, where he decoded intelligence reports. He recounts decoding a conversation with the chief of naval operations about what candidate the navy should back to become the future chair of the Joint Chiefs of Staff. This conversation convinced Murphy that the president had little autonomous military power. Indeed, the president did not even have control over his own chief military officer. Instead, in true pluralist fashion, competing interest groups influenced the appointment. As Murphy puts it, "I had seen a lot of intelligence stuff, which led me to believe the world was highly decentralized. As Herb Kaufman said to me one time . . . I said, 'That's a great title, *Who Governs?*,' and he said, 'No, it isn't.' He said the question is, 'Does anybody govern?'" (interview, November 30, 1997).

Another pre-Yale influence that promoted pluralism was the appeal of professionalism. Some students valued the department's emphasis on a professional social science, rather than on policy advocacy or speculative theory. Of course, the American model of "fact-based" professionalized public policy goes back to the late nineteenth century, specifically to Richard Ely's institutional economics (Bledstein, 1976: 328–29). Many early-twentieth-century reformers wished professional social science to replace the outworn practice of enthusiastic but unreliable policy advocacy (see Bender, 1993). The Yale department's distinction from many other political science departments of the late 1950s lay partly in its embrace of professional social science as opposed to direct policy advocacy. But there was no inherent opposition between the two approaches. Indeed, precisely because it did not enter directly into the political fray, a professional social science might ultimately achieve truly lasting reform. It might provide political reformers with truly "objective," "scientific" knowledge to support their reform efforts.

As we saw in the case of Aaron Wildavsky, the professional social science model appealed to some students at Yale. Another example is Harvey Starr. Starr distinguishes between Yale, which pursued "social science research," and the rest of the Ivy League, which preferred a "policymaker mode." Professional social science education at Yale appealed to Starr because it allowed him to separate his *preferences* about American politics from his *study* of American politics. Although the late 1960s altered his thinking about American politics, it did not shake his belief in Yale social science (interview, June 9, 1998). As Starr explains, the professional education he received at Yale "fit my temperament. . . . It fit with my predisposition to step back and analyze stuff. . . . You know, in many ways, I'm small 'c' conservative, I've never been impulsive. I've always been cautious." Perhaps it isn't surprising that, in a letter to Bruce Russett in 1971, Starr wrote: "After 4 years I've come to feel quite close to Mother Yale—something that doesn't register until you leave" (Starr to Russett, September 28, 1971, YUDPS).

For many students, the most crucial arena of pluralist improvisation was the classroom. After all, whatever their differences, all students shared classroom experience; therefore, the classroom offered a kind of laboratory for pluralist improvisations. One such improvisation concerns the sheer intellectual quality of classes. Stimulating classes obviously encourage students to accept the ideas their instructors propound, including, in this case, pluralism. More subtly, classes indirectly reflect upon the regime a legitimating discourse promotes. Thus, classes that are rewarding indirectly convey the image of an intellectually satisfying, supportive political regime. By contrast, poor classes discourage adherence to the political regime a legitimating discourse promotes.

Classes also were microcosms for pluralism's specific premises. For example, did students feel they could challenge their instructors?

128

If so, the classroom became an improvisation of a pluralistic, egalitarian, tolerant regime, as opposed to a monolithic, hierarchical, dogmatic system of elite-controlled "truth" (Bourdieu and Passeron, 1990). Did teachers provide models of scholarly dedication that reproduced the devotion to gradual improvement characteristic of the pluralist politician? Did teachers respect evidence and verifiable knowledge, a stance that turns classroom discourse into the very model of pluralist policy debate? Or, by contrast, were teachers rash generalizers, passionate ideologues, or uncontrolled speculators, who tried above all to impose their own systems of truth on students? That is, in Lindblom's phrase, did instructors approach intellectual problems "synoptically" or incrementally? Were they prophets or pluralists?

Lastly, what about instructors as human beings? Did they inspire respect and confidence in their students? Did they demonstrate—as pluralism stipulates—that the right leader at the right time could make a crucial difference? Personal charm is a significant attribute of pluralist political leadership; consider, for example, Richard C. Lee, whom William Miller describes as "an interesting fellow . . . nobody is bored by city government as he carries it out," or Franklin Roosevelt (1966: 198). How, if at all, did the personal appeal of faculty in the classroom operate at Yale?

Most pluralist students remember their classes fondly. In fact, pluralist students' overall estimation resembles pluralism itself: just as pluralism sees the American political system as good but not great, so do pluralist students characterize their classes as good but not great. A typical recollection is that of a prominent Canadian political scientist who studied at Yale from 1964 to 1968, then returned to Canada to teach. Now widely respected as a leading scholar of Canadian political institutions and constitutional issues, this scholar states that he was "pleased" with his classes. "I would say that I enjoyed that experience." This measured response improvises pluralism's own moderation. As we will see in chapter 5, it differs sharply from the response of many nonpluralist students, who disliked their classes at Yale.

Many pluralist students comment on specific improvisations of pluralism in the classroom. Take, for example, the premise of elite tolerance. Arthur Goldberg recalls his first seminar with Robert Dahl: "He would challenge everything you said, practically. But he would do it as though you were a colleague . . . and in very short order, people treat you as a colleague, [and] you try to behave like a colleague." Goldberg implies that Dahl's respectful disagreement narrowed the gap between teacher and student, promoting the free flow of ideas prized by pluralists.

Other pluralist students remarked on the comparatively democratic atmosphere of classes. Constance Citro, who attended Yale in the mid-1960s and became senior study director for the Committee on National Statistics at the National Academy of Sciences, initially complains that Yale faculty did not treat women students equally to men. She reports a view "widely shared among the women students that the general view of the faculty was that the women weren't really serious, you know" (interview, February 5, 1998). Nevertheless, in "their classroom demeanor, there wasn't too much of, well, I am the top person here, and you are just the peon. There was very little of that." So, at least within the classroom, gender discrimination gave way to teaching that improvised pluralist themes.

Pluralist students also say that their teachers and their fellow students generally proceeded with caution, care, and respect for evidence, a style of thinking consistent with pluralist reform, rather than ideological fervor. Not all pluralist students admired this style, however; in fact, some found it self-serving. For example, Sara Stewart, who studied at Yale in the late 1960s, observes ruefully:

> I remember another thing that we used to sneer at somewhat and laugh at about was the Yale approach of always covering yourself ahead of time. . . . You never commit and say, "Well now, I really think that this is so"; you'd say, "One could say that blah, blah, blah, blah." And I remember one student . . . made some comment like that, and somebody attacked him, and he says: "Wait a minute, I didn't say I said that. I said one *could* say that." I thought, "That's the Yale way carried to extremes." (Interview, April 27, 1998)

Most pluralist students also found at least some of their instructors inspiring as personalities. For example, Joel Aberbach, who ascribes his influential book *Race in the City* (Aberbach and Walker, 1973: 5) to his Yale experience, comments that although Dahl and Lane were "brilliant" thinkers, more impressive was their "immense dedication to what they were doing and willingness to write and rewrite and re-rewrite, think and rethink, and re-rethink, until their ideas were crystal clear" (interview, September 16, 1997). Dedication to exacting scholarship improvises upon the political vocation of the professional pluralist leader.

Descriptions of individual instructors also support the argument that pluralist students respected faculty at Yale. With two principal exceptions, faculty presented models of openness to pluralist students. Although some faculty members evoked mixed feelings among pluralist students, this dissatisfaction pales in comparison to majority rejection among students who *resisted* pluralism. Quick thumbnail sketches of individual scholars convey the measured approval pluralist students extend toward faculty.

The better-known Yale scholars displayed quite different teaching styles. Students comment favorably, for example, on Robert Dahl's "gravitas." Dahl combined scrupulous politeness to students with a sharply critical sense. He rarely lectured, preferring dialogue; in fact, undergraduates at Yale regarded Dahl as a poor lecturer. Indeed, according to one anonymous informant, Dahl was among the few Yale professors whom undergraduate students did not applaud at the end of a semester.

However, Dahl's reputation as a graduate teacher was mixed. When the topic interested him, he could run an extremely coherent, incisive, Socratic seminar. However, he sometimes seemed disinterested in the material or the class; then students recall him as passive and even lazy. For example, Patrick Morgan recalls a friend stating a common opinion of Dahl among students: "He used to complain about Dahl running his seminars . . . that's what they used to say. I would say, 'Gee, maybe I ought to take one with Dahl,' but they would say 'Don't bother. Just read this stuff; you're not going to get much by sitting in his class.'"

No doubt one reason for the mixed verdict on Dahl was his "detachment," to use Fred Greenstein's term. Even when deeply engaged intellectually, Dahl seemed imperturbable and self-controlled. His distant demeanor perhaps embodied his philosophy of social science, especially his absolute dedication to neutrality in the classroom. For example, Maureen Covell, a Canadian scholar whose 1986 article on Belgium is pluralist in its reformism and incrementalism (1986), recalls one seminar in which Dahl explicitly refused to discuss the ongoing student protests. "He felt that as a neutral political scientist he ought not get involved" (interview, February 3, 1998). (Interestingly, according to Covell, Dahl himself actually took part in one protest march.)

Two faculty members who exceeded Dahl in presenting a low-key image were Robert Lane and Herbert Kaufman. Some students attributed Lane's cryptic teaching style to the psychoanalytic skills he had learned from Yale psychologist John Dollard. However, once they adjusted to his laconic, sometimes elliptical, wry, and subtle style, many students enjoyed his classes. By contrast to the urbane Lane, Kaufman presented himself as a *naif*. As Joel Aberbach describes Kaufman admiringly, "You know, Herb had this 'Aw, shucks' kind of approach, this 'Gee, I don't understand what's going on here. What do you guys think?' And yet . . . he had a wonderful ability to guide people towards deeper thinking about whatever the subject happened to be." Despite some criticisms, pluralist students speak well of all three men; clearly their classroom conduct improvised upon diverse pluralist themes.

In contrast to Dahl, Lane, and Kaufman, Charles Lindblom and Karl Deutsch were extremely forceful classroom characters. Lindblom was caustic and drove some students to distress. One student claims that Lindblom chose a victim in each class and then goaded the unfortunate student mercilessly. Nor did Lindblom always tolerate opposing points of view. John Witte, who entered Yale in 1971, provides a vivid description of Lindblom's pedagogical style. According to Witte:

> His seminar was extraordinarily lazily run. . . . Basically read four or five books, and you had a book a week, and he would let the class talk first. Then he would sort of give his interpretation, and that was it. And there was a little bit of give and take, but not too much. But he loved to argue, and he didn't like it if you didn't argue with him. So he had that kind of personality. (Interview, July 7, 1997)

In the classroom, Lindblom was contrary. Witte recounts that once, when the students responded enthusiastically to Galbraith's *The New Industrial State,* Lindblom attacked the book. But in the next class, when the students attacked Miliband's neo-Marxist *The State in Capitalist Society,* Lindblom defended the book. Judging by Witte's account, Lindblom's personal inclination was toward contestation and debate, both of which—in moderation—are consistent with pluralist theory.

In contrast to Lindblom, Deutsch indulged in long, rambling, dazzling speculations on whatever topic struck his fancy. He astonished many students with his capacity to deploy and synthesize diverse ideas. However, the substance of his arguments was often less compelling than his enthusiasm and style. Deutsch's pedagogical disorganization was legendary. Students recall that classes often ended with Deutsch in full rhetorical flight, continuing to theorize as he slowly moved toward the outside world. Deutsch blended European speculative philosophy with American social science (some said "scientism"), a style that allowed little systematic dialogue with students.

For the most part, these faculty members—and most others—taught in a pluralistic fashion. With the exception of Deutsch and, to a lesser degree, Lindblom, none dominated the classroom in an authoritarian fashion. Most encouraged different points of view and cultivated a cautious, skeptical, but receptive, intellectual style. Even Deutsch's flights of fancy were meant to be inclusive. Deutsch presented himself as a generous thinker inviting students to an intellectual feast. On balance, these were good but not great teachers; like the pluralist system, they had flaws; but by and large—at least to the pluralist students—their pedagogy improvised pluralism well.

Gabriel Almond and Harold Lasswell were the two major exceptions to this generally pluralist style of teaching. Many pluralist students complained that Almond was defensive, insecure, and unresponsive to student questions. Some also thought him arrogant. For example, an anonymous ex-student who spent two years at Yale before moving to Washington as a civil servant, recalls Almond critically. As Almond's teaching assistant, he had written a seminar paper for Almond that drew on Lindblom's work. "And I worked my tail off on that thing and cranked out what I thought was a pretty interesting framework, and Almond sort of thought that I just dashed it off, which p.o.'d me, because it wasn't the case at all. . . . And he trivialized Lindblom" (interview, March 16, 1998). Almond's departure from Yale clearly removed a nonpluralist teacher from the department.

A second, less clear-cut exception was Harold Lasswell. By the time Lasswell arrived at Yale, he had jettisoned his earlier, pessimistic, elitist analysis of politics. As Seidelman and Harpham put it, "World War II and its aftermath sparked Lasswell to reinterpret his past works in the light of a new 'value consciousness' that replaced 'therapy' with a 'developing science of democracy'" (1985: 141). Lasswell expounded this new democratic science to his classes. Yet the classes themselves did not improvise the democratic science he preached. Nor were they pluralistic. Laurel Files states flatly that, "[Lasswell] was one of the worst teachers in the classroom. . . . People used to sit and count how many times he said 'Oh,' or whether he said something, or whether he was going to finish the sentence he started." While Files's observation suggests that Lasswell was diffuse, Douglas Rosenthal describes him as "really kind of rigid and ossified in his thinking by the time I was there." In fact, sometimes Lasswell simply read drafts of manuscripts on which he was working. The tedium of this procedure was not relieved by the arcane jargon Lasswell had developed. Moreover, he left little time for student discussion. In short, in the classroom Lasswell was no pluralist pedagogue.

Yet Lasswell did profoundly influence some students, for whom he remains a seminal figure, almost an icon. William Ascher and Garry Brewer were two such persons; they formed with Lasswell an extracurricular seminar in political development, which examined, among other things, the process of decision making ("Development Decision Seminar," 1969, box 6, folder 14, YUDPS). According to John Fitch, an admiring Lasswell student, "Yale gave us money to go have dinner with Harold Lasswell about once a month." To Ascher, Brewer, Ron Bruner, Douglas Durasoff, Fitch, and a few others, Lasswell's ideas were a revelation. In class Lasswell was Buddha-like, spinning delicate spider webs of abstractions that trapped many students; outside of class, however, he was—for some—a great force.

Nor was Lasswell's influence confined to the academic. Indeed, it was Lasswell's blessing that inspired Brewer to become a founding father of Vietnam Veterans against the War. Brewer states: "If you asked [Lasswell] straightaway, he would tell you. And he thought the [Vietnam] War was a dreadful thing" (interview, January 20, 1998). Thus, from a pluralist standpoint, Lasswell as teacher and mentor was a paradox.

To summarize: for pluralist students, the classroom was generally a site of pluralist improvisation. With a few exceptions, instructors generally performed pluralist themes in their teaching. However, pluralist students do occasionally point out the failure of pluralist premises in the classroom. As one anonymous scholar puts it, "There wasn't a lot of openness to the critique [of pluralism]. . . . When I was there [in the late 1960s], I think the department was still pretty defensive of the approach" (interview, May 8, 1998). Thus, pluralism—though dominant—was neither complete nor consistent in the Yale classroom.

Pluralist students are rather more divided about their experience with faculty outside the classroom. Some remember the faculty as sociable and accessible, traits that fit pluralism; others, however, recall the faculty as reserved and capricious. Moreover, in questions of departmental authority, pluralism in student-teacher relations clearly reached its limits. Although the department did react flexibly in the late 1960s to student demands, modifying its examination and recruitment policies, it did not cede any decision-making authority to students. Harvey Starr remembers vividly that in 1967,

> Graduate students were attempting . . . to get more graduate student input to recruitment and searches and other things like that. I remember a big meeting in HGS, and graduate students were talking and talking, and there were faculty there, including Dahl. . . . Everyone was throwing back his democratic theory at him, and he said, "Yeah, that's fine, but these aren't democracies." Which I thought was cute because, you know, he had written all these things about how people should run whole countries, but this wasn't how he was going to run his department.

Thus, faculty often improvised variations on pluralism in the classroom and in social relations with students. But students had no place within their governing coalition.

GENDER AS FAULT LINE

One structural cleavage that divides pluralist students is gender. A majority of women pluralists felt mistreated at Yale. Yet despite perceiving discrimination—surely an anti-pluralist improvisation— women were no less likely than men to incorporate pluralism. Let us explore this complex topic further.

Female pluralist graduate students criticized faculty on many grounds, such as faculty disinterest in recruiting more female graduate students, unequal faculty mentoring and attention, little assistance in seeking jobs, outright exclusion from important departmental benefits, sexism in pluralist writings, discriminatory grading, derogatory remarks, and, at the extreme, outright sexual misconduct. To be sure, not every woman reported grievances, and very few experienced most of these complaints. Nevertheless, the majority of pluralist women resented some aspects of their treatment.

Some women charge that faculty did not try to recruit women into the graduate program. In 1964, when she arrived at Yale, Maureen Covell observed something that other women also mentioned— namely, that the three women in her class held Woodrow Wilson fellowships, not Yale fellowships. The Wilson fellowship paid Yale a sum of money for each of its student recipients. Yale would only spend its own money on women graduate students after they had proven themselves in their first year. As Covell describes the Woodrow Wilson pointedly, "We referred to it as our dowry."

Some women also complained about discriminatory faculty remarks. For example, when Sarah Morehouse came to Yale in 1955, she remembers having a strange discussion with her graduate adviser. According to Morehouse, who was then living in Fairfield, Connecticut: "He said he envisioned a lot of housewives from Fairfield coming at him with mops and brooms. And it almost seemed to me that this was an odd thing for him to say . . . that made me think he's thinking of me in a very different way from the way I think of myself as a graduate student. And I thought, 'I don't think this is a very professional thing for him to say to me.' "

As late as 1965 some faculty derogated women in classes. An anonymous informant recalls, "One person in particular who would use examples in class of, you know, someone who is utterly uninformed about politics would be the housewife in Dayton. . . . And, um, computers are like women, fast, dumb, and fickle. You know, that sort of thing" (interview, May 8, 1998).

Other women complained about the absence of supportive supervision by faculty. For example, according to Elinor Bowen, "Nobody on the faculty there ever mentored me. Now maybe that would have happened had I stayed longer, because remember I changed schools. But I have a suspicion . . . that the women didn't get mentored." Bowen believes that faculty formed helpful relationships with men rather than with women.

Bowen also asserts that she was the victim of discrimination. The department denied her request for funds to complete her dissertation at Yale. The justification offered was that she had married and was no longer residing in New Haven; however, she claims that married men who were not in New Haven did receive support. She claims to have been "written off altogether" by two directors of graduate studies—David Barber and Herbert Kaufman.

Some women students believe they received less help than men in the search for academic jobs. According to Constance Citro, "In general, there was no follow-up. My getting finished with my thesis and my finding a position and a career essentially were my own doing." Citro claims that other women told essentially the same story, a contention my interviews support.

One anonymous woman student charges that faculty discrimination extended to grading. She states, "I knew I had done a super good job in this one course. . . . And I went into the professor and, in effect, was told that I had gotten a High Pass, and that the professor would raise it to a High Pass Plus, but that never would he give a woman an Honors, because he just didn't want to encourage that kind of thing in the discipline."

Finally, several students report inappropriate behavior by two faculty members, first in the early 1960s and again in the late 1960s. In both cases unwanted and uninvited sexual overtures allegedly took place. Moreover, many women report a common belief among women that sexual impropriety was widespread in faculty-female student relationships. However, only a minority of women actually report personal experiences of this sort; again only two faculty members are named. Nevertheless, the sense of anger and helplessness—even at a thirty-year remove—is palpable.

Needless to say, these recollections are at odds with pluralism's emphasis on the representation and incorporation of minorities. Yet, interestingly, these anti-pluralist perceptions are unrelated to women's reaction to pluralist theory. By contrast, as we will see, every other anti-pluralist perception distinguishes between pluralist and nonpluralist graduate students. Why did aggrieved women graduate students not connect their anti-pluralist treatment to their assessment of pluralist theory?

Several factors may explain this fact. First, the majority of pluralist women felt they were treated equally to men in classes. The discrimination they experienced, therefore, did not encompass the most sensitive arena of competition between the sexes. Moreover, with but one exception, women did not report discrimination in grades. These factors may have deterred women from rejecting pluralism.

Moreover, most women received support from male graduate students. Almost all commented that male students treated them as colleagues engaged in a joint intellectual enterprise. Some state that their male peers were conscious of—and irritated by—gender discrimination by faculty. In typical pluralist fashion, female and male graduate students forged bonds that somewhat cushioned women from faculty abuses. These coalitions therefore improvised pluralism against anti-pluralist improvisations by faculty.

Finally, women may not have articulated their anger in *ideological* terms. Feminism's ideological articulation of gender discrimination did not really penetrate until the 1970s. Moreover, the anti-war movement—not gender discrimination—took pride of place in the late 1960s. Prior to the 1960s, women graduate students may have considered their treatment at Yale "normal"—that is, consistent with women's usual subordinate position in society. Nor did women perceive gender discrimination in pluralist theory itself, a position some would later disclaim. For example, Nan Keohane comments, "In retrospect, I'm sure there were ways in which being a woman put me in a minority, and as I've gone back and looked at some of the work that we read, I realize that we were swallowing some very dubious generalizations about women. But that was part of the culture."

THE COMFORT OF COLLEAGUES

As just mentioned, friendships with male colleagues may have compensated somewhat for the discrimination many women experienced at Yale. Indeed, relations among graduate students emerge as a singularly important improvisation of pluralism at Yale. Pluralist graduate students are especially positive about their colleagues. By contrast, students who did not incorporate pluralism are ambivalent about their fellow students. Thus, graduate student relations mediated the incorporation of pluralism at Yale.

For one thing, pluralist students perceived high intelligence among their peers. Two observations, one from the beginning and one from the end of the period, illustrate these views. Nelson Polsby had studied sociology in a graduate program at Brown before coming to Yale. He contrasts Yale graduate students in the mid-1950s with the students he knew in Providence: "What I encountered was really for the first time absolutely first-class graduate students. . . . They had views about everything, and they were smart." Polsby singles out Greenstein, Wildavsky, and Wolfinger among his contemporaries. His intellectual solidarity with other graduate students is manifest.

Polsby's evaluation resembles that of Gary Jacobson, who studied at Yale in the late 1960s. Jacobson remarks: "You learn quickly in graduate school that the quality of the other graduate students is really what makes things go. . . . The main intellectual excitement really came from being around a group of, I thought, retrospectively, very, very smart, interested folks." Jacobson observes that he and his graduate student friends "hung out a lot together." Thus, informal socializing reinforced the intellectual camaraderie of the graduate experience.

That graduate students should think each other bright is hardly surprising. But the very obviousness of this consciousness is precisely the point. On what is this shared consciousness founded other than mastery of the theoretical frameworks propounded by teachers? Ultimately, command of pluralist theory becomes one standard by which intelligence is measured. Thus, the shared perception of intelligence among pluralist students is politically consequential; it favors the reproduction of pluralist discourse.

Some students connected high intellect to pride in having been accepted into a merit-based elite. The feeling of personal accomplishment not only bolstered self-confidence but also favored group solidarity (for a critique, see Kelly, 1995: chapter 2). Stanley Bach, who left academic life for a job in the Congressional Research Service of the Library of Congress, provides a good illustration of this phenomenon: "To Yale's credit, I think their attitude was, if we have accepted you, we're satisfied that you can make it, and you are here as a junior colleague to be trained. You are an apprentice to be trained. You are one of us, unlike what I gather the tenor of graduate student life is like at a place like Harvard, at least was then" (interview, September 29, 1997).

Robert Axelrod echoes this sense of meritorious elitism, and he adds that, "The students were really very good and highly selected, and so . . . we could learn a lot from each other." "Learning from each other" reinforced and deepened group solidarity.

Pluralist graduate students also organized supportive group activities. William Flanigan recalls that Polsby, Wolfinger, and other advanced students organized informal gatherings where invited faculty members discussed their work. Flanigan remarks that, at first, these meetings were exclusive, but friction between invited and uninvited students emerged. However, "In a couple more years it did involve everyone."

Some pluralists also remark favorably upon peer collegiality in the classroom. Donald Blake, for example, who has taught at the University of British Columbia since leaving Yale in 1972, observes that in classes, there was "quite a collegial atmosphere, not kind of competitive or cutthroat in any sense. I had heard those adjectives applied to other American graduate schools, like the big ones at Berkeley and, ah, Michigan" (interview, January 13, 1998).

The feeling of mutuality among graduate students could be reassuring, especially for younger, insecure students. Stanley Bach recalls his feeling of intimidation in a first-year seminar with Robert Dahl:

> I hadn't understood very much of what was being discussed, and I said to one of the second-year students that . . . I was ready to pack up and go home. I couldn't hack it here. And he said, very reassuringly, not to worry, that he felt the same way during his first year, and that by the time I was in my second year, I would be throwing around all this jargon as if I knew what I was talking about, too.

Again, there is nothing exceptional about the experiences Bach, Blake, and the others describe. Indeed, they are so common among graduate students that at first they appear unimportant. But they are important, for they constitute repeated improvisations on such pluralist themes as elite tolerance, coalition formation, access to power, and incremental reform. Indeed, they are not only ways of incorporating pluralism but also ways of reproducing the discourse.

Not all pluralists respected their colleagues, however. Some found classes harshly competitive, with students struggling against each other for the favor of faculty. James Toscano, for example, denounces "the arrogance and insipidness not of Lasswell but of the followers and the hangers-on and clingers; it was appalling to me. And there were a number of those, some in my own class." At the same time, Toscano lauds the "collegiality—call it a pluralism—that accepted you as part of the profession." Other pluralist students found their

classmates disappointing intellectually and turned elsewhere for stim-
ulation and sociality. Finally, some disliked the professional detachment of other students, who refused to get involved in real politics.
Nevertheless, these represent minority voices among the pluralists.

In fact, some pluralist graduate students did engage in politics
while at Yale. Though only a minority, these students used politics
to improvise upon the pluralist texts they were reading. A few students turned to city politics. Although they recognized that their New
Haven was not entirely the New Haven of *Who Governs?*, they believed pluralist politics could reform the city. By the late 1960s, the
reign of Richard Lee, the mayor who epitomized pluralist leadership
for pluralist scholars, was coming to an end. Sara Stewart campaigned
for the reform slate opposing Lee. She remembers being thrilled and
surprised that the reformers actually won. Immediately following her
account of these events, Stewart emphasizes how pluralism made
sense to her at Yale, especially pluralism's argument that mobilized
citizens could change American politics. For Stewart, the triumph of
anti-Lee reform improvised upon this pluralist proposition.

Others found that simply living in New Haven improvised pluralism. Donald Emmerson, who concentrated on Southeast Asian politics at Yale in the mid-1960s, lived in the Florence Virtue Homes on
Dixwell Avenue. This was a model low-income, racially integrated
residential development midway between Yale and a large black
ghetto. Emmerson states that he and his wife were not trying to make
an integrationist "statement." "We were not striking a blow for freedom, although I had been tangentially involved in things like the
Freedom Rides and the civil rights movement in the South" (interview, July 9, 1998). Emmerson states that he and his wife "loved" the
area and had both black and white friends there.

But the fear of crime was palpable in Florence Virtue. Emmerson
recounts almost being robbed while working at home. However, this
experience did not disillusion him about the American political system or about pluralism. Emmerson's non-American political focus,
plus his favorable opinion of Florence Virtue, distanced him from
threats to pluralism. Moreover, he states, "I am a moderate." Emmerson's moderation not only balanced the positives and negatives of
Florence Virtue but also improvised pluralism's own moderate ten-
dencies.

Other pluralist students improvised pluralism in political campaigns. Andrew Glassberg exulted at the mayoral victory of New York City reform Democrat John Lindsay (a Yale graduate). Glassberg worked in the Lindsay campaign and subsequently interned in the Lindsay administration. Glassberg groups Lindsay together with Richard Lee in the pluralist tradition. Indeed, he states that his Lindsay experience strengthened his belief in pluralism. Although he subsequently criticized budgeting reforms in New York, in general he remains a proponent of pluralism (1981).

In 1968 Richard Norling left Yale temporarily to campaign for Eugene McCarthy in New Hampshire. Norling recounts, "I was surprised, because I was on a scholarship. I was surprised that no one ever called me in and complained" (interview, April 8, 1998). Norling attributes his good fortune to the department's anti-war feeling. Whatever the reason, the department's action (or inaction) certainly improvised the pluralist norm of tolerance, thereby complementing Norling's own adherence to pluralism.

Finally, some students improvised pluralism in the civil rights movement. These students interpreted civil rights protest not as a repudiation but as an extension of pluralism. For example, Charles McCall took part in sit-ins at Woolworth's in New Haven. McCall admits that he felt friction between this illegal protest and pluralism's argument that there were legal means by which groups could influence the political system. He reconstructs his reasoning at the time:

> Dahl's notion that there are resources lying around in the street seems to me generally good and true today as well as then. But the difference is, when you have an excluded group that is being excluded not only by law but by terrorism, then you've got to mobilize a part of the non-excluded population to push for their inclusion. And the fact that there are votes there to be had is not sufficient.

In fact, McCall believed that protest *supported* pluralism, a point of view he argued vigorously against fellow graduate students Michael Parenti and Louis Lipsitz, neither of whom incorporated pluralism.

Unlike McCall, whose pluralist improvisation dealt with access and reactivity, William Flanigan's civil rights activism improvised upon pluralism's reform premise. Flanigan and Dahl became advisers to activists in the Yale Law School contemplating filing lawsuits over low levels of black voting in the South. Dahl and Flanigan doubted that such suits would stand up; instead, they recommended a typically pluralist strategy of legislative pressure. Flanigan recalls there being a lot of civil rights reform motivation at Yale in the mid-1950s. As he puts it, "By the standards of a decade later, we weren't on the barricades, but there was a lot of concern that people brought to Yale."

Even involvement in protest and insurgent politics during the late 1960s did not alienate pluralist students from pluralism. An example is Robert Axelrod, who took five months off from Yale to campaign for Eugene McCarthy in 1968. Axelrod explains his activity in the context of political reform. As he puts it, "We could build democracy and make things more egalitarian, less elitist, and so on." These goals, he states, are consistent with Dahl's version of pluralism.

Even Garry Brewer, whose deep opposition to the Vietnam War estranged him from his pro–Vietnam War service family, held on to pluralism. Citing Dahl and Lasswell, Brewer argued that the Vietnam War was an aberration, not an indictment of the American political system. As he summarizes his thinking at the time: "We don't always get it right, but that's a heck of a lot better than trying to have one view. So in that sense the pluralist argument was one I kind of intuitively felt was OK, but all of a sudden, it made really good sense to me." Thus, for Brewer the conflict over Vietnam improvised upon the themes of multiple centers of power and elite tolerance in pluralist theory.

CONCLUSION

A majority of Yale graduate students incorporated pluralism. They embraced pluralism at Yale and endorse it today. They apply the discourse fluently and flexibly to many issues. Their pluralism springs from a variety of personal, political, departmental, and social origins. These include many supportive relations with teachers and peers both inside and outside the classroom. Moreover, pluralists employ multiple cognitive devices, such as supplementation and extension, to improvise pluralism. Like jazz musicians, these former students have played countless variations on pluralist themes. They improvised pluralism as they learned it, and they learned pluralism by improvising. Together performance and text—theme and improvisation—invigorated pluralism as a legitimating discourse for the American political regime.

5

Disrupting Pluralism

INTRODUCTION: THE GREEN AND THE BLUE

In Stendahl's *The Red and the Black* there is a struggle for the soul of the hero, Julien Sorel, who is torn between an abortively revolutionary Napoleonic state (the Red) and a reactionary Catholic Church (the Black). Sorel lived in the latter and lusted for the former. He stands as a powerful literary symbol for the conflict between the secular and the sacred.

When Lance Bennett first came to New Haven in the late summer of 1970, he recalls:

> I drove to the middle of town [the New Haven Green] and noticed a courthouse surrounded by armed federal marshals and a procession of placard-carrying protesters marching around the Green. So I parked my bags and went over, and did a little participant observation. . . . I knew that the Bobby Seale trial was going to be held in New Haven. I was just unaware that it was going to be starting up the week I arrived. (Interview, February 6, 1998)

Bennett's experience on the New Haven Green was not unusual that summer. Indeed, as a disillusioned Gail Sheehy would later write, on May 1, 1970, fifteen thousand demonstrators assembled on the Green to demonstrate against Seale's trial, claiming that, "The Panthers were being framed" (1971: 1).

Nor was the Black Panther agitation the only activism in New Haven, at least in Bennett's account. There had long been labor strife between Yale's blue-collar workforce and the university administration. Bennett recalls that by 1970 many students and academics had rallied to the workers' cause. Indeed, as he puts it, "There was constant talk in those days among the students of a general strike."

If Bennett's arrival in New Haven in 1970 so deeply impressed him, no less so did his initial exposure to the Yale political science department that fall. As he recalls the event:

> It was the orientation session for new graduate students, and Wester-field was the director of graduate studies at the time. So he gathered us, and we sat in a circle with no center, with Westerfield notably distinguished in a blue Yale blazer and gray slacks, and I believe a red and blue tie, I don't remember if there was any white highlighting on it. But he then introduced us to our future by saying, "This department has just been named the best department of political science in the country. And you're going to have to work very hard to meet our standards."

Bennett's first encounters with New Haven and Yale—the Green and the Blue—presented him with directly opposed pictures. New Haven vibrated with ideological commitment, racial conflict, and potentially violent social change. But at Yale, at least in the graduate school (Kelley, 1974: 456), there was peaceful scholarly dedication, academic competition, and professional prestige. These characteristics conveyed an implicit message; namely, that Yale represented dignified propriety and intellectual striving, in contrast to the political struggles on the Green. No wonder that, as another respondent, Carolyn Harmon, put it, students often felt an "absolute divorce of the department from the outside world" (interview, June 3, 1998).

The reader may fear that I am about to revisit a familiar scenario: the Same Old Story of the 1960s, where idealistic but naïve students encounter radicalizing political events and jettison legitimating theories, such as pluralism. Not so, however; in fact, the Same Old Story—told both by those who compliment the 1960s (for the Yale version, see Hersey, 1970) and by those who condemn the 1960s (for the Yale version, see Taft, 1976)—is oversimplified. For one thing, Harmon's characterization of Yale refers to 1962, eight years prior to Bennett's arrival in town. Some students, such as Harmon, felt tension between the Yale political science department and "the outside world" long before the late 1960s.

In this chapter I focus on the large minority of former Yale graduate students (46 of 102) who—like Harmon and Bennett—disrupted pluralism as a legitimating discourse. "Disrupters" advanced severe criticisms of pluralism's four main tenets. They have at some time rejected the pluralist argument that, through multiple centers of political power, citizens gain access to political leaders who compromise, bargain, and gradually forge successful, incrementally reformist coalitions. I found that disruption assumes three forms. First, twenty-four former students (23 percent) are *Resisters,* who neither accepted pluralism's arguments during their graduate experience nor do so today. Second, thirteen former students (13 percent) are *Rejecters,* who adopted pluralism at Yale, but who have rejected it since. Finally, nine former students (9 percent) are *Recuperators,* who were unpersuaded by pluralist ideas at Yale, but who have since embraced pluralism.

Yet it would be an oversimplification to draw too sharp a contrast between supporters and disrupters of pluralism. As we have seen, most pluralist students readily admit that they have changed their views of pluralism over time. Reciprocally, many disrupters of pluralism admit that the discourse has had a persistent influence on them. The differences, therefore, are often matters of degree. In fact, although they have interrupted pluralism, few disrupters have abandoned the discourse entirely.

The prevailing fixation on the 1960s should not obscure other, more pervasive yet less dramatic sources of disaffection from pluralism (e.g., J. Miller, 1987). The standard political account of the 1960s misses the ordinary experiences—the many unremarkable experiential improvisations—that moved students away from pluralism. Indeed, the chief argument of this chapter is that dramatic political events were only the most visible part of a larger complex of mundane improvisations that gradually weakened pluralism at Yale (Merelman, 1998). Put differently, because disrupters did not perform pluralism in their everyday lives, they were primed to disclaim pluralism when dramatic political events provided them the opportunity.

My argument is that students who did not improvise pluralism at Yale, like their faculty counterparts, tended to disrupt pluralism as a legitimating discourse. The reproduction of pluralism depended as much on what happened *within* Yale as on what happened *outside the school.*

Of course, the department itself was not responsible for all the tension that disrupters felt between pluralist themes and personal improvisations. Some things were simply beyond the department's control. For example, many male students in the late 1960s confronted the imminent possibility—and, in a few cases, the actuality—

of the draft and military service in Vietnam. These students had personal reasons to reflect deeply on the relationship between pluralism and political events. Given this fact, however, it is striking how relatively few students cite outside forces, such as the draft, to explain their thinking about pluralism. Ultimately, departmental dynamics had as much impact on disrupters as did what one student referred to as the world "outside the window."

For the most part, as we will see, disrupters cited their own experiences within the department in their critiques of pluralism; for example, some never felt personally comfortable at Yale. By contrast, very few pluralist students report being deeply alienated or unhappy at Yale. Moreover, those few pluralists who *were* unhappy attribute their discomfort to superficial aspects of context, not to less tractable matters of temperament. Thus even the *kind* of tension disrupters experienced distinguishes them from pluralists.

Over the years disrupters have examined their views on pluralism's relationship to social, political, and cultural life in America. Tellingly, disrupters are more likely than pluralists to see pluralism either as a *reflection* of American politics or as a *shaper* of American politics. By contrast, pluralists tend to see the discourse as *detached* from the American political regime. In fact, without any prompting, some disrupters actually identify pluralism as a legitimating discourse, a phenomenon I naturally found reassuring. After all, when some of the people who hypothetically "should" share your theory actually do so—while those who "shouldn't" do not—then, rightly or wrongly, you think you are on the right track.

But few disrupters have produced systematic theoretical analyses of, or alternatives to, pluralist discourse. On the whole, disrupters are "rebels without a cause." Like James Dean, the flawed hero of that classic 1950s film, they are clearer about what they don't like than what ought to take its place. Theirs is the story of a moribund pluralist discourse, not of pluralism's replacement by a comparably powerful theory of American politics.

My first task in this chapter is to describe clearly the stances Resisters, Rejecters, and Recuperators adopt toward pluralism. Next, I discuss the many improvisations that placed disrupters at odds with pluralism. I then identify factors that limited the disruption of pluralism. Finally, I analyze briefly those few disrupters whose writing and recollections provide a systematic critique of pluralism.

STANCES OF PLURALIST REFUSAL: REMEMBRANCE OF TIME PASSED

Resisters and Recuperators refused pluralism while they were at Yale. However, their reaction to the discourse took many different forms, and they refused pluralism for multiple reasons. Among those who attended Yale from the 1950s until 1965, opposition to pluralism was primarily intellectual, as opposed to the anti-intellectualism that drove the McCarthy crusade against liberalism (Lasch, 1965: 314–15). But after 1965, actual political events became a major stimulant of opposition; indeed, new forms of political action increasingly convinced students of pluralism's procedural limits. Yet Resisters and Recuperators have in common the fact that improvisations within the department often influenced their view of pluralist themes. Quietly, unobtrusively, but forcefully, performance undermined pluralism for most Resisters and Recuperators. Let us look at some examples of this phenomenon.

George La Noue, a Resister who arrived at Yale in 1959, had graduated from a small college in Indiana. His interests had already crystallized; he wanted to investigate the relationships among religion, constitutional law, and American politics. These interests might at first appear unpromising, given Yale's vanguardist advocacy of modern, behavioral political science. However, La Noue intended to apply behavioral methods to the study of courts. Nor did he feel any tension between religion and behavioralism at Yale, even though Robert Lane wondered aloud to him whether political science was his best choice. While in political science, he took a course in the Yale Divinity School. In fact, though still in graduate school, he became a policy analyst for the National Council of Churches.

What alienated La Noue from pluralism was the possibility that political compromise might undercut basic values, even those in the Constitution. Indeed, he recalls questioning Robert Dahl on this subject in class:

> He was saying that there were no fixed ideas among the Framers about political truth or about the organization of government. There were a series of compromises. And I raised my hand and said, with a certainty I wouldn't have now, wasn't the First Amendment an example of a consensus between Federalists and Anti-Federalists . . . and a certain political truth. And he thought about that for a moment, and he said, "You know, maybe you're right about that." (Interview, March 9, 1998)

La Noue's observation illustrates the discomfort felt by many traditionally trained graduate students as they confronted the skepticism about embedded values implicit in pluralist bargaining and compromise (e.g., Storing, 1962). By contrast, many pluralist students were *attracted* to this skepticism, a fact that supported pluralism's ascent as a legitimating discourse. Ultimately, the emergence of pluralism and behavioralism in the 1950s drove many traditionally inclined students away from Yale.

Whereas La Noue objected to the value relativism of pluralism, Lewis Lipsitz became a Resister because he believed that pluralism did not take inequality sufficiently into account. Lipsitz arrived in New Haven in 1958 from the University of Chicago, after a year practicing journalism. He immediately found himself in a course with Charles Lindblom: "Lindblom was beginning to develop his ideas about what he called 'partisan mutual adjustment' at that time. And you know, I just did not buy this stuff. I was very critical of it. And I tried to be critical of it in class, but I don't feel he ever heard what I was saying at all" (interview, March 29, 1998).

According to Lipsitz, Lindblom tried to illustrate partisan mutual adjustment by citing the success of unsupervised pedestrian traffic flows in crowded New York intersections. Lindblom argued that pedestrians automatically make appropriate adjustments; therefore, a central planner is not needed to direct foot traffic. Lipsitz goes on:

> I remember thinking at the time, and I think I said it to him too, that this goes fine as long as the people adjusting to each other are kind of the same size. But, you know, if a truck comes along, people have to get the hell out of the way. And there's no mutual adjustment that goes on. . . . All of this working depends in a way on the relative equality of the process, and that just seemed to me a wrong assumption about economics or politics.

Lipsitz's egalitarian critique of Lindblom was clearly ahead of its time; relatively few students from the 1950s made comparable arguments. Indeed, Lipsitz's critique surfaced in two influential pieces in the *American Political Science Review* (1964, 1968). His resistance to pluralism therefore ultimately assumed textual forms.

But there is also an improvisational aspect to Lipsitz's resistance. Note how Lindblom's nonresponse to Lipsitz contrasts sharply with Dahl's openness to La Noue's criticism. By ignoring Lipsitz, Lind-

149

blom refused to improvise upon pluralism. Indeed, his nonresponse was a performance of the very inequality to which Lipsitz objected. Significantly, observations of faculty nonresponsiveness are more frequent among disrupters of pluralism than among pluralist students. In general, students who espoused pluralism recall smoother relations with their teachers than do students who disrupted pluralism.

Not until the early 1960s did a few students draw on entire competing literatures or conceptual frameworks, rather than specific ideas, to critique pluralism. An anonymous Resister who came to Yale in 1964 is an example of this later stance. As an undergraduate at the University of Rochester, he had deeply admired Richard Fenno, whose scholarship on Congress was just becoming influential. Fenno took this student under his wing; as a result, he became immersed in Congress, an institution that fits easily within the pluralist paradigm. He also studied at Rochester with Arthur Goldberg, whose graduate education at Yale had imbued him with empiricism, behavioralism, and the pluralist theory of American politics. This student would therefore appear a promising recruit to the ranks of pluralists at Yale.

However, in his junior year this student attended the London School of Economics, where he studied with Ralph Miliband, a leading neo-Marxist scholar (e.g., Miliband, 1969). He soon sensed tension between his interest in Congress, his sympathy for American pluralism, and the neo-Marxism to which Miliband exposed him. Later, when he studied with Dahl at Yale, he reacted sharply against pluralism. "I remember thinking that Dahl was a great admirer of, not critical enough of, the American system, and then I began right from the start to be intrigued with European Marxism" (interview, April 27, 1998). Soon he abandoned the study of legislative politics entirely.

This student gravitated to the study of Italian politics, a lively arena for his emerging fascination with European Marxism. Moreover, he found Joseph LaPalombara receptive to his interest in Marxism; in fact, he characterizes LaPalombara as "affirming." Perhaps LaPalombara's support for the student sustained his residual tie to pluralism; though he says he never took pluralism "really seriously"—charging that at Yale it was "religious almost in its invocation"—neither did he embrace the politics of protest. In fact, he dismissed American protestors as "kind of dopey" and frivolous. In a letter to Joseph Hamburger, director of graduate studies in 1968, he states that he would reluctantly "take a teaching post . . . to avoid participating in a war I find ideologically and strategically unsupportable" (letter to Hamburger, March 7, 1968). Thus, the student did ultimately manifest his opposition to the Vietnam War in a fashion consistent with his intellectual resistance to pluralism.

The ambivalence about pluralism that this ex-student evinces is common among *pre*-1965 disrupters. In the absence of polarizing political events or anti-pluralist improvisations during graduate school, disrupters' critiques of pluralism did not wholly eradicate the discourse. Resisters and Recuperators sensed conflict with pluralism both politically and theoretically; however, they turned away from pluralism coolly and dispassionately, in precisely the way Yale had trained them.

By contrast, *after* 1965 political events began to spur sharp opposition to pluralism. Some Resisters and Recuperators simply lay pluralist theory alongside American politics in the late 1960s and concluded that pluralism was fundamentally in error. Others added their own political experiences to their critique of pluralism. Yet event-driven opposition did not necessarily estrange disrupters from Yale; in fact, some disrupters believed that faculty shared their desire to reconstruct American political thought. For these students, pluralist departmental improvisations moderated opposition to pluralist theory.

An example of this stance is the position of Richard Beth, a Resister who came to Yale in 1966 from an undergraduate education at Princeton. Beth, now a researcher at the Congressional Research Service of the Library of Congress, left academic life after his first job at Boston University. However, he became estranged from pluralism at Yale, not at Boston University. Beth believes that his criticism of pluralism paralleled Robert Dahl's reevaluation of his earlier pluralist work. So Beth did not repudiate the entire Yale intellectual enterprise, but only pluralism. In fact, Dahl served as his dissertation adviser. As Beth explains:

> The focus of my critique was that questions could be raised about how closely American political situations or the American polity approximated the pluralist model. . . . Those are questions that Dahl himself also raised, in fact, really quite vigorously in the following years. And I think he came to do so in part as a result of the critiques that were expressed in part in classes such as the one I was in. (Interview, January 12, 1998)

Clearly, politics "outside the window" of Yale influenced Beth to resist pluralism. But departmental improvisations also mattered; Beth balanced his critique of pluralism against Dahl's intellectual journey in the classroom. Because he envisaged Dahl not as an opponent but as a collaborator, Beth leavened his own opposition to pluralism with Dahl's improvisation of pluralist reform. In short, Dahl's openness allowed Beth to temper his resistance. As Beth's case shows, pluralist improvisation provided a *habitus,* that is, a deeply embedded set of customs that hinders a purely intellectual critique from mutating into political rebellion (Bourdieu, 1977).

According to John Gunnell, Robert Dahl's work in the 1960s lacked "an articulate concern about linking political science to political practice" (1995: 222). Beth certainly sensed this lack; in fact, it formed the core of his opposition to pluralism. But Gunnell misses something that Beth grasped: namely, that Dahl himself and other Yale scholars were equally unhappy about the gap between pluralist theory and American practice. In turn, Dahl's discomfort contributed to a pluralist improvisation—his positive response to student critiques—that softens Beth's resistance to the discourse. Again, improvisation and personal experience shape the disruption of pluralism.

For Beth's classmate Nathaniel Beck, political events had a more personal element. Beck's political activism strongly affected his critique of pluralism. Of the forms of opposition I have described, Beck's most approximates pure event-driven radicalism. But even Beck's case needs to be understood in the context of departmental improvisations.

On the face of it, Beck would seem an unlikely Resister. He came to Yale from the University of Rochester, where he had done a combined mathematics and politics undergraduate degree. He describes himself at Rochester as "a gung-ho rationalist," committed to a mathematical/econometric approach to politics. This background clearly did not dispose him to break with pluralism. Nor has Beck produced research that sharply criticizes the American political system. Most of his large body of influential work concentrates on Congress, economic policy, and electoral cycles; in fact, a 1982 *American Political Science Review* article actually reproduces pluralism's multiple centers of power premise (1982). Thus, Beck demonstrates how disrupting a legitimating discourse does not necessarily generate oppositional theories or texts. In fact, Beck exemplifies Henry Aaron's caustic observation about quantitative, economically trained social scientists, whose techniques make it "almost impossible to identify policies that may be necessary, but not sufficient, to achieve some objective" (1978: 156). Given these facts, why did Beck resist pluralism?

The answer is that the clash between Beck's political outlook and his Yale education proved personally traumatic. As he describes himself at Yale:

> Remember, I had gone to school straight out of college . . . so I was just very tired of school. And the war was going on, and the second year I had gotten very interested in politics . . . anti-war work. And this disjunction, I'm sure you've heard this a lot, between sort of doing political science and interest in politics was very great. And for those of us who were interested in mathematical modeling . . . that most apolitical of this stuff . . . was doubly great. And so my second year was just sort of a lost year. . . . Remember, I was very young; I didn't really have an adult experience at Rochester. So I was learning about sex, drugs, rock and roll. (Interview, June 1, 1998)

Beck took part in a New Haven anti-war group called the American Independence Movement. He also participated in local politics and in union organizing in New Haven. Significantly, he uses the phrase "looking at the city through my eyes at that time" to explain his opposition to pluralism. Based on his personal experiences, he concluded that Dahl's *Who Governs?* was "dead wrong."

But if Beck demonstrates how the 1960s drove some students away from *pluralist* political science, he is also a good example of how opposition to pluralism did not generate a critique of *political science*. In the excerpt above, Beck distinguishes between "doing political science" and having an "interest in politics." This distinction implies that being a political scientist—because it is not a manifestation of "interest in politics"—is not a political activity. No wonder Beck still considers mathematical modeling the "most apolitical of stuff."

This distinction may help Beck to pursue the sort of political science he learned and respected at Rochester and Yale. Once the traumatic political events that caused him to oppose pluralism had subsided, he returned to political science with vigor. His disruption of pluralism occurred, but his resistance also typifies the ambivalence that characterizes many of pluralism's opponents. Again, disruption is not necessarily abandonment.

STANCES OF PLURALIST REFUSAL: THE ANALYSIS OF THE PRESENT

Resisters and Rejecters also do not believe that pluralism can explain aspects of contemporary American politics. Unlike pluralists, who affirm the discourse's continuing utility, disrupters—aside from Recuperators—decline to apply pluralism to the current political landscape. Although they sometimes refuse pluralism on quite narrow grounds, they do not give pluralism the benefit of the doubt, as do adherents of the discourse.

There is, also, an important rhetorical difference between the stances of contemporary affirmation and contemporary refusal. Pluralists often affirm the discourse in *formal* terms; that is, they generally cite certain discursive characteristics (such as pluralism's breadth or its flexibility) as grounds for affirmation. By contrast, those who decline to use pluralism usually do so for *substantive* reasons; that is, they focus on the *political* inadequacies of pluralism. Of course, affirming pluralism formally is no less political than refusing pluralism substantively; in fact, the formal quality of pluralist affirmation has helped pluralism to survive politically. However, the substantive focus produced by pluralism's critics generates unusually explicit and varied arguments.

For example, some criticize pluralism's inability to deal with important political issues, such as persistent racial conflict. One, a policy adviser to former Baltimore mayor Kurt Schmoke (himself a Yale undergraduate), states that in Baltimore racial politics defies the compromises and coalition formation described by pluralism. Instead, as this Resister, puts it, "Black ethnicity, if I could use that term, becomes the basis of power. . . . How do you generate the cooperation of other people in your city to kind of work within this institutional framework now? I think that there is a lot of strain there, and a lot of polarization with that" (interview, March 6, 1998). He strongly doubts that pluralism can comprehend black identity and multiculturalism (cf. Dawson, 1994).

Although some who refuse pluralism cite single political issues, such as race or the rise of the Christian Right, others take a more comprehensive stance: namely, that pluralist politics excludes *many* issues. To these disrupters, such early critics of pluralism as Bachrach and Baratz (1962), Schattschneider (1960), and others were essentially correct; contrary to pluralist theory, important issues often do not even reach the political agenda. Peter Eisinger, an ambivalent Rejecter, focused on this problem while he was still at Yale. Indeed, his early research concerned the questions of access and protest in urban politics (e.g., Eisinger, 1972). Although Eisinger states that pluralism is "still powerful enough to provide some starting points for understanding the democratic process," the question of system openness continues to vex him. As he puts it, "The pluralists have never taken into account the power or the anticipated reactions by others in response to the perceived reputation for power and reputation for influence. I've at times found it convincing that powerful actors limited the agenda" (interview, July 9, 1997).

Finally, some who decline to use pluralism today share the same cognitive strategies pluralist students use, but they do so in order to discredit, not to affirm, the discourse. Take, for example, the strategy of cognitive segmentation. Peter Stillman, a Rejecter, states that pluralism cannot handle the issue of identity politics. In fact, in 1974 Stillman argued that Hegel provided a strong critique of the liberal individualism that underlay pluralism (1974). Today Stillman segments pluralism into two parts: its useful opposition to elitist or Marxist theories of society and its problematic part, which touches on identity politics. He complains that "pluralism can sort of break down into groups or identity politics. What is it that holds the country together in a pluralist society?" (interview, April 29, 1998).

For Stillman, the virtue of pluralist politics (the vitality of interest groups) is also its vice (the development of identity politics). The problem is that pluralism provides no common set of values to hold competing interest groups together. Therefore, interest group competition can mutate into identity politics, which, in turn, causes fragmentation, not pluralist compromise and measured reform. In short, the fatal flaw of pluralism is that it applies *too* well, spurring group formation that ultimately threatens national unity.

Some who refuse pluralism today apply broad ideological critiques to the discourse. In discussing Lindblom and Cohen's *Usable Knowledge* (1979), Bruce Berman, a Resister who studied at Yale from 1965 to 1971, comments on American political science's ideological character. Berman concedes that Lindblom's incrementalism did describe the Kenyan colonial administration Berman investigated in his dissertation. But this fact does not salvage pluralism for Berman today. As he puts it: "*Usable Knowledge,* which I think is a wonderful book, where he makes the remark, 'Gee,' somehow he's struck by the fact that American political science never really dealt effectively with the issues of race and class. And I thought, 'There's no mystery to that. It was built into the perspective, which was one of its problems'" (interview, May 10, 1998). Berman regards Lindblom's observation as evidence that American political science, including pluralism, has worn ideological blinders. No wonder he declines to apply pluralism to contemporary politics.

Martha Logsdon, a Resister, was Berman's contemporary at Yale, where the two studied comparative politics. Unlike Berman, she describes pluralism as myth, not ideology. She resisted pluralism at Yale because, as she puts it, she then espoused "a much more class-based analysis of American politics" (interview, March 18, 1998). But she also observes that "Americans like to believe that everybody sort of has access some way. It's a fairly comforting theory about American politics, which I think does serve the interests of the powers-that-be. . . . Pluralism is really a myth, but it's a myth that legitimates the way things are." Logsdon is careful not to assert that pluralism emerged *because* it serves "the powers-that-be." In that sense, she does not offer a reductive ideological critique. Rather, she claims that pluralist ideas are "comforting" to "the powers-that-be." She therefore sees pluralism as a legitimating discourse, not as an ideology.

But only a few who refuse to apply pluralism to contemporary American politics search successfully for alternative paradigms of political analysis. Two examples illustrate this uncommonly ambitious discursive stance.

Lance Bennett found the study of political institutions and democratic processes at Yale inadequate to his emerging perspective. As he puts it, "I did run up against what I considered to be paradigmatic boundaries that I wasn't comfortable with intellectually." By his own account, Bennett's search for an alternative paradigm led him to the Yale political psychology program, and later in his career to interdisciplinary work in political communication. His published work is prolific and generally critical of pluralism (e.g., 1996), although he no longer seeks a grand paradigm and feels comfortable combining political communication with a return to "my old political psychology roots."

Bennett has found an intellectual alternative to pluralism; other disrupters, however, have become skeptical about all conceptual frameworks. When Rufus Browning, a Rejecter, graduated from Yale in 1960, he did not feel strongly attached to pluralism or, indeed, to any theory of American politics. In fact, his 1984 book *Protest Is Not Enough* actually presents a pluralist picture of race and urban political incorporation (see also Browning, Marshall, and Tabb, 1972). Today, however, he reinforces his earlier uncertainty about pluralism with arguments borne of thirty years experience in and out of academia. Browning is an eloquent exponent of theoretical relativism in the study of politics.

I asked Browning my standard question, namely, whether pluralism is or is not a good picture of contemporary American politics. He replied: "It is a reasonably good picture, but it's a picture of only one side. And there are other reasonably good pictures. . . . I see for me the metaphor of the mountain. Here's the mountain, and you look at one side of it, it looks very different than the other side" (interview, January 25, 1998). Browning believes that pluralism peers at the mountain very closely—"decisions and the like." But this micro-analytic perspective ignores the "underlying geologic structure." For Browning, conceptual relativism reduces the value of pluralism. As he puts it, "Instead of searching for the truth, we weren't doing that at all. We were fleshing out a particular perspective, and . . . there are other perspectives that have their own validity." Browning's position undermines not only pluralism but also *any* legitimating or challenging discourse.

Finally, some disrupters refuse pluralism because it cannot handle qualitatively novel aspects of American politics and culture. For example, Richard Beth believes that recent dialogue between academics and the educated public has disintegrated. He attributes this development to the professionalization of the social sciences, a phenomenon he first observed at Yale (interview, January 12, 1998; for a pertinent theory, see Fuchs, 1992, especially chapter 8). Mary Curzan, a Rejecter who held many congressional staff positions, feels that negotiation between interest groups no longer characterizes Washington politics. As she puts it, "We've now got a kind of politics here where there is no balance," a phenomenon she attributes to "the decline of political parties or the entry of emotional, nonnegotiable issues" (interview, February 12, 1998). And Belden Fields, a Resister who has taught at the University of Illinois since leaving Yale in 1965, argues that pluralism's presumed consensus on "the rules of the game" does not comprehend contemporary cultural politics, which is dominated by "ethnic or gender or sexual orientation" (interview, January 16, 1998).

PLURALISM REPELLED

In the previous chapter, I described how many graduate students incorporated pluralism through behavioral improvisations at Yale. I now turn to the way disrupters *repelled* pluralism at Yale. I argue that, by virtue of earlier socialization and education, many disrupters were predisposed to dislike pluralism. But in addition, disrupters tended not to experience Yale as a pluralist arena. Also, many interpreted their political activities as anti-pluralist statements. Finally, both personality and social structure distanced disrupters from the pluralist core of Yale. In summary, where pluralist students overwhelmingly improvised on pluralist themes at Yale, disrupters of pluralism often created entirely different compositions.

Several aspects of prior education and socialization tilted disrupters against pluralism. Religion, regional origins, race, and parental politics essentially *marginalized* some disrupters at Yale. Consider, for example, Douglas Bennett and James C. Scott. The two men shared certain characteristics, such as Quakerism, that predisposed them to resist pluralism. Yet no single phenomenon by itself explains how the two became disrupters.

Douglas Bennett, a Recuperator, has had a long commitment to Quakerism. Indeed, when I interviewed him he was president of Earlham College, a Quaker institution. He came to Yale from another Quaker college, Haverford. Quakerism, of course, has a proud tradition of promoting racial equality; moreover, it also endorses pacifism, a stance of particular pertinence during the Vietnam War, when Bennett attended Yale. Yet, surprisingly, Bennett does not mention Quakerism in connection with Yale or pluralism.

Instead, Bennett traces his resistance to pluralism to his undergraduate teacher Peter Bachrach, a well-known critic of pluralism.

As Bennett puts it, he came to Yale "sort of warmed up on issues of pluralism" (interview, October 30, 1998). Bennett also cites his high school years, during which he was an exchange student in Ecuador. "If there's a sort of short, powerful kick in my life that nudged me in a very different direction, it was living for four months in Guayaquil and seeing poverty, the likes of which I had absolutely no idea existed." Given this mix of factors, it is not surprising that Bennett "was largely a critic of [pluralism]" at Yale.

Bennett's criticism took quite tangible forms. Before coming to Yale, he decided that he would refuse induction into the military. Along with several other political science graduate students, Bennett was arrested on the day that the U.S. government mined Haiphong Harbor, when his leafleting blocked traffic in New Haven. Nor did he keep quiet within the department. In 1969 he co-authored "Obstacles to Graduate Education in Political Science," based on a national survey of graduate schools that he conducted. "Obstacles" called for greater educational collaboration between students and faculty. The study characterized the recent Yale reform of the examination system as a model for national consideration. Obviously, Bennett's activist resistance to pluralism took many forms.

But Bennett also illustrates the complexities of repelling pluralism. He admits that pluralist improvisations at Yale impressed him favorably. In particular, his exposure to Robert Dahl moderated his objections to pluralism. He recounts that in one class a student belligerently confronted Dahl. According to Bennett, the student "kind of bludgeoned him intellectually, I mean just sort of took after Robert Dahl." But, says Bennett, it was "stunning" that Dahl did not become defensive; instead Dahl "said a lot more thoughtful things than we thought he might have up his sleeve to say." Thus, "Dahl that day became a kind of intellectual hero to me." Today Bennett describes himself as "less a critic of pluralism" than he was as a graduate student. In fact, he has recuperated pluralism. Certainly Dahl's performance of pluralism is consistent with Bennett's recent embrace of the discourse.

Like Bennett, James Scott has Quakerism in his background. And unlike Bennett, he cites Quakerism as a source of his resistance to pluralism. As he puts it, "I always had this Quaker left-wing politics and, as a Quaker, it wasn't a big deal for me to get arrested" (interview, May 15, 1998).

Scott, a Resister, is today a leading student of comparative politics; his works articulate a populist, anti-pluralist position on state formation, modernization, and third-world politics. Rather than viewing political leaders as responsive to pluralist interest groups, Scott argues that ordinary citizens must constantly resist oppressive elites who normally exclude them from power (e.g., 1998, 1990). Scott is one of the few Yale graduates whose work contains a comprehensive countertheory to pluralism. Interestingly, Scott now teaches at Yale.

As a graduate student between 1961 and 1965, Scott was "rather inclined to the elitist critiques of Dahl, even though it wasn't work that I did myself." He attributes his "Left politics" not only to Quakerism but also to his family. "My father was a sort of rabid Democrat, and I was the only Democrat in my little Quaker school." Prior to coming to Yale, he took part in civil rights politics and served as vice president of the National Student Association. In the early 1960s NSA took a progressive position on most national and international issues, even while—as was later revealed—the Central Intelligence Agency secretly funded NSA in hopes of opposing Soviet-supported international youth organizations (Saunders, 1999).

Scott's resistance to pluralism at Yale extended not only to Dahl but also to Gabriel Almond. Initially, Scott was intimidated by Almond's arcane terminology; however, he soon asserted himself. "It was in Almond's class, and I remember sitting in that class and being totally mystified, and having had a little index card with me, and I started copying down the words I didn't understand. After I accumulated three or four of them I actually in my complete naïveté raised my hand, and asked Almond if he could explain what the following four words meant." Almond was not amused, and Scott became alienated by comparative politics in the Yale department.

Unlike most disrupters, Scott has created a theoretical challenge to professional political science. In *Seeing Like a State* (1998) Scott analyzes "high modernism," which, he argues, attempts to repress local, indigenous cultures. He characterizes the book's critique of high modernism as "absolutely" a broadside against social science as he experienced it in graduate school. He considers social science in this form a "thin schematic simplification that kind of does violence to the actual shape of social life." Thus, the resistance to pluralism that began in Scott's youth has generated an anti-pluralist text that treats social science—including pluralism—as not only a set of ideas but also as a form of political domination.

Bennett and Scott illustrate the broad range of early experiences that predisposed disrupters to oppose pluralism at Yale. For most disrupters, early experiences produced a feeling of *marginalization* vis-à-vis pluralism (see Douglas, 1995). For example, many southerners at Yale felt marginal to pluralist discourse, as did African Americans, and also many white students for whom issues of race were important. Let me provide some examples.

Theodore Lowi, a Resister, whose influential *The End of Liberalism* (1969) sharply attacked pluralism, attributes his resistance to his "outsider" status. He traces his marginality to being a southern Jew, whose family had been in Alabama since the mid-nineteenth century. As he describes it, "I felt I'd come from a sort of underprivileged, third-world country" (interview, March 23, 1998). He believes his southern origins separated him from such northern Jews as Wildavsky, Polsby, and Greenstein. He states simply: "I came at these things in a different way. I always felt myself an outsider."

Not surprisingly, Lowi's outsider consciousness focused on race. As a native southerner, he understood how deeply entrenched racial domination in the South actually was. He doubted the pluralist argument that racial interest groups "could really have the beneficent effect that . . . was thought to be from the systemic standpoint." He believed that only insurgent social movements, not pluralist interest groups, could change the South. So he returned to Alabama from New Haven to campaign in 1958 for a Labor Party candidate.

Other southerners also felt marginalized at Yale, less because of racial issues than because Yale's secular liberalism clashed with their own religious conservatism. Joseph Retzer, a Rejecter, came to Yale in 1965 from Vanderbilt University; he interrupted his graduate career to serve a year in Vietnam. Retzer was initially drawn to pluralism; however, personally he was unhappy at Yale. As he puts it, "I was from a relatively conservative religious, southern-type culture, and pretty shy, and I didn't really feel real comfortable" (interview, April 10, 1998). He returned South for a year to teach at a black college (Vorhees College in South Carolina), where he took part in civil rights activism. The Vorhees improvisation impelled him to develop a critique of pluralism; increasingly, he perceived the political

√√ playing field to be unfairly tilted against the weak. Interestingly, he attributes this critique partly to his conservative religious upbringing, which made him—even in his hometown of Arlington, Virginia, an outsider among his peers. Thus, initially for religious reasons in Arlington, then for regional reasons at Yale, and finally for political reasons at Vorhees, Retzer saw himself as "an outsider among [my] peers. That may have made it easier for me to start critiquing political science later on."

The few African Americans at Yale also were dismissive of pluralism. Donald Stewart, a Recuperator, spent only the years 1959 and 1960 in the department; ultimately, he went on to head the Educational Testing Service, which administers Graduate Record and Scholastic Aptitude Tests. Although Stewart was personally comfortable at Yale, he disliked New Haven, which he describes as "a dreadful place to live" (interview, May 20, 1998). Stewart explains his distaste for New Haven in racial terms, but he also "saw elements of poverty and disorder in New Haven," which upset him. Ultimately, he concluded that pluralism could not handle the question of race adequately. In addition, as he puts it, "I had a longing for some identification with social movements and developments that had an impact on people of color." His search took him first to Europe, then for two years to Africa, and then into foundation work in the United States. As he concludes wryly, "I needed to find myself and go off in this world where I thought I could become another Ralph Bunche, or whatever." In short, for Stewart, personal improvisations and racial consciousness trumped pluralist theory.

Unlike Stewart, an anonymous African American completed the graduate program in political science. A Resister, he received his Ph.D. in 1969, after being at Yale off and on throughout the 1960s. He perceived race and poverty not only as a black man but also from the vantage point of the New Haven anti-poverty program, where he worked for three years (see Talbot, 1967: chapter 15). He drew more critical conclusions about pluralism than did Yale scholars of New Haven. For one thing, he sensed "the inattention to race" in *Who Governs?* Although pluralists correctly analyzed policy consensus, he believes they missed the systemic bias in this process (see also Domhoff, 1978). A political elite actually manipulated consensus; the general public did not arrive at its own decisions. Ultimately, he believes, pluralism entailed "a lot of the acceptance of the status quo without looking behind it" (interview, March 6, 1998).

This sensitivity to racial issues stimulated criticism of some Yale faculty. The ex-student argues that Nelson Polsby and Gabriel Almond were biased and inflexible teachers. Polsby advanced only his own version of pluralism; Almond promoted only his own approach to comparative politics. Nor does he exempt Robert Dahl from criticism. "Dahl would never get out of his pluralistic framework about the dispersal of power and everybody has influence, which to my way of thinking was wrong. . . . Everybody didn't have influence, or if you had influence, it didn't matter greatly."

Like Stewart, this ex-student felt caught between social change, on the one hand, and pluralist political science, on the other. When New Haven experienced racial turmoil in the 1960s, he "was involved with the city, and the section around New Haven Hospital was the hot spot for political activists." He expected that the issues he was confronting daily in New Haven would show up in the classroom. But they did not. He concluded that, rather than modifying pluralist theory, Yale political science preferred not to confront racial conflict.

Of course, Quakerism and minority racial status were rarities among Yale graduate students. But there were more common sources of marginalization among disrupters of pluralism. A natural place to begin, of course, is the student's political heritage. It is by now a truism that most student radicals in the 1960s were acting out political beliefs learned from their parents (e.g., an early study is Flacks, 1971). Given this fact, one might expect students from left-wing families to feel marginalized at Yale and to react by resisting pluralism.

On close examination, this expectation turns out to be simplistic and, in some cases, actually runs counter to the facts. Although a left-wing family background did often stimulate resistance, the real impact of family was not in politics per se, but rather in many early experiences that set the student on a course away from pluralism. By itself, a left-wing family heritage did not ensure the disruption of pluralism.

Of course, some disrupters do attribute their resistance directly to family political ideology. A case in point is Robert Grey, a Resister who came to Yale in 1961 and left in 1964; Grey has spent his entire teaching career at Grinnell College in Iowa. As an undergraduate at

Wesleyan University, Grey studied with E. E. Schattschneider, whose *The Semi-Sovereign People* (1960) took a skeptical view of pluralism. Grey also absorbed C. Wright Mills and Floyd Hunter's versions of elite theory at Wesleyan. But as he puts it, "These books [only] tend to confirm ideas I had" (interview, April 24, 1998). Although he thought pluralism at Yale an "interesting challenge, and to some extent persuasive," he observes, "I don't think I ever bought into the pluralist description."

Grey came from "a family of old communists." His father organized automobile workers in the Detroit sit-down strikes of the 1930s. Therefore, the Mills and Hunter books were only "part of my lullabies, as it were." Grey describes himself as "a radical critic" early in life, a stance he maintained at Yale. In fact, in recent years he has become "more and more antagonistic to a pluralist vision." As he sums it up, "My radical family heritage and all the evidence I see around me suggests we have a radical, almost a Marxist vision of the way the political system operates as a far more accurate representation than a pluralist vision."

So direct a family political heritage is unusual. More typical is the filtering of family influences through intellectual traditions and local circumstances. A case in point is Edgar Litt, a Resister, whose work on ethnic politics and political cynicism in America began to appear soon after he graduated from Yale in 1960 (1963). Like Grey, Litt was influenced "by the Jewish socialist tradition." However, unlike Grey, he characterizes this influence as "indirect." The significance he attributes to his familial tradition is not its socialism, but rather the fact that it exposed him to the writings of New York Jewish intellectuals, such as Daniel Bell and Nathan Glazer. Clearly, for Litt, the New York intellectuals played a role in creating resistance to pluralism.

But what exactly is this role? After all, the New York intellectuals gradually *rejected* socialism and moved toward pluralism, even conservatism (e.g., Kristol, 1983: 12). So it must not have been their politics alone that appealed to Litt. Rather, the New York intellectuals provided an eclectic alternative to disciplinary professionalization and objective social science at Yale. (Indeed, Litt still recalls his classmate Wildavsky's wry remark that New Haven might as easily have been in Wyoming instead of only sixty miles from New York City.) Like Wildavsky and Polsby, Litt also became professionalized at Yale. Yet, unlike his two friends, Litt found professionalization uncomfortable.

In resisting pluralism, Litt maintained his connection to the politically engaged, New York Jewish intellectual tradition—even though he encountered that tradition only secondhand as an adolescent in Baltimore, Maryland (interview, March 19, 1998).

Grey and Litt illustrate the way in which familial political ideology sometimes created an ideological barrier against pluralism. Other familial influences are equally as strong, but counterintuitive. For example, Daniel Levine, a Recuperator, who has long taught Latin American politics at the University of Michigan, also resisted pluralism at Yale; in fact, he characterizes himself as a "radical student." However, unlike Grey and Litt, he *opposed* the politics of his family. In a biting condemnation, he states that, "My surviving parents are sort of right-wing racists"; by contrast, he describes himself as "the radical black sheep of my family" (interview, March 16, 1998). His family apparently propelled Levine *away* from their politics. Levine instead turned to his New York radical adolescent milieu and to an early—and uncommon—interest in social theory. These two influences supported his resistance to pluralism. Indeed, he is the only person I interviewed who employed the term "social theory" to explain why he "just never could swallow [pluralism] completely."

Politically unconventional religious traditions (Quakerism), marginal regions (the South), marginal family political traditions (Jewish radicalism), and political marginality itself all predisposed students to resist pluralism. Other features of social background also produced marginality. A good example is Jan Deutsch, a Resister who took classes in political science while a law student at Yale and presently teaches in the Yale Law School. In 1968 Deutsch engaged in a heated exchange about pluralism with Nelson Polsby that appeared in print (see J. Deutsch, 1976: 169–98). Deutsch had already debated pluralism in classes at Yale. Even today, Deutsch states, "I don't think that argument is dead." Deutsch's principal complaint against pluralism is its scientific pretensions:

> See, from Nelson's point of view . . . Yale was doing pure anthropology. I mean their vision of themselves was that social science was a coherent body of experiential life. And they were doing to politics precisely what the anthropologists did to culture . . . except anthropology, because they don't have "science" in the title of the department, are much more cognizant of something that the Yale people simply ignored. (Interview, February 17, 1998)

165

Deutsch argues that pluralism was not self-critical and that it protected the status quo. In his 1968 article, Deutsch criticized "the ultimate source of the failure of *Who Governs?*" He identifies this failure as the emphasis on process in the study, which "does not permit an assessment of whether the system is operating within proper limits, whether the community agenda is an equitable one, for any such assessment . . . would require the postulation of 'real' as opposed to perceived interests" (1976: 178). In essence, Deutsch is charging that pluralism lacked true reformist capacity.

Certainly this is a quite subtle critique for so young a scholar. How does Deutsch explain his unusual perspective? "I am an immigrant," he responds. "The culture wasn't natural. I had to consciously adjust." Deutsch implies that, as an immigrant, he approached pluralism as a distinctly American discourse that fulfilled particular American needs. Indeed, he compares Polsby's pluralism to Freudianism. "Nelson . . . thinks like the Freudians back then [in the 1950s]. That when you have science you have truth." Once again, a marginal social identity—that of immigrant—promoted resistance to pluralism.

In the previous chapter, I described upwardly mobile students who used pluralism to escape from their ethnic, working-class origins. But *conscious* awareness of class and ethnicity usually worked *against* pluralism. The most striking example of this point is Michael Parenti, a Resister whose prolific neo-Marxist writings on American politics germinated while he was still a graduate student at Yale in the late 1950s and early 1960s. In a recent memoir of his working-class, Italian childhood in New York City, Parenti describes a recurrent dream he had in the late 1960s. In the dream he returns to the East Harlem brownstone of his childhood. He interprets the dream as symbolizing the painful split he felt between his professional life as an academic and his working-class, Italian youth. Yet the dream reconciles his opposed selves: "The working-class Italian youth and the professional-class American academic were to live under the same roof. I had come home to two worlds apart. Never quite at home in either, I would now have the best of both. Once I understood the message, the dreams stopped" (1996: 269).

At Yale, Parenti recalls, his working-class consciousness spurred his resistance to pluralism. Indeed, he uses class not only to explain his antipathy to pluralism but to describe a confrontation he had with

Polsby over pluralism. As he puts it, "Well, I come from a working-class background. I felt I was a little more sensitive to the question of class deprivation than most of the people I was dealing with. Polsby's father was a doctor" (interview, April 14, 1998). Parenti singles out Polsby because of an earlier confrontation the two had when they were graduate students at Brown University. At Brown, Parenti organized a chapter of the NAACP; Polsby complained to Parenti that the NAACP was an "extremist group" and would be "provocative." According to Parenti, Polsby preferred the formation of an Urban League chapter.

Parenti cautions that too much not be read into his class origins and states, we "don't know how much [one] can generalize things like that." I certainly agree; no single factor—religion, class, race, family political tradition—can explain why some students incorporated pluralism, and others disrupted it. Yet individual aspects of socialization did stimulate *improvisations* that powerfully influenced student reactions to pluralism. For disrupters, these improvisations created intellectual and social marginality.

My concept of marginalization differs from traditional sociological uses of the term. By marginalization I do not refer to demographic or ethnic minorities. To be sure, there is demographic marginality among disrupters. For example, of the thirty-six Jewish male graduate students I interviewed, 59 percent were disrupters, as compared to only 34 percent (sixteen) of the forty-eight male non-Jews. Thus, Jewish marginality did provide a foundation for the disruption of pluralism. But of the small number of women I interviewed (seventeen), more are pluralists than disrupters. Thus, by itself, sociological marginality is never determinative; demographic and ethnic marginality only favors *improvisations* of marginality. It is these improvisations that ultimately lead people to disrupt pluralism.

As the previous chapter reveals, graduate student pluralists were generally satisfied with teaching and classes at Yale. By contrast, students who disrupted pluralism have a more mixed view of classes and teachers. They often found classes unsatisfying; in addition, they recount instances in which teachers violated pluralist themes. Finally, Resisters, Rejecters, and Recuperators display an edge of bitterness that is missing in pluralist students.

Nevertheless, I stress that the picture is *mixed,* not uniformly negative. In fact, some of the most vociferous disrupters of pluralism remember their teachers and classes fondly. A striking case in point is Catherine MacKinnon, a Resister who did graduate work in political science at Yale in the late 1960s and early 1970s and later received her doctorate. MacKinnon is a leading feminist legal scholar; her gender-based analysis of American politics is at great variance with pluralism (e.g., MacKinnon, 1987). She observes, "My work substantively became what it is largely in opposition to pluralism. But it was Dahl's practice of pluralism that allowed that, encouraged it even. Which is, ultimately, what the practice of pluralism is supposed to be about, and in my experience there with him, actually was" (personal communication, October 7, 1998).

Nor is Dahl the only recipient of such compliments. Deane Neubauer, a Rejecter who has taught at the University of Hawaii for many years, remembers that Robert Lane extended himself, "helping me through some difficult stuff I was having personally" (interview, June 8, 1998). Neubauer describes Lane as "gracious." Bruce Berman, a Resister who attended Yale in the late 1960s, recalls that Joseph LaPalombara not only engaged in classroom debates on Vietnam but also modified his earlier hawkish views. "LaPalombara I can remember at times being defensive, but at other times being willing to listen and certainly to argue the issues. And I think trying to distance himself at some point from his earlier involvements. He had in fact, very early on, '59 or '60, been part of a Michigan State group that went to advise South Vietnam on issues of public administration." And Hugh Heclo, a well-known public policy scholar, states (e.g., Heclo, 1977) that the faculty at Yale, especially Dahl and Lindblom, not only encouraged but also welcomed criticism (interview, June 3, 1998).

Still, disrupters are more negative about classes and teachers than are pluralists. Indeed, many disrupters scornfully single out particular instructors by name. Daniel Levine, for example, states that he "detested" Lindblom and dropped his course. "[Lindblom] was an abusive, dominating, authoritarian person who liked to humiliate students. I disapprove of graduate instructors who get their kicks by making people embarrassed." Note how Levine accuses Lindblom of improvisations (e.g., "authoritarian") that directly contradict pluralism.

Other disrupters made equally disparaging statements about faculty. Michael Leiserson, for example, remarks that Karl Deutsch, for whom he served as a teaching assistant, liked only "nice little girls" in graduate classes; that Deutsch refused to admit his mathematical errors when they were pointed out to him; and that Deutsch left it to his underlings, such as Leiserson, to correct his teaching mistakes (interview, April 27, 1998). Michael Wald, a Resister who took political science courses while in the Law School and who now teaches law at Stanford, voices a common criticism of Lasswell. "I took a course from Lasswell and [Myres] McDougal in the Law School. I actually took it twice . . . because I figured I must have missed what they were saying the first time" (interview, July 9, 1998). Wald considers Lasswell "fairly incomprehensible." Another student complains that in class Robert Dahl used "to come in and say, 'Well, what did you think of the readings?' I did not find that useful." Robert Grey believes that Frederick Watkins wrote an unflattering recommendation letter about him because of a collision between "the patrician New England as opposed to the sort of lower-middle-class Jewish style. He didn't think I was an appropriate representative of Yale University."

I recount these observations not to cause pain, but rather to describe the gap many disrupters perceived between pluralist themes and departmental improvisations. Levine's accusation that Lindblom was authoritarian; Leiserson's condemnation of Deutsch's high-handedness; Wald's assessment of Lasswell's obscurity; Dahl's lack of pedagogical leadership; Grey's charge that Watkins acted in a discriminatory fashion—these are all allegations that instructors did not improvise their own pluralist themes. Put simply, they did not practice what they preached. Pluralism opposes authoritarianism; yet, according to Levine, Lindblom was authoritarian. Pluralist leaders accept criticism; yet, according to Leiserson, Deutsch refused criticism. Pluralist political leaders communicate their ideas effectively; Lasswell, says Wald, did not. Pluralist leaders—such as Richard Lee—take policy initiatives; yet Dahl seemed passive in the classroom. Pluralism opens doors to energetic citizens; Watkins, according to Grey, did not.

Some disrupters go farther: they believe that Yale simply did not value good teaching, especially as compared with research. Penny Gill, a Resister who was part of a large contingent of comparativists at Yale in the mid- to late 1960s, is especially vocal on this point. Gill observes that Robert Dahl was the "rare" instructor who would actually talk to students in the hallways. By contrast, most faculty were "totally disinterested in any kind of teaching . . . anything that would take any time away from their non-Yale professional career" (interview, January 26, 1998). Indeed, Gill recalls that, among the junior faculty dismissed in the late 1960s were "several with reputations as being really good teachers." According to Gill, their firing sent "a message about what counted and what didn't count."

Gill also felt that Yale did not prepare her well for dissertation research. Partly in response to the shortcomings of their Yale training, she and other comparativists compiled written ruminations about their field experience. In her contribution, Gill wrote: "I found that I had to discard, temporarily, the heavy baggage of theory I carried from graduate school, until I could sort out some of the raw evidence myself and ask some of my own questions. Too many of the categories and too much of the jargon seemed heavily dependent upon the American political experience for them to be initially useful in Norway" (Martin, 1971: 4).

Disrupters also criticize specific features of teaching. One glaring deficiency, according to some former students, was the lack of mentorship. Robert Grey observes that he never became anybody's mentee, even at the dissertation stage. Although the faculty were not unfriendly, "I didn't have any sense that they welcomed graduate students coming to consult them and spend time, you know, to talk to them about anything."

In pluralist theory elected leaders broker coalitions, a task that requires them to guide citizens, interest groups, and other politicians. Yet this is precisely what, according to Grey, many faculty at Yale would not do for their students. Thus, poor mentorship represents another failed improvisation on pluralist themes.

Other disrupters objected to faculty who encouraged divisive, fragmenting competition. As we saw in the last chapter, some pluralist students remark favorably on the *absence* of competition in the classroom. Others, like Polsby, *welcomed* classroom competition, finding it intellectually stimulating. By contrast, many students who disrupted pluralism denounce classroom competitiveness at Yale.

George La Noue states that competitiveness had a destructive effect in his classes. He maintains that "in every seminar we were ranked. . . . There was a ranking system, so you were number four in a nine-person seminar, or whatever." La Noue believes that ranking students strained relationships among graduate students. So lasting was the effect of this experience that during his many years at the University of

Maryland, Baltimore, he has actively discouraged competition among students. He attributes this practice partly to his Yale classes.

Disrupters also criticize faculty members who were unwilling to discuss current political controversies, such as the Vietnam War. Jeffrey Romoff, a Resister who left Yale without a Ph.D. in 1970 and now heads the Medical Center at the University of Pittsburgh, is particularly forceful on this point. He contrasts the "artificiality" of pluralism and behavioralism at Yale with the "real-live passion about perspectives" in his undergraduate career at City College of New York. He offers an example concerning H. Bradford Westerfield. Romoff wanted to use the war in Vietnam to illuminate some ideas in the assigned reading. However, "I was advised, or the class was advised, you know, that don't do that because you have to be sufficiently distanced and objective in order to, in fact, understand exactly what happened" (interview, April 6, 1998). Romoff concluded that faculty "absolutely" prevented contemporary issues from emerging in classes.

Disrupters complained more than pluralists about the gap between contemporary politics and classroom discussion, another fact that highlights the connection between improvisations and pluralist themes. According to pluralism, the political system responds to contemporary issues. Responsiveness serves two functions: it reassures concerned citizens, and it permits the political system to cope with challenges. But to many disrupters like Romoff, classes did not improvise upon these two pluralist themes. The resulting gap inserted itself into the disruption of pluralism.

Finally, some disrupters were disappointed that Yale taught no radical theoretical alternative to pluralism. According to Bruce Berman, "The perspective that most of us operated from was an interior critique of most . . . theories. We didn't have a very powerful radical apparatus that challenged it root and branch. There wasn't Marxism there." Not until Shlomo Avineri visited Yale in 1966 did the department offer students a well-regarded scholar of Marxism. Indeed, to some students Avineri became a kind of hero. Peter Stillman, for example, attributes his skepticism about pluralism to Avineri's courses on Hegel and the young Marx.

To be sure, few other political science departments offered students much radical thought. Moreover, this criticism of Yale may be unwarranted. Certainly Sidney Tarrow took radical social movements seriously; indeed, Tarrow's scholarship reflects his opposition to pluralism. Nevertheless, perception, not fact, is what matters. From the perspective of its student critics, the department did not improvise upon the pluralist theme of tolerance. The resulting irritation helped to disrupt pluralism.

Women disrupters are especially biting about the department, more so than women pluralists. The formers' perceptions of discrimination are extremely personal and emotional. For example, not only did Barbara Feinberg, a Recuperator who was at Yale from 1959 to 1962, learn that "women were treated differently than men," but she also comments ruefully upon the pain this revelation caused her. "Nice old me didn't realize that these things [benefits] were available until after the fact, but I really felt like a second-class citizen . . . and an outsider" (interview, February 11, 1998). As she sums it up, "I was not made comfortable." For an anonymous female Rejecter who left Yale in the late 1960s, lingering guilt feelings remain. Like Feinberg, she too believes that "women were not taken as seriously as men." She adds, "[I feel] interminably guilty about not completing, since they may have thought that I proved them right" (interview, July 12, 1998).

Other women disrupters recount traumatic personal experiences at Yale. Carolyn Harmon, a Recuperator, remembers "the moment I discovered that the bright male student gets encouragement through a friendly pat on the back, but the bright woman gets a hand on her knee from the professor I most respected and hoped to work with" (personal communication, June 27, 2002). Penny Gill reports on her initial exposure to Yale, an account that, at thirty years' remove from the events, remains riveting:

> Can I tell you what happened the very first day in New Haven? A kid from Milwaukee, I had never been to an Ivy League school, I had never met anybody that I knew who had been to an Ivy League school. This was a big, big, big move. And there was an opening cocktail party or reception for new graduate students, and the department was there. And there was a reception line, and . . . I was at the end of the line, and I shook [unnamed]'s hand, and he looked me right in the eye; and he said—this is a direct quote—"What is a sweet young thing like you doing wasting all your beautiful juices in graduate school?" And that was my welcome to graduate school.

Mary Curzan also perceived gender discrimination and heard about—but did not personally experience—sexual overtures. She recalls that in several classes, one with Fred Greenstein and one with Harold Lasswell, "I would say something. They'd say, 'That's nice, Miss Hanna.' They paid no attention, and a male would say it two sentences later, and it would be a brilliant idea." Though she did not feel angry at the time (and is surprised at herself now for *not* doing so), Curzan gradually withdrew from class participation. Eventually, she concluded that she was "studying in a vacuum," a fact that perhaps limited "the depth of my involvement" in political science. Curzan eventually left academia entirely.

Some women disrupters joined the feminist movement, through which they developed a strong consciousness of gender issues. In both respects, they differed from women who incorporated pluralism. Jessica Wolf, a Rejecter, is a good example of this phenomenon. Wolf recalls being in the first consciousness-raising group at Yale; she also attended a conference in New Haven that introduced Kate Millett to Gloria Steinem. Though Wolf believes faculty considered her a serious graduate student, she remarks, "There always was an attitude that . . . men were the real ones that counted. . . . In fact, it was said of me in a letter of recommendation, intended to be positive, you know, 'she thinks like a man.' And that's an example of what I found quite offensive" (interview, May 19, 1998).

Finally, partly in opposition to pluralism at Yale, Catherine MacKinnon developed her sophisticated feminist analysis of American politics. Nevertheless, she commends Yale for "taking her seriously intellectually." But she also distances the department psychologically; she explains that the political developments of the early 1970s—not the political science department—formed the primary context of her graduate school life. Of pluralism she remarks caustically, "Women have never been any sort of the 'plurality' that pluralism understood make up American democracy" (personal communication, October 7, 1998). And though she is complimentary to Yale, she feels "less affection for those who tried to destroy me professionally and personally."

The previous chapter describes how most student pluralists forged strong social bonds with their peers. By contrast, a surprisingly large group of disrupters are critical of their fellow students and describe themselves as socially isolated at Yale.

Some disrupters objected to superficial status distinctions. For example, Nathaniel Beck recalls "a horrible seminar with a whole bunch of other graduate students, all of them looking like they came from Ivy League schools and came to class in their tweed jackets." Speaking of an earlier period, George La Noue remembers feeling intimidated by undergraduates who were "shoe" (i.e., well dressed and wealthy; for a portrait, see Trillin, 1993); by contrast, La Noue was quite "unshoe" (my term), coming from "a blue-collar family and a very small college." La Noue also resents the fact that rankings in graduate seminars created "a tight-knit cohort" of successful students from which he was excluded; partly for these reasons he created a network of friends outside of political science.

Place of residence in New Haven also influenced the formation of social bonds. Some students lived in the Hall of Graduate Studies, where they took classes together, ate evening meals together, and socialized regularly with each other. Other students lived off-campus, dispersed in housing at greater or lesser remove from the university. Although limited to two years of residency in HGS, students who lived there often forged lasting relationships with each other. Harvey Starr, a pluralist student, believes that students who lived in HGS had an easy time socially; by contrast, those who lived off-campus, he thinks, were "more adrift." Joseph Retzer, who rejected pluralism, felt that had he lived in HGS he would have been more socially comfortable at Yale. Donald Forbes, a student of comparative politics in the late 1960s, remembers HGS particularly fondly. "I . . . very much liked the community of political scientists there" (interview, February 17, 1998). Significantly, Forbes embraced pluralism at Yale; only later, after he left HGS, did he reject it, objecting to its "reigning ideas or ideologies." In 1988 Forbes published a thoughtful critique/appreciation of Dahl, in which he concluded, "Radical as some of his practical suggestions may be, Dahl accepts the overall pattern of contemporary political and academic life with surprisingly few reservations" (1988: 244).

The social situation for women students was especially difficult. For one thing, women's strained relations with faculty sometimes carried over to their relations with male graduate students. Barbara Feinberg, for example, felt that "my fellow graduate students, I didn't think were very welcoming. I don't know if it's because they saw me as competition or what it was." Mary Curzan attributes her silence in graduate classes partly to male students. As she puts it, "If I ever did speak in class, if I ever said anything critical, people looked so wounded at some level other than the intellectual level that it was . . . an awkward experience."

Certainly many women—even Disrupters—did build strong friendships with men in the graduate program. Carolyn Harmon, for one, recalls warmly the collegiality and friendship of male graduate students. However, women who disrupted pluralism did not establish as strong a set of social networks as did women who embraced pluralism.

Some female disrupters saw their fellow students as narrow and prematurely professional. Martha Logsdon is quite scathing on this subject: "I have to say that graduate students in political science were what at the time I used to call robots. . . . I mean Rostropovich played at Yale, and I couldn't find anybody in political science who would go to a concert. I thought they were sort of unidimensional." Logsdon, like La Noue, eventually developed a social life outside the department.

Philip Singerman, a Recuperator who attended Yale in the late 1960s, strongly objected to cliquishness among students. Singerman left academia and served as assistant secretary of commerce for economic development in the Clinton administration. He describes an "inner circle" of graduate students around Robert Dahl. These students took themselves "very seriously"; these "professionals" formed friendships that excluded nonprofessional students. Singerman describes his reaction to pluralism at Yale as "critical from the Left." However, Singerman has recovered pluralism; he now considers the discourse a good description of the American political process (interview, April 13, 1998).

By the late 1960s, tight social bonds between graduate students no longer automatically favored the transmission of pluralism. Indeed, for some disrupters, *rejection* of pluralism became a motive for forming social relationships. Stephen Hellman, a Recuperator, and Penny Gill, both comparativists at Yale in the late 1960s, established "our own sort of seminar of people," who "vetted each other's research projects." Hellman and Gill objected to the paucity of courses on Marxism (see also Hellman, 1978). Their informal counter-organization created bonds among the student critics of pluralism. The seminar emphasized "relating . . . ethical and moral concerns to your research," another topic these students found absent at Yale (Hellman interview, March 6, 1998).

175

For some disrupters, personality problems apparently contributed to anti-pluralist improvisations. By contrast, pluralist students almost never mention their personalities in the context of Yale. I believe the troubled introspection among some disrupters reflects the power of pluralism at Yale. Since pluralism was "normal" in the department, opposing pluralism placed the student beyond the range of psychological comfort. Alternatively, personal unhappiness may have fostered alienation both from pluralism and from other students. Either way, psychological turmoil clearly stimulated the disruption of pluralism.

The range of personal tribulations is wide. At one extreme, there are cases of diagnosed and treated psychiatric disorder. More common, however, are expressed feelings of shyness, loneliness, and alienation. In a couple of cases, homosexuality estranged disrupters from life at Yale. Significantly, these personal revelations do not appear in interviews with pluralists.

In the previous chapter I discuss how political involvement supported pluralism for some pluralist students. Given the tenor of the times, one might expect that by the late 1960s political activism would work *against* pluralism at Yale. However, this is another oversimplification in the "Same Old Story" about the 1960s. Actually, political experience during the late 1960s generated many different reactions among disrupters. Still, despite these complications, participation in politics by disrupters generally did create opposition to pluralism.

Two paired comparisons establish this point. Peter Eisinger recalls working in the primary campaign of Robert Cook, a "left-wing" insurgent Democratic candidate running for mayor against Richard Lee. Recall that Sara Stewart—a pluralist who is discussed in the previous chapter—also participated in insurgent Democratic politics in New Haven. Stewart interpreted her activity as a vindication of pluralist politics; in fact, her candidate won. By contrast, Eisinger remembers that the Lee machine "utterly demolish[ed] the insurgency." While Eisinger denies that the loss affected his thinking about pluralism, he still uses the machine's effective mobilization in his teaching. Eisinger must have found himself in something of a quandary. Machine politics pluralist style had vanquished the "left-wing" insurgency he supported. In effect, therefore, though Eisinger was personally and politically uncomfortable with pluralism, he had to admit that pluralist politics was powerful. Perhaps this incongruity and resulting discomfort stimulated Eisinger later to reconsider pluralism, as Stewart never did.

A second comparison is between an anonymous Resister and Andrew Glassberg, a pluralist. While he was at Yale in the early 1960s, the Resister worked for Community Progress, Incorporated, the local poverty agency. Like Glassberg, he was attracted to the John Lindsay mayoralty campaign in New York, though Glassberg actually *worked* for Lindsay, and the Resister did not. Glassberg interpreted the Lindsay campaign as a vindication of pluralism. By contrast, the Resister interpreted it as inconsistent with pluralism. Why the difference? Perhaps partly because the Resister, a black, was acutely sensitive to issues of civil rights, on which he faulted pluralism. And perhaps partly because, unlike Glassberg, he did not join the Lindsay campaign, an improvisation that might have overcome his resistance to pluralism. For these reasons his interest in the Lindsay campaign became an anti-pluralist expression.

Finally, even prior to the late 1960s some disrupters engaged in protests that challenged pluralism's theme of access. Belden Fields, for example, remembers that he "carried around a petition opposing" the American invasion of the Dominican Republic. In 1961, Robert Grey and James Scott took part in the Fair Play for Cuba Committee. Grey recalls, "Our fellow Yale graduate students sort of looked at us strangely"; Scott remembers that when he and Grey tried to rally the department for a *New York Times* article in support of Cuba, "The faculty mobilized against us." Thus, in these many ways, disrupters repeatedly improvised political activities that challenged pluralism.

THE PLURALISM THAT REMAINS

Despite their disaffection, the majority of disrupters retain some ties to pluralism in forms said and unsaid. To begin with, only a minority of disrupters have abandoned all traces of pluralism. Though disrupters reject most pluralist themes, they usually hang on to one or two. Moreover, they apply pluralist analysis to at least some subjects. Thus, their orientations toward pluralism fall on the same continuum as those of pluralists; disrupters simply sit at the other end of a common dimension.

The pluralist theme that remains most persuasive for disrupters is tolerance. Many disrupters praise faculty with whom they dis-

177

agreed. Two examples illustrate this phenomenon. As we have seen, Douglas Bennett strongly opposed pluralism. Indeed, Bennett's classmates still speak admiringly of his willingness to accept the legal consequences of his opposition to the Vietnam War. Yet, as mentioned earlier, Bennett deeply appreciated Dahl's tolerant response to antipluralist criticism. Bennett also lauds Robert Lane's intellectual curiosity and openness. Bennett chose a dissertation topic that was "a colossal mistake" professionally: whether "the behavioral project of observing things could actually in some serious way observe meaning." Rather than reject his risky idea, Lane encouraged him and served as an active, if not assertive, dissertation adviser. True, the dissertation put Bennett "in a little bit of professional peril." Nevertheless, it demonstrated that Yale valued intellectual curiosity, not just professional success.

Bruce Payne, a Resister, also compliments Lane's intellectual tolerance. "I was in disagreement with some deeper parts of his outlook," says Payne, "but [Lane] was tolerant, he was intelligent" (interview, June 2, 1998). In fact, like Bennett, Payne sometimes found Lane's intellectual tolerance frustrating, possibly because Lane's "almost psychiatric method" evaded pointed debate.

Faculty tolerance sometimes took active and practical forms. When the New Haven police arrested Nathaniel Beck, who was protesting the Cambodian invasion, "Bob Lane bailed us out. He said it's the best thing, this was the smartest thing you've ever done. He said when he was at Harvard he got arrested for the dining hall workers." Thus, Lane not only tolerated but also endorsed Beck's action. Today, says Beck, he finds himself in "roughly the same position" as Lane. "So whenever my students complain about I'm being too conservative, I say, 'Let me tell you about the days when . . . ,'" in effect reproducing what Lane had told him. Beck's memory of Lane's tolerance mitigates his resistance to pluralism.

While improvisations by faculty continue to tie many disrupters to pluralism, things *unsaid* also limit disruption. One potential generator of opposition that does *not* emerge often is deeply personal frustration or unhappiness. Strikingly few disrupters mention any serious emotional turmoil at Yale that goes beyond the classroom. Put differently, few disrupters connect the *entirety* of their emotional lives to pluralism or to Yale. A conspicuous exception to this common pattern, however, is Jessica Wolf. Wolf projects many of her emotional struggles onto her Yale experience. She states that graduate students at Yale wanted "empowerment," "respect" from faculty, and "to be bigger grownups." She describes her political activities, in part, as adolescent rebellion against authority, that is, "telling parents, giving parents what-for." She recounts a vivid "cameo moment" during the 1968 Democratic presidential convention. Her father, she says, was "horribly offended" by the protests; by contrast, she felt like "cheering on the student protesters." Finally, her spontaneous emotional reaction to Yale today is "anxiety."

Wolf employs a large number and variety of emotionally freighted terms to describe Yale. Had other students responded to Yale with Wolf's degree of emotional intensity, pluralism would have been more completely disrupted. Of course, comparable emotions may exist among other disrupters. However, the fact that they did not appear in the interviews leads me to doubt the emotional power of resistance to pluralism.

Also unstated is a political analysis of the department. Disrupters almost never describe pluralism as anything but a theory of the American political system. They did not visualize the department itself as a testing ground for pluralism. Nor do they "unmask" pluralist discourse as a language by which faculty jockeyed for departmental prestige, status, and power (Small, 1999). Only Jeffrey Romoff—one of the most alienated Resisters—introduces a power analysis of the department. Romoff's observations deserve extended quotation:

> Actually, the greatest lesson was to understand that there existed parallel cultures. I soon found out, particularly when we got involved in the politics of getting the comprehensive exam waived. . . . You know, it was my first experience in understanding that the Department of Political Science was a more realistic base of politics and power than their reports about politics and power in society. . . . People were vested and for real. They were invested about getting their promotion handled. They were invested about who was in charge. They loved people, they hated people, they resented people, they were in competition with people, they sought power. They did all the things human beings do in real-life political situations. Whereas when they wrote about these things, they were sterile, and compact, and dissociated.

Romoff's dissection of the department explicitly targets the gap between pluralist themes and faculty improvisations. No other disrupters developed so sophisticated a political analysis of the department.

Finally, most disrupters do not use alternative theories or discourses to attack pluralism systematically. Disrupters' criticisms generally emerge in an ad hoc haphazard fashion. Typically disrupters call attention to specific substantive mistakes in the discourse, such as pluralism's inability to capture racial conflict. The most conspicuously missing critiques involve class and ethnicity. Few disrupters apply a class analysis to pluralism; indeed, few even *use* the concept of social class. In addition, very few disrupters employ a feminist analysis; only Catherine MacKinnon recalls thinking systematically in feminist terms at Yale. More surprising is the comparative absence of C. Wright Mills's readily available elitist critique of pluralism. While elitism was pluralism's major target, it was also the most available countertheory to pluralism. Disrupters mention individual elitist works, but few advanced an elite theory themselves. Nor do we find many references to radical or conservative thought. Few mentioned, say, Progressivism, or the socialist political tradition, or the New York Intellectuals, as starting points from which to attack pluralism. Even fewer attacked pluralism from the conservative perspective of, say, a William Buckley in *God and Man at Yale* (1951). Finally, though a considerable number of disrupters discuss their encounter with Marxism in the late 1960s, few actually apply a Marxist analysis either to pluralism or to the American political system.

In short, even for disrupters pluralism defined the terrain of theoretical struggle. This fact constitutes a further—and often decisive—way by which legitimating discourses exert control over political debate (Rose, 1999; Gilens, 1999).

CREATING ALTERNATIVE THEORIES

Despite the residual ties to pluralism exhibited by most disrupters, a few develop both in the interviews and in their writing alternative political theories. In addition, some spontaneously advance the argument that pluralism is a legitimating discourse. Few actually use the term *legitimation* in relation to pluralism, but some claim that pluralism rationalized political events, stabilized the American political system, or deterred the creation of oppositional theories. In effect, these characterizations conceptualize pluralism as a legitimating discourse. They also prepare the way for alternative theories.

Of course, the sociology of knowledge has long treated some academic theories as legitimating discourses. In fact, writers have made this argument about pluralism, or about prominent structural-functionalist scholars, such as Talcott Parsons, associated with pluralism. For example, Murray Edelman writes of the 1950s and 1960s, "Pluralism certainly eased the consciences of public officials and academics, who could justify the exercise of power as a response to the concerns and enthusiasms of political, military, and industrial elites (1997: 103). David Hollinger describes functional sociologist Robert K. Merton as contributing to legitimation "in the era of World War II" and in the postwar building of a sociological profession (1996: 80). Alvin Gouldner argues that by ignoring the Great Depression, Talcott Parson's sociological theory assisted capitalism to survive (1970: 194–95). Finally, according to William Buxton, Parsons hoped that "the commitment of the social sciences to the culture of the Cold War order would have a great potential bearing on the state of public consciousness" (1985: 135). Disrupters might have relied on this literature in order to treat pluralism as a legitimating discourse.

But no disrupters refer to this literature, although more make comparable arguments than do pluralist students. For pluralists to question the disinterested, objective status of their own ideas would be uncomfortable. By contrast, it is easier for disrupters than for pluralists to develop a legitimation analysis of pluralism. Indeed, questioning pluralism no doubt impelled disrupters to wonder about why the discourse persuaded so many of their fellows. A legitimation argument is one response.

Disrupters offer many versions of this legitimation argument. Penny Gill, Ed Litt, and Erwin Hargrove provide illustrations. Hargrove, a Resister, some of whose well-known works on the presidency evaluate pluralism skeptically (e.g., Hargrove, 1974: 178), graduated from Yale in 1963. Hargrove characterizes pluralism in the 1950s as "talking about the Eisenhower presidency." As he puts it, "I think that political science reflects more ideology than people will admit. And . . . our work was really kind of articulating the political stability of the 1950s" (interview, February 20, 1998). Gill describes political development theory at Yale in the 1960s as "a response to the American victory at the end of the Second World War." She claims that her comparativist friends at Yale explicitly referred to pluralism in these terms. Finally, Ed Litt argues that some of his pluralist class-

181

mates retain an interest in legitimating the political regime. Speaking of Nelson Polsby, Litt remarks, "You know . . . if you run an institute for government at Berkeley, you need to have some faith that it's worthwhile, and it's not being subverted from Oakland with the Black Panthers, or God knows what."

Both Lewis Lipsitz and Hargrove analyze pluralism as a stabilizer of the American political system. Lipsitz observes that, because of McCarthyism, left-wing ideas had "kind of gone underground"; he feels that pluralists wanted "to duck our heads down a bit" and ignore major issues that might have caused conflict. Hargrove makes the same point more forcefully. Pluralism, he says, covered up "social fissures," at least for a while.

Finally, Hugh Heclo, an anonymous Resister, and Jeffrey Romoff argue that pluralism marginalized competing theories of American politics. The Resister states that in classes he had to read *The Civic Culture* "about eight times"; the book, he concluded, "was religious almost in its invocation," suggesting that the book was regarded as an article of faith, not reason. Hugh Heclo argues that pluralism blinded students to the Christian roots of social reform. Therefore, people have underestimated religious identity as a political force. He remarks, "That is a function, I think, of Yale education." Finally, Jeffrey Romoff describes political science at Yale as "a game of normal science" and a "referential body of knowledge." He remarks caustically that he learned "how not to have more than one or two marvelously created ideas, for which I was usually criticized."

Did disrupters believe pluralism had an impact beyond the academy? A belief that pluralism influenced American political attitudes, public policy, or politicians obviously attributes considerable power to the discourse. These attributions might impel scholars to question the desirability of pluralist power and to develop alternative theoretical perspectives. Also, because disrupters are critical of pluralism, they might well consider the broader impact of the discourse.

By contrast, pluralists are not motivated to think about the discourse's influence beyond the academy. Pluralism presented itself to students as, above all, a politically disinterested, empirically grounded, essentially scientific description of American politics. Students who incorporated pluralism therefore had little reason to consider the discourse's larger political ramifications. As a result, they would be unlikely to seek other discourses—or, indeed, to theorize broadly at all.

I examined these questions via my "$64,000 question," which asked whether pluralism was a response to political events, an autonomous academic theory, or a politically influential body of ideas. Almost half of the disrupters attributed a "shaping" power to pluralism, and only a quarter thought the discourse an autonomous academic theory. By contrast, almost half the pluralists characterized the discourse as autonomous, and fewer than a third believed that pluralism influenced American politics.

Two interviews illustrate the differences between those who attribute broad power to pluralism and those who do not. In answer to my question, Michael Kraft, a Recuperator (e.g., Kraft, 1984), remarks that political scientists exert "not very much" influence beyond the academy. He cites as an example the failure of environmental policymakers to take political scientists seriously. He concludes, "I don't think that what academics did at Yale in the sixties or late fifties had much impact on the larger society" (interview, March 13, 1998).

By contrast, Martha Logsdon characterizes pluralism as "a myth, but it's a myth that legitimates the way things are." As she tells it, "Those pluralistic ideas, whether they're coming out of Yale or not, are very comforting to an elite who feels, you know . . . I think our society teaches us we . . . need to have some democratic element to what we're doing. And it becomes, you know, you can say, 'Well, look the academics say we're a pluralist society. Everybody has a shot.'"

Kraft has concluded that pluralism did not penetrate the major channels of American political culture. Logsdon, however, believes pluralism assisted a political elite to consolidate its power. Although both Kraft and Logsdon are disrupters of pluralism, Kraft has recuperated pluralism. Logsdon, however, is a Resister and a strong critic of the discourse. Their differing views of pluralism's influence are consistent with Kraft's return to pluralism and Logsdon's continuing estrangement.

In sum, many disrupters possess ideas that seem favorable to the creation of theories opposed to pluralism. But have they done so? What have they written? And what about pluralist students? Have they produced new pluralist works? The answers to these questions are clear. Some pluralist students have written important extensions of pluralism, and some disrupters have produced major theoretical critiques of, and alternatives to, pluralism. But most have done neither.

Several pluralist students have produced major elaborations of the discourse. These extensions include Joel Aberbach's research on competing elites in pluralist democracies (Aberbach, Putnam, and Rockman, 1981); Robert Golembiewski's organization theory (e.g., 1962); Arend Lijphart's theory of consociational democracy (1975), with its emphasis on elite bargaining; Nelson Polsby's studies of American political institutions; Aaron Wildavsky's research on incremental budgeting; Fred Greenstein's studies of the presidency; Raymond Wolfinger's research on voting and ethnic politics; and, most recently, Robert Putnam's influential work on "social capital," (1993), which he characterizes as "doing the same kind of thing I would have been taught at Yale" (interview, April 24, 1998). Of these scholars only Aaron Wildavsky offered a major theoretical *alternative* to pluralism; Wildavsky in his later years advanced cultural theory, which treats subcultures as "alternative ways of life," not as pluralist interest groups (Thompson, Ellis, and Wildavsky, 1990).

By contrast, some disrupters have produced important theoretical alternatives to pluralism. Among these are Theodore Lowi, whose neo-institutionalism criticizes the pluralist state; Lance Bennett, whose research supports an elitist, rather than a pluralist, perspective; Donald Forbes, whose research on ethnic relations disputes the tolerance premise of pluralism (1997); Erwin Hargrove, with his innovative analysis of presidential leadership (1998); Catherine MacKinnon, with her feminist theory of American politics; Michael Parenti, with his Marxist analyses of American politics; and James Scott, whose blend of Gramscian neo-Marxism, elite theory, and historical sociology has strongly influenced the study of comparative politics.

In sum, important pluralists and disrupters among Yale graduate students continue to conduct a major dialogue within American political science. Pluralists adapt and revivify pluralism as a legitimating discourse; disrupters challenge pluralism with oppositional theories. Most important, the dialogue itself has its origins not in disembodied intellectual ruminations but in systematically different improvisations at Yale itself.

6

Embodying Pluralism

INTRODUCTION: EMBODYING A DISCOURSE

Inspired by Michel Foucault, some contemporary cultural scholars discuss the "inscription" of ideas on people's bodies (e.g., Bonnell and Hunt, 1999). Perhaps relishing the shock the body metaphor produces, these writers contend that ideas are not only mental phenomena but also regulators of the most intimate practices. The body becomes a battleground of competing philosophical systems, legal rules, moral norms, dominant ideologies, legitimating discourses, and oppositional beliefs. These cultural forms manifest themselves not only as the ideas we have but also as the most personal things we do, such as eating, making love, praying, or even playing games.

Though often obscure, hyperbolic, and exaggerated, these observations are insightful. In this chapter I too inquire into the "embodiment" of a discourse, namely, pluralism. Specifically, I investigate the way disrupters and pluralists embody pluralism today both in texts (their writings) and improvisations (their occupational conduct). I consider these texts and improvisations reproductions of the pluralist discourse originally encountered at Yale.

In so doing, I follow Michael Schudson (2001), who argues convincingly that politics is, among other things, a distinct "cultural practice" embodied in concrete acts such as voting, speechifying, parading, and protesting. It is through these practices that ideas and theories such as pluralism help to constitute everyday political life, in a form I have elsewhere called "mundane political culture" (Merelman, 1998).

The difference between this approach to pluralism and that of other writers on the subject is illustrated by a glance at Rogers Smith's recent analysis of political science in America. In Smith's account, by the end of the 1960s scholarly criticisms of pluralism had relegated the discourse to the sidelines, its place taken by new empirical approaches, such as rational choice and historical institutionalism. Indeed, in his concluding sections—"The Discipline Today" and "Prophesying without Honor"—the term *pluralism* does not even appear. In short, he argues that pluralism is dead (Smith, 1997).

By contrast, in my account pluralism survives, even among some who resisted pluralism as graduate students and still find it problematic today. In fact, pluralism is embodied in two ways: in contemporary texts and improvisations, and in former students' interpretations of these texts and improvisations. As mature participants within the political culture, as scholars of politics, and as self-reflective citizens, these Yale students continue to enact pluralist discourse.

I do not discount Smith's argument; of course, there is in political science a "new institutionalism," a theory of rational choice, a "constructivism," and even a resurgence of cultural analysis. These texts are now producing their own improvisations, their own embodiments. Yet this fact does not dispute my basic contention, which is that to understand a legitimating discourse, we must do more than investigate ideas; we must connect ideas to *context*. We must investigate the lived realities of actors. In so doing, it is worth remembering that bodies are simultaneously the *targets* of power and the *agents* of power. Power constrains people; at the same time, people exert power to *produce* constraints (Foucault, 1995). Bodies are simultaneously disempowered and empowered. A legitimating discourse not only restricts students but also arms them with intellectual and material resources. Constraints and resources intertwine to produce writing and action, theme and improvisation.

But how does the embodiment of a discourse transform constraint into opportunity, turn subject into actor? How do those who encountered pluralism at Yale many years ago embody the discourse today? By what means has pluralism survived? There are, I think, three answers to these questions: psychological, social-psychological, and sociological. In the case of psychology, the key mechanism is cognition; in the case of social psychology, the key mechanism is identity; and in the case of sociology, the key mechanism is Bourdieu's "habitus."

Regarding psychology, recent research yields strong evidence that political education in high school and university shapes adult political attitudes and behaviors. Niemi and Junn (1998) demonstrate that even a single course in high school civics increases students' political knowledge, comprehension, and participation. Nie, Junn, and Stehlik-Barry (1996) show that higher education raises verbal proficiency, which, in turn, stimulates political engagement, interest in politics, attentiveness to politics, and political participation. The result is what the authors call "democratic enlightenment." Nie, Junn, and Stehlik-Barry also demonstrate that higher educational levels accurately predict long-term increases in political tolerance. Thus, both high school political education and college education generally improve political cognition among adults.

If formal education has lasting effects on the general public, these effects must be especially strong for political scientists. If this observation seems obvious, this very fact makes it too important to omit. The point is simple: there is every reason to believe that the pluralism learned at Yale has continued to influence Yale students long after their departure from New Haven.

These lasting cognitive effects are supported by sustained intellectual performance through the life span. Douglas Powell (1994: chapter 4) demonstrates that such cognitive abilities as verbal inference, reasoning, and spatial relations remain comparatively stable from ages twenty-five to fifty-five. Serious cognitive declines set in only during the later years. Thus, most former graduate students at Yale still possess the cognitive abilities necessary to employ pluralism in a sophisticated fashion. Verbal memory also remains powerful into late middle life; therefore, pluralists and disrupters likely remember enough to employ pluralist discourse effectively.

Clearly students will have employed pluralism variously in their careers. Pluralists have adapted the discourse to new circumstances; disrupters have rejected, resisted, or recuperated pluralism in reaction to these same circumstances. Again, cognitive psychology helps us to understand this process. Political scientists are, after all, *experts* in political discourses. According to Tennant and Pogson (1995: 45), experts employ ideas with greater flexibility than novices. Moreover, according to Fiske, Kinder, and Larter (1983), experts, unlike novices, are able to adapt their theoretical framework to conflicting information. Therefore, it is only to be expected that Yale students will use pluralism in many different ways, thus enhancing its power through multiple improvisations and many different embodiments of the discourse.

Yet this formulation artificially separates thinking, writing, and practice; pluralism is not a set of finished texts "played out" in contemporary practices or improvisations. Rather, new improvisations alter pluralism as text. There is a dialectical relationship between text and improvisation; improvisations not only *enact* pluralism but also *create* pluralism *anew*. To understand this dialectic, I turn to Lave and Wenger's conception of "situated learning."

According to Lave and Wenger, learning occurs in communities of practice, not in isolation. Lave and Wenger studied several types of skilled practitioners, such as midwives, tailors, navy quartermasters, and butchers. They discovered that learning is "situated" in contexts that draw actors, practices, and ideas together in mutually supportive ways (as reported in Tennant, 1997: 73). Similarly, political scientists, even those who pursue nonscholarly careers, are immersed in distinctive communities of practice. In these communities, political discourses such as pluralism are daily reconstituted. For those who are scholars, "pluralism" is no longer just the discourse they learned at Yale, but also the discourse they embody in such improvisations as establishing a scholarly record, attending conferences, creating a distinctive intellectual mark, editing manuscripts, or even writing books that incorporate new forms of pluralist theory. And for non-scholars pluralism emerges as they talk to politicians, run organizations, and try to make sense of ongoing political events. These improvisations embody pluralism.

"Identity" most effectively captures the social-psychological component of this process. Identity provides personal continuity amid the flux of experience and the vicissitudes of the life course. Although identity's exact components are contested, all students of the concept agree that identity holds fragments of the individual's life cycle together. Moreover, recent longitudinal investigations, such as that of Miriam and Clark (Tennant and Pogson, 1995: 95–96), reveal stability in the way individual adults respond to important life events. These patterns are the empirical manifestations of identity.

Graduate students at Yale between 1955 and 1970 undoubtedly made pluralism part of their identities. Although pluralism probably is not the strongest aspect of their self-conception, it is part of the "tacit knowledge" (Tennant and Pogson, 1995: 60–61) that they carry with them. In short, whether they are disrupters or pluralists, pluralism has helped to make them who they are.

But there are also social forces that affect situated learning and personal identity. The social foundations of pluralist embodiment reside in what Bourdieu calls a "habitus," which he defines as "a system of shared social dispositions and cognitive structures which generates perceptions, appreciations, and actions" (1998: 270). The key word in this definition is *shared.* Yale graduates share social positions with like-minded others, who are also engaged in teaching, scholarship, political activity, and political occupations. Discourses such as pluralism are the coin of these realms, the currency by which actors exchange ideas, perform tasks, reward and punish each other, and, in the most literal sense, create society.

Former Yale students, whether practitioners or scholars, expect each other to be conversant with pluralism. In addition, practitioners share a habitus that often requires advising politicians, running organizations, and exerting influence. Performing these tasks may call upon pluralist ideas and may even produce new improvisations of pluralism. This formulation modifies Russell Jacoby's pessimistic view of intellectuals and politics. Jacoby (1987) argues that previously "independent intellectuals" have retreated to universities, thereby removing themselves from politics (but see Robbins, 1993: 173). Jacoby ignores the fact that more and more political actors are university-educated. Although these academically trained political actors are not *scholars,* they certainly exert power; moreover, their habitus forces them to use all the relevant ideas at their disposal, including pluralism (see also Barnes, 1995: 104–5). So the *indirect* power of pluralist academics may be great.

Finally, we should not doubt whether pluralism exerts enough *emotional* force to motivate continued embodiment. At Yale, pluralism became enmeshed in emerging identities, personal conflicts, and the complex emotions of confidence, rejection, and success. There is no reason to expect the emotional resonance of pluralism to disappear as people build careers, become adults, create families, and engage the political world.

This emotional connection to pluralism is social as well as individual. Pluralism, after all, is part of American political history; as Erik Erikson pointed out (1969), personal identity and transformational politics are often closely linked. Pluralism was not simply a dry set of texts and improvisations distinctive to Yale students or to American academia. Instead, as Wilfred McClay observes, "American pluralism was a 'normative concept,' a kind of golden mean between Left and Right authoritarianism—the true and only liberal antithesis to totalitarianism" (1994: 224). Pluralism opposed fascism and Soviet Marxism. Pluralism was therefore a fighting doctrine in the Cold War. Thus, personal struggles over pluralism among graduate students at Yale shaped the major political conflicts of their time. Surely this fact gives students reason to embody the discourse throughout life, even though the Cold War has ended.

To summarize: this chapter describes the way former Yale graduate students embody pluralism in texts and improvisations. Pluralism remains alive for these former students, appearing in multiple contexts of "situated learning." Also, pluralism helps them to constitute personal identity. Finally, pluralism penetrates their occupational habitus. These improvisations upon pluralism—pluralism's embodiment—keep the discourse alive.

POSITIONAL EMBODIMENTS OF PLURALISM

Positionally, pluralism is embodied when the Yale degree or attendance assists graduates to achieve valuable academic or professional jobs. Ensconced in such positions, they possess enhanced opportunity to employ pluralist discourse. However, described in this way, positional power is unduly objective. Occupying a valuable position is not the only way to embody pluralism positionally. Positional power is also *subjective*, namely *consciously attributing* career achievement to having attended Yale. This subjective conviction enters the student's habitus. It manifests itself, for example, in statements that cite Yale as partly responsible for the individual's success. In fact, such statements are themselves improvisations that diffuse Yale pluralism broadly.

In order to investigate positional embodiment, I asked my interviewees to talk about whether Yale had any effect on their job opportunities and their career achievements. I considered "position" to include both actual jobs and explicit attribution of achieved position to Yale. The conclusion I draw from this analysis is unsurprising in general, but surprising in details. The positional embodiments of Yale pluralism are broad but not deep; nor does it matter much whether a student is a pluralist or a disrupter. Positional improvisations affect pluralism's legitimating power only slightly.

Many factors favored Yale graduates in the achievement of positional power. Foremost, of course, was the academic reputation and institutional prestige of Yale itself. "In student placement during the 1960–72 period, Rochester's political science program was second only to Yale's; Yale placed 62 percent of its total placements in American Council of Education-related departments, and Rochester placed 58 percent (Amadae and de Mesquita, 1999: 280). In addition, as Thomas Bender has pointed out (1993: 56), in the early twentieth century a new form of professionalism transformed universities. Money began to flow to universities in order to finance the education of future professionals. In political science Charles Merriam of the University of Chicago provides an example of convergence between a new professional class and expanded scholarly disciplines (Karl, 1974). By the end of the Second World War, universities such as Yale were poised to benefit from the new professionalism (Bender, 1997). Moreover, the new professionalism provided many job opportunities for Yale political science graduates both within and without the academy (for sociology, see Turner and Turner, 1990: chapter 4).

Also, as Lacey and Furner indicate (1993: 52), thanks to the Cold War federal research support for the social sciences dramatically expanded. These new funds provided even more positions for Yale graduates to fill. Indeed, for much of the 1950s and 1960s Yale graduates enjoyed a seller's market for their skills. And as more academic institutions strove to become research institutions, there were many attractive jobs for Yale graduates.

Finally, alterations within the structure of political science increased positional opportunities. The academic institutionalization and professionalization of political science encouraged mutual dependence and network formation among scholars (Fuchs, 1992: 81). The new networks disseminated information about good jobs and opportunities, fundable research, and so forth. No longer were political scientists isolated seekers of truth; now they assisted each other in building careers. All these developments augmented the already impressive advantages Yale graduate students enjoyed.

As of July 1997, of the 256 students who attended Yale graduate school in political science between 1955 and 1970, twenty-seven held positions at major research universities, by which I mean universities

191

rated among the top twenty graduate political science programs as of 1995 (Ranking research, 1995: 736). These programs mainly include Ivy League universities, several branches of the University of California, a few large land grant universities in the Midwest, and a handful of universities in the South, such as the University of North Carolina and Duke. I added two major Canadian universities, York University and the University of Toronto, to this list. Thus, the vast majority of Yale graduate students have not achieved positional power in the most prestigious political science programs.

Of course, this record does not take into account the publications of Yale graduates. Nor does it count scholars who held positions at major institutions at times other than July of 1997. Nor does it make allowances for the twenty-three former students who left academia. Finally, it does not demonstrate an unusually low or high level of positional success, for I have no comparable data on the graduates of departments other than Yale. Nevertheless, if a major academic political science position is our standard, no more than 10 percent of (27 of 256) Yale graduates had "made it" in academia by 1997.

Of the graduates I interviewed (approximately 40 percent of the total who matriculated between 1955 and 1970 at Yale), I missed only three of twenty-seven who held positions at major research institutions. Were these twenty-four disproportionately pluralists? Not at all. Pluralists do outnumber disrupters at these institutions (15 to 12), but this majority is proportional to the entire population I interviewed. Clearly pluralist discourse has not enjoyed a decisive advantage positionally in major research universities. Moreover, pluralist students were no more likely than disrupters to gain positions in the very top universities. In short, there is little evidence of a pro-pluralist bias in the career trajectories of Yale graduates.

Certainly graduates stated that a Yale degree had a positive impact on their careers. However, the perceived impact was limited. For example, only a substantial minority of graduates (approximately one-third) remarked that attending Yale had helped them get their first jobs. After this initial step, however, the Yale influence diminished rapidly. Donald Forbes typifies a quite general view among the graduates: "I just felt [the Yale advantage] those first few years. Anyone who had come from Yale was at a real advantage. But then eventually it just . . . the whole atmosphere changed, and I grew away from that, and people started seeing me in . . . not so much as a graduate of a famous department of political science, but just for who I was" (interview, February 17, 1998).

In addition, very few graduates believe their relationships with other Yale students have improved their careers. Only a few attribute grants, publications, or conferences to Yale connections. Although many Yale graduates describe enduring friendships with fellow Yalies, few believe these friendships have conveyed material rewards. Thus, even in network form, Yale did not provide much positional power to its graduates.

Nor, for the most part, did pluralists enjoy advantages over disrupters in first job placements. The Yale department apparently did not favor pluralists in its recommendations, at least as perceived by graduates. This is a significant fact, for recommending pluralists over equally meritorious disrupters in the job market—though risky if Yale were perceived as discriminatory—would certainly have diffused pluralist discourse more widely.

However, there are two notable exceptions to this generalization. Michael Parenti and Michael Leiserson explicitly attribute setbacks in their careers to Yale. Indeed, they identify by name pluralist graduate students at Yale who, they believe, impeded their careers. Moreover, disrupters in general are more likely than pluralists to complain that the department did little for them in the job search. On balance, however, though Yale did secure many of its graduates good first jobs, this process provided little advantage to the long-term embodiment of pluralism.

EMBODYING PLURALISM IN SCHOLARSHIP

In Elizabeth A. Kelly's words, universities are not only where "so much of the struggle for democracy has taken place," but also "public spheres in their own right" (1995: 88). If Kelly is correct, then recent concerns about the "demise" of the public sphere are misplaced. Although most academic scholars choose not to address the lay public, they still take part in civic debate. Their teaching and research connect them to the public through their students, through the texts their students read, and through their own writings. As a result, former graduate students at Yale who have pursued an academic career are well placed to diffuse pluralism widely as a legitimating discourse.

193

Nor has disciplinary professionalization removed the motivation to propound broad theories of politics, such as pluralism. To the contrary, as Bruce Robbins points out, a professionalized university education is saturated with theory. "The original sense of 'profession' was a declaration of belief made upon entry into holy orders; to enter into membership was to announce shared theory" (1993: 34). The legitimacy of a profession rests not only upon fulfilling a publicly valuable calling, but also upon the theory that underlies the calling. Ultimately, the difference between the academic political scientist and the politician is not that the latter practices politics and the former does not, but rather that the political scientist *theorizes* about politics, whereas most politicians do not.

Obviously, legitimating discourses benefit from the support academic scholars give them. As Michael Schudson points out (1989: 64), "rhetorical force" influences whether a cultural object—such as a legitimating discourse—penetrates a political culture. Rhetorical force depends on communication; the classroom, the monograph, the textbook, the article—all communicate the rhetorical force of a discourse. And high-status communicators, such as academics, increase the rhetorical power of a discourse. Thus, academic scholarship— teaching and writing—are important means by which, rhetorically, Yale graduates can diffuse pluralism.

To investigate the embodiment of pluralism in scholarship, I naturally asked those Yale graduates in academia to reflect upon the influence, if any, of pluralism on their research and their teaching. In addition, however, I asked graduates who had *left* academic life to talk about the influence of pluralism on their work lives. Did knowledge of pluralism help Mary Curzan to understand Congress when she worked on Capitol Hill? Did pluralism assist Stanley Bach to make sense of the Library of Congress? Did pluralism shape Jeffrey Romoff's leadership of a major university hospital, or Donald Stewart's administration of the Educational Testing Service?

Such questions to nonacademics might initially seem odd. How, after all, can one realistically trace the occupational impact of academic theories learned many years ago? But to understand a legitimating discourse, we must pursue its most subtle manifestations. The question seems strange not because it is irrelevant, but because it has not been asked very often. In fact, like Moliere's M. Jourdain, who suddenly discovered he had been speaking prose all his life, some

Yale graduates suddenly discovered in their conversations with me that they had been speaking "pluralism" all their occupational lives.

I pointed out earlier how few Yale graduates present full theories of pluralism in their writings. However, some Yale graduates do conceive of their scholarship as an extension of Yale pluralism. Let us look at two important cases.

Joel Aberbach regards pluralism as a major influence on his writing. He mentions, especially, pluralism's "general theoretical approaches, and its appreciation for politics and in method" (interview, September 16, 1997). He also describes his work on political elites as "imprints of my Yale experience," citing specifically his approach to elite relationships, bargaining, multiple centers of power, and elite competition. According to Aberbach, his writing reflects Yale pluralism's "fundamental appreciation for the value that political life had in society. And I think I've retained that."

I asked Aberbach whether his 1973 book suggested that Yale pluralism had overlooked the crisis in race relations. Was the book intended to be a criticism of pluralism? Not necessarily, according to Aberbach. He points out that the book is about political trust among blacks, a subject Aberbach had tackled in his Yale dissertation. Moreover, Aberbach reminded me that the book's last chapter "put a great emphasis on . . . the need for policymakers to shape policies in a way that de-emphasized race." He traces this argument to pluralism's emphasis upon cross-cutting social cleavages. Thus, not only does Aberbach trace his writing to Yale pluralism, but he also improvises conversationally upon pluralism.

Like Aberbach, Robert Putnam also connects his work to Yale pluralism. In fact, Putnam describes three such connections. First, he adamantly argues that pluralism was reformist, as is his own work (Uchitelle, 2000). As he put it to me: "I've not looked back at the texts, but I think as a matter of the culture of the place, I think it's wrong to describe the work or the teaching of Dahl or Lane or Lindblom or any of those folks as celebratory" (interview, April 24, 1998). Later he adds that it is "not an accurate account to say that the mood of that place was scientific, detached from worries about how the system was actually operating." Thus, the reform premise ties Putnam to Yale.

Second, Putnam describes himself as engaged "nowadays not on strictly what you would call social science, but convening, and first of all doing a lot of public speaking, and secondly convening a group of community leaders from across the country . . . to contribute to a national discussion about how to reinvent civil society." Putnam believes this activity is consistent with Yale pluralism. "I don't think this is some kind of rejection of my Yale roots in 'antiseptic' social science; it seems to me I'm doing the same time that I would have been taught at Yale to do . . . that the notion of engagement is not antithetical to the Yale training I had."

Third, Putnam considers his concept of "social capital" an affirmation of Yale pluralism. "It doesn't quite say Dahl was right, although it certainly does not say Dahl was wrong. It's quite consistent with all that. It actually does say Almond and Verba were right . . . so it's not like this is a kind of a linear, you know, parental connection." In making these connections, Putnam also improvises conversationally on pluralism at Yale.

Aberbach and Putnam, however, are exceptions to the general tendency of Yale graduates to embody only *particular* aspects of pluralism. From one point of view, the fragmentation of pluralism as a comprehensive theory represents a significant decline in influence. At the same time, fragmentation has not destroyed but rather has transformed pluralism. Today, as embodied in the accounts of most Yale graduates, pluralism is a flexible, relatively uncontroversial, regularly employed body of ideas. In fact, the intellectual fragmentation of pluralism has freed the discourse from the heated debates that swirled around it in 1970. Now it circulates widely and unmarkedly through a broad range of scholarship.

One pluralist influence on scholarship is programmatic and methodological. Some Yale graduates employ pluralism as a set of ideal methods for analyzing political problems. They value pluralism's presumed logical rigor, conceptual clarity, and, above all, testability. Russell Murphy discusses this aspect of pluralism in his career: "I think [pluralism] has [been influential]. I think if you move away from pluralism per se and more towards the empirical and, i.e., the testable hypotheses, the ideal that leads to, I think that has continued to shape my own writing, scholarship, and certainly has shaped my own teaching" (interview, November 30, 1997).

Pluralism as a model method of investigation is not confined to scholars but extends also to some Yale graduates who entered public service. For example, William Bacchus has combined pluralist scholarship on American foreign policy (e.g., 1974) with a long career at the State Department. He claims that the methods of elite interviewing and participant observation that he learned from Lasswell at Yale have proved of great service. Indeed, these methods have sensitized him to the State Department's increased use of "spin." In fact, the methods he learned at Yale have transformed Bacchus's conception of the State Department.

Other Yale graduates draw on particular substantive claims of pluralism. For example, Stephen Hintz states that the pluralist theory of decision making helps "to place in context an awful lot of what I have done and thought" (interview, March 9, 1998). Hintz has been a political activist, serving in the Wisconsin City Management Association, where he consults with cities around the state. In this capacity he finds the idea of a civic culture "a theme that I could draw upon."

As we can see, no single premise of pluralism predominates among Yale graduates. Instead, they appropriate those aspects of the discourse that are most pertinent to their activities. In so doing, they extend pluralist arguments into new policy areas. Consider, for example, Herbert Alexander's remarks on his influential campaign finance research. Pluralism, he notes, argued that "any group, moneyed or not, that had a prime policy consideration could find a way to get its views heard. And, you know, I saw money in that context" (interview, September 18, 1997). Interestingly, Alexander disparages the "unidimensional kind of analysis that Common Cause does, that, just to get money, and doesn't look at the other variables, like party loyalty, like constituency interests, like personal views, principles." In fact, Alexander attacks campaign finance reformers who "don't seem to recognize that there are other factors besides money that influence the outcome of policy decisions." Because of pluralism, Alexander treats political money as but one political resource among many. Thus, pluralism not only stimulated Alexander's original research on money in politics but also restrains his enthusiasm for programmatic, rather than incremental, finance reform.

Nonacademics have also applied substantive aspects of pluralism to their work. Indeed, some political practitioners have used pluralism to facilitate career transitions. An example is Richard Norling, who believes that Barber's study of the Connecticut legislature eased his adjustment to becoming a subcommittee staff director in the House of Representatives. According to Norling: "I think [Barber] has a sense of what was really happening, and he could still analyze it. . . . But he had a sense of what really went on. . . . And so, you know, I had a little bit of a sense. Of course, the first six months you're totally green in an institution like that, where a lot of old timers know how things work. But I think that background helped prepare me to pick it up" (interview, April 8, 1998).

Finally, many Yale graduates trace their abiding research interests back to pluralism at Yale. For Joel Aberbach, it is the study of elites; for Herbert Alexander, it is the problem of political money; for Arend Lijphart, it is the investigation of consociational democracy; for Douglas Chalmers, it is the analysis of nongovernmental organizations in Latin America; for Douglas Durasoff, it is comparative politics as a power struggle; for William Flanigan, it is the history of electoral behavior; for Lance Bennett, it is political communication; for Rufus Browning, it is budgetary policy; for Belden Fields, it is the problem of majority tyranny; and so on. As this list suggests, both pluralists and disrupters frame their subjects in relation to pluralism. In so doing, they have extended pluralism into many new scholarly realms, such as political communication. Even as pluralism has fragmented, the discourse has stimulated new scholarship.

Given these facts, it is surprising how little impact pluralism has had on teaching. Only one fourth of the Yale graduates state that pluralism has played a major role in their instruction; moreover, even these few mention pluralism only in passing. Rare, indeed, is the graduate who offers a full, careful description of pluralism in his teaching, as does Leroy Rieselbach: "I teach Congress in what we now talk about as a kind of distributive model of congressional politics, pork barrels, pluralistic bargaining, and negotiations among separate power centers, and all the rest of that. And, you know, I've subsequently subjected that kind of stuff through more rigorous critiques of alternative models" (interview, April 25, 1998).

Why do so few Yale students mention the teaching of pluralism? Partly, of course, because of newer theories, which take pride of place. Also, I think, because scholarly identity is bound up primarily in writing, not teaching. But in so defining themselves, scholars undoubtedly weaken the diffusion of pluralism. Ironically, the value of professional research that so many absorbed at Yale inhibits the teaching of pluralism, the legitimating discourse they also learned at Yale.

EMBODYING PLURALISM IN CULTURAL MEMORY

As Rieselbach's concluding sentence implies, many Yale graduates no doubt insert pluralism into newer political theories. It is a temptation—regularly reinforced by conventional intellectual histories—to treat new theories as if they were separate from old. Theories become "opponents" of each other, or are "consistent" with each other. But whether opposed or consistent, theories are considered essentially *different* from each other. From this conventional standpoint, pluralism has given way to new theories, has fallen out of contemporary political science, and has lost the legitimating power it had.

But this conception of theoretical evolution ignores cultural memory, that is, the way groups of people recall and reconstruct their past (Schudson, 1992; Schwartz, 1996). Moreover, our reconstructions of the past affect the way we comprehend the present—and plan for the future. Thus, cultural memory shapes contemporary intellectual development. Cultural memory tilts contemporary theoretical choices in one direction rather than another. Thus, if academics choose new theories they believe are consistent with pluralism, then pluralism continues to indirectly help legitimate the American regime. In turn, these privileged discourses not only provide historical continuity to political science but also take on some of the legitimating functions pluralism previously performed. For the scholar, there is a clear psychological benefit in this process: the comforting sense of continuity and the conviction that political science produces cumulative knowledge. Meanwhile, the political regime benefits from the production of political discourses that do not contest its basic processes (see also Verdery, 1991: 138).

For these reasons I asked my respondents about the connections between pluralism and recent theories, such as rational choice, the new institutionalism, and postmodernism. Significantly, they excluded postmodernism, the approach of these three that most challenges the American political regime. Postmodernism, after all, has specifically attacked dominant groups and promoted the subordinate perspectives of racial minorities and women. It is significant, therefore, that respondents *include* rational choice and the new institutionalism, which are comparatively more friendly to the American regime than is postmodernism. Thus, their cultural memory indirectly defends the American political system.

199

Rational choice is presently a powerful paradigm within political science (e.g., see Bates, 1998). Although rational choice is skeptical about the state, it retains and even expands the regime's—and pluralism's—professed belief in the rationality of citizens. By contrast, postmodernism contests individual rationality and denies any referential equivalence between material reality and ideas. Thus, postmodernism and rational choice not only sharply oppose each other but also offer contrasting visions of the regime. Rational choice endorses the regime weakly; postmodernism challenges the regime (McCarthy, 1996: 102).

By and large, Yale graduates believe rational choice is consistent with pluralism—even a natural "inheritor" of pluralist ideas. This improvisation undoubtedly assists rational choice to gain ascendance in political science. To be sure, most Yale graduates do not warmly welcome rational choice. Nevertheless, by coupling pluralism to rational choice, they endorse this newer theory and also support a discourse that weakly legitimates the regime.

By contrast, Yale graduates are hostile to postmodernism. For one thing, fewer are knowledgeable about postmodernism than about rational choice; as a result, sheer ignorance becomes a mechanism of exclusion. But in addition, Yale graduates sever pluralism from postmodernism, which means that postmodernism, with its oppositional properties, becomes marginalized.

The primary argument graduates use to connect pluralism to rational choice is that the two discourses share a commitment to science. By contrast, graduates construe postmodernism as hostile to science and, therefore, to pluralism. This reasoning characterizes both pluralists and disrupters. Consider two examples.

Pluralist Donald Emmerson discusses the relationship between rational choice and pluralism in the context of the behavioral revolution: "Rational choice represents a reiteration under slightly different guise of the same impulse that drove the particularly extreme fringes of the behavioral revolution . . . the desire . . . to bring destiny . . . by the forelock, you know, kind of a forcible conquest of nature as a subjection of nature to regular laws. . . . It was called the behavioral revolution then; it's called rational choice now" (interview, July 9, 1998). For Emmerson, the search for empirical laws is a principal characteristic of political science. This search draws together the behavioral revolution—his particular interpretation of the Yale experience—and rational choice. Postmodernism has no place in this enterprise.

James Scott, a Resister, makes a similar argument. Scott sees a sharp contrast between postmodernism and rational choice. He feels "sure" that rational choice is closer than postmodernism to pluralism. Of rational choice he observes, "It's in a sense the behavioralist program carried further to a kind of deductive, formal methodology" (interview, May 15, 1998). By contrast, postmodernism repudiates "this idea that things are sort of out there like rocks, and that we're not constructing them." Indeed, Scott equates rational choice's condemnation of other theories as "unscientific, unrigorous, and so on" with Yale pluralism's "implicit contempt for . . . previous work as unscientific, methodologically sloppy."

The construction of a link between pluralism and rational choice is both a discursive improvisation and a political choice. Pluralism lends its support to a weakly legitimating political discourse—rational choice—and denies support to an oppositional political discourse, namely, postmodernism. Tying rational choice to pluralism leaves intact the calculating, self-interested, goal-maximizing individual of the liberal democratic regime. By contrast, tying postmodernism to pluralism would undermine liberal democratic faith in the calculating, self-interested, goal-maximizing individual. In this way, the cultural memory of pluralism supports the American political regime.

EMBODYING PLURALISM IN PRACTICE

Nonacademic graduates also embody pluralism in their occupations. These embodiments take three forms: in the framing of tasks, in communicating with other actors, and in making policy decisions. Many former Yale students do in fact discuss pluralism's impact in precisely these three ways.

In this section I focus mainly on twenty-three Yale graduates in public service careers. These nonacademic practitioners are an important part of pluralism's story; after all, they bring pluralism out of academia and into the world of government. When they respond to the world as pluralists, they help to create a pluralist world. When their co-workers respond positively to their pluralist improvisations, the co-workers, too, become part of pluralist discourse. Pluralism thus becomes more than a textual theory *about* American politics; it actually *becomes* American politics, all the more powerful because it is lodged in ongoing, unmarked practices, and not in the debated (and debatable) writings of scholars.

A majority of practitioners—proportionately more of pluralists than disrupters—do in fact use pluralism to frame their work. For example, I asked Arnold Kanter about his contacts with bureaucrats and policymakers in the State Department; I inquired whether these actors behaved "as if they were in a sense pluralists." He responded: "The more astute bureaucrats do. Although they would never articulate it as such. . . . They speak in terms that you would recognize as a kind of pluralist perspective. I mean the idea of having to build bureaucratic coalitions, the idea of trying to aggregate interests, and sort of forge a winning coalition in order to prevail on a policy" (interview, March 24, 1998). Because bureaucrats conform to pluralism, Kanter can navigate easily in the bureaucratic world. Thus, he embodies pluralism both in the meaning he gives his work and in the relationships he forges with policymakers.

Richard Ayres employs pluralism in an intensely emotional way. He recounts an incident that epitomizes pluralism's emotional resonance:

> Shortly after I came to Washington and I was then at ERDC [Environmental Resources Defense Council], there was a guy who was, I guess he was in the White House for a while, and then he was at DOE [Department of Energy] for a while. . . . He was always on the other side of issues that I was involved in. And at one point he sent me a copy of this book called *The Monkey Wrench Gang*. . . . This was a tale of how people finally took things into their own hands and started blowing up transmission towers in the West, and bulldozing things, and saving the environment this way. And I remember being really incensed at the guy. . . . I was mad enough to write him a letter about it and say, you know, "The thing that really makes me angry about that is it says nothing. It's a copout. It's the way you think about it if you're too lazy to actually change things. Changing things takes work, not just running around blowing things up." (Interview, October 14, 1997)

Ayres accepts the pluralist argument that real change is incremental and gradual. His comment not only frames environmental policy pluralistically but also recounts an earlier pluralist improvisation.

Ayres and Kanter are pluralists, but even disrupters sometimes frame the political environment in pluralist terms. I asked Mary Curzan to talk about whether what she learned at Yale had affected her work in Washington. She responded, "I have just lived in a political environment most of my adult life, and it's part of your conversation, it's part of the backroom stuff, you know" (interview, February 12, 1998). Curzan believes that politics in Washington conforms to pluralism's basic premises. As she puts it, "It would resemble them . . . it would resemble them." Although Curzan herself is critical of pluralism, she perceives that others in Washington adhere to pluralist theory. Interestingly, her remark sustains the very discourse she has rejected.

Framing one's work conceptually is essentially a psychological phenomenon. By contrast, actually employing pluralist language to communicate with others reproduces pluralism socially, not just in the mind. Actors who communicate with each other in pluralist terms develop a stake in the discourse; after all, pluralist ideas help hold their relationship together. Indeed, multiple acts of pluralist communication may hold together an entire occupational culture (see also Hall, 1993).

Curtis Lamb offers a good illustration of this phenomenon. Lamb describes how his architectural practice draws him into politics. I asked him whether politicians communicated with him in the language of pluralism. He replied: "I think they would have described what they were doing . . . would have been coming out of primarily an incremental, pluralist perspective . . . that there are lots of forces here, and, you know, I'm trying to balance them" (interview, March 19, 1998). Lamb also believes that pluralism has given him an appreciation of politicians. "What I felt was that I could understand these people and, by extension, kind of empathize, even if somebody was telling me that a project couldn't move forward. I could see where they were coming from. I didn't have to personalize it; I could see things . . . sort of the swirl of forces." Finally, Lamb asserts that pluralist discourse *influences* politicians. As he puts it, "Exceptions from zoning and lobbying with the alderman . . . was quite a natural activity." In short, pluralist ideas are an unacknowledged lingua franca of American politics.

Robert Lyke states that pluralism has given him a distinctive perspective on tax policy, the subject he has pursued at the Congressional Research Service. Pluralism offers tax policy a human dimension that economics lacks. Moreover, the pluralist perspective resonates with relevant congressional actors. I asked Lyke if these actors shared his pluralist assumptions, to which he replied, "I would think so. Yes, and even kind of explicitly." He continues, "Some of the sharper members and some of the sharper staff directors think about these issues very much like I think people who would go through Yale or any other public policy school. . . . Only because I think it helps them sort out the different perspectives and help them weigh things in balance" (interview, March 6, 1998).

Even disrupters have applied pluralism to do their jobs. As we have seen, Carolyn Harmon was deeply critical of pluralism during her graduate years. Yet once she arrived in Washington she observed that major policy actors behaved like pluralists. Moreover, she preferred pluralist politicians to politicians who violated pluralist norms. Notice the contrast she draws between Elliot Richardson, secretary of the Department of Health, Education, and Welfare in the Nixon administration, and Patricia Harris, who held the equivalent job for Jimmy Carter.

Harmon praises Richardson as "one of my true heroes." She continues:

> I attended his staff meetings, that is, all of the agency chiefs that reported to him monthly, or biweekly. So I saw him in action quite a bit dealing with issues of public welfare, AFDC, Head Start, Medicaid, and Medicare, you know, the range of education issues. He understood . . . could balance interests and be concerned with good management of programs in order to make them better. And when dealing with people who were not the brightest lights on the tree, managed to make his displeasure known without humiliating them. (Interview, June 3, 1998)

Richardson's ability to balance interests, forge compromises, manage programs, and mollify other politicians epitomized a leadership style that fits Richardson's pluralism, the theory Harmon learned at Yale, initially resisted, and then afterward recovered. By contrast, Patricia Harris, "a rather nasty woman," could not cope with her job. Unlike Richardson, "She did not have a grasp of what needed to be done." In short, she did not play pluralist politics effectively.

Finally, Yale graduates embody pluralism as they make policy decisions. More than half of the former Yale students who left academia for government or the nonprofit sector describe using pluralism in decision making. Still others embody pluralism in voluntary associations. Of course, the theoretical implications of these embodiments are uncertain. How many improvisations are enough to sustain a discourse? Nevertheless, the frequency of pluralism's application is suggestive; moreover, the breadth of employment is impressive.

Constance Citro describes her use of pluralist ideas as study director at the National Academy of Sciences. The NAS provides expert research to Congress and the executive branch on policy issues, such as how to measure poverty. Citro must coordinate multidisciplinary study groups of scientists who often disagree with each other; for example, statisticians and nonstatisticians have quite different approaches to the poverty problem. She must mediate and reconcile these differences. To do so, she relies on her Yale education:

> And so the work that I do as a study director is often involved with trying to apply those [Yale] principles, those lessons from how a political organization, like, say, a congressional committee, worked to trying to make these study groups work more effectively. You'll see when conflicts are coming up, see what kinds of information the group in one discipline needs to understand what the other one is [doing]. . . . Because then these academy reports, they don't always get listened to, but they get listened to more than the typical . . . (Interview, February 5, 1998)

Indeed, Citro attributes the awards she has won "to what I learned at Yale." In her remarks there are echoes of the pluralist tolerance premise, which, as Robert Wiebe points out, "shaped American political culture decisively at mid-century" (1995: 222), when Citro was coming of age.

Although Citro relies upon specific pluralist ideas about conflict and compromise, other Yale graduates draw upon pluralism as an overarching decision framework. Beginning with his work at the Connecticut League of Cities, Philip Singerman used pluralism as an "analytic approach." Though critical of pluralism at Yale, he remarks, "In retrospect my academic training was excellent. . . . It gave me perspective . . . on the day-to-day reality, and it still does" (interview, April 13, 1998). Later, as assistant secretary of commerce, Singerman recovered the pluralist approach he resisted at Yale.

Even Rejecters sometimes enact pluralism indirectly. An example is Jessica Wolf, who has pursued mental health policy in Connecticut. Although she rejects pluralism, she maintains a positive view of behavioralism. As she puts it, "I think that, to [behavioralism's] credit, the focus on doing rigorous studies . . . is a good one. I've had very high standards over the years in terms of what I do, you know, in my work. . . . It wasn't so much what we learned about politics because of the behavioral approach, but it certainly helped teach me how to think about good work" (interview, May 19, 1998). Wolf maintains that the behavioral approach "may have helped me in the course of my career."

In summary, via task framing, communication, and policymaking, many Yale graduates have embodied pluralism in their government work. Although these embodiments are unmarked and sporadic, they help form the *habitus* of political actors in the United States. In this form, they not only sustain pluralism but also buttress the American political regime.

BODILY INFIRMITIES

As a legitimating discourse, pluralism survives through diverse positional, scholarly, and practical embodiments. These embodiments take myriad forms, including, for example, research, prestigious academic status, cultural memory, and pluralist communication patterns. Nevertheless, like its aging embodiers, pluralism suffers bodily infirmities. Pluralism does not invigorate all Yale graduates; indeed, some attribute to pluralism a distinctly dark side. To comprehend the embodiment of pluralism fully, we need to investigate these bodily infirmities.

Although most disrupters embody some pluralism, they are profoundly ambivalent about this fact. This is hardly surprising. For disrupters, embodying pluralism creates an ideological dilemma, that is, a set of "contrary themes" (Billig et al., 1988: 31) in which positive and negative beliefs coexist in mutual discomfort. By contrast, pluralists have *only* positive things to say about embodying the discourse. Note, however, that outright avoidance or condemnation of pluralism is rare. On balance, therefore, pluralism's infirmities are not disabling. Pluralism may not stride with the vigor of youth, but neither is it incapacitated; it simply moves with the hesitation of increasing age.

A rare disrupter who views her Yale experience entirely negatively is Penny Gill. When I asked Gill about the influence of Yale and pluralism on her career, she responded, "Well, I always laugh and say I'll tell this story on myself. That Yale taught me how to teach. And everyone who knows me knows how I hated my time at Yale. And people say how could that possibly be. And I say every single thing Yale did, I do exactly the opposite" (interview, January 26, 1998). Gill particularly objects to Yale's elevation of research over teaching. To Gill, Yale is the Other against which she consciously rebelled.

More common among disrupters, however, is ambivalence. For Belden Fields and George La Noue, career choices and professional achievements reflect negatively on Yale. As we have seen, La Noue was drawn to the intersection of religion, law, and politics and, especially, to civil rights issues. He felt that Yale political science offered him little along these lines; he therefore turned first to the Yale Law School and then, later, to politics. As he puts it rather bitterly: "Actually, I had to do that almost to spite Yale, because there—maybe I was fortunate—but there was no one teaching constitutional law in the political science department. . . . I had to make my own way" (interview, March 9, 1998).

While La Noue developed "almost to spite Yale," Belden Fields states that Yale graduates' eventual academic status depended partly on their stance toward pluralism. When I asked Fields whether Yale graduates who became pluralists were favored in their career development, he responded immediately, "Oh, sure . . . I think if you accepted that relatively uncritically and formed research projects of that kind, and you came up and you found the circulating elites, that your career was much better than if you found a class dimension to it" (interview, January 16, 1998).

Nevertheless, Fields and La Noue are still ambivalent; they embody pluralism positively as well as negatively. Fields, for example, acknowledges heavy reliance on pluralism in his early teaching career, and La Noue acknowledges that his Yale degree opened doors to him. Thus, in Billig's dilemmatic form, the two disrupters continue to embody pluralism.

Some disrupters have developed their research and teaching in conscious opposition to Yale. For example, Bruce Payne, a Resister, became deeply interested in political ethics and in the education of policymakers. Initially, he believed that his Yale education was help-ful. However, eventually he had to pursue "another direction." As he explains, "I got deeply interested in questions of character, partly in an argument with Dave Barber, whom I'd had as a young professor at Yale, and who I thought had a really terribly attenuated notion of what character meant" (interview, June 2, 1998). Barber's "kind of four-by-four matrix view of psychological character" dissatisfied Payne; in reaction, he taught courses that avoided social science, in favor of novels, short stories, and philosophical essays.

Bruce Berman's conflict with pluralism surfaced with the last chapter of his dissertation, which, as he put it, "was veering away from Yale." "I remember Bill Foltz telling me that the concluding chapter of my thesis was very controversial. There were quite a num-ber of people upset because it was dabbling in dependency theory at the time" (interview, May 10, 1998). Subsequently, Berman turned to political culture, which he thought Yale also ignored. These devel-opments had personal repercussions; he and Joseph LaPalombara, a member of his dissertation committee, have not spoken since gradu-ate school.

But Berman and Payne also embody pluralism positively. Payne states that Charles Lindblom's writings on public policy deeply influ-enced his early teaching and research. And Berman contends that Karl Deutsch's *Nationalism and Social Communication* (1953) is "a very, very sophisticated theory" of cultural community. On balance, therefore, both Berman and Payne embody pluralism ambivalently.

Finally, some disrupters consider pluralism a flawed guide. For example, on the basis of his experience in Baltimore one Resister calls into question Lindblom's incrementalism. The problem, as he explains, is that politicians do "think incrementally, but I think in terms of political pronouncement there's a disconnect." Politicians achieve public attention, he believes, only by raising people's expecta-tions exponentially beyond incremental rewards. Political discourse is inflated, not incremental. A debilitating gap emerges between polit-ical promise and political performance, a gap that pluralism does not explain (see Hart, 1994: chapter 6).

Drawing on his experience in the Environmental Protection Agency, Joseph Retzer criticizes pluralist arguments about interest groups. Retzer agrees with pluralists that environmentalist and indus-try interest groups both have access to policymakers. However, "If you just look at the manpower from industry and environmental groups that EPA deals with, you can see that the environmentalists are stretched thin" (interview, April 10, 1998). Industry interest groups are flush with lobbyists and are always well represented at hearings; meanwhile, "The same person from the Friends of the Earth shows up at four different groups." In short, though the system provides access, its playing field is not level.

Yet Retzer praises pluralism's impact on his teaching and commends Yale for helping him secure his EPA job. The aforementioned Resister states that his Yale training served him well as an academic administrator. Thus, both men embody Yale pluralism ambivalently. Their disruption of pluralism has become a dilemma they embody day by day.

CONCLUSION: PLURALISM IN THE EMBRACE OF HISTORY

As we can see, the embodiment of pluralism assumes multiple forms. As professionals, as scholars, as teachers, and as political actors, Yale graduates embody pluralism in their careers, in decision making, in comprehending political science, and in interpreting American politics. For some, pluralism remains a trustworthy map of the political world. For others, pluralism is a valuable career asset. For still others, pluralism is an unresolved dilemma. But for virtually all, pluralism is a vital force.

This conclusion is not without irony. After all, as David Robertson reminds us, "The behavioral method that provided the epistemological foundation of pluralism was strongly anti-historical. . . . By the mid-1960s the widespread acceptance of behavioral assumptions shattered the link between history and political studies" (1994: 118). Robertson cites Dahl's 1961 article "The Behavioral Approach in Political Science" to support this claim. But now pluralism itself is part of American political history, a history that is not dead but is alive and ever-changing. Even scholars who try to turn their backs upon history do not escape but merely change the past. The irony is plain: pluralism is trapped in the very history it attempted to flee.

This observation is simply a restatement of the double-sided approach to pluralism I have pursued in this study. Pluralism consists of texts *about* politics and improvisations *of* politics. To comprehend pluralism requires that its textual and its improvisatory "faces" be comprehended and theorized together.

The principal purpose of this chapter is more modest, however. I have only described how pluralism is embodied and, therefore, continues to help legitimate the American political regime. Those who embrace pluralism embody the discourse easily and confidently. Those who have disrupted pluralism embody the discourse, albeit ambivalently. From a political standpoint, the confident application of pluralists almost certainly trumps the dilemmatic struggle of disrupters. The fragmentation and uncertainty of pluralism's opponents, coupled with the relative coherence and confidence of its adherents, keeps pluralism vital. No wonder continuity rather than disabling conflict is the norm in politics; it is easier to legitimate than to oppose a political regime.

What happens, however, when major political events challenge pluralism and the American political regime? How do Yale graduates interpret these events? And how do their interpretations affect pluralism itself? These are the questions to which I now turn.

7

Pluralism Besieged

INTRODUCTION: TROUBLE IN MIND

In his 1962 study of the "American common man," Robert Lane observed that "unless a traditional way of looking at things is regularly reinforced by the experience of living men, it will gradually be extinguished" (1962: 89). Lane's observation prefigures the basic argument of this study, namely, that pluralism—to which Lane contributed substantially—is not only a set of ideas but also a means by which "living men" and women conduct their political lives. This chapter considers one aspect of lived political experience among Yale graduate students: the confrontation between pluralism and political conflict. The question is how, by utilizing pluralism, Yale students interpret the anti–Vietnam War movement, militant black politics, and today's "identity politics" of gender, race, and religion (e.g., Goldberg, 1993; Jacobson, 1998). These phenomena have spawned violent and nonviolent protest, mass action, uncompromising interest groups, and attacks on regime institutions. To help legitimate the American political regime, pluralism must repel this "siege." Can Lane's "living men" explain these events pluralistically? Or do the events overwhelm pluralism, "extinguishing" its legitimating power?

The movements of the 1960s and contemporary identity politics have disturbed many former Yale students. Some become quite passionate as they talk about these phenomena. Robert Putnam, for example, recalls with horror the night in 1967 that Martin Luther King was assassinated. In New Haven, he says, "We could see fires from the rioting in the sky" (interview, April 24, 1998). The rioting was "politically threatening. . . . It was a different kind of politics from what we had both studied and known to be fair." He concludes, "What that glow in the sky on that evening of the Martin Luther

211

King assassination conveyed was a sense that there was something happening in American politics that was not encompassed by the conceptual framework that we were all working with."

Almost as palpable is an anonymous ex-student's anger and anxiety about the contemporary Christian Right: "The Religious Right in Iowa has largely taken over one party and is foisting its views on the entire society because the next generation does not involve itself in political participation" (interview, March 31, 1998). She states firmly that the Christian Right is "inconsistent" with pluralism.

But neither Putnam nor this ex-student is a disrupter. Instead, both defend pluralism from these troubling events. In turn, their statements actually *reproduce* pluralist discourse. Other former students, however, cannot reproduce pluralism successfully to explain these phenomena. These latter Yale scholars—to use Robert Lane's term—"extinguish" pluralism (1962: 89).

Pierre Bourdieu asserts that "The question of the legitimacy of the state, and of the order it institutes, does not arise except in crisis situations" (1999: 70). But not all crises erode legitimacy. Instead, legitimating discourses—such as pluralism—may capture and disarm the crisis. The theoretical question, therefore, is how to conceptualize the discursive confrontation between pluralism and the conflicts I asked my informants to discuss. How should we think about this confrontation?

Essentially a legitimating discourse is an interpretive framework that people impose upon the stream of political events. During normal political times, the framework works so smoothly that individuals are rarely even conscious that they are constructing a particular version of the world. During these times the discourse is transparent and invisible; the interpretive framework is "common sense." The world is untroubled.

However, serious political conflicts subject a legitimating discourse to stress. Suddenly the framework's categories, its central actors, its basic explanations, its predictions, no longer seem obvious. Now users of the discourse must improvise upon it consciously and imaginatively. If they succeed in doing so, not only will the discourse survive, but it will also help subdue the conflicts. Successful improvisations "normalize" conflicts; gradually, challenges lose their earlier menace. However, when improvisations exceed the capacity of a legitimating discourse, not only will the discourse collapse, but the legitimacy of the political system will also suffer.

In order to conceptualize how actors use a discourse to confront conflict, I propose the idea of narrative. As actors improvise a discourse, they compose a narrative, which is nothing more than a convincing story about the troubling events (e.g., Parish, 1996; Brass, 1997).

A narrative is related to the more familiar concept of "schema." A schema, according to Fiske and Taylor (1991: 98), is "a cognitive structure that represents knowledge about a concept or type of stimulus, including its attributes and the relations among those attributes." The schema concept appears often in political psychology and has been helpful in understanding, among other topics, audience reactions to televised news (Iyengar, 1991) and to female political candidates (Hitchon and Chang, 1995).

Why do I prefer narratives to schemas (see also Reeher, 1996: 30–35)? The reason is simple: schemas are only the building blocks of narratives. By themselves, schemas lack the dynamic, "story" qualities that people apply to politics. A schema is pre-existing, settled "knowledge" about familiar situations. By contrast, I asked my respondents to discuss political conflicts that arguably challenge pre-existing knowledge. Therefore, my respondents had to build narratives on the spot, with more or less help from schemas. For example, although Putnam possesses a schema for blacks and protesters, he must use this schema to make up a *story* about the relationship between black protest and pluralism. This story, not its schematic elements, constitutes the politically significant performance of a discourse.

I believe there are two "grand narratives," or stories, that former graduate students at Yale have made up about the Vietnam War, violent black protest, and contemporary identity politics. The first narrative is scientific; that is, it employs rhetorical devices typically found in scientific literature and practice. By and large, those who create these scientific narratives are pluralists; indeed, one reason people remain pluralists is because, for them, scientific narratives work effectively.

A second grand narrative is fictionlike. Unlike *real* fiction, fiction*like* narratives are stories that use fictional devices to analyze actual events. The fictionlike narrative is not necessarily less true or false than the scientific narrative; rather, it simply employs different rhetorical styles and devices. Former Yale students invent fictionlike narratives when they believe that political conflict overwhelms pluralism. Because they can no longer improvise within the accepted confines of pluralist discourse, they invent new stories and new themes. To do so, they adopt rhetorical devices characteristic of—and best illustrated by—fiction.

For the most part, disrupters invent fictionlike narratives. Disrupters have concluded that certain political events overcome pluralism; therefore, disrupters are literally thrown back on their own literary and political devices. Fictionlike narratives appear when established discourses—including both pluralism and its ally, science—fail. Then there is leeway and motivation for students to construct imaginative, if conjectural, fictionlike narratives.

The scientific narrative and the fictionlike narrative have different political implications. The scientific narrative often conceals the most threatening aspects of political conflict; as a result, though pluralist discourse survives, the conflicts themselves may not vanish. By contrast, fictionlike narratives are highly idiosyncratic. As a result, they produce little political unity among their users. Fictionlike narratives therefore cannot overthrow science or pluralism. I discuss the consequences of this fact at the end of the chapter.

CONSTRUCTING A SCIENTIFIC NARRATIVE
OF PLURALISM

An important preliminary procedure scientists undertake is to isolate a phenomenon for study. For example, microbiologists extract samples or assays of biological material for laboratory analysis. To do so, they separate these materials from their natural origins (Latour and Woolgar, 1986: 59 ff.). The creation of an assay—an isolated, "pure" sample—involves "distancing," by which I mean extracting an object from its everyday context and subjecting it to special treatment prior to detailed examination. Distancing protects the phenomenon from uncontrolled, contaminating, and possibly dangerous contact with other phenomena. An analogous type of distancing occurs when political scientists transform real political conflicts into objects of scientific study. In so doing, the political scientist also insulates the theoretical discourse—in this case pluralism—that guides the study. Distancing objectifies the subjectively uncomfortable experience of political conflict and in the process defends pluralism against attack.

Many Yale students distance real political conflicts from pluralism. Indeed, some explicitly introduce the concept of distancing as scientific reasoning about pluralism. One way they do so is to define political conflicts as purely *personal* experiences that do not compromise pluralism. Conceptualizing threatening events as "only" uncomfortable personally reduces the *political* threat to pluralist theory.

For example, William Ascher distances the Vietnam War from pluralism. Ascher responds to my question about the impact of racial and Vietnam protests in New Haven by observing:

> We were pretty insulated from what was going on, certainly in New Haven, and we were all going to be scientists. And I think it was very observational in orientation, rather than really challenging or revolutionary. . . . I think that we were growing more skeptical of pluralism as it was practiced in the U.S. But that was more on the level of personal politics than on the level of theory in my mind. (Interview, May 20, 1998)

Notice how Ascher's conception of "personal politics" distances pluralism from the Vietnam War protests, even as it says nothing about his own view of Vietnam.

Harvey Starr provides another example of distancing. Starr observes that Yale taught him above all else to be a "social scientist," not a policymaker. Social science also distanced him from American politics. As a result, the 1960s only "affected the way I thought about American politics, but not about the way I thought about *studying* American politics" (interview, June 9, 1998; emphasis added). Thus, Starr distances pluralism—conceived as the *study* of American politics—from his beliefs about the *substance* of American politics. As regards contemporary identity politics, Starr performs another kind of distancing. In this case, he refers directly to pluralism, not to social science. Today, he admits, pluralism *is* being challenged. Still, pluralism remains useful as a "broad way of coming at politics" and therefore is "not bad." Here Starr expands and blurs pluralism, distancing it from the specifics of identity politics. From this sufficiently distant perspective, identity politics does not necessitate the abandonment of pluralist theory.

Distancing often distinguishes between the general and the particular. In this form, pluralism serves as the general argument; particular political conflicts are only individual cases. As science, pluralism concentrates on the former; therefore, specific conflicts cannot overcome the discourse. Willard Witte, who spent one year at Yale before turning to economics, practices this form of distancing. As he puts it: "If you are trying to look for fundamental foundations of behavior, you intentionally focus away from specific idiosyncratic kinds of influences. . . . because you are focusing upon general principles, you don't want to draw your conclusions from specific instances" (interview, May 11, 1998).

Although Witte's distinction between the fundamental and the specific maintains pluralism, it is also problematic. As Thomas Kuhn's (1962) discussion of scientific paradigms makes clear, to label specific cases "idiosyncratic" is to remove beforehand any capacity they might have to dispute a discourse. In fairness, Witte perceives tension between the political conflicts I mentioned and pluralist theory. In fact, he comments wistfully that, "In some ways that lack of connection with real-world events is probably one of the things I would've liked to have seen *more* of" (emphasis added). Witte actually wants *more* distance between pluralism and the real world, not less.

It should be said that treating pluralism as "general principles" uncompromised by specific conflicts is not true to behavioralism—the research method associated with pluralism. The behavioral revolution intentionally moved political science away from legal abstractions, institutional blueprints, and moral norms. It urged the study of "political behavior as such . . . what people did and actually undertook" (Farr, 1995: 202). The behavioral approach was radically empiricist. It rested upon observable and verifiable events, not formulas or principles. Ultimately, a behavioral theory must explain real phenomena. To exempt pluralism from specific political conflicts is to violate the scientific framework upon which pluralism depended.

Fully one-fourth of the pluralist graduate students practiced one or another form of distancing. By contrast, tiny percentages of disrupters engaged in distancing. Most disrupters concluded that pluralism could not survive certain political conflicts. To the contrary, these conflicts overwhelmed pluralism.

Distancing fences off a particular discursive space within which science is to proceed undisturbed by troubling phenomena. Indeed,

216

this is precisely the mission of a scientific laboratory (Latour, 1999: chapter 2). At the extreme, distancing takes on physical manifestations in defense of pluralism. A case in point is Stanley Bach's vivid recollection of one Yale political scientist who distanced his classroom from Martin Luther King Jr.'s assassination:

> I was in my room in HGS [Hall of Graduate Studies], and I heard about [the assassination]. . . . I just couldn't sit there by myself. And I remember walking over to the classroom part of HGS and, um, interrupting a seminar, thinking everyone would really want to hear this news, and everything would come to a halt. I forget who it was or what the seminar was about, but the professor couldn't understand why I had interrupted him and couldn't understand what could possibly justify interrupting a political science seminar. (Interview, September 29, 1997)

Some pluralists use the rhetorical device of *moderation* to protect pluralism from contemporary identity politics. I asked Richard Norling, who gravitated from Yale graduate school to congressional aide to software designer and finally to candidate for county office in Maryland, about the possible challenge identity politics posed for pluralism. Norling contrasts pluralism's moderation with the moral extremism of identity politics. He then uses this contrast to suggest the limitations of the Christian Right. Ultimately, he concludes that a moderate politics—exemplified by pluralism—remains an appropriate stance: "New movements sometimes get a moral fervor about them, which helps them gain ascendancy, at least part way. . . . One other thing that has happened to the Religious Right is that the moral fervor is so strong it actually turns some people off and it keeps them from getting to a majority" (interview, April 8, 1998).

Although Norling does not actually mention pluralism, his remarks are a response to my question about identity politics and pluralism. Implicitly, therefore, he asserts that pluralism is a moderate alternative to the Christian Right. He then proceeds to moralize about *moderation,* giving it—and pluralism—the normative edge over the Christian Right. For example, he characterizes the "40 percent of independents" as "decent people," an appellation he denies to the Christian Right. If "decent people" perceive too much "moral fervor," they "sort of step back." In other words, being moderate, independent, and stepping back—the pluralist response—becomes the "decent" thing to do. Thus, what Norling begins as scientific distancing via moderation metamorphoses into moral evaluation, both of which protect pluralism.

The distancing language of moderation need not be *explicitly* normative. Consider, for example, Curtis Lamb's analysis of the 1960s. According to Lamb, who characterizes himself as "very involved" in Vietnam War protests, domestic turmoil "just showed how kind of off center things could get at the collective level . . . how off center they could get within this country" (interview March 19, 1998). The phrase "off center" implies a departure from moderate, centrist, pluralist equilibrium. The pluralist system failed to sustain this equilibrium; therefore, protests emerged. But Lamb's comment is not purely descriptive, for he believes the protests were intended to *return* politics to the pluralist center. Otherwise, he says, politicians would be in a position to "destroy the world." Lamb's explanation justifies the protests, therefore, as an attempt to move the system back to the pluralist center and prevent further "off-center" politics. For Lamb, the protests did not *repudiate* pluralism; in fact, the protests attempted to *save* it.

In the natural sciences, distancing requires the use of specialized equipment, not just the naked eye. Latour and Woolgar call this the process of "materialization" (1986: 238). Thus, a biologist first places a bacterium on a slide and then uses a microscope to examine the slide. By analogy, a political scientist first distances identity politics and then uses a theory to examine it. The question I posed, of course, is whether pluralism is the best instrument for the analysis. Just as only certain microscopes allow the biologist to observe the bacterium clearly, so perhaps only certain political discourses truly illuminate identity politics. Perhaps pluralism is the wrong microscope through which to observe identity politics. For the most part, however, pluralist former students denied this possibility. For them, pluralist discourse was an appropriate microscope. How did they come to this conclusion?

Partly, they practice "differentiation," by which I mean they used the pluralist instrument for very few tasks. The former student limits pluralism to only those political phenomena the discourse illuminates, avoiding the phenomena it misses. The result is a workable, if limited, theory.

For example, Donald Blake—like Willard Witte—distinguishes

between pluralism as a general theory and pluralism as an explanation of particular events. Pluralism doesn't apply to individual events; therefore, although New Haven erupted in race riots on the day Blake arrived in the city, this event did not threaten his belief in pluralism. True, the riots affected his thinking about pluralism "a little bit." But he improvises a form of differentiation. "But I don't recall . . . any kind of negative transference to the sort of research that had been done in a particular area. . . . It was, you know, an impact more on my personal day-to-day life, but not my intellectual life" (interview, January 13, 1998). For Blake, pluralism is an instrument that only applies to "intellectual life," not personal experiences. Therefore, specific political experiences cannot overturn pluralist discourse.

Where Blake *narrows* pluralism, William Ascher *broadens* it. To Ascher, pluralism was a *telescope,* not a microscope. Pluralism applied to an entire political system, not particular conflicts. As he puts it, "The question is, is there something rotten with the situation that we're dealing with such difficult issues that we're pitting citizens against one another, or is there something fundamentally wrong with this system per se? And I don't think I ever had that latter view." For Ascher, pluralism effectively handles broad "system" questions; therefore, it did not need to be abandoned.

Leroy Rieselbach develops an epistemological version of differentiation. Rieselbach differentiates between predictive theory and explanatory theory. True, pluralism did not predict protest in the 1960s, but its purpose is to *explain,* not to predict. As he puts it, "Our notion was that you had to try to be explanatory. That [theory] is the explanation and prediction—the latter being quite difficult, the emphasis tended to fall on the former, after-the-fact explanation of empirical events" (interview, April 25, 1998). In short, because pluralism is only an explanatory instrument, the unpredicted emergence of protest does "not really" threaten the discourse.

Another form of differentiation shrinks the territorial scope of pluralism. For example, Laurel Files argues that contemporary identity politics is no more dangerous to pluralism than were the unthreatening politics of the 1960s. Files believes that identity politics is simply an intensification of "Middle America" politics. She then proceeds to differentiate territorially; pluralism may have been "espoused there in [New Haven], but that doesn't mean that even at the time it was reflecting what was real for 'Middle America'" (interview,

February 25, 1998). Thus, pluralism extends only to selected regions; in this form, Files retains her support for pluralist analysis today, albeit in a limited form.

Differentiation draws lines between pluralism and specific political conflicts, but it pays little attention to the several parts of pluralism. A related improvisation *reduces* pluralism to specific substantive claims, selects the one claim that seems to work, and then concludes that this claim salvages the entire theory. Where differentiation does not peer into pluralism's interior, reduction focuses on specific pluralist assertions. Where differentiation employs a single, all-purpose low-resolution pluralist "microscope," reduction employs several high-resolution pluralist instruments. Let me provide two examples of reduction.

In his response Arthur Goldberg reduces pluralism to leadership. Goldberg observes that "the kind of insights that you got out of both Yale and Rochester" helps us understand political leadership. Pluralism describes two types of leaders. "There is one sort of person who gets a lot of gratification . . . out of confrontation, out of public display, out of in-your-face kind of exercises" (interview, February 25, 1998). These protest leaders are "tremendously helpful in getting certain issues on the agenda." However, "Those people generally don't make it into the policymaking arena because those are not tactics that work well with people who have to compromise, negotiate, and live with the policy they make." Hence, protest leaders give way to policymakers. Goldberg explains that this theory of leadership is "part of the kind of stuff we learned." For Goldberg, then, arguments about leadership protect pluralism from political conflict.

Arend Lijphart reduces pluralism to its arguments about competing political elites. As he summarizes his current thinking about pluralism:

> Pluralism . . . is a valid, but partial, explanation of how American politics works. . . . It was an antidote [for elite theory], but there's obviously a great deal of elite control that can exist kind of side by side with pluralism. . . . Pluralism says there is not one governing elite; what you have are lots of competing elites. . . . The original pluralists also said that these competing elites do not compete on an equal basis . . . plus there are groups that are underrepresented or unrepresented, and so pluralism is certainly not an ideal way of running a democracy. (Interview, June 12, 1998)

For Lijphart, pluralism does not rule out protest politics. Competing but unequal elites may generate political alienation and social protest. Nor do multiple elites assure equality to even fully mobilized protest groups. Pluralist democracy is real, but limited. Pluralist theory remains valid, but reduced in scope.

The core of any scientific narrative, of course, is explanation or causal inference (King, Keohane, and Verba, 1994). Distancing, differentiation, and reduction are merely steps toward causal explanation. The narrative test of pluralism, therefore, is how well it explains the conflicts of the 1960s and contemporary identity politics. Those pluralists who explain these threatening phenomena causally develop what Barry Barnes calls a "realist strategy" of science. First, they accept only empirical reality and then insert "a body of knowledge"— in this case pluralism—that is "kept in being as an all-embracing, irrefutable sense-making system capable of making out any and all future events or observations as routine and unsurprising" (1995: 115). Though pluralists do *not* claim the discourse is irrefutable, they do adopt a realist strategy, and they do routinize challenging events. Let me provide some examples of this causal narrative.

Many pluralist respondents merely extend specific elements of pluralism to cover identity politics. For example, Robert Axelrod observes that pluralism always focused on ethnicity and leadership; therefore, "I don't see it as such a big leap to have considered the implications for, say, racial identities, and . . . do you look to Martin Luther King or Louis Farrakhan as your leaders" (interview, February 3, 1998). Racial identities are just like any other ethnic identities, and, of course, ethnic groups choose different kinds of leaders. Therefore, so-called radical black politics fits easily within a pluralist framework of explanation.

Charles McCall offers a more complex causal explanation as he considers the Christian Right and black identity politics. The Christian Right poses no problem for pluralism: "This is again the notion of seeing resources which they can mobilize and change public policy in the way they favor, and finding a couple of charismatic people to entrepreneurially put this together" (interview, March 31, 1998). Besides "fundamentalist Christians are not united in any real way politically." Fundamentalist Christians are a typical pluralist interest group struggling to hold itself together politically.

Black identity, however, is a more serious challenge to pluralism;

McCall admits that "the cross-cutting cleavages" aspect of pluralism does not apply to race. Black identity is the distinctive outgrowth of economic discrimination and a "kind of social tyranny which forces people to spend most all of their social lives identifying with a single group." McCall's argument implies that blacks do not choose identity politics; indeed, if economic and social circumstances were different they would eschew identity politics and behave in a pluralistic fashion. Thus, although pluralism doesn't actually *explain* black identity, pluralism remains the *normal* and *preferred* course of action for all social groups. Hence, the explanatory power of pluralism remains intact.

As McCall's response illustrates, pluralist explanations are most successful when they combine various elements of the discourse, such as cross-cutting cleavages, political resources, and entrepreneurial leadership. A particularly good example appears in William Liddle's response to my question about whether affirmative action or majority/minority electoral districts conflict with pluralism's "rules of the political game." Liddle sees no such challenge; instead, these "are the tensions of a democratic society." True, these policies create conflict, but pluralist debate will triumph. "The answer to that is the pragmatic answer that you work them out on the margins. You have a debate between Lani Guinier and Bill Clinton. . . . Sometimes she wins and sometimes she loses" (interview, May 20, 1998). In short, such pluralist processes as debate, incremental gains, bargaining, and trade-offs ultimately moderate identity politics.

Sometimes, however, pluralists violate Barnes's "realist strategy." For example, David Seidman, who was at Yale from 1966 to 1970 before entering the Justice Department, essentially defines identity politics out of existence. Seidman is no realist; to him, identity politics is not what it appears to be at all. Identity groups only *seem* to advance "nonnegotiable" demands that run contrary to pluralism. However, "One can always view that as a tactic. Most of these things do at some level get compromised" (interview, April 21, 1998). In short, identity politics is just a cover for pluralism (e.g., Katznelson, 1996: 174–75).

Finally, not all explanatory narratives meet elementary canons of logic or King, Keohane, and Verba's standard of falsifiability (1994, 100–105). For example, one ex-student takes logically inconsistent positions on identity politics. She argues that the Christian Right, though highly ideological, is consistent with pluralism. By contrast, multiculturalism and feminism harm the Democratic Party, a pluralist institution. Although the party has survived as "a pluralist hodgepodge of coalitions," multiculturalism and feminism have hurt the Democratic Party (interview, April 4, 1998). The ex-student is inconsistent; she argues that identity politics on the Right is compatible with pluralism, but that Left identity politics violates pluralism. Apparently, identity politics has contradictory effects. Perhaps she reached this logically shaky conclusion because she so disliked the theoretical abstractness of pluralism at Yale. For her, practice, not theory, matters; in any case, pluralist politics survive, which for her is the important thing. In short, she pragmatically constructs an explanatory narrative that, no matter how logically suspect, does protect pluralism.

While scientific narratives dominate defenses of pluralism, other narratives also protect the discourse. In fact, some arguments are emotive, rather than scientifically "rational." For example, a few respondents argued that pluralism helped them deal with the pain they felt about race or the Vietnam War. Others "pathologized" identity politics, characterizing it as an unhealthy deviation from "normal" American politics. These latter pluralists resemble those ordinary Americans for whom, in Robert Wiebe's words, "Flag-burners and draft-dodgers, feminists and homosexuals, armed rioters for Black Power and armed militants for Indian power, whole armies of the other seemed to rise just behind the hippies in the late 1960s and early 1970s" (1995: 230). Lastly, a few pluralists circumvented, avoided, or ignored my questions about identity politics. (I choose, no doubt for my own protective reasons, to regard these nonresponses as forms of psychological denial, rather than judgments on the questions themselves.)

What are the political consequences of a scientific defense of pluralism? Does the scientific narrative strengthen the political regime? I think the scientific narrative presents both advantages and disadvantages politically.

One advantage of the scientific narrative is that it yields compact and comprehensible arguments, as illustrated in the cases just examined. Moreover, it focuses on empirical *evidence* about identity politics and the events of the 1960s. In addition, the scientific narrative is flexible; its most imaginative practitioners construct ingenious arguments in defense of both pluralism and the political regime. Most important, any form of *scientific* legitimation buttresses a political regime. After all, despite challenges from religion, science remains the most highly prized form of contemporary knowledge; therefore, using science to defend pluralism strengthens the American political regime.

Nevertheless, the scientific narrative is not *powerfully* legitimating. Paradoxically, the very discursive techniques—distancing, differentiation, reduction, and causal explanation—that compose the scientific narrative may induce political quiescence rather than mobilization. Certainly few pluralists seem deeply aroused or engaged by the political challenges I asked them to discuss. Having concluded that science supports both pluralism and the political regime, most assume that the political system is safe. Therefore, they adopt a stance of political disengagement. In short, the detachment that is a prerequisite to the scientific narrative spills over to political action. Just as pluralists think of themselves as detached observers of politics, so also are they coolly calculating political actors. Theirs is not the politics of passion in defense of the American regime.

CONSTRUCTING A FICTIONLIKE
ANTI-PLURALIST NARRATIVE

Disrupters see the 1960s and identity politics as more powerful challenges to pluralism than do pluralists. Therefore, disrupters find the scientific narrative inadequate to the task of explanation. As a result, disrupters create an alternative narrative, one that is reminiscent of fictional genres, not of scientific explanations. "'Genre fiction' refers to a range of fiction identified as non-mainstream . . . subdivided into the marketing categories of science fiction, fantasy, romance, horror, western, detective thriller, and so on" (Talbort, 1995: 38). The genre narratives disrupters construct contain such typical fictional devices as dramatic conflict, personalization, evocation of emotion, and character development. However, unlike most works of fiction, these fictionlike narratives do not have neat resolutions. Instead, the struggle between pluralism and severe political conflict persists. As a result, fictionlike narratives are not as decisive as scientific narratives. Therefore, rhetorical defenses of pluralism carry more political power than do rhetorical challenges to pluralism.

Constructing a fictionlike narrative requires that disrupters first discredit the scientific defense of pluralism. This is less difficult than it may seem; according to William Gass, "For most people, fiction is history; fiction is history without tables, graphs, dates, imports, edicts, evidence, laws; history without hiatus—intelligible, simple, smooth" (1970: 30). Many disrupters reject the distance pluralists maintain between pluralism and severe political conflict. For disrupters, scientific detachment gives way to personal engagement. Few disrupters employ distancing at all, and of these few, most reject the insulation of pluralist discourse from political challenge.

Instead, many disrupters argue that pluralism should make no distinction between theory and practice. In place of distancing, disrupters want pluralism to adopt *praxis,* a fusion of theory and practice (on praxis, see Barrett, 1991: 38). Philip Singerman provides a vivid illustration of this phenomenon. He recalls with disdain a statement made by one of his teachers, Fred Greenstein, about the Vietnam War: "Greenstein said, 'I am not a hawk, I am not a dove, I'm an owl.' One of my friends said that means he sleeps during the day. And I thought that was very insightful" (interview, April 13, 1998). Although Singerman notes that LaPalombara, Dahl, and Lane were "supporters" of anti-war students, he is not placated. As he puts it, "It didn't translate directly into their work. And, you know, we would want them to, you know, we wanted our Godlike teachers to be leaders on this important political issue, and they were unable to." In short, pluralists refused to abandon their scientific detachment in favor of praxis.

After rejecting distancing, disrupters begin to develop fictionlike narratives of engagement. Two such narratives draw upon the detective story, which identifies criminals, and satire, which ridicules vice. Both share a concern with *exposure* and *revelation,* that is, discovering the truth behind pretense. Masters of satire, such as Evelyn Waugh (*Scoop, A Handful of Dust, Decline and Fall*), and the detective story, such as Graham Greene (*England Made Me, The Ministry of Fear*), reveal the disreputable reality behind the veil of respectability. They also argue that power—whether in the form of bourgeois manners (Waugh) or conspiracies (Greene)—crushes the individual. Max Weber's reflections on intellectuals in politics resemble the arguments of satirists and detective novelists. Weber argued that intellectuals were not Greenstein's disinterested "owls" who merely observed political events from afar. Like others, intellectuals protected and promoted their group interests as "carriers of . . . 'knowledge'" (Sadri, 1992: 88).

Some disrupters, such as Jeffrey Romoff, construct narratives of exposure (not unlike those of Waugh or Greene) to attack pluralism. Indeed, Romoff tries to expose all political science, not just pluralism. He argues that political science simply follows trends in popular culture. For example, to Romoff, rational choice is "very reflective of Jerry Springer. . . . I don't consider the academic world legitimating. I consider the academic world as necessarily *needing* legitimation, since it is made up of the same people that watch Jerry Springer" (interview, April 6, 1998). Academics are really just like other people. But, unlike other people, they pretend to be experts or intellectuals. Political discourses, such as rational choice and pluralism, help maintain this necessary fiction. Thus, Romoff exposes academic discourse as a quest for power, not for truth.

Theodore Lowi also creates a narrative of exposure. He claims that pluralism was an effort to elevate political science professionally in response to the New Deal and the growth of the American state (see also Lowi, 1992). He observes that, "All theories in social science are ideologies. That doesn't mean they don't have a scientific base to them" (interview, March 23, 1998). Referring specifically to pluralism, he argues that V. O. Key, David Truman, and Robert Dahl had just "come out [of the war], and they had to make sense of all that stuff in a way that's both comparable with what they experienced, and that is realistic. Political science had become a realist profession, whereas before it had been a reformist and a political theory, traditionalist, and reformist kind of thing." As a new "realist profession," political science had to accommodate the social changes wrought by the war. Pluralism achieved accommodation by legitimizing not only the political regime but also professional political science.

Lowi also composes an exposure narrative about pluralism and identity politics. Identity politics does not "disprove" pluralism; after all, pluralism is an ideology, not scientific theory. Therefore, it cannot really be disproved. Of course, identity politics is also an ideology. "Just like pluralism was an adjustment to the reality of the modern state . . . identity politics is to me a psychologizing and a different form of normalizing the pluralist ideology. . . . I think identity politics is a way of saying, 'Stop the world. We want to get on.'" Thus, pluralism and identity politics are both ripe for narratives of exposure.

Though they are powerful fictional genres, satire and detective stories typically eschew strong emotion. Satire appeals to the head, not the heart, of the reader. And Greene's spy stories are deliberately impersonal; his characters exist in what critics have dubbed "Greeneland," a bleak, emotionally barren no-man's land of anti-heroes. Yet disrupters have experienced personal anguish in the confrontation between political challenges and pluralism. Satire and detective narratives cannot assuage this pain; they are too "cool," deliberate, "objective," and ironic. Thus, some disrupters turn to other fictional genres.

There are several literary models for narrating emotional turbulence. In the hands of a skilled writer such as Sigmund Freud, even the psychological case history becomes emotionally gripping. Freud's notes on such patients as "Little Hans" and "The Wolfman" are model narratives of personal pain. Interestingly, some Yale undergraduates published their own case histories of the trauma they experienced during the late 1960s (Gecan, 1972).

One fictional genre that unites personal trauma and political ideas is fantasy or, better, phantasmagoria. Fantasy fiction uses grotesquery and hallucination to develop its stories. For example, Ralph Ellison's *Invisible Man* narrates the politics of race as a surrealistic, traumatic, "pilgrim's progress." In Salman Rushdie's *Shame*, Pakistan's political history metaphorically becomes a hallucinatory descent into personal madness. And in D. M. Thomas's *The White Hotel* Freud's case history of a traumatized hysteric (Anna B.) serves as the fictional medium for the author's hallucinatory rendering of Nazism.

Interestingly, some disrupters also construct narratives of trauma. For example, Joseph Retzer describes himself as "very angry" after serving in Vietnam: "It definitely changed my views about the American government" (interview, April 10, 1998). So profound was the experience that it generated Retzer's dissertation topic, in which he emulated his adviser Robert Lane by interviewing in depth sixteen Vietnam veterans. Retzer's personal trauma produced case histories of political trauma. These narratives projected Retzer's painful rejection of pluralism into scholarship.

Bruce Payne's trauma narrative also springs from personal experience. "I had, after all, gotten beat up and shot at in Mississippi . . . and I was worried about the possibility that people would be killed, quite rightly" (interview, June 2, 1998). Drawing upon his fears, he urged political scientists to become politically active, especially because, among blacks, "the anger is growing." But his effort failed, and he "ended up feeling very badly about that." From these events he concluded the absence of "the appropriate intellectual passions that might have directed us in ways that would have been more helpful." Payne's narrative of trauma does not end like Retzer's. In the fashion psychiatrists recommended, Retzer converted his pain into generativity, that is, a dissertation. Payne did not and turned instead to a non-scholarly academic career.

When I asked Penny Gill to reflect on contemporary identity politics and pluralism, she too constructed a trauma narrative. Her "gut reaction" is that pluralism cannot handle the culture wars; she traces this failure back to the Vietnam War and the civil rights movement. Moreover, she again introduces her emotions when she observes, "We were deeply worried about racism" (interview, January 26, 1998). Her response is not that of a dispassionate scientific observer, but of a distraught political participant (hence the use of "we"). In fact, she recalls the specific political events that traumatized her. "You know, Martin Luther King and Bobby Kennedy were shot while I was sitting with friends at Yale eating dinner. Those are the events I'll never forget." Thus, Gill imposes a trauma narrative on the struggle between pluralism and the culture wars; this narrative's repetition ("I'll never forget") demonstrates to her the weakness of pluralism.

Not surprisingly, some disrupters construct trauma narratives that contain life-changing decisions. For Nathaniel Beck, the "big thing" was the Black Panther trial in New Haven, which disillusioned him about pluralism and academia as a whole. He decided to abandon an academic career or, at best, to use academia only as "a base to do other stuff." In fact, he did not intend to complete his dissertation fieldwork in Washington. Eventually, however, Beck recovered from his trauma, resumed his dissertation, and created a successful academic career (interview, June 1, 1998).

Unlike Beck, Jessica Wolf was permanently transformed by political trauma. According to Wolf, the 1960s burst upon her in a "cameo moment," namely, as she watched the television broadcasts of the 1968 Democratic convention. Afterward, she became "increasingly disenchanted with . . . American political structures" and decided not to pursue an academic career. As she summarizes her reaction to the 1960s: "It wasn't something I articulated to myself. But I did, I did want to do something that made a difference. That was clear. I was worried that being in academia was not necessarily the best fit for me" (interview, May 19, 1998).

So far, these trauma narratives have ended relatively well; the storytellers seemingly emerge whole and unregretful. A few disrupters, however, narrate less heartening stories of personal trauma. These disrupters claim that their traumas injured them permanently in professional terms. Their narratives resemble the "confessional" autobiographies that have recently become popular in American literature (e.g., Susanna Kaysen, Barbara Harrison, Paula Vogel). In these stories the author "tells all" about how those she trusted and loved victimized her. The victim suffers disabling trauma and never entirely recovers. Three disrupters adopt the confessional narrative to discuss the 1960s and pluralism.

Richard Beth offers a comparatively mild version of the confessional genre. After Beth graduated from Yale, he joined the political science department at Boston University. Having rejected pluralism, he turned to radical politics. He remarks that, "It was easy for the department to see me as just another of those radicals," more interested in revolution than in scholarship. He admits that his scholarly record at Boston was marginal, but he feels the university penalized him for his political activities. He describes a subtle form of victimization:" It's probably very easy for a lot of other people to be looked at as not serious political scientists because they weren't doing the mainstream stuff, you know, and I admit to not being real interested in doing what you would even call 'normal science'" (interview, January 12, 1998).

Ever so gently, Beth blames "mainstream" political science, including pluralism, for his troubles at Boston. He implies that the confrontation between political events and pluralism harmed his career.

Michael Parenti and Michael Leiserson produce bitter confessional narratives. Both claim that pluralist scholars intentionally singled them out for career punishment. Leiserson believes that his rejection of pluralism and his political activism at Berkeley incurred the wrath of tenured faculty, including second-generation Yale pluralists in the Berkeley department. He claims that his pluralist mentors at Yale were more tolerant than his pluralist colleagues at Berkeley; the latter, he says, only wanted "bureaucratic behavioralists" in the department. He states that he was warned to fit into a "Yale slot" in the Berkeley department. He attributes his not receiving tenure at Berkeley to political retaliation. Moreover, he believes that Berkeley blacklisted him for other academic jobs (interview, April 27, 1998).

Most of those in a position to know firsthand what happened at Berkeley deny Leiserson's charges. However, an anonymous junior faculty colleague of Leiserson's at Berkeley agrees with his account; indeed, this scholar suspects that by voicing his suspicion about the Leiserson affair, he hastened his own departure from Berkeley. My desire, however, is neither to support nor refute Leiserson. I am only illustrating the way collisions between political events and pluralism sometimes generate powerful anti-pluralist confessional narratives.

Michael Parenti offers a similar confessional narrative, although, unlike Leiserson, he exempts Yale scholars from his charges. Nevertheless, he contends that his radical political activities at the University of Illinois cost him academic jobs and ultimately drove him from academia entirely. As he puts it: "I took out my file and realized I had applied to about a hundred, or about a hundred and twenty places, you know, and I had been turned down by departments where I had outpublished the entire department" (interview, April 14, 1998). Parenti claims his "left-class analysis" had crossed a "serious line." Therefore, most universities would not hire him.

In contrast to confessional narratives, highly cerebral fictionlike narratives also emerge out of the confrontation between pluralism and political challenges. A "cerebral" narrative is the opposite of a "sentimental" narrative. Sentimental narratives foreground feeling as opposed to thought. The confessional narrative, the passionate condemnation of pluralist distancing, and the narrative of trauma are all sentimental, for they emphasize emotions. By contrast, cerebral narratives call on literary genres such as satire; these narratives ridicule pluralist ideas on grounds of theoretical inadequacy, not personal experience. Thus, cerebral narratives argue that political events constitute intellectual rather than emotional challenges to pluralism.

One cerebral narrative portrays the struggle between pluralism and severe political conflict as the struggle between order and disorder. Some fictional models of this narrative are novels about early-twentieth-century anarchism. Several novelists portrayed anarchism as revealing the superficiality and fragility of civilized society. Two powerful literary exemplars of this anarchist narrative are Joseph Conrad's *The Secret Agent* and Henry James's *The Princess Casamassima*, both of which chronicle bungled acts of terrorism directed against British liberal democracy.

Some disrupters construct versions of these anarchist narratives.

This narrative genre especially appeals to critics of the elite consensus or "rules of the game" premise in pluralism. In these narratives, pluralist procedural consensus symbolizes social order, and identity politics symbolizes the forces of destruction. Let me provide two examples.

When I asked Rufus Browning about pluralism and contemporary identity politics in California, where he lives, Browning constructed an anarchist narrative. He argues, "When Dahl in *Who Governs?* writes about the rules of the game and a consensus on rules of the game, it seems to me in that kind of phraseology, he sort of excludes the possibility of some of the kinds of cultural politics we now have" (interview, January 25, 1998). Interestingly, by introducing the term *phraseology* Browning calls attention to the deliberately rhetorical aspect of pluralism. The substance of his argument, however, portrays a struggle between pluralist order and cultural disorder.

Lance Bennett develops a more extended version of the anarchist narrative. First, Bennett traces identity politics to "socialism and Marxism . . . in the sixties." Next, according to Bennett: "I think that you can sort of encapsulate the mainstream response against diversity and identity politics as basically a liberal, pluralistic response. Saying that the people who are lobbying for diversity simply haven't played the game successfully, and now they want to change the rules. And here the rules basically look like pluralism" (interview, February 6, 1998).

Bennett believes that identity politics poses a unique challenge to pluralism. Unlike the socialist movements of the 1960s, identity politics offers a "kind of cultural alternative." Bennett recognizes that identity politics threatens established political order ("the rules"); moreover, he associates this order with pluralism. Bennett's reconstruction retraces the narrative steps of Joseph Conrad's *Under Western Eyes*, which is a fictional study of bomb-throwing Russian revolutionary socialists in turn-of-the century Geneva. To be sure, no bomb throwers appear in Bennett's or Browning's narratives. Nevertheless, the narratives they construct closely resemble that of Conrad, their literary predecessor.

The anarchist narrative targets the pluralist premise of elite consensus. A related narrative does not focus initially on pluralist premises, but instead on unprecedented political *issues*. Where the anarchist narrative proceeds deductively—testing a premise against

231

events—the issue narrative proceeds inductively, moving from specific problems to premises. The issue narrative is pragmatic; it starts with a concrete problem, from which it then draws anti-pluralist conclusions.

Many who develop issue narratives are deeply concerned about the problem in question. In particular, they are frustrated that pluralism has ignored the problem. These narratives find their counterparts in the genre of social reform fiction, such as Frank Norris's *The Octopus*, Dickens's *Hard Times*, or Steinbeck's *The Grapes of Wrath*. All these novels decry the injustices ordinary people suffer at the hands of the powerful. Let us call this the "Joad narrative," after the heroic family of evicted farmers in *The Grapes of Wrath*.

Two disrupters who advance the Joad narrative are James Scott and George La Noue. In discussing identity politics and pluralism, La Noue immediately targets the issue of immigration. As he puts it, "I don't ever recall at Yale a discussion about the force of immigration in American life, and now, for example, in the civil rights area, immigration is such an important part of the problem" (interview, March 9, 1998). La Noue doesn't advocate any particular policy on immigration; nor does he explicitly condemn pluralism for failing to consider immigration. Nevertheless, the immigration issue motivates La Noue to challenge pluralist theory.

James Scott sensed the weakness of pluralism as he completed his Yale dissertation, which he subsequently published as *Political Ideology in Malaysia: Reality and the Beliefs of an Elite* (1968). He now dismisses the book, calling it a "bad dissertation" mired in the paradigm he learned at Yale. He attributes his rejection of this paradigm to "getting involved in questions of corruption" while doing fieldwork in Malaysia. In reaction, he undertook subsequent research on patron-client relationships in Malaysia. This research convinced him that "a career devoted to understanding the peasantry and peasant rebellion was a worthy way to spend your life" (interview, May 15, 1998). Ultimately, the issue of corruption helps to explain Scott's gradual rejection of pluralism.

Other disrupters construct more explicitly judgmental Joad narratives than does Scott. For example, Michael Kraft observes that two years into course work at Yale, he and some other students became interested in environmental issues. The students formed a discussion group, which drew the conclusion—epitomized in an influential book by their fellow student William Ophuls (1977)—that pluralist incrementalism could not deal with environmental degradation. Kraft acknowledges, however, that Charles Lindblom, chair of Ophuls's dissertation committee, did not object to Ophuls's anti-incrementalist argument (interview, March 13, 1998). Less forgiving than Kraft in his Joad narrative is Michael Parenti, who sharply contrasts the academic "question of whether or not Dahl's study of New Haven really meant this or that" with the stark fact that "you've got a CIA war waged in Mozambique where two million people were killed." In view of the Mozambique disaster, "all this" (i.e., pluralism) is simply "irrelevant."

Finally, some disrupters construct *ironic* narratives about pluralism and identity politics. Irony is a figure of speech that deliberately advances meanings directly opposed to those literally expressed. Irony is, of course, a favorite literary device of many authors; Jane Austen is a particular master. One need only recall how Austen's superbly intelligent heroine Emma causes harm to her friends through her benignly intended, but ill-considered, actions. Some disrupters employ irony when they argue that, despite being hostile to identity politics, pluralism actually spawned the politics of identity. For example, Peter Stillman claims, "Pluralism can sort of break down into groups or identity politics. What is it that holds the country together in pluralist society?" (interview, April 29, 1998). Stillman observes that pluralism legitimates the proliferation of interest groups. But without a common set of values, interest groups based on group identity alone eventually develop. Without any overarching values, pluralism inevitably destroys itself.

Perhaps the most cerebral of all fictionlike narratives argues that because pluralism overlooks emotions or does not predict identity politics or simply is no better than other theories, it fails as a scientific theory. Although these narratives attack pluralism on its own scientific grounds, these are not *scientific* narratives. Instead, they rely on the emotive and affective power only fiction conveys.

One such narrative contends that pluralism fails the scientific tests of prediction and explanation. According to Robert Grey, pluralism does not explain the decline of political participation in America. Pluralism, Grey contends, has always underestimated mass attitudes by focusing too heavily on competing political elites. Therefore, it never considered "whether the basic character of democracy is not some-

233

how almost fatally compromised by the character of present-day mass attitudes, what I'm calling demobilization. But nobody was asking that kind of question then" (interview, April 24, 1998). Grey essentially argues that because pluralism does not predict demobilization, it is a failed theory of liberal democracy.

Michael Kraft extends this narrative to identity politics. He notes:

> There wasn't much emphasis back then on potential for ideological politics or identity politics to arise. They had that kind of confidence that mainstream political dialogue was fine, and that elites were in agreement; there was some consensus about the rules of the game. So in that sense I don't think it prepared us well for the rise of the New Right, and the . . . fundamental disaffection with politics.

Finally, Steven Wolinetz generalizes this narrative to political science as a whole. Considering identity politics, Wolinetz remarks on the gap between general theories of politics and specific political events or institutions. Theory and reality do not come neatly together; therefore, political science is a limited instrument. "The whole drive for an empirical political science . . . could never have been a complete view of political science" (interview, May 18, 1998). To support his point, Wolinetz cites Karl Deutsch's research. According to Wolinetz, Deutsch's global theories did not match the empirical data. "Yet Deutsch's projects kept going on collecting all this data that I was never clear whether he understood it, or how it was going to fit into things. There was a lack of a kind of integrated point of view." Wolinetz implies that the gap between pluralist theory and empirical reality has been filled by new political movements—such as identity politics—that further undercut political science.

Of course, the predictive and explanatory failures of social science are a favorite topic among writers on intellectuals and politics. For example, Etzioni-Haley writes, "It is not that [the intellectuals] have not been successful [in some cases] in having their ideas accepted and their knowledge implemented. It is merely that these ideas . . . have not always worked well" (1985: 2). Indeed, Charles Lindblom has commented scathingly on social science's inability to provide "usable knowledge" for policymakers or the general public (1990).

The fictional counterpart to these critiques is the dystopian novel. In this genre scientific knowledge produces unpredicted and disastrous social effects. One powerful example is H. G. Wells's *The Island of Dr. Moreau,* in which a deranged scientist creates a race of amoral, violent, hybrid beasts, half human and half animal. Another is, of course, Mary Shelley's *Frankenstein,* in which Dr. Frankenstein's monster exacts revenge upon his creator. Perhaps the argument that pluralist thought is not predictive or explanatory should therefore be called the "science fiction" narrative.

Another fictionlike narrative calls attention to emotion and faith. According to this narrative, pluralism does not comprehend the affective and normative dimensions of identity politics. The conflict between pluralism and identity politics is, therefore, a conflict between "sense and sensibility." Indeed, Jane Austen's *Sense and Sensibility* is the fictional equivalent of this narrative. *Sense and Sensibility* compares two competing paths of conduct—feeling and thought. Contrasting heroines reflect and embody these opposing principles. Pluralist reason ("sense") is limited because it cannot eradicate identity's ("sensibility's") passion and faith.

Mary Curzan presents a sophisticated version of the sense and sensibility narrative as she ponders how ordinary people respond not only to pluralism but also to political science:

> Let's put the morality issue over here on the side. Even if I myself might be willing to die for civil rights or whatever it is or, God knows, racism, Nazism, whatever. Let's put that to the side, and let's talk about it this way. I think because they do talk about it this way . . . they had no understanding of the emotional reaction that just talking about it this way caused . . . a fundamental distrust of a person who would talk this way. (Interview, February 12, 1998)

In short, political science's "sense"—its propensity to analyze coolly and not to condemn—offends the moral "sensibilities" of ordinary people. People do not want their moral convictions "put . . . to the side" in the name of science.

Although Curzan herself does not choose between sense and sensibility, most disrupters do take sides. Like most disrupters, Hugh Heclo chooses sensibility, focusing on the same academic/popular opinion gap that Curzan analyses. Heclo argues that academics cannot be neutral as educators; nor can the state simply balance opposing educational philosophies in pluralist fashion. Academics and the state must take a stand. Heclo puts it this way: "I mean, damn it, there is a difference whether or not you teach our kids sex education in the school. And whether or not the power of government is put behind a particular viewpoint, government is not neutral whatever it does" (interview, June 3, 1998). Heclo thus explicitly rejects a value-free model of education. Moreover, he acknowledges that this model "might possibly have made it difficult to talk about what was emerging, culture wars for Americans."

By contrast to Heclo, Carolyn Harmon's narrative tilts in favor of sense, not sensibility. Though she resisted pluralism at Yale, Harmon has since embraced the discourse. Indeed, she hopes that the civic culture component of pluralism overcomes identity politics. Identity politics, she says, "makes me very nervous. It verges on cultural pluralism, which is something which I think, even then, we recognized as not a good idea. If you don't have one common civic culture, cultural pluralism is going to make it very difficult to continue to function as a democracy" (interview, June 3 1998). Harmon is cautiously optimistic that identity politics will fade over time.

In the sense and sensibility narrative, disrupters describe a powerful emotional struggle between opposing approaches to life. But the substantive principles in the struggle are only implied; rarely do they emerge explicitly in discussion. However, some disrupters do offer substantive philosophical arguments about the identity politics/pluralism confrontation. These are narratives of *ideas*, not character or emotions. In narrative terms, the ideas themselves become characters. This narrative draws on a fictional tradition that includes such classics as John Bunyan's *Pilgrim's Progress*, Dostoyevsky's *The Brothers Karamazov*, and Thomas Mann's *The Magic Mountain*. In these three works, the novel becomes an arena for philosophical debate, while action and plot take second place.

The hallmark of this "novel of ideas" narrative is its use of philosophical arguments. One version of the narrative pits science against identity politics. When I asked Nathaniel Beck about identity politics on California campuses, he constructs precisely this narrative. He admits to not "liking that stuff [identity politics] at all." He explains that, "In terms of political science, I have difficulty trying to figure out what it is that someone's gender or gender orientation makes much difference. . . . I've become much more of a scientist . . . the scientific method sort of doesn't much depend upon the person." In short, Beck finds science stronger intellectually than identity. Science, he claims, is simply the most persuasive set of ideas we possess.

Another novel of ideas narrative consists of a debate between pluralism and competing theories of American politics, such as Marxism or multiculturalism. Jan Deutsch offers the richest and most revealing illustration of this narrative. As Carl Boggs has pointed out, Marxism actually did not present a coherent approach to America in the 1960s until the decade itself had ended (1993: 120). Perhaps this is why Deutsch, in his 1968 *Stanford Law Review* article that attacked *Who Governs?*, mentions the New Left, C. Wright Mills, power elite theory, and "social stratification theorists" (1976: 252), but not Marxism.

However, when I asked Deutsch about pluralism and contemporary identity politics, he constructs a debate involving Marxism, among other theories. Specifically, Deutsch argues that "what Marxism was then [in his 1968 piece], multiculturalism and deconstruction are now." Deutsch feels that he is "fighting exactly the same battles" now as he did in 1968 against Nelson Polsby, who falsely believed "there is a pure version of science here." Deutsch argues that Dahl repudiated pluralism in his later work on Yugoslavia, which Deutsch characterizes as "multicultural" (interview, February 17, 1998). Deutsch's narrative consists of a debate between, on the one hand, Marxism, multiculturalism, deconstruction, and identity politics, and, on the other hand, pluralism and science. Thanks to the passage of time, Deutsch now grasps the full theoretical implications of his earlier attack on pluralism. Perhaps his example explains why there are so few novel of ideas narratives among disrupters. Maybe it requires a historical perspective and much political change—as well as ample textual debate—to introduce philosophical themes into the everyday conversations of political scientists.

CONCLUSION: SCIENCE AND FICTION
IN PLURALIST DISCOURSE

Is it possible to advance any tentative conclusions about scientific narratives that defend pluralism, or fictionlike narratives that attack pluralism? More important, can we draw from this analysis any insights about the power of legitimating discourses in a political regime? I believe so.

Scientific narratives produce coherent, compact improvisations on pluralist themes. These improvisations have sustained a core of pluralists who maintain their legitimating views into our own time. But these scientific narratives appeal to only a small majority of former Yale students. Further, the scientific narrative is limited and cautious. Therefore, pluralists often find themselves on the defensive as they confront political challenge. The scientific narrative is stronger on argument and logic than on passion and political empowerment; it generates a stable, reasonable text, but little political will to advance or protect the political regime. In short, the scientific narrative is long on political talk and short on political action. It therefore contributes only modestly to pluralism's legitimation of the American political system.

Fictionlike narratives suffer from opposite problems. They are long on political action but short on political logic. The fictional devices disrupters employ to elevate identity politics over pluralism are evocative and emotionally vibrant. However, no coherent argument emerges; nor does any particular method of analysis predominate. It is in the nature of fiction that it does not provide as unified a set of narratives as does science. Such disparate fictional genres as satire, science fiction, personal confession, Joad narratives, and novels of ideas do not constitute a coherent discourse. True, the fictionlike narratives may disrupt a political regime, but they can neither sustain change nor legitimize a *new* political system. The result is that, for all its limitations, pluralism remains a valuable legitimating discourse for the American political regime.

8

Pluralism in the Web of Culture

INTRODUCTION: LEGITIMATING DISCOURSES AND POLITICAL CULTURE

So far I have analyzed Yale pluralism without paying much attention to other political discourses. Now is the time to insert Yale pluralism into the web of American political culture. The key question I ask is whether Yale pluralism entered a receptive cultural environment. After all, the influence of any particular legitimating discourse depends on the political culture as a whole. What was the position of pluralism in American political culture during the 1950s and 1960s? What role in the culture did pluralism play? And what actual contribution did Yale make?

In order to investigate these questions, I examined a sample of journalistic and educational texts that reached politically active and powerful Americans during the period 1950 to 1970. In these writings did pluralist ideas play a conspicuous role? If so, then the version of pluralism advanced at Yale fell on fertile cultural ground. Although I make no claim that Yale pluralism *created* a pluralist political culture, Yale would certainly have contributed its share to a larger web of culture that legitimized the American political regime. I agree with Dennis Wrong, who writes about sociological ideas and the public, that "Whatever the original source of the idea, the fact that it is shared by experts and their subjects or clients may reinforce its authority in the eyes of both" (1998: 137).

What does social theory lead us to expect about pluralism in the political culture of American leaders? It is possible that pluralism occupied a position of *cultural hegemony,* by which I mean both quantitative and qualitative domination. In explicating typical neo-Marxist theories of cultural hegemony, Chris Jenks writes, "All elements of the superstructure contrive to exert ideological hegemony within the culture, from religion, to education, the mass media, law, mass culture, sport and leisure, and so on" (1993b: 83). Ben Agger asserts that there is a monopoly of "glitzy, Manhattanized postmodernism" (1992: 75) in contemporary culture, a condition he refers to as hegemonic. The hegemonic hypothesis stipulates that, as a discourse that favors those with power, pluralism dominated the political culture of leaders. The hegemonic position is certainly plausible; after all, as I earlier argued, those with power are indeed disposed to seek out and embrace comforting political discourses, such as pluralism (see also Schram, 1995; Madison, 1999).

In its original form, cultural hegemony refers to "the securing of consent, the struggle for the 'hearts and minds' of the *people*," (Barrett, 1991: 55; emphasis added), not elites. However, pluralism in the general public is not the focus of this study. I concentrate solely on the beliefs of power holders. I therefore limit the hegemonic model to the politically active minority of Americans. In this form, a hegemonic hypothesis predicts that pluralism dominated the political culture of politically active Americans from 1950 to 1970. This prediction is consistent with my earlier discussion of legitimating discourses, in which I argued that although legitimating discourses did not *necessarily* achieve hegemony, this possibility remains open.

Neo-Marxism is not alone theoretically in predicting the hegemony of pluralism among politically active Americans. As Abercrombie, Hill, and Turner pointed out (1980: chapter 2), Parsonian structural functionalism also predicts value consensus among political leaders. As these authors put it, "In Parsonian sociology, if a collectivity exists, then it *must* possess an integrated system of values" (50). Moreover, as William Buxton shows, Parsons's system of integrated values favors established social institutions (1985: 49).

From a purely practical standpoint, a plausible hegemonic argument can also be mounted for pluralism in the political culture of leaders. We should naturally expect elites to promote and embrace pluralist ideas, given pluralism's legitimating qualities (for empirical evidence, see Huber and Form, 1973). Leaders exert some power over print journalism; moreover, they take an active interest in the college education of their children. It therefore is plausible that they should try to infuse pluralism into journalism and, to a lesser degree, American government textbooks. True, the First Amendment and judicial decisions protect free intellectual exchange. Moreover, political leaders must also respect the pluralist norm of tolerance for other discourse. Yet, although these factors might inhibit political leaders, opportunities remain for them to influence political culture in a pluralist direction.

In fact, as Timothy Cook (1998) has shown, American political leaders have long exerted some control over journalists. After all, journalists cannot do their jobs without relying on political elites for crucial information. Just as labor unions cannot make financial demands that would bankrupt employers, so also journalists must accept some ideas that support rather than destroy politicians. As a result, political authorities may be able to create pluralist hegemony within their own political culture.

However, a plausible contrary hypothesis can also be propounded. Political competition in liberal democracies may produce multiple visions of American politics, preventing the hegemonic reign of pluralist values. Indeed, perhaps competition for power among leaders will eventually encourage some to charge that the political regime does not conform to pluralist standards. Pluralism would then have to compete on an equal footing against anti-pluralist discourses, which portray the regime as unrepresentative, corrupt, intolerant, unaccountable, tyrannical, and unreformable. Under these conditions, legitimating discourses, including pluralism, would become only one voice among many in the political culture of American leaders.

How might so heterogeneous a political culture emerge? As Mannheim pointed out, political competition in liberal democracies reveals underlying social cleavages (Longhurst, 1988: 133). Political competition therefore requires that politicians not only directly assail each other but also indirectly attack whole sectors of society. Therefore, political competition is inherently dangerous. Indeed, it may cause politicians to actually *become* intolerant, unresponsive, irrational, and, above all, power-hungry.

Moreover, political leaders often *do* violate the pluralist norms they profess in public. They regularly try to silence opponents, prevent or excessively accelerate change, abuse power, and ignore public demands. Journalists and scholars regularly uncover and publicize these transgressions, adding them to the web of political culture. In-

241

deed, revealing the failures of pluralist politics supports journalists' and educators' own claims to legitimacy. Hence, a heterogeneous political culture is arguably a natural consequence of a vigilant press and pluralist political competition.

In addition, according to some social scientists, the media became increasingly "adversarial" beginning in the 1960s. Pointing to growing amounts of negative political news, writers such as Thomas Patterson (1993) and Joseph Cappella and Kathleen Hall Jamieson (1997) argue that journalists believe they are morally and intellectually superior to politicians. Therefore, they increasingly derogate the political process. As a result, the political culture becomes even more heterogeneous.

Finally, some political leaders may believe they have more to gain than to lose from accusing their opponents of illegitimate anti-pluralist behavior. Such accusations are bound to be emotionally powerful and may stimulate a rapid infusion of partisan support. By contrast, the harms such claims might do to the political system are conjectural and distant. Thus, it may seem rational in the short term for political competitors to question legitimating discourses such as pluralism, which appear to cover up for an unjust political regime.

Some recent research supports this fragmentation hypothesis. For example, the general public often holds the media responsible for spreading negative views of government. According to Diana Mutz (1998: 118), when asked what caused them to doubt whether government could be trusted, 72 percent of Mutz's sample named media. Although Mutz believes the media are *not* adversarial, her findings are consistent with a fragmentation hypothesis. Clearly, in contemporary American political culture legitimating discourses such as pluralism compete against challenging discourses such as religious fundamentalism and identity politics. Might not a comparable fragmentation have existed in the 1950s and 1960s?

The plausibility of both the hegemonic and the fragmentation hypotheses suggests the need for a third, more nuanced approach, which I call a "figure-ground model." In this model, pluralism retains pride of place. All things being equal, newspapers, magazines, and textbooks will generally depict political leaders cooperating in pluralist fashion to protect the political system. Political competitors will not engage in the risky politics of regime delegitimation. Therefore, journalists and educators will downplay violations of such legitimating discourses as pluralism. However, sometimes policymakers may be unable to prevent bitter partisan and group conflict that does challenge pluralist norms. When such conflict occurs, it engulfs the political and media landscape, resembling showers of brilliant meteors against a night sky. These conflicts provide anti-pluralist "figures" that draw public attention away from the pluralist "ground." The result is an outburst of division in American political culture.

The figure-ground model gains support from research on media "indexing." Gadi Wolfsfeld (1997), Lance Bennett (1994), and Daniel Hallin (1984) demonstrate that media coverage of the Vietnam War and the Arab-Israeli conflict took its cue from the conduct of leaders. So long as leaders agreed on policy, the media did not question their adherence to regime norms such as pluralism. However, when leaders disagreed publicly on these deeply felt issues, the media adopted an oppositional stance, questioning both conformity to and the workability of pluralist norms. The pluralist hegemony that political leaders normally enjoyed disappeared, its place taken by fragmentation and division. Indeed, for a time delegitimation flashed brilliantly against the duller legitimating ground of pluralism.

The figure-ground model may have a distinctive composition and rhythm. Compositionally, pluralist images may dominate most policy arenas for long periods. Magazines, newspapers, and textbooks may consistently portray these policy arenas in pluralist terms. Indeed, such treatment may become so regular and reliable that people simply take it for granted. This pluralist imagery may be compared to the background in Gestalt psychology's figure-ground perceptual illusions.

But a few policy controversies generate charges that politicians are violating their constitutional duties or flouting regime norms. Other policy struggles may suggest that in practice pluralism simply does not work. These controversies challenge pluralist hegemony. Perhaps newspaper coverage of Joseph McCarthy portrayed violations of pluralist tolerance. Or perhaps coverage of political scandals, such as the Bobby Baker or Billie Sol Estes affairs of the 1960s, portrayed politicians selling out their constituents in favor of "fat cats." Media and textbook attention to these events will seize public attention. Although usually briefer and more specialized compositionally than pluralist coverage, these anti-pluralist images undermine pluralist hegemony. These then become the spectacular anti-pluralist figures that flash against the pluralist ground.

What do these remarks suggest about the political culture of leaders in the 1950s and 1960s? A hegemonic hypothesis predicts that pluralism will dominate magazine, newspaper, and textbook depictions throughout the period. A fragmentation hypothesis predicts the opposite, namely, that pluralism will constitute a minority of all depictions all the time. Finally, the figure-ground hypothesis stipulates that pluralism will constitute a modest majority of all images; however, a few political events—involving severe controversy or scandal—will generate cultural fragmentation.

No doubt Yale's academic pluralism would operate differently in each of these theoretical contexts. Obviously, when pluralism is hegemonic in the political culture, Yale's message would resonate broadly. But in such a culture Yale pluralism may not be much needed or noticed. Conversely, Yale pluralism would struggle in a heterogeneous political culture, where loud oppositional voices challenge it. Perhaps Yale pluralism would be most crucial in a figure-ground model. In such a political culture Yale's pluralist message would be both visible and valuable to political leaders. When these leaders confront periodic anti-pluralist outbursts, they may well appreciate an expert academic discourse that restores their self-confidence.

LEADERS' POLITICAL CULTURE: TEXTS IN CONTEXT

By the 1950s and 1960s political leaders in the United States were overwhelmingly university-educated. Granted, relatively few of these leaders would have encountered the college textbooks of the day, except perhaps for those published in the early 1950s. Nevertheless, the leaders' *children* would have been reading these texts and perhaps discussing them with their parents. Moreover, many of these books would have been in the homes of the powerful. I therefore regard these texts as part of the political culture to which leaders were indirectly exposed during the period.

What picture of American politics did the major freshmen American government texts of the 1950s and 1960s present? The answer to this question is straightforward: American government texts were the most thoroughly pluralistic component of leaders' political culture during the period. In these texts, pluralism achieves a position of cultural hegemony.

This conclusion emerges from a systematic examination of thirteen freshman American government texts widely used during the period. Each text was scrutinized to identify subject matter pertinent to the four pluralist premises. The material surveyed included descriptions of power distribution in the United States and characterizations of political leaders as either tolerant or intolerant, as mutually cooperative or divisive, as ideological zealots or coalition builders. In addition, coders examined discussions of policymaking. Were policymakers reactive and responsive to public preferences and interest groups? Or were they pictured as ideological visionaries who ignored public preferences? Finally, what about government's accomplishments? Was government sluggish, static, and passive? Or, contrariwise, did the system generate dramatic, radical change? Or was the political system incrementally reformist, moving slowly forward in response both to public pressures and to leaders' initiatives?

As just stated, the answers to these questions were unambiguously pluralist. Most texts characterized the distribution of power in the United States in terms of multiple competing groups, rather than in terms of a monolithic power elite. Most texts described leaders as tolerant, cooperative, coalition builders and power brokers. In addition, most texts portrayed policymakers responding evenhandedly to the public's preferences. Finally, most texts described policymaking in incrementally reformist terms.

Consider, for example, Ogg and Ray's early (1950) description of power in the United States: "An exceedingly large share of the American electorate has avenues of influence and control over national and state governments through the medium of voluntary associations" (13). Ogg and Ray did not alter this pluralistic depiction in several subsequent editions of their popular text.

A more complex statement of the multiple centers of power argument may be found in Burns and Peltason's widely used *Government by the People* (1957). Burns and Peltason recognize that there is an unequal distribution of power among competing interest groups. They also comment on the limited power of most citizens, who are *not* represented by interest groups. Nevertheless, in 1957 they still describe lobbyists and interest groups as "a sort of 'third house'" (265) for the people. Moreover, Burns and Peltason describe politics as "largely a conflict among competing groups with conflicting ideas of what is in the 'general interest'" (241). Thus, Burns and Peltason clearly reject a power elite explanation of American politics. Instead, they paraphrase Dahl's *Preface to Democratic Theory:* "How, then, can government govern? How do we get things done? If the majority does not rule, who does? The answer is that we are government by *shifting coalitions of minorities* rather than by *simple majorities.* Under this system government *can act only with the consent of the several major interests in society"* (555).

Unlike Ogg and Ray, Burns and Peltason become progressively more critical of pluralism in subsequent editions of their text. For example, in 1969 they portray interest groups as maintaining the status quo against such forces of change as the Black Power movement (253–72). In 1966, Burns and Peltason stated that, "The real problem raised by the activities of interest groups in America is their frequent failure to represent broader segments of the community, organized or not" (304). Three years later, in their 1969 edition, the authors are even more unhappy about interest groups. They state that interest groups actually exclude deprived Americans; therefore, the poor "are more likely to emphasize political techniques that bypass conventional group politics—direct action, separatism, and violence" (272). Thus, by 1969 Burns and Peltason imply that pluralism does not produce orderly political change in America. In short, Burns and Peltason become progressively less sanguine about pluralism.

However, other authors explicitly recommend pluralism in their texts. For example, the 1965 edition of Redford, Truman, Hacker, Westin, and Woods's *Politics and Government in the United States* offers a perfect statement of pluralism as a legitimating discourse:

> The Negro struggle for political and social equality demonstrates that the techniques of group politics are available to those at the bottom of the social ladder. With all the inequities and imperfections of the system, its performance commands considerable respect. Until we come across some fine philosophers (or technicians) whom we are prepared to make into kings, a good case can be made for staying with political pluralism. (232)

In addition to reproducing the multiple power centers premise in pluralism, most texts argue that policymaking in the United States is reactive and disjointed, rather than planned, visionary, or centrally directed. For example, Adrian and Press write in *The American Political Process* (1965: 612), "Federal programs are designed to give a little to almost everyone. . . . The detail of domestic policy is not the result of a carefully devised plan; it is a response to many pressures." This passage combines the multiple centers of power argument with incrementalism and reactivity. "Many pressures" evokes a pluralistic distribution of power. Programs that "give a little to almost everyone" without a "carefully designed plan" are the very essence of incrementalism. Finally, *"response"* (my emphasis) suggests that the political system reacts to pressure.

A particularly strong version of the reactivity premise appears in Carr, Bernstein, and Murphy's *American Democracy in Theory and Practice* (1963). In the following passage the authors explicitly reject assertions that American political leaders are either self-interested power seekers or ideological zealots:

> Activities of the government are undertaken *in response to the wishes and needs of the American people.* The government does not maintain these activities merely for the sake of spending money, of regulating people's lives, or of giving civic servants something to do. Generally it acts *in response* to pressures created by misfortunes or dissatisfactions of groups of citizens. (612; emphasis added)

Of the four major pluralist themes, these texts pay least attention to the question of tolerance among leaders. Indeed, the subject of leadership itself rarely appears. Instead, the texts typically fold characterizations of leadership into sections on political parties, interest groups, and the presidency. The absence of attention to leadership is revealing, for it implies that competing institutions and interest groups leave political leaders with little autonomous power. This assumption, in turn, suggests that leaders are accountable to others in the United States.

The relative invisibility and apparent weakness of leaders does not trouble most authors. Consider, for example, Irish and Prothro's 1965 discussion of political parties. Parties, according to the authors, "serve to moderate differences among opposing groups" (208) and to build coalitions before a general election. By implication, party *leaders* are simply expert coalition builders, not program initiators. A more elaborate, though similarly modest, characterization of American political leadership appears in Austin Ranney's *The Governing of Men* (1971).

Ranney describes American political parties as "broker" rather than "missionary" or "ideological" parties (329–30). As the term *broker* suggests, American political parties make deals "among the conflicting demands of interest groups" (330). At this point Ranney explicitly takes up the topic of party leadership. He states that American party leaders reflect the "cross-sectional character" of political interests. Because leaders come from many backgrounds, they do not represent narrow "segments" of the community (331). Implicitly, the leadership stratum of American political parties is—like the parties themselves—a representative coalition of competing and compromising interests.

Although the texts portray coalition building as a leadership task, they say little about leaders' tolerance for dissent. The texts rarely describe leaders defending the "rules of the game," protecting individual rights, or speaking in support of unpopular minorities. At best, the texts only hint at the theme of tolerance. For example, Caldwell and Lawrence (1969: 122) observe that American political parties often incorporate previously controversial or extreme ideas. This statement implies that party leaders are open to unpopular minority views. However, Caldwell and Lawrence do not develop this argument. Instead, they return to the standard emphasis on coalition building. They observe that openness to unpopular positions demonstrates that the parties are essentially non-ideological coalitions.

The absence of the tolerance premise from most texts is an intriguing phenomenon. Perhaps the authors assume that the fundamental norms and constitutional underpinnings of American democracy are so secure among leaders that a discussion of tolerance is unnecessary. But surely McCarthyism might have given them pause in this regard. Moreover, by 1969—when Caldwell and Lawrence published their book—racial and anti-war protests had generated extensive FBI and CIA surveillance that often infringed on the rights of individual citizens. Caldwell and Lawrence do discuss protest in the 1960s; in fact, they concede that "the American political system may need modification if conflicting political demands amid rapidly changing times are to be successfully met" (1969: 167). Yet they do not focus on political leadership in this context, either as protectors of dissent or as catalysts of change.

The texts do, however, describe the American political system as reformist. Typical assertions of the reform premise may be found in

248

Carr, Bernstein, and Murphy (1963) and Redford et al. (1965). For example, Carr and his colleagues couple the reform premise with the theme of reactivity. "Since democracies usually take action gradually," they write, "the government's response to these needs is slow rather than rapid, reluctant rather than eager, and piecemeal rather than planned" (612). Nevertheless, reform ("response to these needs") presumably occurs. For their part, Redford and his colleagues state that, "On the whole, as our national development demonstrates, pluralist politics has been a highly creative process." Gradually, pluralism corrects imbalances of power (232). Redford et al. single out Congress for particular commendation; they observe, "It is equally clear that the Congress, with all its peculiarities, is neither moribund nor ineffective" (422). In short, again, reform occurs.

By the late 1960s, however, doubt about reform has crept into some texts; by the early 1970s, some writers admit that reform has not solved some important problems. In 1972, Woll and Binstock observe that, despite reform, recurrent systemic failures cause political violence. They cite the Civil War as one conspicuous case (571); moreover, they fear that frustrated African Americans will initiate further violence, rather than accept incremental reform (45).

Most pessimistic of all about reform is Robert Salisbury's *Governing America: Public Choice and Political Action* (1973). Of the texts examined, Salisbury's is the only one that foresees absolute deadlock in pluralist politics. Unlike most authors, Salisbury offers a clear description of "A Pluralist View of America," quoting, perhaps inappropriately, Walt Whitman's "Song of Myself" as a literary example of pluralism (30). Salisbury observes that "the progressive emphasis on structural change as the strategy by which to make government more effective and responsive remains a part of the contemporary American political culture" (30). But Salisbury traces structural change to *Progressivism*, not to pluralism and is actually quite skeptical about pluralism's reform capacity. He asks rhetorically, "How viable is a political system that is honeycombed with organized groups of every description? Such a system may find itself immobilized, unable to respond to a new crisis because its leaders can not break out of the complex balance created by the interplay of decision makers and groups" (99).

But Salisbury's critical tone is an exception to pluralist hegemony in government texts; even in the late 1960s and early 1970s, American government texts retain pluralism as a dominant discourse. Notes of skepticism, concern, and impatience become more frequent; yet, the pluralist message remains generally intact.

Interestingly, specific references to "pluralism" or to the writings of Yale pluralists are not especially common in texts. Only Burns and Peltason and Ranney recommend many works by Yale authors, including books by Deutsch, Dahl, Lindblom, Lane, Lasswell, and Almond and Verba. While this absence weakens the visibility of pluralist discourse, it may actually increase pluralism's legitimating power. After all, this lacuna makes difficult a systematic criticism of pluralism as a whole; meanwhile, individual pluralist themes diffuse widely. Thus, the elision of pluralism itself may facilitate the largely unremarked dispersion of pluralist themes throughout the web of American political culture.

In sum, major pluralist themes dominate American government texts from 1950 to 1970. The only missing themes are those of elite tolerance and vigorous political leadership. However, authors mainly omit—and rarely challenge—these two themes. On balance, therefore, pluralist hegemony prevails in the textbook segment of American political culture.

THE WORLD ACCORDING TO *TIME*

Although American government textbooks offered leaders a pluralist imprimatur in the 1950s and 1960s, for their day-to-day picture of the political system leaders naturally relied on journalism. Therefore, I investigated print journalism that likely reached policymakers on a regular basis during the period. To begin with, I considered every even year's worth of *Time* magazine between 1950 and 1970. In each case, I focused on stories pertinent to pluralism.

By examining even-numbered rather than odd-numbered years, I offer a conservative estimate of pluralist imagery in print journalism. In even-numbered years elections take place; political conflict therefore takes center stage during campaigning. Hence, my findings may underestimate the prevalence of pluralism in American print journalism. If so, Yale pluralism may have entered a somewhat more receptive cultural environment than my findings reveal.

Certainly of all my print sources, *Time* provides the sharpest contrast to the American government texts. *Time* describes the American political system not as pluralist but as fundamentally fragmented, even fractured along partisan, ideological, and organizational lines. *Time* denies that American political leaders are flexible compromisers and argues that the American political system is inaccessible to most citizens. *Time* portrays leaders as corrupt and responsive not to popular concerns but to monied special interests. *Time* also describes a political stratum bitterly divided by charges of domestic subversion and disloyalty; also, many in this stratum have little tolerance for political dissent. In short, *Time* paints a conflictive picture of the American political regime.

Time is also ambivalent about the value of pluralism. For example, it often portrays McCarthyism sympathetically, as if rooting out "subversives" is more important than protecting free speech. It also seems to endorse the divisiveness of ideological polarization. For *Time* in the 1950s and 1960s, politics is an ideological struggle between good and evil. The struggle is fierce, unpredictable, and fateful. It is also beyond pluralist control.

Time's depiction is as much a product of omission as commission. *Time* devotes scant attention to the policies that pluralists highlight, such as urban renewal and education. In addition, *Time* has little to say about policy arenas in which there are confrontations between pluralist and nonpluralist political forces, such as housing policy. As a result, *Time* reverses the pluralist imagery prevalent in American government texts; pluralism is weak, and heterogeneity is the rule.

Between 1950 and 1956, the McCarthy anti-Communist crusade received abundant *Time* coverage. In this coverage the subject of leaders' tolerance played a major role. In fact, the overwhelming majority of *Time*'s 102 "tolerance" stories in my sample concentrated on McCarthy's charges about Communists in government, investigations by the House Un-American Activities Committee (HUAC), loyalty oath controversies, the practice of blacklisting, and possible associations between the Communist Party and other groups, such as labor unions and civil rights organizations. In only 11 of these 102 stories did *Time* portray American political leaders as tolerant of political dissent. Rather, *Time* describes an American leadership that lacks consensus on basic pluralist rules of the political game.

In some articles, *Time* depicts all parties to the McCarthy struggle—liberal and conservative—as equally disposed to violate the plu-

251

ralist norm of tolerance. For example, in a May 15, 1950, story ("Investigations: Other Voices"), *Time* reports on Congress's effort to make Senator McCarthy stipulate a specific number of Communists in the State Department. The article singles out Owen Lattimore, whom McCarthy had targeted in his attacks on the State Department. In a brief two sentences, *Time* manages to characterize all participants—McCarthy, Lattimore, and the Communist Party—as equally intolerant: "Again last week Lattimore took the stand in rebuttal, there showed himself a match for McCarthy—or the *Daily Worker*— in the technique of the vituperative smear. McCarthy, he said, was a professional character assassin" (20).

Time is not a neutral observer of this unsavory confrontation. In its next sentence it states that Lattimore used "Union Square" methods to defend himself. This reference implies that Lattimore is indeed a Communist because the Communist Party often used Union Square for rallies. *Time* thus shifts the onus of intolerance from McCarthy to Lattimore. But the "vituperative smear"—the epitome of intolerance—applies to all segments of the political stratum.

Time's own approach to these conflicts adds to the image of heterogeneity. The magazine treats recurrent outbursts of intolerance as partisan strategies; politicians readily sacrifice tolerance in return for immediate political advantage. For example, this particular article remarks, "So far, McCarthy has charged much, but had proved not one case. But there was little doubt of the political effectiveness of his methods." "Little doubt," of course, implies that the public rewards intolerance; therefore, no rational politician would practice the tolerance norm.

Time persistently emphasizes violations of the tolerance norm. For example, the headline of a March 22, 1954, article on the investigation of Annie Lee Moss, another suspected Communist, is "Committee vs. Chairman," a phrase that immediately frames the story in terms of elite division. The story recounts how Democratic senators on McCarthy's committee used the occasion of Moss's testimony to attack the absent senator. The Democrats charged McCarthy with "convicting people by rumor and hearsay and innuendo" (27). Although superficially the article portrays Democratic senators protecting Moss's rights, the deeper message is that Democrats are getting back at McCarthy for partisan reasons.

Time does not exempt the legal system from its portrayal of division. Even judges do not respect the rights of suspected Communists. For example, on July 26, 1954 ("The Right to Draw Inferences"), *Time* reported that a Los Angeles judge had ruled against twenty-three actors and writers who claimed they had been blacklisted. Noting that the plaintiffs had refused to answer questions before HUAC, *Time* writes, "The Judge concluded that the movie industry and the public would be entitled to draw 'unfavorable inferences' from the plaintiffs' refusal to testify" (12). In short, the Constitution's legal custodians refused to enforce the pluralist norm of tolerance for unpopular political views.

Time concentrated its coverage of tolerance-related stories within the 1950–56 period. It focused on McCarthy, who persistently violated the pluralist norm of tolerance. After 1956, however, *Time* virtually dropped the tolerance theme and turned to a different pluralist premise: open and easy access to responsive politicians. But instead of improvising this premise, *Time* emphasizes how politicians and lobbyists develop corrupt relationships with each other. These relationships violate the pluralist norm of easy and fair *public* access to policymakers. Access, *Time* implies, works mainly to the advantage of the powerful *few;* rarely does *Time* write about ordinary citizens gaining effective access to responsive policymakers.

Of the thirty-three stories that specifically discuss political access between 1958 and 1970, twenty-nine chronicle instances of scandal and bribery. Three particular cases dominate *Time*'s attention: the Sherman Adams scandal in the Eisenhower administration, the Billie Sol Estes scandal in the Kennedy administration, and the Bobby Baker scandal in the Johnson administration.

Some examples of stories about the Estes and Baker cases convey the nature of *Time*'s coverage. On June 1, 1962, *Time* ("Still Digging") reports on the suspicious death of the U.S. Department of Agriculture official who unearthed "the Billie Sol Estes Scandal." The article observes that two Democratic members of Congress from Texas, Congressman J. T. Rutherford and Senator Ralph Yarborough, helped Estes obtain meetings with key Agriculture Department officials at the same time the two received hefty campaign contributions from Estes. Though the story does not explicitly assert that Estes bribed the two men, *Time*'s decision to put "campaign contributions" in quotation marks implies bribery (18–19). Thus, *Time* intentionally creates a stronger impression of corruption than the facts warrant.

253

In 1964 *Time* devoted considerable attention to the Bobby Baker case. Not only does *Time* report on Baker's bribe taking as secretary of the Senate, but the magazine also derides congressional efforts to investigate Baker. For example, *Time* reports that by adjourning the investigating committee, the Democratic Committee chair, Everett Jordan, had "staved off further Baker sessions through Election Day." The article ridicules the committee and its chair:

> In hearings only last week, Jordan actually forgot that he was chairman of the committee, cleared his throat and began: 'Er, Mr. Chairman . . .' A further example of general ineptness came when the committee tried to pursue the charge that Democratic Wheelhorse Matt McCloskey had indirectly made a $35,000 payoff to Baker. They put McCloskey's auditor on the stand, only to discover that they had the wrong auditor. ("Off Again," December 18, 1964: 24)

In this passage, *Time* not only implicates Baker but also implies that members of Congress are incompetent. Indeed, Congress may be trying to cover up the corruption entirely.

Though *Time*'s coverage of these two scandals tarnishes Democrats, *Time* also occasionally targets Republicans. For example, in 1950 it alleges that big business has unfair access to Republican politicians ("Congress: The Sump Pumps," May 8, 1950: 17). In 1956 ("Investigations," April 16, 1956: 25) it reports that an executive in the gas industry has used financial contributions to a Republican South Dakota senator to influence legislation. And in 1958 it devotes many articles to the case of Republican presidential adviser Sherman Adams. *Time* is convinced that the political leaders of *both* parties abuse the pluralist norm of fair public access to responsive politicians.

Time's omission of stories about *legitimate* constituent access to lawmakers reinforces this portrayal. Rarely does *Time* report that ordinary citizens or interest groups operating legally have achieved an appropriate response from members of Congress. True, in 1950 *Time* did report that a mobster actually *failed* to bribe a politician ("Missouri: Murder on Truman Road," April 17, 1950: 21). But only once, in 1954, does *Time* report a successful mass petition being delivered to Congress—tellingly, in support of McCarthy ("Opinion: The Ten Million," November 29, 1954: 13). Only once does *Time* report that a labor union leader has conferred appropriately with a president ("Labor: Man of Steel," July 9, 1956: 15). Only once does *Time* report that a large interest group has legitimately influenced congressional debate ("Medicaid for the Aged," May 9, 1960). And only once does *Time* report that a major civil rights leader (its "Man of the Year," Martin Luther King Jr.) has gained appropriate access to the president (January 3, 1964). In short, for *Time*, access typically corrupts, rather than legitimates, the political system.

In addition, *Time* virtually ignores policy arenas celebrated by pluralists. For example, in the ten even-numbered years I sampled between 1950 and 1970, *Time* published only eleven stories about public housing. True, ten of these eleven stories portray public housing in a pluralist fashion. One, for example, reports that Lyndon Johnson responded quickly to Mississippi blacks protesting limited public housing funds ("Poverty: Capital Camp," April 15, 1966: 26). Nevertheless, this single pluralist policy arena cannot compete against the anti-pluralist scandals and elite intolerance that *Time* stresses.

Time also ignores two policy arenas to which Dahl paid particular attention in *Who Governs?*: school board elections and urban redevelopment. Of course, school board elections are local or state affairs; therefore, it is understandable why only three *Time* stories discussed the subject. But urban redevelopment was a major federal initiative throughout the period. Yet *Time* devotes only seven stories to the subject; moreover, although these articles produce a modestly pluralistic pattern, they contain little in-depth analysis.

If we lay the *Time* coverage alongside the textbook content we have examined, the figure-ground political culture model begins to emerge. *Time*'s depictions of public policies and the texts' depictions of the regime provide a pluralist background. However, *Time*'s sporadic anti-pluralist eruptions of scandal and intolerance flash brilliantly against this pluralist foundation. Yale pluralism thus enters a political culture that is receptive to its major arguments but that contains powerful challenges.

MAGAZINES BEYOND *TIME*

Though beginning their decline with television's ascent, general magazines for an educated public still flourished between 1950 and 1970. There were widely read middle-brow weeklies, such as *U.S. News and World Report* and *Newsweek*. There were self-consciously highbrow periodicals, such as *Saturday Review* and *The Nation*. There were sectarian magazines, such as *Commonweal* and *The Christian Century*. There were explicitly political journals, such as *The Reporter* and *The New Republic*. And there were popular family-oriented magazines, such as *Look, Life,* and the *Ladies Home Journal*. Thus, beyond *Time,* American political leaders could draw upon a diverse mix of magazine voices. What place did pluralism occupy in the wider world of magazine journalism?

In order to answer this question, I examined all the magazine articles mentioned in even-numbered years from 1950 to 1970 by the *Readers Guide to Periodical Literature* under the headings of public housing, urban renewal, and power. The total number of such articles came to 123 for the ten years of analysis. My examination of these 123 articles reveals a weakly pluralist majority. These magazines presented a more skeptical picture of the American political system than did American government texts, but they also offered a more pluralistic message than did *Time*. Indeed, this examination reveals the true extremity of *Time*'s anti-pluralist coverage.

Although these periodicals contained few stories about power as such, these few are revealing. As a group they exhibit some of the same reservations about pluralism that *Time* exhibited. Of the eighteen articles on power, ten took a pluralist line, and eight were decidedly nonpluralist. Interestingly, magazines directed at an intellectual and activist audience, such as *Saturday Review* and *Commentary,* took a no more skeptical view than did family-oriented publications such as the *Ladies Home Journal* or *Look*. Both intellectuals and ordinary middle-class citizens could read some counterpluralist, oppositional discourses. In short, on balance, magazine stories about power present a quite ambivalent image of pluralism.

The academic power elite debate did not escape these magazines. In fact, one stalwart of the power elite argument—Floyd Hunter—made his case in *The Nation* ("The Decision Makers: Can You Name Them?" August 21, 1954 [179]: 148–50). Throughout the period *The Nation* offered a strong voice of anti-pluralist discourse; the magazine published several stories that explicitly attacked the premise of multiple centers of power, including one by political theorist C. B. MacPherson ("Bow and Arrow Power," January 19, 1970 [210]: 54–56).

However, academic proponents of pluralism also had their say—

and in a larger circulation magazine than *The Nation.* In *U.S. News and World Report,* Alexander Heard—described as "a leading political scientist"—explicitly attacked the power elite thesis (July 1, 1963 [55]: 58–60). Under the belligerently titled headline "What's All This about a 'Power Structure' in U.S.?" Heard explicitly advanced the pluralist thesis: "I do not feel that we have in this country a 'power structure' in the sense of an all-powerful group at work behind our public officials, deliberately manipulating the course of events. What we do have, if the term is to be used, are 'power structures' plural. There are many structures of influence and power, and sometimes they work at cross-purposes" (58).

Heard points out that the most important though often overlooked of these structures is the electoral process, the process in which most ordinary citizens take part. Thus, Heard adds the access-reactivity theme to the multiple centers of power premise. In addition, he asserts that, by proceeding in pluralistic, coalition-building fashion, presidents are making racial progress. For Heard, not only reactivity but also incremental reform is alive and well.

Not everyone agrees with Heard that pluralism can solve the racial crisis. An exchange in *Newsweek* during a two-week period in 1966 reflects this disagreement. Louis Harris, the Democratic pollster, first advances a comparatively optimistic pluralist prognosis about race. In "The New Coalition—Wave of the Future?" (July 25, 1966 [68]: 24), Harris analyzes Democratic election victories in Virginia and Mayor John Lindsay's success in New York City. Harris believes these elections symbolize a new coalition that "is reform-minded, wants to reject the old, and is solidly against segregation as a way of life. The components of the coalition are white residents of the suburbs, . . . better educated city dwellers, and Negroes, many of whom were voting for the first time." To explain these voting patterns, Harris introduces the pluralist theme of cross-class political coalitions: "The Virginia election appears to be a harbinger of the future, in which the most and least privileged join hands to form political power, irrespective of region or party label." In short, coalition politics pluralist-style generates racial progress.

Two weeks later *Newsweek*'s resident conservative columnist, Raymond Moley, comes to very different conclusions about racial politics and pluralist reform. Moley argues that white politicians courting black voters have created "unattainable expectations" ("Pattern of

Revolution," August 8, 1966 [68]: 84). As a result, writes Moley, responsible black leaders have lost control of the civil rights movement. Violent radicals, such as Floyd McKissick and Black Power advocate Stokely Carmichael, have taken their place. Moley traces Black Power back to the American Communist Party's advocacy of black autonomy in 1932. Although Moley concedes that the future is unpredictable and that "the new militancy" may wane, he argues that an "irrational climate" surrounding race could stimulate "sporadic outbursts." According to Moley, "The slow process of alleviating housing deficiencies and unemployment" may fail. Pluralist compromise and incremental reform will probably not resolve racial conflict in America.

Thus, the magazines are uncertain about pluralist coalition building involving race. However, they do generally agree that popular political participation is increasing. Pluralism has at least stimulated activism among growing numbers of ordinary citizens. The economist Sumner Slichter advances an interesting argument to this effect in the *Saturday Evening Post* ("The Power Holders in the American Economy," December 13, 1958 [231]: 34–35). A more powerful statement of the position appears in a May 1970 *Fortune* article. In "More Power to Everybody," Max Ways claims that "a thrust for greater participation replaces the old drive for independence" (May 1970 [81]: 172). Ways attacks "dogmatic Marxists" and the New Left, who underestimate the recent increase in political participation. Indeed, Ways compares the current participation revolution to the liberal revolutions of the eighteenth century. He points out that in industry workers are increasingly sharing decision-making power with executives. In the military, foot soldiers now share command decisions with officers. In the economy, corporations must respond to greater consumer activism. Thus, not just in politics, but all across society, public participation has increased, checking the power of leaders. In short, pluralist access and reactivity have empowered ordinary citizens.

Also, unlike *Time*, other magazines regularly cover policy areas emphasized by pluralists. Moreover, these stories offer a modestly optimistic picture of pluralism in action. The subject of urban renewal provides a case in point. Not until the mid-1950s did magazines begin to seriously cover municipal improvement and urban renewal. However, as urban renewal became an established program, a stream of stories emerged. Of forty-one articles on the subject between 1956

258

and 1970, twenty-five offered a pluralist assessment of urban renewal. Most such articles portrayed urban renewal as a creative reformist response to urban deterioration; most argued that interest groups and concerned citizens did influence urban renewal policymakers; and most also depicted policymakers stitching together winning urban renewal coalitions. Thus, most articles identified effective pluralism in urban renewal policy.

To be sure, not all these stories *endorsed* urban renewal. For example, a *Readers Digest* article of 1964 ("The Sad Little Story of Wink," October 1964 [85]: 97–100) describes how, through successful pluralist lobbying, one Texas town obtained federal urban renewal funds. However, the article goes on to condemn Washington bureaucracy for poor planning and inefficiency. The story chronicles the saga of Wink, Texas, an impoverished town that applied for urban renewal funds. Facing bureaucratic roadblocks, the town's leaders appealed informally to Vice President Johnson, who secured an instant positive response from the housing and home finance administrator. Soon urban renewal money began to flood into little Wink. To this point, the story is one of classical pluralist access and reactivity. However, the article then proceeds to attack the urban renewal bureaucracy for overselling the program, town planners for destroying houses without replacing them, and unnamed politicians and local citizens who perhaps profited illegally from the failed project. Thus, while *pluralism* works, urban renewal may not.

However, some stories rhapsodize about pluralism and urban renewal. For example, although a *U.S. News and World Report* article ("A Trillion Dollars to Save the Cities?" October 3, 1966 [61]: 73–77) regrets the high price tag for urban reconstruction, the story praises the federal program. The article highlights effective lobbying by local officials, including Mayors Cavanaugh (Detroit), Lindsay (New York), and Lee (New Haven). It also describes the lobbying efforts of city planners. Then the article presents urban renewal as a breathtakingly promising reform. It praises urban renewal projects already completed in Hartford, Pittsburgh, Washington, D.C., Philadelphia, and San Francisco. It cites these projects as proof that urban renewal can transform urban areas, deliver high-quality architecture, and improve transit patterns. It concludes on a quite hopeful note: "Now Congress is showing signs of concern. Money is beginning to pour out to stimulate mass transit. There are proposals by President

Johnson for money to remake demonstration cities and for new towns." Thus, in urban renewal the pluralist system appears to work.

Other articles describe effective pluralist coalition building and bargaining in urban renewal. For example, barely two weeks after the above story in *U.S. News and World Report, Newsweek* recounts President Johnson's tactics in assembling a winning House coalition to pass his Demonstration Cities Program. According to the article ("Congress: Weaver's Trade," October 24, 1966 [68]: 42–44), the administration feared that some Democratic members of Congress opposed to "racial balancing" might torpedo the program. Therefore, Postmaster General Lawrence O'Brien asked a number of doubtful Democrats what they needed in their districts. Soon strategically placed post office, sewer, and other pork barrel projects began to flow to these districts. Moreover, LBJ spent two days on the phone persuading wavering Democrats. Finally, a classic pluralist compromise was struck: the Johnson administration accepted an amendment that, in return for Democratic votes, prohibited school busing in Demonstration Cities areas. Ultimately, pluralist horse trading produced a valuable piece of reform legislation.

But a substantial minority of articles criticizes pluralist politics in urban renewal. Some stories claim that urban renewal does not touch the real problems of cities. For example, a 1962 *Commentary* article (Abe Gottlieb, "The Gray Areas of American Cities," April 1962 [33]: 339–42) argues that urban renewal should rehabilitate existing housing; instead, the program has concentrated on slum clearance and new building. Why has rehabilitation lagged? Partly because Americans want new, not rehabilitated, housing. Partly because planners and social scientists do not know how to revitalize neighborhoods. Partly because red tape and inadequate incentives have slowed the Federal Housing Administration. But, most important, politicians don't support rehabilitation programs. Thus, the politics of urban renewal does not produce the effective reform that pluralism promises.

In a *Commentary* piece published six years later, David Danzig and Jon Field offer an especially biting assessment of urban renewal and pluralist politics ("The Betrayal of the American City," June 1968 [45]: 52–59). Danzig and Field agree with Gottlieb that Americans do not like old housing or urban life. However, they concentrate on recent suburbanization, which they attribute mainly to "the concentration in the cities of a black population with an exaggerated dependence on government" (53). This concentration has created a feeling of political hopelessness. Danzig and Field note that, in the last year alone, Congress considered over two hundred bills that dealt with "the urban crisis, but only six passed, and these provided minimal help." The fact is that federal policy favors suburbs over cities. As a result, pluralist politics *exacerbates* rather than *alleviates* the urban problem. Indeed, in urban policy leaders are increasingly turning to coercion rather than to pluralist politics. Danzig and Field conclude that supporters of urban renewal have not created an effective reform coalition. Why? Because blacks lack the power to create real change, and "no segment of white society is seeking to mobilize the immense political power of the cities behind their common self-interest" (59). In short, according to Danzig and Field, a successful pluralist urban politics has yet to emerge.

Thus, the picture of pluralism is mixed. The magazines depict urban renewal as an arena in which interest groups and average citizens often influence policymakers. The public is able to extract funds and assistance for slum clearance and new building. Moreover, urban renewal has produced some significant and useful reforms. In addition, political leaders have forged winning coalitions in support of urban renewal. So, in many respects, the pluralist politics of compromise and access often works. But a lack of planning, existing anti-urban policies and biases, and, above all, racial animosities impede needed programs, such as housing rehabilitation. The result is that pluralist politics has yet to solve the urban crisis.

The magazines also take a modestly pluralist approach to the issues of public housing and municipal improvement. Of forty-four articles on public housing, twenty-eight pictured the federal program as an arena of successful pluralist policymaking. However, not surprisingly, the same criticisms of pluralism that appeared in stories about urban renewal reemerge in articles about public housing.

One subset of purely descriptive articles simply reports facts about low-interest mortgage loans and cooperative housing aid programs in the early 1950s. During these years, the magazines portray public housing as a beneficial extension of veterans assistance programs, such as the GI Bill. Importantly, these favorable stories about public housing concentrate on whites of modest income. In the 1950s the magazines frame public housing as a manageable, sensible federal program capable of improving life for Americans.

During the 1960s public housing becomes an arena in which political leaders forge powerful pluralist coalitions to effect significant reform. For example, a 1968 *New Republic* article ("Home Building," March 9, 1968 [158]: 8–9) focuses on President Johnson's housing policy. The article describes Johnson's creation of the Department of Housing and Urban Development (HUD), his pioneering of rent supplements for the poor, and his Model Cities Program. The article also recounts how Johnson persuaded private industry to join the federal government in support of public housing. Finally, the story observes that New York governor Nelson Rockefeller also supports public housing; thus, public housing produces cooperation that cuts across party lines. In short, the *New Republic* sees pluralism working reasonably well in housing policy.

Some stories about public housing also highlight the pluralist theme of easy public access. For example, in a 1966 *Christian Century* article ("Housing for the Nation's Poor, II: Are Rent Supplements the Answer?" January 12, 1966 [83]: 44–47), Lyle E. Schaller not only praises public housing but also argues that, through rent supplements, the 1965 Housing and Urban Development Act "provides the churches with a powerful weapon to use if they want to be involved in helping solve the nation's housing problems." Schaller claims that private interest groups, including coalitions of black and white clergy and congregations, have the opportunity to influence public housing for the better.

Nevertheless, racial conflict clouds the performance of pluralism in public housing. As early as 1954, in a *Commonweal* article ("The Housing Scandal," July 2, 1954 [60]: 311–13), Michael Harrington calls attention to the racial aspects of public housing. He argues that racial divisions destroyed the modest housing initiative put forth by the Eisenhower administration. According to Harrington, the Supreme Court decision that outlawed segregation in public housing alienated southern Democrats from the program. Harrington doubts that private business or the political parties will pick up the slack. In short, a nascent pluralist reform coalition in support of public housing has dissolved. Harrington concludes: "Private business has demonstrated time and again that it cannot begin to solve the [housing] problem. And in 1954, the issue of racial segregation and the deep split within both political parties has once again inhibited any real public action."

By 1966 some writers use public housing programs to criticize all arenas of pluralist politics. For example, Herbert Gans argues in *Commonweal* ("Doing Something about Slums," March 18, 1966 [83]: 688–93) that, "Housing schemes can do little to help the poor, and the real need for effective anti-poverty programs." In fact, public housing stigmatizes the poor "and reduces further their dignity and their ability to live as they choose" (689). For Gans, public housing is bound up with race and class politics in the United States; pluralism simply cannot cope with these issues. The new Demonstration Cities Program has promise, but the powerful combination of racial and class anxieties will prevent a successful pluralist compromise. "As always, the prime inadequacy is financial; the net federal subsidy for this program will be only 2.3 billion dollars over six years" (692–93). Although Gans concedes that an upsurge of political pressure from average citizens might free up more money, he is pessimistic. In a pluralist system, he implies, the poor do not benefit.

To conclude, according to magazine journalism, in specific domestic policy arenas pluralist politics is the norm and often works effectively. Yet pluralist politics cannot overcome deep conflicts over race and class. Issues of race and class flash brilliantly against the background of everyday pluralist politics. Together race and class destroy pluralist hegemony and put in its place the figure-ground model of leaders' political culture.

THE NEW YORK TIMES: ALL THE PLURALISM THAT'S FIT TO PRINT

As the newspaper of record in the United States, the *New York Times* reaches many politically active citizens. Indeed, the *Times* is probably the most widely read print component of leaders' political culture. What picture of the American regime did the *Times* present between 1950 and 1970? In particular, how did it represent pluralism during the period?

In order to investigate this question, I considered every Sunday *Times* for the eleven even-numbered years between 1950 and 1970. I focused on stories about the pluralist themes of access-reactivity and tolerance among political leaders. In addition, I analyzed stories about three policy areas analyzed by pluralists: public housing, urban

263

redevelopment, and school board decisions. The sample for my discussion comprises a total of 455 articles.

As might be expected, the *Times* devoted considerable attention to issues of tolerance and political access during the period. Indeed, its distribution of stories closely tracks that of *Time* magazine. Moreover, like *Time,* it paints a predominantly anti-pluralist picture of access-reactivity and elite tolerance. However, the *Times* deviates markedly from *Time* in its depiction of McCarthyism. Moreover, it devotes more attention than *Time* to civil rights, free speech, and individual liberty. As a result, the *New York Times* presents the theme of tolerance as a contested terrain between pluralist and nonpluralist politics. While two-thirds of the 218 articles that deal with tolerance take a nonpluralist position, leaders are not completely intolerant partisans.

One aspect of the *Times* coverage that somewhat counters political intolerance is the paper's stories about academics and intellectuals who successfully defend themselves against McCarthyism. In addition, the *Times* identifies political leaders who speak out in favor of free speech and against McCarthy. For example, on March 12, 1950, the *Times* reports on the National Lawyers Guild's opposition to loyalty programs in the federal government (Murray Illson, "Loyalty Program Upheld, Attacked," 80). Two weeks later the *Times* reports that college faculty decry loyalty oaths (3), that a priest has deplored McCarthy's "extremism" (3), and that a loyalty oath protest is scheduled at the University of California, Berkeley (Lawrence E. Davies, "Berkeley Campus Sets Oath Protest," April 2, 1950). These stories provide a discernible counternarrative to the dominant anti-pluralism of *Time*'s tolerance coverage.

Moreover, throughout the twenty-year period, the *Times* ran stories about political leaders and private citizens trying to *promote* tolerance. For example, in 1960 the *Times* reported that "President Eisenhower asked today that each American 'examine his conscience' in a movement to end racial, religious and other unworthy discriminations" ("President Issues Tolerance Plea," November 13, 1960: 43). According to the article, the president spoke out to commemorate the 160th anniversary of the Bill of Rights. While these occasional stories do not nullify the impact of McCarthy, they do add a dose of pluralism to the tolerance theme.

Finally, in the late 1960s the *Times* sometimes reported that political leaders actually supported the rights of unpopular protesters and dissenters. The *Times* ran stories about the Air Force dropping curbs on free speech (May 15, 1966: 10), Barry Goldwater's strong assertion of free speech rights against President Johnson (June 2, 1966: 40), the end of the loyalty oath (January 11, 1970: E6), a Tennessee court's freeing of a presidential heckler (June 14, 1970: 45), and a court's ruling against the censorship of a student newspaper (July 12, 1970: 27). Thus, the *New York Times* softened the dominant picture of leader intolerance.

However, on the matter of access and reactivity, the *New York Times* closely resembles *Time* magazine's anti-pluralism. Not only does the *Times* (understandably) cover the same instances of corruption that *Time* reported, but the paper also provides deeper anti-pluralist analyses. For example, in a long article about the New York state legislature, David K. Shipler writes that lobbyists "have become indispensable parts of the process of making law" ("Lobbyists Play a Key Role in Albany Lawmaking," February 11, 1970: 1). Although legislators and the author present lobbying as basically beneficial, the article worries that some lobbyists "are regarded as more influential than many Assemblymen or Senators" (1). In addition, not all lobbyists are equal; business groups generally prevail over others. Shipler writes, "Some legislators cite this lack of well-organized opposition to moneyed interests as the major deficiency of the lobbying process" (60). In sum, contrary to pluralism, unelected and unrepresentative lobbyists wield vast amounts of unequal power.

But the *Times* does at least report that some labor unions are also influential. In particular, the United Auto Workers and the Coal Miners under John L. Lewis represent workers effectively. Still, the *Times* confines its favorable coverage of unions to the early 1950s. Later in the period, the *Times* paints a grimmer picture of access and reactivity. Increasingly, like *Time* magazine, the newspaper features scandal, corruption, exclusion, and backstage deals rather than open and fair relations between ordinary citizens, large interest groups, and politicians.

The *Times* does provide a distinctively pluralist portrayal of public policy in the United States, however. In the three policy areas I examined—public housing, urban redevelopment, and school board politics—the *Times* published a steady stream of pluralist stories between 1950 and 1970. Of 198 stories on these topics, 150 (three-quarters) described an active, vital pluralist process. The *Times* often profiled citizen groups that effectively opposed objectionable proposals. These stories generally describe policymakers being forced to alter their programs by citizen action. Other articles chronicle successful efforts by local representative bodies—such as school boards—to influence state policies on behalf of ordinary citizens. The abundance of these stories undoubtedly reflects the metropolitan arena of local *Times* coverage. However, the pluralist tilt of the coverage cannot be explained by its New York setting; the *Times* also reports pluralist stories about these policy issues outside New York City.

For example, in 1970, the *Times* described strong citizen opposition to federal housing programs in several cities around the United States (John Herbers, "Federal Housing Projects Stir Strong Opposition across U.S." June 14, 1970: 67). The article describes numerous local meetings and protests against Operation Breakthrough, a HUD program to provide federal assistance to ten cities. In Wilmington, Delaware, "There have been about twenty public hearings and meetings in which the citizens have contended that the project would overload sewers, crowd schools, decrease property values, and take away a large area of open space." Protesters objected to scattered-site, low-cost housing that would have moved blacks into predominantly white areas. Although these protests describe the racial animosities that limit pluralist reform, at least citizen involvement provides access to policymakers. Moreover, politicians react in typically pluralist fashion. The article reports that in St. Louis, "As a result [of protests], the City Council defeated a bill required for the project."

The *Times* reports many other cases of influential citizen opposition to policies aimed at helping minorities. For example, in 1970, the *Times* describes a previously obscure bill in the New York State Senate, which has stimulated sudden, effective local opposition in Brooklyn. "When community groups outside the [black] Bedford-Stuyvesant, Crown Heights and Brownsville areas of the project learned of the bill after its passage by the State Senate on Tuesday, an immediate outcry arose" (Paul L. Montgomery, "Atlantic Avenue Renewal Stirs Dispute in Brooklyn," April 5, 1970: 1). The predominantly white, middle-class protesters contacted their legislators in opposition to the renewal project. According to the article, state lawmakers not only attended local protest rallies but also planned to delay the bill in the legislature.

Racial minorities also play the pluralist game. For example, a July

1960 story reports that opposition by minorities has slowed plans to renew the Adams-Morgan neighborhood in Washington, D.C. The article states that a coalition of Adams-Morgan minority citizen groups has met with planners and expressed its opposition to the project. As a result, the plan "has run into trouble" (Bess Furman, "Urban Renewal in Washington Stalled as Its Neighbors Protest," July 31, 1960: 59).

Education policies are especially likely to stimulate the pluralist representation of minority groups. For example, in 1962, the *Times* reported that a Chicago alderman was responding to pressure exerted by local black organizations. He hoped to prevent the board of education from spending local tax dollars that would maintain racial segregation in schools (Donald Janson, "Chicago School Board Accused of Pursuing Racial Segregation," January 21, 1962: 62). A combination of sit-ins, testimony at city council hearings, and legal suits by black parents have produced articulate pluralist representation.

To summarize, the reservations of the *New York Times* about leader tolerance and reactivity do not extend to policymaking. According to the *Times*, pluralism is alive and well in many spheres of public policy. Thus, pluralist policymaking contains a background against which anti-pluralist outbursts occur. The *Times* thus contributes substantially to a figure-ground model of pluralism in the political culture of American leaders.

CONCLUSION: TWO CHEERS FOR PLURALISM

E. M. Forster, in his World War II BBC radio broadcasts, argued that liberal democracy, flawed though it was, still merited two out of a possible three cheers. Certainly, argued Forster, liberal democracy was superior to fascism and socialism. Forster's enthusiasm for liberal democracy was tempered and sober; as he put it, "Democracy is not a Beloved Republic, and never will be. But it is less hateful than other forms of government, and to that extent it deserves our support" (1951: 69).

The evidence reviewed in this chapter supports a like verdict about pluralism in American political culture. Pluralism formed the background of leaders' political culture during the 1950s and 1960s. Although newspapers, magazines, and textbooks targeted serious weaknesses in pluralism, there were plentiful, if unspectacular, pluralist descriptions of public policy. Only *Time* magazine deviated entirely from this figure-ground pattern.

The figure-ground pattern described here differs sharply from other characterizations of American political culture during the 1950s and 1960s. Certainly there was no hegemonic pluralist consensus during the period. Instead, the terrain of political discourse was sporadically contested. Moreover, contrary to those who characterize the 1950s as bland and quiet, the decade witnessed plenty of debate about pluralist politics.

Likewise, the evidence does not support those who argue that the 1960s shattered a pluralist consensus and created fragmentation. Instead, if anything, pluralist depictions of the American political regime actually increased in the late 1960s. After all, the 1960s produced no national counterpart to McCarthy, nor counterparts to the Billie Sol Estes and Bobby Baker scandals that mocked the pluralist access-reactivity premise. In fact, American political culture looks about as pluralist in the late 1960s as it did in the early 1950s. In that sense, Yale pluralism was indeed part of a vital pluralist discourse during the entire period.

Yet pluralism never achieved hegemony for two reasons: some segments of the American Right, as illustrated by *Time* magazine, opposed pluralism bitterly; also, pluralism confronted searching and thoughtful critiques from the Left, as manifested in *Commentary, Commonweal, The New Republic,* the *New York Times,* and a minority of American government textbooks. The Right—for example, *Time* magazine—disdained pluralist politics, seeing it as riven by ideological struggle, corruption and scandal, partisan maneuvering, and inept policymaking. Meanwhile, the Left hammered pluralism for its subservience to business interests, its mistreatment of racial minorities, and its refusal to confront anti-democratic structural inequalities.

Still, these critiques never derogated pluralism entirely. For one thing, critics rarely attacked pluralism on *normative* grounds. Few critics claimed that pluralist politics was in its very essence immoral. Only *Time* hinted that congressional scandals were perhaps the inevitable consequences of a morally bankrupt—as opposed to inept— political system. Likewise, few Left critics questioned the *goals* of pluralism or of the American regime. Most voices agreed that citizen access to responsive politicians, tolerance among leaders, reform policies, and competing centers of power are worthy things. Only rarely did critics suggest that real reform might require greater centralization, or that unequal access to politicians signaled a fundamentally vicious political regime.

The sole exception to this generalization is *Time*'s coverage of domestic anti-Communism, which did actually attack pluralism on moral grounds. Americans, *Time* implies, should recognize that there is a fateful moral struggle between the Communist movement and American nationalism; in this struggle there is no room for the compromises, tolerance, reactivity, and incremental reformism of pluralism. Pluralism, *Time* suggests, is simply not capable of winning the ideological war against Communism.

But even this is a limited attack on pluralism, for neither *Time* nor the Left proposes a serious alternative to pluralism. In fact, the American government textbooks—which, after all, offer more room for theoretical debate than do newspapers or magazines—discuss few significant substitutes for American pluralist politics. Thus, pluralism persists; Yale's legitimating discourse resides within—and reinforces—a moderately receptive political culture.

9

The Legitimation Dilemma

PLURALISM AT WORK

The argument of this study is essentially contained in the following anecdote, told by Fred Greenstein to the author:

> Dahl kind of lackadaisically put together a course in which the idea was to read the leading current works. We read Truman one week, and Dahl brought in a brilliant, constructive, destructive propositional analysis of Truman, which he never published, but showed all the contradictions in Truman. We read some of the voting studies, and so on. After six weeks, Dahl said, "I think that is everything that is interesting and current in political science. Is there any reason to continue having these meetings?" Everybody had these temper tantrums, and I said why don't we read this new book distributed by some of the book clubs, Mills's *Power Elite,* and Dahl came in with the first draft of the ruling elite piece, and then he brought in the head of redevelopment in New Haven, Ed Logue, to talk about what were the realities in New Haven politics, and the following year he said to Wolfinger and Polsby that he got a big grant from the Ford Foundation. He was going to study power in a city, and would they like to work with him. (Interview, July 23, 1997)

As this anecdote illustrates, pluralism as text and improvisation came to life in the ordinary experiences of its progenitors at Yale. Indeed, Greenstein's anecdote depicts all four premises of pluralism simultaneously at work. The students' temper tantrums and Greenstein's bold suggestion opposed Dahl's initiative to end the class prematurely; thus, "followers" (students) challenged the leader (Dahl), thereby improvising the competing centers of power premise. In turn, Dahl reacted positively by considering Mills's new book, thereby keeping the course alive. Dahl's action also improvised the tolerance premise; indeed, he brought a voice critical of pluralism—that of Mills—into classroom discussion. The ultimate result was incremental reform, in the emergence of *Who Governs?*, an important contribution to the pluralist analysis of American politics. In turn, pluralism itself was a reformist departure from traditional institutionalism in political science.

How then has Yale pluralism worked? I count thirty-nine specific ways, as described below.

Thirty-Nine Ways that Yale Pluralism Worked

1. Through the production of pluralist texts.
2. Through pluralist occupational experiences early in a career (Dahl, Kaufman, Lane).
3. Through effective pluralist practice regarding minority groups, such as Jews.
4. Through the use of pluralism to solidify a department (e.g., the Kendall affair; department reaction to the 1960s).
5. Through successful recruitment of new pluralist faculty (Mayhew, Lasswell).
6. Through senior faculty improvisations of pluralism.
7. Through rebuff of external challenges to pluralism (Lane and Russett promotions).
8. Through junior faculty compliance with pluralism (Dix, Calleo).
9. Through reactive responsiveness to students.
10. Through department enforcement of pluralist "rules of the game," such as tolerance.
11. Through the construction of a pluralist department identity.
12. Through the development of cognitive mechanisms for reproducing pluralism (e.g., segmentation).
13. Through the production of reformist pluralist leadership (Fesler, Dahl).
14. Through the "scientizing" of pluralism in narratives.
15. Through a feeling of success among pluralist graduate students.
16. Through student observation of pluralist improvisations by faculty.
17. Through student improvisations of pluralism.
18. Through early socialization experiences that favored pluralism among students.

19. Through flexible interpretations of pluralism among students.
20. Through making pluralism "obvious" to students
21. Through student personal experiences that confirmed pluralism.
22. Through the student's development of cognitive mechanisms (e.g., supplementation, exemption) for defending pluralism.
23. Through the application of pluralism to new political issues.
24. Through the application of pluralism to social and occupational relations.
25. Through the embodiment of pluralism in political decision making.
26. Through the complementarity between a student's personal identity and pluralism.
27. Through the student's desire to move from the periphery of society to the center.
28. Through the appeal of professionalism to students.
29. Through the absence of convincing oppositional discourses.
30. Through supportive political experiences.
31. Through the slight positional advantages enjoyed by pluralists.
32. Through the establishment of strong peer networks among pluralists.
33. Through pluralism as a scholarly legacy or cultural memory.
34. Through the self-confidence pluralists developed.
35. Through pluralism's "distancing" of students from intellectual challenges.
36. Through students refraining from radical political action because of pluralism.
37. Through pluralism becoming a moral norm.
38. Through the application of "realism" to empirical observations.
39. Through pluralism becoming the "ground" of political culture.

Yet, despite its length, we should not be overly impressed by this list. After all, mine is not a Foucaultian account of an encompassing, triumphant legitimating discourse. As I have shown, even in the most favorable political circumstances—a period of Cold War, following upon American victory over discredited discourses such as fascism and Marxism; an economy awash with new prosperity and expanded opportunity; and a domestic political environment (until the late 1960s) of consensus on moderate policies among the leaders of both political parties—pluralism never achieved hegemony in American political culture. Indeed, it did not even capture the allegiance of enough Yale political scientists to sustain itself at that institution. Thus, not only have "recent Marxists . . . greatly exaggerated the degree to which the supposed 'ideological hegemony' of the bourgeoisie perpetuates capitalism" (Wrong, 1998: 104–5), but also a most promising legitimating political discourse in academia cannot be counted on to strongly fortify the American political regime.

Why is this so? Why is it difficult to produce and sustain powerful legitimating discourses in the United States, especially in universities? Certainly there was no lack of subtlety in pluralism. As Benjamin Barber points out, pluralism enjoyed "scientific serendipity," that is, it did not preach moralistically. According to Barber, pluralism argued that American democracy was "*descriptively* superior to the democracy of . . . other nations" (1998: 206; emphasis added). This scientific message was as powerfully legitimating as it was unobtrusive. Yet it did not dominate the cultural terrain even before the 1960s. By the late 1960s it could not successfully protect the reformist national state it legitimated.

Garry Wills advances one possible explanation for pluralism's limitations. Wills argues that the 1960s dethroned an Ivy League Establishment "that informally decreed what political positions were serious, marginalizing all others" (1998: 28). This Establishment, according to Wills, defined politics in ways congruent with pluralism. For example, it screened out conflictive "cultural" arguments about religion, race, class, and gender. Even though it was centrist and did incorporate ethnic and racial minorities into American politics, the Establishment eventually shattered. The center did not hold. Instead, radicals of the Right and Left seized control of American politics. As a result, says Wills, for the last two generations politics has steadily escaped Washington—the institutional home of pluralism.

Even if Wills is correct about a pluralist Establishment during the mid-twentieth century, there remains the question of whether Establishment control is typical of American politics or an aberration. Wills is clear on this subject; the mid-twentieth century was "a deviation, one caused by the need to respond to a long-continuing crisis (Depression, World War, Cold War), in which elites were given emergency powers" (57). In fact, elsewhere Wills claims that the dominant mythology of American politics has held that "Government is . . . at best, a necessary evil, one we must put up with while resenting the necessity. . . . Americans believe that they have a government which is itself against government, that our Constitution is so distrustful of itself as to hamper itself" (1999: 15). If Wills is correct, any legitimating discourse for power holders—even one as comparatively democratic as pluralism—will lack complete acceptance in the United States.

Should this possibility be entirely surprising? Not really. After all, Weber, who argued famously that the Western state would increasingly depend upon rational-legal doctrines, never asserted that rational-legal legitimation would be complete. Even Wilhelmian Germany—far more a rational-legal society than the United States—throbbed with alternative ideologies of personal charisma, traditional religiosity, folk customs, and aesthetic escapism (Scaff, 1989). Weber recognized that power holders were always engaged in struggles to establish their legitimacy and even to rationalize their power to themselves.

No wonder power holders so often resort to nondiscursive forms of legitimation. For example, power holders often comfort themselves in the belief that they are providing important material benefits to citizens. Distributing tangible rewards is undoubtedly a source of satisfaction and self-confidence. Who can resist being a "public servant," rather than a self-interested power holder? Providing material benefits to needy constituents is gratifying; so what if there is no legitimating discourse to explain theoretically why or how the process of distribution actually occurs? This absence is no great loss—at least so long as there remain benefits to be distributed, and inefficiency and corruption do not weaken power holders.

Or power holders can comfort themselves by offering symbolic satisfactions to citizens (Edelman, 1988). Previously unrepresented constituents may derive vicarious pleasure from seeing one of "their own" achieve a position of power. Or perhaps the symbolic "politics of recognition" (Gutmann, 1992) embodied in speeches, public celebrations, memorials, holidays, proclamations, and so on will reassure power holders that they do, in fact, care about ordinary citizens. Also, repeated incessantly, rhetorical invocations of patriotism and the Constitution may persuade power holders that they indeed *are* patriotic and respectful of the Constitution, rather than manipulative and exploitative. Who needs a legitimating discourse to explain and justify all the smoke and mirrors—at least until challenges to symbolism surface, and dissident groups begin to point out that the emperors are not wearing any clothes?

Or power holders can tell themselves that they are experts, and therefore deserve to rule. Perhaps they possess specialized expertise in an area of public policy, or they are experts in the process of governance. In fact, claims of expertise resemble legitimating discourses. Legitimating discourses are simply the expert analyses offered by academics and journalists, rather than by politicians or bureaucrats. Moreover, power holders may view their own experiences as peculiarly authenticating; they may boast of their "hands-on," insider practical wisdom, as opposed to the theories of the intellectual in the ivory tower. Still, purely practical expertise cannot transcend the power holder's own experience. Therefore, legitimation *via* practical expertise fails eventually. Then, in the absence of a legitimating discourse, the power holder may not know just what went wrong, why, and what should be done next.

Or power holders may develop tunnel vision and concentrate on their own particular policy area, ignoring all others. They may perceive "their" policy as more successful than the regime as a whole. They may cast themselves as "good soldiers" who work on a meritorious program. Somehow there has evolved a winning formula for, say, Social Security, or defense procurement, or bilingual education. Why worry if the relationship between this policy and others is poorly understood? So what if academics do not justify the policy or the regime as a whole? But just as no man is an island unto himself, neither is a governmental program an island unto itself. It is necessary to set priorities among programs; power holders must therefore cooperate across specialized policy spheres. When the regime itself comes under fire, power holders will profit little from saying, in effect, "Well, the government as a whole may be lousy, but my program works fine." In short, sooner or later even the most myopic power holder will search for a legitimating discourse.

Finally, power holders may comfort themselves because even during periods of political turmoil majorities of the population may remain quiescent and seemingly undisturbed. Like Richard Nixon, they may conclude that the "silent majority" is on their side; their opponents are an unrepresentative, radical minority whom they can consign to an enemies list. After all, during the height of student protests at Yale, in 1968, when "the university's blue collar workers went on strike, students crossed the picket lines to keep the cafeterias running" (Frum, 2000). In fact, future Republican president George W. Bush was apparently a member of the silent majority at Yale between 1964 and 1968. Bush "was a noncombatant in these upheavals. . . . In short, while some students took to the barricades, Mr. Bush took to the bar" (Kristof, 2000). "Taking to the bar" may not be a ringing vote of confidence in the powers-that-be, but it is certainly not support for insurgents. Eventually, however, majority quiescence and passivity proves cold comfort to power holders, as the events of the late 1960s demonstrate. Look what happened to Lyndon Johnson and Richard Nixon; the "silent majority" did not save them.

When all is said and done, leaders need legitimating discourses. Pluralism worked for a time by generating texts and practices that power holders could use to transcend their identities as public servants, symbolic leaders, policy experts, or good soldiers. Indeed, pluralism brought these identities together theoretically into a legitimate structure of rule. But, as the saying goes, "That was then. What about now?"

NEW LEGITIMATING DISCOURSES?

In a recent polemic, Morris Berman decries "the celebration of ignorance that characterizes American culture today" (2000: 41). Berman, like many recent others who diagnose the "cultural decline" of contemporary American life, expresses despair about the role of American intellectuals. Nor do politicians escape this attack. Indeed, to return briefly—and perhaps unfairly—to George W. Bush, Frank Bruni writes that the Republican standard-bearer flaunted his "disdain for intellectualism." Bruni grants that anti-intellectualism is not a new phenomenon in the United States; nevertheless, "Mr. Bush's sustained promotion of it—along with his tendency to throw stones at ivory towers and challenge any suggestion that book learning could trump horse sense—is unusually aggressive" (2000). Given these descriptions, one might reasonably expect the decline of pluralism to have created a vacuum of legitimating discourses for the American political regime.

Not so, however. Indeed, two convergent phenomena promote the creation and dissemination of new legitimating discourses. The first phenomenon, of course, is the need for legitimation among power holders, a disposition they indulge—albeit reluctantly sometimes—by indirectly promoting and financing promising academic research and writing. Of course, by "promising" I refer to academic efforts that are likely to favor their own power.

The second phenomenon is the desire of academics to make sense of politics. After all, regardless of pluralism's weakened condition, power holders continue to rule, and politics goes on. How is the political regime to be theorized *after* pluralism? The study of political power is especially enticing today precisely because the regime that pluralism legitimated has changed, thanks to the challenges that began in the 1960s. The decline of pluralist discourse parallels the transformation of the pluralist regime into . . . what? How exactly does the political system work today? And what new legitimating discourses do academics offer in answer to this question?

Political scientists have in fact produced several new legitimating discourses. These discourses capture different features of the contemporary American political regime. Their variety reflects the complexity of the current regime. The regime does not operate consistently across its various sectors; therefore, it promotes several competing legitimating discourses. None of these discourses covers as much ground as did pluralism nor enjoys as broad acceptance. However, each has perhaps penetrated more deeply into specific policy areas than did pluralism. Most significantly, all of these discourses lack a crucial component—the promise of effective citizen influence on government—that pluralism indirectly offered. For this reason, the new discourses cannot replace pluralism.

Certainly the most ambitious potential successor to pluralism is the theory of rational choice. Rational choice theory legitimates those power holders who favor the privatization of government services, and who believe the market rather than the state best provides social benefits. The theory of rational choice supports a slimmed-down state that defers whenever possible to the market. It relies upon a new faith in economic theory, as exemplified by John Mueller's confident observation: "Economists, I suggest, now basically have reached a substantial and probably correct consensus about how economies work, and they are able to prescribe policies that have a good chance of enhancing an economy's ability to grow. . . . Now the economists' advice is increasingly being accepted by decision makers." According

277

to Mueller, this "economic science" includes the truth that "economies do best when the government leaves them substantially free" (1999: 99–100).

Jill Quadagno argues that American public policy now reflects the "correct consensus" Mueller celebrates. There is, says Quadagno, the "ascendance of a neo-conservative ideology, which depicts the welfare state as an impediment to a free market" (1999: 4). Quadagno describes a new "capital investment welfare state," in which government facilitates private savings and investments, rather than offering direct social insurance. Power holders with capital investment as their major goal will certainly enjoy the support of rational choice theory, which explains that the state is inefficient, "rent seeking"—that is, "creating opportunities for profits higher than would be obtained in an open, competitive market" (Ostrum, 1998: 3), averse to broad consumer choice, and, necessarily coercive in order to force "free riders" into compliance.

Like pluralists, rational choice theorists have applied their arguments to many different political institutions, including Congress and executive agencies (e.g., Segal, 1997; Moe, 1984). Furthermore, recent rational choice theory takes account of inconvenient empirical findings, such as the fact that people often exhibit more trust than narrowly conceived rational self-interest predicts. In fact, according to Elinor Ostrom (1998), rational choice actually now legitimates the reciprocal trust that supports collective action, including that of the state. Thus, if trust, as well as free riding, becomes "rational," the theory of rational choice will give politicians more to do than simply devolve their functions to the market or to capital investment.

Yet even an expanded rational choice theory is a flawed legitimating discourse. For one thing, most rational choice theory is so mathematically dense that power holders must find it inaccessible. In this respect, it differs sharply from pluralism. More important, even with the trust mechanism included, rational choice theory subordinates government to the market. At best, government's job remains to stimulate the market and private investment; thus, in a regime legitimated by rational choice theory the "era of Big Government *is* over," as President Bill Clinton put it. Indeed, rational choice theory may not even empower a restricted set of political power holders. People who are not already trusting or cooperative tend to avoid collective action and social choice dilemmas (Ostrom, 1998: 12). Given this fact, rational choice theory does not relieve politicians of the need to exert power through coercion. By contrast, pluralism's emphasis on socialized consensus and adherence to "rules of the game" could convince power holders that theirs was, in fact, a benign and shared exercise of rule, not naked domination.

Another potential successor to pluralism is historical institutionalism. As Ira Katznelson's recent review of this approach makes clear (1998), historical institutionalists try to explain American politics in terms of state capacity, rather than in terms of the strategies of individuals (as in rational choice theory) or group competition (as in pluralism). Katznelson shows that some historical institutionalists intend to produce legitimating discourses for politicians. Indeed, he quotes a leading example of historical institutionalism—Finegold and Skocpol's *State and Party in America's New Deal* (1995)—to support his contention. Finegold and Skocpol claim "to grasp the true choices and the action possibilities that face . . . makers of the public policies for the future" (quoted in Katznelson, 1998).

According to historical institutionalists such as Finegold and Skocpol, the key to American politics is the state's variable ability to dominate interest groups, social classes, and individual actors. Historical institutionalists argue that effective public policies depend above all on the expertise, resources, authority, and beliefs of politicians in positions of institutional authority. Thus, for historical institutionalists, unlike rational choice theorists, the state can be the most effective of all social forces. Power holders will no doubt find this message comforting and reassuring.

Finegold and Skocpol's treatment of the National Recovery Administration (NRA) and the Agricultural Adjustment Administration (AAA) during the New Deal illustrates why historical institutionalism would appeal to holders of power. The authors argue that the AAA succeeded because the Department of Agriculture "was, so to speak, an island of state strength in an ocean of weakness" (1995: 58). For example, historically the department had recruited and trained a core group of agricultural economists, who were able to shape the implementation of farm legislation during the New Deal. By contrast, the NRA suffered from "the historically explicable absence of relevant administrative strength in the U.S. national state" (58). Therefore, the NRA never surmounted the fragmenting forces of industrial interest groups. The NRA never achieved control of the manufacturing economy, as the AAA did the agricultural economy. In short, the implied message Finegold and Skocpol deliver to power holders is clear: "Build the state, and become powerful. Not only can you do so, but only if you do so will significant political progress occur in America."

Just as rational choice theory has its contemporary political embodiment in privatization and the "capital investment welfare state," so also does historical institutionalism have its embodiment in, for example, the *National Performance Review* (1994), which was intended to increase the efficiency of government. President Clinton was also fond of historical institutionalism. Though he proclaimed the era of "Big Government" to be dead, the president argued that a small government could remain powerful, once it became streamlined, flexible, and focused. Desperately searching for whatever legitimation he could muster, Clinton alternately grasped market initiatives based on rational choice (e.g., the North American Free Trade Agreement [NAFTA]; welfare reform) and historical institutionalism's support for the state (the Reinventing Government Program; proposed comprehensive national health care; the Human Genome Project).

Nevertheless, like rational choice theory, historical institutionalism is a flawed legitimating discourse. For one thing, as Katznelson (1998: 195) points out, its emphasis upon "path-dependence"—the tendency of history to constrain institutions—discourages politicians who hope for reform. Office holders who believe they are prisoners of the past hardly experience the freedom felt by pluralist politicians, who maneuver flexibly between interests to form progressive political coalitions.

In addition, historical institutionalism removes from politicians the pleasure that comes from assisting interest groups. Responding to needy citizens is gratifying for a policymaker, even if, in so doing, the policymaker's own autonomy is reduced. It cannot be pleasant for power holders to constantly field the complaints of disappointed interest groups and constituents, who feel they have been overlooked, deceived, and coerced. Indeed, interest group weakness often produces arrogance among policymakers. And arrogance—like pride—goes before a political fall, as the AAA discovered when the Supreme Court invalidated the original Agricultural Adjustment Act.

A third potential successor to pluralism, surprisingly enough, is multiculturalism. Though it is primarily an oppositional discourse created by disempowered ethnic groups, multiculturalism can also become a legitimating discourse, as the case of Canada shows. In conformity to multiculturalism's "soft" version—which urges more positive images of women, gays, and ethnic minorities—some holders of power in the United States have now become, in effect, multiculturalists. For example, the United States National Park Service now devotes itself to celebrating ethnic minorities through the reconstruction of historical sites (Rhea, 1997). In addition, officials who enforce affirmative action programs gain support from multiculturalism's "hard" version—that is, the argument that public policies should distribute material benefits explicitly along ethnic lines. Indeed, according to one of affirmative action's more vociferous opponents, Frederick Lynch, the symbol of "diversity" now empowers political leaders who would welcome multicultural discourse in political science (1997).

In fact, relatively few political scientists have advanced a multicultural theory of American politics. However, some political theorists, such as Iris Marion Young (1990), have advanced strong normative arguments in support of multiculturalism. Moreover, in one of the most influential recent articles in American political science, Rogers Smith (1993) identifies an ethno-racial tradition in American political culture. Indeed, in a recent historical study (with Philip Klinkner) of American racial politics, Smith urges policymakers to overcome "our inherited racial inequalities" (Klinkner, 1999: 347). Although Smith does not advocate multiculturalism as a solution, he nevertheless provides useful ammunition to power holders committed to distributing government benefits along ethnic and racial lines.

Yet multiculturalism suffers more severe disabilities as a legitimating discourse than do rational choice or historical institutionalism. Proponents of the latter two discourses can cite many powerful public policies to support their theories. But aside from affirmative action's production of a black middle class (Patterson, 1997: 147), proponents of multiculturalism have yet to provide convincing policy in support for their theories. Moreover, rational choice and historical institutionalism offer clear definitions of a compelling national interest (ever-increasing prosperity in the rational choice case; a powerful state in the historical institutionalism case). By contrast, multiculturalism has yet to articulate a transcendent national interest to which ethnic and racial groups should subordinate themselves. Therefore, multiculturalism legitimates only a few power holders in contemporary American politics. No wonder that multiculturalism is the most peripheral of contemporary legitimating discourses. Nor is it any surprise that few political scientists advance the discourse.

In some areas of public policy, these three legitimating discourses compete against each other on relatively equal terms, supporting different policies and power holders. Public education provides a particularly good example of this discursive conflict. Beginning with Chubb and Moe's *Politics, Markets, and American Schools* (1990), proponents of rational choice theory have offered legitimation to educational policymakers, including President Bush, who advocate private school choice "accountability," voucher programs, and the charter school movement. Recent research by Paul Peterson and Mark Schneider offers some empirical support to such programs. The school choice movement, like rational choice theory, emphasizes the virtues of unfettered competition. Proponents argue that private educational entrepreneurs in competition with each other and with public schools can produce higher-quality education than can public schools alone. Peterson also claims that educational achievement in choice schools surpasses that for comparable students in nonchoice schools (Peterson and Noyes, 1996; Howell and Peterson, 2002). In addition, Schneider (Schneider et al., 1997) argues that parental participation increases in choice schools (for a challenge to Peterson, see Witte, 2000). Both findings legitimate the choice movement.

For its part, historical institutionalism supports a different set of new educational policies: national standards and high-stakes achievement testing. As Eva L. Baker (1994) has shown, the powerful national standards and testing movement is very much a top-down, state-driven phenomenon. Baker demonstrates that experts, such as professional educators, national organizations of academics, testing specialists, and federal administrators, have propelled the testing and standards movement forward. Prestigious presidential commissions have also promoted national educational standards. Elected politicians have supported the movement not in response to an aroused public opinion or powerful interest groups representing concerned parents and teachers, but rather because of pressure from educational professionals and technocrats. Indeed, the standards and testing movement had to overcome the entrenched opposition of the National Education Association, the largest interest group of teachers in the country. National standards and testing inevitably centralize American education, empowering educational bureaucrats, testers, and state administrators. In short, just as historical institutionalism argues, a strongly committed state apparatus backed by technical experts can reform even America's most decentralized government program—public education.

Finally, proponents of multiculturalism have reformed educational curricula in an effort to "celebrate" ethnic diversity and to incorporate and reward ethnic minorities. Indeed, in many classrooms and schools, multiculturalism is now the conventional pedagogical wisdom. As Nathan Glazer puts it, "'We are all multiculturalists now.' Of course, we are not all multiculturalists, but one would be hard put, if one works in schools and with black school children . . . to find someone who is not" (1997: 160). Multiculturalism in its legitimating version supports the power holders implementing these reforms. In sum, multicultural curricula improvise multicultural theory; educational vouchers improvise rational choice; and national standards and testing improvise historical institutionalism. Thus, contemporary educational policy is a cornucopia of discursive legitimation.

THE LEGITIMATION DILEMMA

Undoubtedly there are virtues associated with the discursive competition between rational choice, historical institutionalism, and multiculturalism. Each discourse legitimates a particular subgroup of power holders; together the three endorse most of those who currently control public policy. Thus, the political regime enjoys more diverse support than any single legitimating discourse—even one as popular as pluralism—can provide.

Also, competition between the three legitimating discourses prevents power holders from becoming a single unified elite. Take, for example, educational policy. Proponents of school choice may sometimes find it difficult to ally with supporters of national standards. If all students must take the same tests, then schools will offer little choice of curricular goals. As a result, school choice's promised variety of school offerings diminishes. Many proponents of multiculturalism also reject school choice, reasoning that relatively few of the low-achieving minorities they represent will be able to attend choice schools. If the bulk of minority, low-income students must remain within traditional public schools, why divert scarce resources to the minority choice programs? Finally, even when proponents of all three discourses subscribe to the same policy, such as national standards, they will assign the policy different priorities. In short, discursive competition inhibits smooth cooperation and total domination among power holders.

The virtue of modest cleavage among power holders is that it prevents the accumulation of unified political power at the apex of the political system. As a result, power holders will find it difficult to impose unpopular policies on resistant citizens. In sum, discursive competition may prevent tyranny, which the Founding Fathers—and, certainly, Yale pluralism—believed to be the greatest danger to any political system.

Finally, discursive competition may raise the quality of public policy. Debate over policies that improvise rational choice, historical institutionalism, and multiculturalism will force proponents of particular policies to make especially strong arguments. Vigorous debate among power holders might also catch the public's attention, thereby democratizing the political process. In short, competing legitimating discourses might create a more attentive, vocal, and influential public.

But something is missing from this picture. Contrary to my argument, despite the rise of these new discourses, the public's engagement in politics has actually declined since the heyday of pluralism. Moreover, public trust in political institutions is also much lower than it was during the 1950s and 1960s (but see Brooks and Cheng, 2001). Indeed, the grim descriptions of Americans' political disengagement are now themselves embedded in American political culture. These descriptions constitute a mocking countermelody to the tunes the three competing legitimating discourses are playing.

There are as many diagnoses of the public's current disenchantment with politics as there are descriptions of the phenomenon. Some of the most frequently mentioned culprits include Watergate and the Vietnam War; the decline of grassroots political parties (Putnam, 2000: 42–47); the withering of "social capital" (Putnam, 2000: 42–47)); negative election campaigns (Cappella and Jamieson, 1997); and the adversarial tone of the mass media (Patterson, 1993). I believe, however, that an additional factor should be added to this list: the absence of a democratically expansive legitimating discourse.

284

Consider, in this regard, rational choice theory. It endorses democratic participation through the market, not through government. But if the market consistently outperforms the state, why should average citizens become politically engaged?

Or take historical institutionalism. Finegold and Skocpol demonstrate that New Deal agricultural policy overcame "the expressed demands of well-organized farmers" (1995: 159); at the same time, "The governmental units that offered access to the agricultural underclasses . . . were dismantled" (163). If a strong state does not represent either the organized or the unorganized, why should ordinary citizens become politically engaged?

Or, finally, consider multiculturalism. Among the three competing discourses, multiculturalism would appear to be the only one that explicitly values the public's political engagement. Indeed, it urges ethnic minorities to increase their participation in politics. However, one ethnic group's expanded power may be seen as another's reduced power. Take an economic example. Despite contrary evidence, many white males believe that affirmative action deprives them of access to education and employment (Patterson, 1993, 148). One possible reaction to this belief is to become politically alienated rather than participatory.

Now consider pluralism at Yale. Although pluralists considered low participation to be normal in politics, pluralism indirectly promoted participation. The reactive premise promised that politicians would respond to organized citizens. The multiple centers of power premise gave competing groups of leaders an incentive to mobilize ordinary citizens. The reform premise foresaw programs that would benefit formerly marginalized groups, increasing their capacity to participate effectively. Finally, the pluralist idea of "anticipated reactions"—namely, that politicians had reason to fear even the unorganized—suggested that politicians were never wholly removed from public influence. In short, unlike rational choice theory, historical institutionalism, or multiculturalism, pluralism at Yale endorsed broad citizen political engagement.

But if this is so, why did pluralism's critics in the late 1960s claim that it did *not* foster political participation? To its critics on the left, pluralism failed the most crucial test of democracy; it did not establish participatory mechanisms for popular rule. Indeed, the New Left depended on precisely this assumption; it drew a sharp distinction between "participatory democracy" and pluralist democracy (Students for a Democratic Society, 1962: 47). The New Left proposed participatory democracy; it distrusted the limited, traditional forms of participation favored by pluralism.

Nor is this conflict over citizen participation absent from contemporary political science (e.g., Kahane, 2000). Today theorists of communitarianism, "deliberative democracy," and social capital make the participatory argument, in opposition to the proponents of rational choice, historical institutionalism, and (where it enjoys political power) multiculturalism. Significantly, few power holders strongly promote policies to advance communitarianism, deliberative democracy, or even social capital. These participation-enhancing theories mainly serve as oppositional, not legitimating, discourses.

It is no accident that most legitimating discourses regard citizen participation with ambivalence and even skepticism. Nor is it any accident that pluralism, rational choice, and historical institutionalism enjoy more acceptance among the powerful than participatory democracy, communitarianism, deliberative democracy, and social capital theory. Indeed, for those with power, citizen participation creates a chronic, and perhaps insoluble, legitimation dilemma.

What is this dilemma? On the one hand, holders of power want the public to support their policies. Indeed, in a liberal democracy, public acclamation ultimately provides the strongest form of regime legitimation. And virtually by definition, only widespread citizen participation can assure public acclamation. Certainly today's legitimating discourses would benefit from more public enthusiasm. Without public acclamation, how can we be certain that citizens approve of market-based attacks on "Big Government"? Without public acclamation, how can we know that the state has actually imposed its reform policies successfully? And how, without public acclamation, can we be sure that multiculturalism has truly empowered ethnic minorities?

On the other hand, citizen participation presents dangers to power holders. By definition, participation introduces new voices into the political arena. Who can know for certain what these new voices will say? Once the genie of participation is set loose, it may disrupt the political regime and attack those who control the regime.

In short, the legitimation dilemma is the contradiction between *stimulating* citizen participation to build regime legitimation and *limiting* citizen participation lest it disrupt political rule. By balancing effective citizen participation with effective rule, pluralism managed this dilemma during the 1950s and 1960s. Pluralism's successors have not been as fortunate.

Today's decline of citizen participation coincides with what Giddens (1990) calls "the disembedding of social systems." Disembedding is the "'lifting out' of social relations from local contexts of interaction and their restructuring across indefinite spans of time-space" (21). A related process is abstraction, which is the control over social structures exerted by impersonal processes and distant experts (22–77). The disembedding and abstraction of social systems obviously demands that people be willing to trust unseen and unknown others. Yet the absence of legitimating discourses impedes such trust. After all, why should people trust power holders with whom they are neither encouraged nor able to interact? The virulent combination of participation-*limiting* legitimating discourses and trust-*demanding* social systems may help explain the public's current estrangement from governmental institutions.

Recently Robert Dahl has indirectly addressed the legitimation dilemma. He identifies "a democratic paradox," namely, the fact that "in many of the oldest and most stable democratic countries, citizens possess little confidence in some key democratic institutions. Yet most citizens continue to believe in the desirability of democracy" (2000: 35). Dahl explains this paradox by arguing that citizens do not consider democracy to be primarily institutional, but rather "the fundamental political rights and opportunities that . . . are intrinsic elements of democracy" (38). Citizens continue to endorse democratic values, but they do not believe that political institutions deliver democratic rights and opportunities. Dahl worries that "Dissatisfaction with the way their government works might in the long run weaken the confidence of some citizens in the value of . . . democracy and thus weaken their support for democracy" (39). And he asks: "Has not the time arrived when political scientists, constitutional lawyers, and others who are concerned about the future of democracy should take up this challenge and look for feasible ways of remedying the defects that so many citizens see in the way their governments operate?" (40).

In effect, Dahl is calling for political scientists to advance more oppositional than legitimating discourses. After all, without increased participation, citizens will likely remain dissatisfied with their political institutions. Yet, if my argument is correct, no legitimating discourse—including Dahl's version of Yale pluralism—can ever privilege citizen participation above all else. Only *oppositional* discourses elevate citizen participation to a position of primacy. But as Yale pluralism illustrates, most political scientists do not embrace oppositional discourses. Indeed, faced with participatory challenges within their own institutions, they even prefer a discursive vacuum to oppositional discourses. Thus, while political scientists—indeed, academics in general—often do speak truth *to* political power, they rarely speak the truth coherently and effectively *against* political power. Political scientists may, as we earlier heard Rogers Smith say, wish "to aid American democracy, however deep their reservations might run about its current form" (1997: 273). But, as Smith concedes, these desires are "perpetually unfulfilled." The experience of pluralism at Yale suggests that these desires are doomed to frustration in perpetuity.

Appendix
Bibliography
Index

Appendix
Chief Works by Yale Political Scientists, 1950–1975

Almond, Gabriel
The Civic Culture (with Sidney Verba; 1965)
Comparative Politics (with G. Bingham Powell; 1966)
The Politics of the Developing Areas (1960)
The Appeals of Communism (1954)

Barber, James David
Citizen Politics (1969)
An Introduction to Political Analysis (with Robert Lane and Fred
    Greenstein; 1962)
The Lawmakers (1965)
The Presidential Character (1972)

Dahl, Robert A.
After the Revolution? (1970)
Modern Political Analysis (1963)
Pluralist Democracy in the United States (1967)
Political Oppositions in Western Democracy (edited volume; 1966)
Politics, Economics, and Welfare (with Charles Lindblom; 1953)
A Preface to Democratic Theory (1956)
Social Science Research on Business (with Mason Haire and Paul
    Lazarsfeld; 1959)
Who Governs? (1961)

Deutsch, Karl
Nationalism and Social Communication (1953)
The Nerves of Government (1966)

Greenstein, Fred
The American Party System and the American People (1970)
Children and Politics (1965)
An Introduction to Political Analysis (with Robert Lane and James
    David Barber; 1962)
Personality and Politics (1969)

Kaufman, Herbert
The Forest Ranger (1960)
Governing New York City (with Wallace Sayre; 1960)
Politics and Policies in State and Local Governments (1963)
Time, Chance, and Organizations (1974)

Lane, Robert
Introduction to Political Analysis (with James David Barber and
    Fred Greenstein; 1962)
The Liberties of Wit (1961)
Political Ideology (1962)
Political Life (1959)
Political Man (1972)
Political Thinking and Consciousness (1969)
Public Opinion (with David Sears; 1964)
The Regulation of Businessmen (1966)

Lasswell, Harold
The Future of Political Science (1963)
Politics (1958)
Power and Society (with Abraham Kaplan; 1950)
Power, Corruption, and Rectitude (with Arnold Rogow; 1963)

Lindblom, Charles
The Intelligence of Democracy (1965)
The Policy-Making Process (1968)
Politics, Economics and Welfare (with Robert Dahl; 1953)
A Strategy of Decision (with David Braybrooke; 1963)

Muir, William
Prayer in the Public Schools (1967)

Murphy, Russell
Political Entrepreneurs and Urban Poverty (1971)

Polsby, Nelson
Community Power and Political Theory (1963)
Congress and the Presidency (1964)
Presidential Elections (with Aaron Wildavsky; 1964)

Wildavsky, Aaron
Dixon-Yates (1962)
Leadership in a Small Town (1964)
The Politics of the Budgetary Process (1964)
Presidential Elections (with Nelson Polsby; 1964)

Wolfinger, Raymond
The Politics of Progress (1973)

Bibliography

Aaron, Henry J. 1978. *Politics and the professors: The Great Society in perspective.* Washington, D.C.: Brookings Institution.

Aberbach, Joel D., Robert D. Putnam, and Bert A. Rockman. 1981. *Bureaucrats and politicians in western democracies.* Cambridge: Harvard University Press.

Aberbach, Joel D., and Jack L. Walker. 1973. *Race in the city: Political trust and public policy in the new urban system.* Boston: Little, Brown.

Abercrombie, Nicholas, Stephen Hill, and Bryan S. Turner. 1980. *The dominant ideology thesis.* London: Allen and Unwin.

———, eds. 1990. *Dominant ideologies.* London: Unwin Hyman.

Adrian, Charles R., and Charles Press. 1965. *The American political process.* New York: McGraw-Hill.

Agger, Ben. 1992. *The discourse of domination: From the Frankfurt School to postmodernism.* Evanston, Ill.: Northwestern University Press.

Alexander, Herbert E., and Rei Shiratori, eds. 1994. *Comparative political finance among the democracies.* Boulder, Colo.: Westview Press.

Alexander, Jeffrey C. 1988. Culture and political crisis: "Watergate" and Durkheimian sociology. In *Durkheimian sociology: Cultural studies,* edited by Alexander. Cambridge: Cambridge University Press. Pp. 186–224.

Alker, Hayward R. 1996. *Rediscoveries and reformulations: Humanistic methodologies for international studies.* New York: Cambridge University Press.

Almond, Gabriel A. 1954. *The appeals of communism.* Princeton: Princeton University Press.

———. 1960. *The politics of the developing areas.* Princeton: Princeton University Press.

Almond, Gabriel A., and G. Bingham Powell Jr. 1966. *Comparative politics: A developmental approach.* Boston: Little, Brown.

Almond, Gabriel A., and Sidney Verba. 1965. *The civic culture: Political attitudes and democracy in five nations.* Boston: Little, Brown.

Althusser, Louis. 1969. *For Marx.* Translated by Ben Brewster. New York: Pantheon.

Amadae, S. M., and Bruce Bueno de Mesquita. 1999. The Rochester school: The origins of positive political theory. In *Annual review of political science,* vol. 2, edited by Nelson Polsby. Palo Alto: Annual Reviews. Pp. 269–95.

Archer, Margaret. 1996. *Culture and agency: The place of culture in social theory.* Rev. ed. Cambridge: Cambridge University Press.

Aronowitz, Stanley. 1988. *Science as power: Discourse and ideology in modern society.* Minneapolis: University of Minnesota Press.

Axelrod, Robert. 1986. An evolutionary approach to norms. *American Political Science Review* 80:1095–111.

Bacchus, William I. 1974. Diplomacy for the '70s: An afterview and appraisal. *American Political Science Review* 68:736–48.

Bachrach, Peter, and Morton S. Baratz. 1962. Two faces of power. *American Political Science Review* 56:947–52.

Baer, Michael A., Malcolm E. Jewell, and Lee Sigelman, eds. 1991. *Political science in America: Oral histories of a discipline.* Lexington: University Press of Kentucky.

Bailey, F. G. 1977. *Morality and expediency: The folklore of academic politics.* Oxford: Basil Blackwell.

Baker, Eva L. 1994. Researchers and assessment policy development: A cautionary tale. *American Journal of Education* 102:450–78.

Balkin, J. M. 1998. *Cultural software: A theory of ideology.* New Haven: Yale University Press.

Ball, Terence. 1993. American political science in its postwar political context. In *Discipline and history,* edited by Farr and Seidelman. Pp. 207–23.

———. 1995. An ambivalent alliance: Political science and American democracy. In *Political science in history,* edited by Farr, Dryzek, and Leonard. Pp. 41–66.

Barber, Benjamin R. 1998. *A passion for democracy: American essays.* Princeton: Princeton University Press.

Barber, James David. 1965. *The lawmakers: Recruitment and adaptation to legislative life.* New Haven: Yale University Press.

———. 1969. *Citizen politics: An introduction to political behavior.* Chicago: Markham.

———. 1972. *The presidential character: Predicting performance in the White House.* Englewood Cliffs, N.J.: Prentice Hall.

Barber, William J. 1997. Reconfigurations in American academic economics: A general practitioner's perspective. *Daedalus* 126 (winter): 87–105.

Barnard, F. M. 1991. *Pluralism, socialism, and political legitimacy: Reflections on opening up Communism.* Cambridge: Cambridge University Press.

Barnes, Barry. 1995. *The elements of social theory.* Princeton: Princeton University Press.

Barrett, Michele. 1991. *The politics of truth: From Marx to Foucault.* Cambridge: Polity Press.

Bates, Robert H. 1998. *Analytic narratives.* Princeton: Princeton University Press.

Bauman, Zygmunt. 1987. *Legislators and interpreters: On modernity, postmodernity, and intellectuals.* Ithaca: Cornell University Press.

Bay, Christian. 1958. *The structure of freedom.* Stanford: Stanford University Press.

Beck, Nathaniel. 1982. Parties, administrations, and American macroeconomic outcomes. *American Political Science Review* 76:83–93.

Beetham, David. 1991. *The legitimation of power.* Atlantic Highlands, N. J.: Humanities Press International.

Bender, Thomas. 1993. *Intellect and public life: Essays on the social history of academic intellectuals in the United States.* Baltimore: Johns Hopkins University Press.

———. 1997. Politics, intellect, and the American university. *Daedalus* 126 (winter): 1–39.

Bennett, Douglas, et al. 1969. Obstacles to graduate education in political science. *PS: Political Science and Politics* 2 (fall): 622–42.

Bennett, W. Lance. 1994. "The News about Foreign Policy." In *Taken by storm: The media, public opinion, and U.S. foreign policy in the Gulf War,* edited by Bennett and David Paletz. Chicago: University of Chicago Press. Pp. 12–43.

———. 1996. *The governing crisis: Media, money, and marketing in American elections.* 2d ed. New York: St. Martin's Press.

Berezin, Mabel. 1997. *Making the fascist self: The political culture of interwar Italy.* Chicago: University of Chicago Press.

Berger, Bennett. 1995. *An essay on culture: Symbolic structure and social structure.* Berkeley: University of California Press.

Berman, Morris. 2000. *The twilight of American culture.* New York: Norton.

Berns, Walter. 1997. The assault on the universities: Then and now. In *Reassessing the sixties: Debating the political and cultural legacy,* edited by Stephen Macedo. New York: Norton. Pp. 157–84.

Billig, Michael. 1995. *Banal nationalism.* London: Sage.

———. 1998. *Talking of the royal family.* London: Routledge.

Billig, Michael, et al. 1988. *Ideological dilemmas: A social psychology of everyday thinking.* London: Sage.

Birch, David, et al. 1974. *Patterns of urban change: The New Haven experience.* Lexington, Mass.: D.C. Heath.

Bledstein, Burton. 1976. *The culture of professionalism: The middle class and the development of higher education in America.* New York: Norton.

Boden, Deidre. 1994. *The business of talk: Organizations in action.* Cambridge: Polity Press.

Boggs, Carl. 1993. *Intellectuals and the crisis of modernity.* Albany: State University of New York Press.

Bonnell, Victoria, and Lynn Hunt. 1999. Introduction. In *Beyond the cultural turn: New directions in the study of society and culture,* edited by Bonnell and Hunt. Berkeley: University of California Press. Pp. 1–35.

Boudon, Raymond. 1989. *The analysis of ideology.* Translated by Malcolm Slater. Cambridge: Polity Press.

Bourdieu, Pierre. 1977. *Outline of a theory of practice.* Translated by Richard Nice. Cambridge: Cambridge University Press.

———. 1988. *Homo academicus.* Translated by Peter Collier. Stanford: Stanford University Press.

———. 1999. Rethinking the state: Genesis and structure of the bureaucratic field. In *State/culture: State formation after the cultural turn,* edited by George Steinmetz. Ithaca: Cornell University Press. Pp. 53–76.

Bourdieu, Pierre, and Jean-Claude Passeron. 1990. *Reproduction in education, society, and culture.* Translated by Richard Nice. London: Sage.

Branch, Taylor. 1988. *Parting the waters: America in the King years, 1954–1963.* New York: Simon and Schuster.

Brass, Paul R. 1997. *Theft of an idol: Text and context in the representation of collective violence.* Princeton: Princeton University Press.

Braybrooke, David, and Charles Lindblom. 1963. *A strategy of decision: Policy evaluation as a social process.* New York: Free Press.

Brint, Steven. 1994. *In an age of experts: The changing role of professionals in politics and public life.* Princeton: Princeton University Press.

Brooks, Clem, and Simon Cheng. 2001. Declining government confidence and policy preferences in the U.S.: Devolution, regime effects, or symbolic change. *Social Forces* 79:1343–75.

Browning, Rufus P., Dale Rogers Marshall, and David Tabb. 1972. Minorities and urban electoral change: A longitudinal study. *Urban Affairs Quarterly* 15 (December): 206–28.

———. 1984. *Protest is not enough: The struggle of blacks and Hispanics for equality in urban politics.* Berkeley: University of California Press.

Bruni, Frank. 2000. Bush's unusual pitch: I don't know. *New York Times,* June 4.

Brym, Robert J. 1980. *Intellectuals and politics.* London: Allen and Unwin.

Buckley, William F., Jr. 1951. *God and man at Yale: The superstitions of academic freedom.* South Bend, Ind.: Gateway Editions.

Burns, James MacGregor, and Jack Walter Peltason. 1957 [1963, 1966, 1969]. *Government by the people: The dynamics of American national government.* 3d, 5th, 6th, 7th ed. Englewood Cliffs, N.J.: Prentice Hall.

Buxton, William. 1985. *Talcott Parsons and the capitalist nation-state: Political sociology as a strategic vocation.* Toronto: University of Toronto Press.

Caldwell, Gaylon, and Robert M. Lawrence. 1969. *American government today.* Rev. ed. New York: Norton.

Cantor, Norman. 1991. *Inventing the middle ages: The lives, works, and ideas of the great medievalists of the twentieth century.* New York: Morrow.

Cappella, Joseph N., and Kathleen Hall Jamieson. 1997. *Spiral of cynicism: The press and the public good.* New York: Oxford University Press.

Carr, Robert Kenneth, Marver H. Bernstein, and Walter F. Murphy. 1963. *American democracy in theory and practice: National, state, and local government.* 4th ed. New York: Holt, Rinehart and Winston.

Ceaser, James W. 1990. *Liberal democracy and political science.* Baltimore: Johns Hopkins University Press.

Cetina, Karin Knorr. 1999. *Epistemic cultures: How the sciences make knowledge.* Cambridge: Harvard University Press.

Chubb, John E., and Terry M. Moe. 1990. *Politics, markets, and American schools.* Washington, D.C.: Brookings Institution.

Cohen, Mark Nathan. 1998. *Culture of intolerance: Chauvinism, class, and racism in the United States.* New Haven: Yale University Press.

Coleman, James S., et al. 1966. *Equality of educational opportunity.* Washington, D.C.: U.S. Office of Education.

Collins, Randall. 1998. *The sociology of philosophies: A global theory of intellectual change.* Cambridge: Harvard University Press, Belknap Press.

Connolly, William. 1984. The dilemma of legitimacy. In *Legitimacy and the state,* edited by Connolly. New York: New York University Press. Pp. 222–49.

Cook, Timothy E. 1998. *Governing with the news: The news media as a political institution.* Chicago: University of Chicago Press.

Cormack, Mike. 1992. *Ideology.* Ann Arbor: University of Michigan Press.

Coser, Lewis. 1984. *Refugee scholars in America: Their impact and their experiences.* New Haven: Yale University Press.

Covell, Maureen. 1986. Regionalization and economic crisis in Belgium: The variable origins of centrifugal and centripetal forces. *Canadian Journal of Political Science* 19 (June): 261–81.

Cruz, Consuelo. 2000. Identity and persuasion: How nations remember their pasts and make their futures. *World Politics* 15 (April): 275–312.

Dahl, Robert A. 1956. *A preface to democratic theory.* Chicago: University of Chicago Press.

———. 1961a. The behavioral approach in political science: Epitaph for a monument to a successful protest. *American Political Science Review* 55 (December): 763–72.

———. 1961b. Equality and power in American society. In *Power and democracy in America,* edited by William V. D'Antonio and Howard J. Ehrlich. South Bend, Ind.: University of Notre Dame Press. Pp. 73–91.

———. 1961c. *Who governs? Democracy and power in an American city.* New Haven: Yale University Press.

———. 1963. *Modern political analysis.* Englewood Cliffs, N.J.: Prentice Hall.

———. 1967. *Pluralist democracy in the United States.* Chicago: Rand McNally.

———. 1970. *After the revolution? Authority in a good society.* New Haven: Yale University Press.

———. 1997. A brief intellectual autobiography. In *Comparative European politics: The story of a profession,* edited by Hans Daalder. London: Pinter. Pp. 68–79.

———. 2000. A democratic paradox? *Political Science Quarterly* 115:35–41.

———, ed. 1966. *Political oppositions in Western democracy.* New Haven: Yale University Press.

Dahl, Robert A., Mason Haire, and Paul F. Lazarsfeld. 1959. *Social science research on business.* New York: Columbia University Press.

Dahl, Robert A., and Charles E. Lindblom. 1953. *Politics, economics, and welfare.* New York: Harper Torchbooks.

Dant, Tim. 1991. *Knowledge, ideology, and discourse: A sociological perspective.* London: Routledge.

Dawson, Michael. 1994. *Behind the mule.* Princeton: Princeton University Press.

Deutsch, Jan G. 1976. *Selling the people's Cadillac: The Edsel and corporate responsibility.* New Haven: Yale University Press.

Deutsch, Karl. 1953. *Nationalism and social communication.* 2d ed. Cambridge: MIT Press.

———. 1966. *The nerves of government.* New York: Free Press.

Domhoff, G. William. 1978. *Who really rules? New Haven and community power reexamined.* New Brunswick, N.J.: Transaction Books.

Douglas, Ann. 1995. *Terrible honesty: Mongrel Manhattan in the 1920s.* New York: Noonday Press.

Downs, Anthony. 1957. *An economic theory of democracy*. New York: Harper and Row.

Downs, Donald Alexander. 1999. *Cornell '69: Liberalism and the crisis of the university*. Ithaca: Cornell University Press.

Easton, David, John G. Gunnell, and Michael B. Stein. 1995. Introduction: Democracy as a regime type and the development of political science. In *Regime and discipline: Democracy and the development of political science,* edited by Easton, Gunnell, and Stein. Ann Arbor: University of Michigan Press. Pp. 1–27.

Edelman, Murray. 1988. *Constructing the political spectacle*. Chicago: University of Chicago Press.

———. 1997. Veiled uses of empirical theories. In *Contemporary empirical political theory,* edited by Kristen Monroe. Berkeley: University of California Press. Pp. 100–112.

Eisenberg, Avigail. 1995. *Restructuring political pluralism*. Albany: State University of New York Press.

Eisinger, Peter. 1972. The conditions of protest behavior in American cities. Discussion Paper 108-72. Madison: Institute for Research on Poverty, University of Wisconsin–Madison.

Erikson, Erik H. 1969. *Gandhi's truth: On the origins of militant nonviolence*. New York: Norton.

Esman, Milton J. 2000. *Government works: Why Americans need the feds*. Ithaca: Cornell University Press.

Etzioni-Halevy, Eva. 1985. *The knowledge elite and the failure of prophecy*. London: George Allen and Unwin.

Ewing, Cortez A. M., and Jewell Cass Phillips. 1962. *Essentials of American government*. New York: American Book.

Eyerman, Ron. 1994. *Between culture and politics: Intellectuals in modern society*. Cambridge: Polity Press.

Farr, James. 1995. Remembering the revolution: Behavioralism in American political science. In *Political science in history,* edited by Farr, Dryzek, and Leonard. Pp. 198–225.

Farr, James, John S. Dryzek, and Stephen T. Leonard, eds. 1995. *Political science in history: Research programs and political traditions*. Cambridge: Cambridge University Press.

Farr, James, and Raymond Seidelman, eds. 1993. *Discipline and history: Political science in the United States*. Ann Arbor: University of Michigan Press.

Fearon, James D., and David Laitin. 1996. Explaining interethnic cooperation. *American Political Science Review* 90 (December):715–35.

Fesler, James. 1997. Back to normalcy. Chapter 7, unpublished manuscript, August 25.

Finegold, Kenneth, and Theda Skocpol. 1995. *State and party in America's New Deal*. Madison: University of Wisconsin Press.

Fiske, Susan, and Shelly E. Taylor. 1991. *Social Cognition*. 2d ed. New York: McGraw-Hill.

Fiske, Susan T., Donald R. Kinder, and W. Michael Larter. 1983. The novice and the expert: Knowledge-based strategies in political cognition. *Journal of Experimental Social Psychology* 19:381–400.

Flacks, Richard. 1971. *Youth and social change.* Chicago: Markham.

Flanigan, William, and Nancy H. Zingale. 1998. *Political behavior of the American electorate.* Boston: Allyn and Bacon.

Forbes, H. D. 1988. Dahl, democracy, and technology. In *Democratic theory and technological society,* edited by Richard B. Day, Ronald Beiner, and Joseph Masciulli. New York: M. E. Sharpe. Pp. 227–47.

———. 1997. *Ethnic conflict: Commerce, culture, and the contact hypothesis.* New Haven: Yale University Press.

Forster, E. M. 1951. *Two cheers for democracy.* New York: Harcourt, Brace, and World.

Foucault, Michel. 1995. *Discipline and punish: The birth of the prison.* 2d ed. Translated by Alan Sheridan. New York: Vintage Books.

Fowler, Robert Booth. 1991. *The dance with community: The contemporary debate in American political thought.* Lawrence: University Press of Kansas.

———. 1999. *Enduring liberalism: American political thought since the 1960s.* Lawrence: University Press of Kansas.

Frum, David. 2000. George Bush's 60's were real, too. *New York Times,* June 4.

Fuchs, Stephan. 1992. *The professional quest for truth: A social theory of science and knowledge.* Albany: State University of New York Press.

Fuller, Steve. 1993. Disciplinary boundaries and the rhetoric of the social sciences. In *Knowledges: Historical and critical studies in disciplinarity,* edited by Ellen Messer-Davidow, David R. Shumway, and David J. Sylvan. Charlottesville: University Press of Virginia. Pp. 125–48.

Galbraith, John Kenneth. 1958. *The affluent society.* Boston: Houghton Mifflin.

Gass, William H. 1970. *Fiction and the figures of life.* New York: Knopf.

Gecan, Michael, ed. 1972. *Seen through our eyes.* New York: Random House.

Gerth, H. H., and C. Wright Mills, eds. and trans. 1958. *From Max Weber.* New York: Oxford University Press.

Giddens, Anthony. 1979. *Central problems in social theory: Action, structure, and contradiction in social analysis.* Berkeley: University of California Press.

———. 1990. *The consequences of modernity.* Stanford: Stanford University Press.

Gilens, Martin. 1999. *Why Americans hate welfare: Race, media, and the politics of anti-poverty policy.* New Haven: Yale University Press.

Glassberg, Andrew. 1981. The urban fiscal crisis becomes routine. *Public Administration Review* 41 (January, special issue): 165–71.

Glazer, Nathan. 1997. *We are all multiculturalists now.* Cambridge: Harvard University Press.

Goldberg, Arthur S., and John R. Wright. 1985. Risk and uncertainty in the durability of political coalitions. *American Political Science Review* 79 (September): 704–18.

Goldberg, David Theo. 1993. *Racist culture: Philosophy and the politics of meaning.* Oxford: Blackwell.

Goldfarb, Jeffrey C. 1998. *Civility and subversion: The intellectual in democratic society.* Cambridge: Cambridge University Press.

Golembiewski, Robert T. 1962. *The small group: An analysis of research concepts and operation.* Chicago: University of Chicago Press.

Gouldner, Alvin. 1970. *The coming crisis of Western sociology.* New York: Basic Books.

Gramsci, Antonio. 1971. *Selections from the prison notebooks.* London: Lawrence and Wishart.

Greenstein, Fred I. 1965. *Children and politics.* New Haven: Yale University Press.

———. 1969. *Personality and politics.* Chicago: Markham.

———. 1970. *The American party system and the American people.* Englewood Cliffs, N.J.: Prentice Hall.

Gunnell, John G. 1993. *The descent of political theory: The genealogy of an American vocation.* Chicago: University of Chicago Press.

———. 1995. The declination of the "state" and the origins of American pluralism. In *Political science in history,* edited by Farr, Dryzek, and Leonard. Pp. 19–41.

Guttman, Amy, ed. 1992. *Multiculturalism and the politics of recognition.* Princeton: Princeton University Press.

Hahn, Carole L. 1998. *Becoming political: Comparative perspectives on citizenship education.* Albany: State University of New York Press.

Halberstam, David. 1993. *The fifties.* New York: Villard Books.

Hall, Peter A. 1993. Policy paradigms, social learning, and the state. *Comparative Politics* 23:275–96.

Hallin, Daniel C. 1984. The media, the war in Vietnam, and political support: A critique of the thesis of an oppositional media. *Journal of Politics* 46:2–24.

Hamilton, Anne Wing. 1999. Bureaucrat bashing in Russia and the United States: A comparison of the cultural construction of negative images of authority. Ph.D. diss., University of Wisconsin–Madison.

Hargrove, Erwin C. 1974. *The power of the modern presidency.* New York: Knopf.

———. 1998. *Idealism in presidential leadership: Appealing to the better angels of our nature.* Lawrence: University Press of Kansas.

Hart, Roderick P. 1994. *Seducing America: How television charms the modern voter.* New York: Oxford University Press.

Hartz, Louis. 1955. *The liberal tradition in American.* New York: Harvest.

Heclo, Hugh. 1977. *A government of strangers: Executive politics in Washington.* Washington, D.C.: Brookings Institution.

Hellman, Stephen. 1978. The Italian CP: Stumbling on the threshold? *Problems of Communism* 27 (November-December): 31–48.

Hersey, John. 1970. *Letter to the alumni.* New York: Knopf.

Hitchon, Jacqueline C., and Chingching Chang. 1995. Effects of gender schematic processing on the reception of political commercials for men and women candidates. *Communication Research* 22 (August): 430–58.

Hollinger, David. 1996. *Science, Jews, and secular culture: Studies in mid-twentieth-century American intellectual history.* Princeton: Princeton University Press.

Howell, William, and Paul E. Peterson. 2002. *The education gap: Vouchers and urban schools.* Washington, D.C.: Brookings Institution.

Huber, Joan, and William Form. 1973. *Income and ideology: An analysis of the American political formula.* New York: Free Press.

Hudson [Lane], Helen. 1966. *Tell the time to none.* New York: Dutton.

Irish, Marion D., and James W. Prothro. 1965. *The politics of American democracy.* 3d ed. Englewood Cliffs, N.J.: Prentice Hall.

Iyengar, Shanto. 1991. *Is anyone responsible? How television frames political issues.* Chicago: University of Chicago Press.

Jacobson, Gary C. 1985–86. Party organization and the distribution of campaign resources: Republicans and Democrats in 1982. *Political Science Quarterly* 100 (winter): 603–25.

Jacobson, Matthew Frye. 1998. *Whiteness of a different color: European immigrants and the alchemy of race.* Cambridge: Harvard University Press.

Jacoby, Russell. 1987. *The last intellectuals: American culture in the age of academia.* New York: Basic Books.

James, David Ray. 1981. The transformation of local state and class structures and resistance to the civil rights movement in the south. Ph.D. diss., University of Wisconsin–Madison.

Jay, Martin. 1973. *The dialectical imagination: A history of the Frankfurt School and the Institute of Social Research, 1923–1950.* Boston: Little, Brown.

Jenks, Chris. 1993a. *Culture.* London: Routledge.

———, ed. 1993b. *Cultural reproduction.* London: Routledge.

Jewell, Malcolm E., and Sarah M. Morehouse. 1996. What are party endorsements worth? A study of preprimary gubernatorial endorsements. *American Politics Quarterly* 24 (July): 338–62.

Kahane, David. 2000. Pluralism, deliberation, and citizen competence: Recent developments in democratic theory. *Social Theory and Practice* 26:509–25.

Kalman, Laura. 1986. *Legal realism at Yale, 1927–1960.* Chapel Hill: University of North Carolina Press.

Karl, Barry D. 1974. *Charles E. Merriam and the study of politics.* Chicago: University of Chicago Press.

Katznelson, Ira. 1996. *Liberalism's crooked circle: Letters to Adam Michnik.* Princeton: Princeton University Press.

———. 1997. From the street to the lecture hall: The 1960s. *Daedalus* 126 (winter): 311–33.

———. 1998. The doleful dance of politics and policy: Can historical institutionalism make a difference? *American Political Science Review* 92 (March): 191–99.

Kaufman, Herbert. 1960. *The forest ranger: A study of administrative behavior.* Baltimore: Johns Hopkins University Press.

———. 1963. *Politics and policies in state and local governments.* Englewood Cliffs, N.J.: Prentice Hall.

———. 1974. *Time, chance, and organizations: Natural selection in a perilous environment.* Chatham, N.J.: Chatham House.

Kelley, Brooks Mather. 1974. *Yale: A history.* New Haven: Yale University Press.

Kelly, Elizabeth A. 1995. *Education, democracy, and public knowledge.* Boulder, Colo.: Westview.

Kernan, Alvin. 1999. *In Plato's cave.* New Haven: Yale University Press.

King, Gary, Robert O. Keohane, and Sidney Verba. 1994. *Designing social inquiry: Scientific inference in qualitative research.* Princeton: Princeton University Press.

Klinkner, Philip A., with Rogers M. Smith. 1999. *The unsteady march: The rise and decline of racial equality in America.* Chicago: University of Chicago Press.

Kraft, Michael E. 1984. Political constraints on development of alternative energy sources: Lessons from the Reagan administration. *Public Policy Journal* 19 (December): 319–30.

Kristol, Irving. 1983. *Reflections of a neo-conservative: Looking back, looking ahead.* New York: Basic Books.

Kuhn, Thomas. 1962. *The structure of scientific revolutions.* Chicago: University of Chicago Press.

Lacey, Michael J., and Mary O. Furner. 1993. Social investigation, social knowledge, and the state: An introduction. In *The state and social investigation in Britain and the United States,* edited by Lacey and Furner. Cambridge: Woodrow Wilson Center Press and Cambridge University Press. Pp. 3–73.

Lane, Robert E. 1959. *Political life.* New York: Free Press.

———. 1961. *The liberties of wit.* New Haven: Yale University Press.

———. 1962. *Political ideology.* New York: Free Press.

———. 1966. *The regulation of businessmen.* New Haven: Yale University Press.

———. 1969. *Political thinking and consciousness.* Chicago: Markham.

———. 1972. *Political man.* New York: Free Press.

———. 1991. *The market experience.* Cambridge: Cambridge University Press.

———. 2000. *The loss of happiness in market societies.* New Haven: Yale University Press.

Lane, Robert E., James D. Barber, and Fred Greenstein. 1962. *Introduction to political analysis.* Englewood Cliffs, N.J.: Prentice Hall.

Lane, Robert E., and David O. Sears. 1964. *Public opinion.* Englewood Cliffs, N.J.: Prentice Hall.

Lasch, Christopher. 1965. *The new radicalism in America: The intellectual as a social type.* New York: Knopf.

Lasswell, Harold D. 1930. *Psychopathology and politics.* Chicago: University of Chicago Press.

———. 1958. *Politics: Who gets what, when, how.* New York: Meridian.

———. 1963. *The future of political science.* Englewood Cliffs, N.J.: Prentice Hall.

Lasswell, Harold D., and Abraham Kaplan. 1950. *Power and society.* New Haven: Yale University Press.

Latour, Bruno, and Steve Woolgar. 1986. *Laboratory life: The construction of scientific facts.* Princeton: Princeton University Press.

Latour, Bruno. 1999. *Pandora's hope: Essays on the reality of science studies.* Cambridge: Harvard University Press.

Layder, Derek. 1994. *Understanding social theory.* London: Sage.

Leiserson, Michael. 1968. Factions and coalitions in one-party Japan: An interpretation based on the theory of games. *American Political Science Review* 62:770–87.

Levin, Daniel Lessard. 1999. *Representing popular sovereignty: The Constitution in American political culture.* Albany: State University of New York Press.

Lijphart, Arend. 1975. *The politics of accommodation.* 2d ed. Berkeley: University of California Press.

Lindblom, Charles E. 1965. *The intelligence of democracy.* New York: Free Press.

304

———. 1968. *The policy-making process.* Englewood Cliffs, N.J.: Prentice Hall.

———. 1971. Yale as a political system. *Yale Alumni Magazine* 34 (March): 9–17.

———. 1977. *Politics and markets: The world's political-economic systems.* New York: Basic Books.

———. 1982. Another state of mind. *American Political Science Review* 76:9–22.

———. 1990. *Inquiry and change: The troubled attempt to understand and shape society.* New Haven: Yale University Press.

Lindblom, Charles E., and David Cohen. 1979. *Usable knowledge.* New Haven: Yale University Press.

Lipsitz, Lewis. 1964. Work life and political attitudes. *American Political Science Review* 58:951–62.

———. 1968. If, as Verba says, the state functions as a religion, what are we to do then to save our souls. *American Political Science Review* 62:527–35.

Litt, Edgar. 1963. Political cynicism and political futility. *Journal of Politics* 25 (May): 312–23.

Longhurst, Brian. 1988. *Karl Mannheim and the contemporary sociology of knowledge.* New York: St. Martin's Press.

Lowi, Theodore. 1969. *The end of liberalism.* New York: Norton.

———. 1992. The state in political science: How we became what we study. *American Political Science Review* 86:1–7.

Lynch, Frederick R. 1997. *The diversity machine: The drive to change the white male workplace.* New York: Free Press.

MacKinnon, Catherine A. 1987. *Feminism unmodified.* Cambridge: Harvard University Press.

Madison, Kelly J. 1999. Legitimation crisis and containment: The "anti-racist white hero film." *Critical Studies in Mass Communication* 16 (November): 399–417.

Mannheim, Karl. 1936. *Ideology and Utopia: An introduction to the sociology of knowledge.* New York: Harcourt, Brace.

Mansfield, Harvey C. 1997. The legacy of the late sixties. In *Reassessing the sixties: Debating the political and cultural legacy,* edited by Stephen Macedo. New York: Norton. Pp. 184–207.

Marcuse, Herbert. 1964. *One dimensional man: Studies in the ideology of advanced industrial society.* Boston: Beacon.

Martin, Penny Gill. 1971. The autobiography of a field research project: The Norwegian labor party. Unpublished manuscript, Indiana University, February.

Marx, Karl and Friedrich Engels. 1970. *The German ideology.* Edited by C. J. Arthur. London: Lawrence and Wishart.

Mayhew, David R. 1974. *Congress: The electoral connection.* New Haven: Yale University Press.

McCarthy, E. Doyle. 1996. *Knowledge as culture: The new sociology of knowledge.* London: Routledge.

McClay, Wilfred M. 1994. *The masterless: Self and society in modern America.* Chapel Hill: University of North Carolina Press.

McFarland, Andrew. 2001. Political pluralist theory reconsidered: Four stages and eleven concepts. Paper prepared for delivery at the annual meeting of the Midwest Political Science Association, April 21.

McLennan, Gregor. 1995. *Pluralism.* Minneapolis: University of Minnesota Press.

McSwite, O. C. 1997. *Legitimacy in public administration: A discourse analysis.* Thousand Oaks, Calif.: Sage.

Meehan, Thomas. 1971. The Yale faculty makes the scene. *New York Times Magazine,* February 7:12.

Merelman, Richard M. 1986. Domination, self-justification, and self-doubt: Some social psychological considerations. *Journal of Politics* 48:276–300.

———. 1998. The mundane experience of political culture. *Political Communication* 15 (October-December): 515–35.

Miliband, Ralph. 1969. *The state in capitalist society.* London: Weidenfeld and Nicholson.

Miller, Arthur, Charles Tien, and Andrew Peebler. 1996. The American political science review hall of fame: Assessments and implications for an evolving discipline. *PS: Political Science and Politics* 29 (March): 73–83.

Miller, James. 1987. *Democracy is in the streets.* New York: Simon and Schuster.

Miller, William Lee. 1966. *The fifteenth ward and the Great Society: An encounter with a modern city.* Boston: Houghton Mifflin.

Mills, C. Wright. 1956. *The power elite.* New York: Oxford University Press.

Moe, Terry. 1984. The new economics of organization. *American Journal of Political Science* 28 (November): 739–77.

Morehouse, Sarah McCally. 1998. *The governor as party leader: Campaigning and governing.* Ann Arbor: University of Michigan Press.

Morrice, David. 1996. *Philosophy, science, and ideology in political thought.* New York: St. Martin's Press.

Moynihan, Daniel Patrick. 1969. *Maximum feasible misunderstanding: Community criteria in the war on poverty.* New York: Free Press.

Mueller, John. 1999. *Capitalism, democracy, and Ralph's pretty good grocery.* Princeton: Princeton University Press.

Muir, William. 1967. *Prayer in the public schools: Law and attitude change.* Chicago: University of Chicago Press.

Murphy, Russell. 1971. *Political entrepreneurs and urban poverty: The strategies of policy innovation in New Haven's model anti-poverty project.* Lexington, Mass.: Heath Lexington Books.

Mutz, Diana. 1998. *Impersonal influence: How perceptions of mass collectives affect political attitudes.* Cambridge: Cambridge University Press.

National performance review: Implementation. 1994. Washington, D.C.: General Accounting Office, United States Government Printing Office.

Nie, Norman, Jane Junn, and Carol Stehlik-Barry. 1996. *Education and democratic citizenship in America.* Chicago: University of Chicago Press.

Niemi, Richard G., and Jane Junn. 1998. *Civic education: What makes students learn.* New Haven: Yale University Press.

Ogg, Frederic A., and P. Orman Ray. 1950. *Essentials of American government.* 6th ed. New York: Appleton-Century-Crofts.

Oliga, John C. 1996. *Power, ideology, and control.* New York: Plenum Press.

Olson, Mancur. 1965. *The logic of collective action: Public goods and the theory of groups.* Cambridge: Harvard University Press.

Ophuls, William. 1977. *Ecology and the politics of scarcity: Prologue to a political theory of the steady state.* San Francisco: W. H. Freeman.

O'Rand, Angela M. 1989. Scientific thought style and the construction of gender inequality. In *Women and a new academy,* edited by Jean F. O'Barr. Madison: University of Wisconsin Press. Pp. 103–22.

Oren, Dan A. 1985. *Joining the club: A history of Jews at Yale.* New Haven: Yale University Press.

Ostrom, Elinor. 1998. A behavioral approach to the rational choice theory of collective action. *American Political Science Review* 92:1–23.

Parenti, Michael. 1996. Political science fiction. In *Dirty truths,* edited by Parenti. San Francisco: City Lights Books. Pp. 221–33.

Parish, Steven M. 1996. *Hierarchy and its discontents: Culture and the politics of consciousness in caste society.* Philadelphia: University of Pennsylvania Press.

Parkin, Frank. 1972. *Class inequality and political order.* New York: Praeger.

Patterson, Orlando. 1997. *The ordeal of integration: Progress and resentment in America's "racial" crisis.* Washington, D.C.: Civitas.

Patterson, Thomas. 1993. *Out of order.* New York: Knopf.

Payne, James L., and Oliver H. Woshinsky. 1972. Incentives to political participation. *World Politics* 24 (July): 518–46.

Peterson, Paul, and Bryan Hassel, eds. 1998. *Learning from school choice.* Washington, D.C.: Brookings Institution.

Peterson, Paul E., and Chad Noyes. 1996. Under extreme duress: School choice success. Unpublished manuscript, Harvard University.

Polsby, Nelson W. 1963. *Community power and political theory.* New Haven: Yale University Press.

———. 1964. *Congress and the presidency.* Englewood Cliffs, N.J.: Prentice Hall.

Polsby, Nelson W., and Aaron B. Wildavsky. 1964. *Presidential elections: Strategies of American electoral politics.* New York: Scribner.

Popper, Karl. 1950. *The open society and its enemies.* Princeton: Princeton University Press.

Posey, Rollin, and Albert Huegli. 1953. *Government for Americans.* Evanston, Ill.: Row Peterson.

Powell, Douglas H., in collaboration with Dean K. Whitla. 1994. *Profiles in cognitive aging.* Cambridge: Harvard University Press.

Powledge, Fred. 1970. *Model city, a test of American liberalism: One town's efforts to rebuild itself.* New York: Simon and Schuster.

Price, David E. 1974. Community and control: Critical democratic theory in the progressive period. *American Political Science Review* 68 (December): 1663–78.

Pride, Richard A. 1995. *The confession of Dorothy Danner: Telling a life.* Nashville: Vanderbilt University Press.

Purcell, Edward A., Jr. 1973. *The crisis of democratic theory: Scientific naturalism and the problem of value.* Lexington: University Press of Kentucky.

Putnam, Robert D., with Robert Leonardi, and Raffaella Y. Nanetti. 1993. *Making democracy work: Civic traditions in modern Italy.* Princeton: Princeton University Press.

Putnam, Robert D. 1996. The strange disappearance of civic America. *American Prospect* 7 (winter): 34–46.

————. 2000. *Bowling alone: The collapse and revival of American community.* New York: Simon and Schuster.

Quadagno, Jill. 1999. Creating a capital investment welfare state. *American Sociological Review* 64 (February): 1–12.

Radosh, Ronald, and Joyce Milton. 1983. *The Rosenberg file: A search for the truth.* New York: Holt, Rinehart, and Winston.

Ranking research doctorate programs in political science. 1995. *PS: Political Science and Politics* 28 (December): 734–36.

Ranney, Austin. 1971. *The governing of men.* 3d ed. New York: Holt, Rinehart, and Winston.

Redford, Emmette S., David B. Truman, Andrew Hacker, Alan F. Westin, and Robert C. Wood. 1965. *Politics and government in the United States: National, state, and local edition.* New York: Harcourt, Brace and World.

Reeher, Grant. 1996. *Narratives of justice: Legislators' beliefs about distributive fairness.* Ann Arbor: University of Michigan Press.

Rhea, Joseph Tilden. 1997. *Race pride and the American identity.* Cambridge: Harvard University Press.

Ricci, David M. 1984. *The tragedy of political science.* New Haven: Yale University Press.

Riker, William H. 1953. *Democracy in the United States.* New York: Macmillan.

————. 1988. *Liberalism against populism: A confrontation between the theory of democracy and the theory of social choice.* Prospect, Ill.: Waveland Press.

Robbins, Bruce. 1993. *Secular vocations: Intellectuals, professionalism, culture.* London: Verso.

Robertson, David Brian. 1994. Politics and the past: History, behavioralism, and the return to institutionalism in American political science. In *Engaging the past: The uses of history across the social sciences,* edited by Eric H. Monkkonen. Durham: Duke University Press. Pp. 113–54.

Rogow, Arnold A., and Harold D. Lasswell. 1963. *Power, corruption, and rectitude.* Englewood Cliffs, N.J.: Prentice Hall.

Rose, Sonya O. 1999. Cultural analysis and moral discourses: Episodes, continuities, and transformations. In *Beyond the cultural turn: New directions in the study of society and culture,* edited by Victoria E. Bonnell and Lynn Hunt. Berkeley: University of California Press. Pp. 217–41.

Ross, Dorothy. 1991. *The origins of American social science.* Cambridge: Cambridge University Press.

Rovere, Richard. 1959. *Senator Joe McCarthy.* New York: Harcourt, Brace.

Russett, Bruce M. 1972. *No clear and present danger: A skeptical view of the United States entry into World War II.* New York: Harper and Row.

Sadri, Ahmad. 1992. *Max Weber's sociology of intellectuals.* New York: Oxford.

Salisbury, Robert H. 1973. *Governing America: Public choice and political action.* New York: Appleton-Century-Crofts.

Saunders, Frances S. 1999. *Who paid the piper? The CIA and the cultural Cold War.* London: Granta Books.

Sayre, Wallace S., and Herbert Kaufman. 1960. *Governing New York City: Politics in the metropolis.* New York: Russell Sage.

Scaff, Lawrence A. 1989. *Fleeing the iron cage: Culture, politics, and modernity in the thought of Max Weber.* Berkeley: University of California Press.

Schattschneider, E. E. 1960. *The semi-sovereign people: A realist's view of democracy in America.* New York: Holt, Rinehart, and Winston.

Schlesinger, Arthur M. 1949. *The vital center: The politics of freedom.* Boston: Houghton Mifflin.

Schlossberg, David. 1998. Resurrecting the pluralist universe. *Political Research Quarterly* 51 (September): 583–615.

Schneider, Mark, et al. 1997. Institutional arrangements and the creation of social capital: The effects of public school choice. *American Political Science Review* 91 (March): 82–94.

Schram, Sanford F. 1995. *Words of welfare: The poverty of social science and the social science of poverty.* Minneapolis: University of Minnesota Press.

Schudson, Michael. 1989. How culture works. *Theory and Society* 18 (March): 153–81.

———. 1992. *Watergate in American memory.* New York: Basic Books.

———. 2001. Politics as cultural practice. *Political Communication* 18 (4):421–33.

Schwartz, Barry. 1996. Memory as a cultural system: Abraham Lincoln in World War II. *American Sociological Review* 61:908–27.

Scott, James C. 1968. *Political ideology in Malaysia: Reality and the beliefs of an elite.* New Haven: Yale University Press.

———. 1990. *Domination and the arts of resistance: Hidden transcripts.* New Haven: Yale University Press.

———. 1998. *Seeing like a state: How certain schemes to improve the human condition have failed.* New Haven: Yale University Press.

Sears, David O. 1990. Whither political socialization research? The question of persistence. In *Political socialization, citizenship education, and democracy,* edited by Orit Ichilov. New York: Teachers College Press. Pp. 69–98.

Segal, Jeffrey A. 1997. Separation-of-powers games in the positive theory of Congress and courts. *American Political Science Review* 91:28–45.

Seidelman, Raymond, with the assistance of Edward J. Harpham. 1985. *Disenchanted realists: Political science and the American crisis, 1884–1984.* Albany: State University of New York Press.

Sewell, William H., Jr. 1992. A theory of structure: Duality, agency, and transformation. *American Journal of Sociology* 98 (July): 1–29.

———. 1996. Political events as transformations of structures: Inventing revolution at the Bastille. *Theory and Society* 26:841–81.

———. 1999. The concept(s) of culture. In *Beyond the cultural turn: New directions in the study of society and culture,* edited by Victoria E. Bonnell and Lynn Hunt. Berkeley: University of California Press. Pp. 35–62.

Shapiro, Ian, and Donald P. Green. 1994. *Pathologies of rational choice theory.* New Haven: Yale University Press.

Shapiro, Ian, and Grant Reeher, eds. 1988. *Power, inequality, and democratic politics: Essays in honor of Robert A. Dahl.* Boulder, Colo.: Westview Press.

Sheehy, Gail. 1971. *Panthermania: The clash of black against black in one American city.* New York: Harper and Row.

Sidanius, Jim, and Felicia Pratto. 1993. The inevitability of oppression and the dynamics of social dominance. In *Prejudice, politics, and the American dilemma,* edited by Paul M. Sniderman, Philip E. Tetlock, and Edward G. Carmines. Stanford: Stanford University Press. Pp. 173–212.

Simpson, Paul. 1993. *Language, ideology, and point of view.* London: Routledge.

Small, Mario. 1999. Departmental conditions and the emergence of new disciplines: Two cases in the legitimation of African American studies. *Theory and Society* 28:659–707.

Smith, Rogers M. 1993. Beyond Tocqueville, Myrdal, and Hartz: The multiple traditions in America. *American Political Science Review* 87:549–67.

———. 1997. Still blowing in the wind: The American quest for a democratic, scientific political science. *Daedalus* 126 (winter): 253–89.

Spillman, Lyn. 1997. *Nation and commemoration: Creating national identities in the United States and Australia.* Cambridge: Cambridge University Press.

Stillman, Peter G. 1974. Hegel's critique of liberal theories of rights. *American Political Science Review* 68:1086–92.

Storing, Hebert, ed. 1962. *Essays on the scientific study of politics.* New York: Holt, Rinehart.

Students for a Democratic Society. 1962. *The Port Huron statement.* Chicago: Students for a Democratic Society.

Swartz, David. 1997. *Culture and power: The sociology of Pierre Bourdieu.* Chicago: University of Chicago Press.

Swidler, Ann. 1984. Culture in action: Symbols and strategies. *American Sociological Review* 51:273–86.

Taft, John. 1976. *Mayday at Yale: A case study in student radicalism.* Boulder, Colo.: Westview Press.

Talbot, Allan R. 1967. *The mayor's game: Richard Lee of New Haven and the politics of change.* New York: Harper and Row.

Talbort, Mary M. 1995. *Fictions at work: Language and social practice in fiction.* London: Longman.

Tarrow, Sidney. 1994. *Power in movement.* Cambridge: Cambridge University Press.

Tennant, Mark, and Philip Pogson. 1995. *Learning and change in the adult years.* San Francisco: Jossey-Bass.

Tennant, Mark. 1997. *Psychology and adult learning.* 2d ed. London: Routledge.

Thompson, Michael, Richard Ellis, and Aaron Wildavsky. 1990. *Cultural theory.* Boulder, Colo.: Westview Press.

Torrance, John. 1995. *Karl Marx's theory of ideas.* Cambridge: Cambridge University Press.

Trillin, Calvin, 1993. *Remembering Denny.* New York: Farrar, Straus and Giroux.

Turner, Stephen Park, and Jonathan H. Turner. 1990. *The impossible science: An institutional analysis of American sociology.* Newbury Park, Calif.: Sage.

Uchitelle, Louis. 2000. Lonely bowlers, united: Mend the social fabric. *New York Times,* May 6: A 15.

Verdery, Katherine. 1991. *National ideology under socialism: Identity and cultural politics in Ceausescu's Romania.* Berkeley: University of California Press.

Walsh, David. 1993. The role of ideology in cultural re-production. In *Cultural re-production*, edited by Chris Jenks. London: Routledge. Pp. 228–50.

Walton, John. 1992. Making the theoretical case. In *What is a case? Exploring the foundations of social inquiry*, edited by Charles C. Ragin and Howard S. Becker. Cambridge: Cambridge University Press. Pp. 121–39.

Ware, Alan. 1998. Dahl in perspective: Assessing a colossus of political science. *Public Affairs Report* 39 (September): 14–16.

Weber, Max. 1958. *The protestant ethic and the spirit of capitalism*. Translated by Talcott Parsons. New York: Scribners.

————. 1978. *Economy and society*. Edited by Guenther Roth and Claus Wittich. Berkeley: University of California Press.

White, Milton. 1966. *A Yale man*. New York: Doubleday.

Wiebe, Robert H. 1995. *Self-rule: A cultural history of American democracy*. Chicago: University of Chicago Press.

Wildavsky, Aaron. 1962. *Dixon-Yates: A study in power politics*. New Haven: Yale University Press.

————. 1964a. *Leadership in a small town*. Totowa, N.J.: Bedminister Press.

————. 1964b. *The politics of the budgetary process*. Boston: Little, Brown.

————. 1989. *Craftways: On the organization of scholarly work*. New Brunswick, N.J.: Transaction Publishers.

Williams, Howard. 1988. *Concepts of ideology*. New York: St. Martin's Press.

Williams, Raymond. 1977. *Marxism and literature*. Oxford: Oxford University Press.

Wills, Garry. 1998. Whatever happened to politics? Washington is not where it's at. *New York Times Magazine*, January 25.

————. 1999. *A necessary evil: A history of American distrust of government*. New York: Simon and Schuster.

Winks, Robin W. 1987. *Cloak and gown: Scholars in the secret war, 1939–1961*. New York: Morrow.

Witte, John F. 2000. *The market approach to education: An analysis of America's first voucher program*. Princeton: Princeton University Press.

Wolfe, Alan. 1997. Two cheers for professionalism: The 1960s, the university, and me. In *Reassessing the sixties: Debating the political and cultural legacy*, edited by Stephen Macedo. New York: Norton. Pp. 184–207.

Wolfinger, Raymond. 1973. *The politics of progress*. Englewood Cliffs, N.J.: Prentice Hall.

Wolfsfeld, Gadi. 1997. *Media and political conflict: News from the Middle East*. Cambridge: Cambridge University Press.

Wolin, Sheldon S. 1960. *Politics and vision: Continuity and innovation in Western political thought*. Boston: Little, Brown.

————. 1997. The destructive sixties and postmodern conservatism. In *Reassessing the sixties: Debating the political and cultural legacy*, edited by Stephen Macedo. New York: Norton. Pp. 129–57.

Woll, Peter, and Robert Binstock. 1972. *America's political system*. New York: Random House.

Wood, Robert C. 1993. *Whatever possessed the president? Academic experts and presidential policy, 1960–1988*. Amherst: University of Massachusetts Press.

Wrong, Dennis. 1994. *The problem of order: What unites and divides society.* Cambridge: Harvard University Press.

———. 1998. *The modern condition: Essays at century's end.* Stanford: Stanford University Press.

Wuthnow, Robert. 1987. *Meaning and moral order: Explorations in cultural analysis.* Berkeley: University of California Press.

Young, Crawford. 1994. *The African colonial state in comparative perspective.* New Haven: Yale University Press.

Young, Iris Marion. 1990. *Justice and the politics of difference.* Princeton: Princeton University Press.

YUDPS (Yale University Department of Political Science Records), YRG 14-FF. Manuscripts and Archives, Yale University Library.

Zerubavel, Yael. 1995. *Recovered roots: Collective memory and the making of Israeli national tradition.* Chicago: University of Chicago Press.

Zunz, Olivier. 1987–88. The genesis of American pluralism. *Tocqueville Review* 9: 201–20.

Index

313